PRICING
RECREATION AND
PARK SERVICES

The Science and the Art

John L. Crompton
Texas A&M University

SAGAMORE
PUBLISHING

Publishers: Joseph J. Bannon and Peter L. Bannon
Sales and Marketing Manager: Misti Gilles
Director of Development and Production: Susan M. Davis
Production Coordinator: Amy S. Dagit
Cover Designer: Marissa Willison

ISBN print edition: 978-1-57167-797-6
ISBN e-book: 978-1-57167-798-3
Library of Congress Control Number: 2016934062

Printed in the United States

SAGAMORE
PUBLISHING
1807 N. Federal Dr.
Urbana, IL 61801
www.sagamorepublishing.com

To the memory of a windy night
on top of The Beacon: Priceless

Contents

Section 1
Multiple Dimensions of the Benefit Principle:
The Functions of Price in the Public Sector

Section 3
Behavioral Pricing: Adapting Price to Fit Clienteles' Perceptions of What Is Acceptable

Preface

In the early 1980s, Ron McCarville and I initiated a substantial research program with the goal of providing a scientific foundation to guide pricing decisions confronting managers and elected officials in public parks and recreation agencies. The timing was fortuitous because it coincided with the tax revolt that erupted in the late 1970s and early 1980s. This transformed the political narrative in the U.S. (and coincidentally in Canada, U.K., Australia, New Zealand, and other countries during the same time). Prior to this shift, those seeking electoral office promised more and better public services in their platforms. After the tax revolt, the emphasis changed to reducing, or at least not increasing, taxes. This was perhaps most prominently and notoriously exemplified by President George H. W. Bush's 1987 pledge: "Read my lips. No new taxes" and his electoral defeat in 1992, which many attribute to his breaking that pledge.

While voters have widely supported this philosophy for the past 30 years, they have simultaneously continued to expect high quality public services. Raising additional revenues from user pricing has been prominent among the multiple strategies adopted at all levels of government to reconcile these ostensibly antithetical mandates.

The research program that McCarville and I undertook endured for about a decade. Since that time, in the past 20 years, other leisure researchers have reported findings, but the number of studies has been relatively small and a sustained research program has not been pursued. Meanwhile, pricing research in other fields has grown exponentially. Hence, the challenge in writing this book has been to review the extensive literatures in the fields of retailing, welfare economics, behavioral economics, psychology, political science and leisure; extract pertinent concepts, principles and research findings that seem likely to inform policy decisions in the different milieu of public leisure agencies; and adapt, modify and integrate them so they fit the context of these agencies.

The insights gleaned and adapted from these literatures have been honed and refined by two filters. First, numerous leisure professionals at the many workshops, presentations and consulting assignments that I have led in the past 20 years have provided frank and generous feedback. Many of the examples used in the book are not accompanied with citations, because they emerged from these professional verbal interactions and their source was not documented.

The second filter was my experience as an elected official. In my years as a councilman and mayor pro tem for the city of College Station (population of 100,000), on multiple occasions, my state-of-the-art knowledge of pricing had to be reconciled and adapted to the political realities of a particular situation. It is one thing to advocate scientifically best practices; it is a different matter to implement them in the political environment of an emotional, volatile, passionate, crowded council chamber. This experience confirmed the central importance of three principles that permeate this book: carefully framing issues so they result in a desired outcome, communicating in non-technical language free from the jargon of economists, and building constituency support before seeking a political decision.

While it would never be publicly stated in such crass terms, the overriding concern of many elected officials is how to "pluck the goose to obtain the most feathers with the least amount of hissing." They can identify the losers from price increases, and while they seek the additional revenue to retain service quality, they fear the wrath of those who are adversely affected.

The crux of controversies associated with pricing frequently revolves around how best to reconcile the two concepts of fairness that guide pricing decisions: The Benefit Principle states those benefiting from a service should bear financial responsibility for its cost, and the Ability to Pay Principle recognizes the public sector's obligation to ensure no residents are excluded from participating because they lack the funds to do so.

In the private sector, the sole criterion considered in pricing decisions is maximizing revenues. Usually, this entails exclusively focusing on responsive target markets. Pricing decisions in the public sector are more complex because the mission is different. Decision makers have to find the price that is "fairest" to all; that is, it best serves the interests of all residents, including non-users and the economically disadvantaged.

Section 1 of the book, comprising Chapters 2 to 4, is focused on issues related to the Benefit Principle. These issues invariably revolve around equity, income redistribution, efficiency and income generation. Resolution or avoidance of controversies requires that managers and elected officials understand these issues so they can rationally explain and justify their pricing decisions to constituents.

In Section 2, comprising Chapters 5 to 8, price elasticity is discussed. This is the economic concept that undergirds differential pricing, which creates the discounts and premiums used to reconcile the Benefit and Ability to Pay Principles. The justifications (or lack thereof) for these price differentials are discussed in detail. If discounts are not offered to the economically disadvantaged, one of two undesirable outcomes will occur: (i) Prices will be set at a level that is too high for them so those whose need is greatest are effectively excluded, which abrogates the Ability to Pay Principle, or (ii) to preclude such exclusion, prices are set at a low level for all, resulting in a large consumers' surplus among those who could pay more, which is an abrogation of the Benefit Principle. In accordance with the Benefit Principle, premiums are charged to capture consumers' surplus and to cover the costs associated with meeting the demands of some users for additional increments of benefits beyond the standard offering.

Chapters 9 to 12, which constitute Section 3 of the book, reflect the emergence of behavioral economics in the 1980s. Prior to that time, the guiding economic framework for pricing decisions comprised the neoclassical concepts of price, demand and utility. This was based on how people ought to behave if they were logical and rational. In contrast, behavioral economics recognizes that people's economic behavior is frequently not rational. It focuses attention on how people actually behave. Subsequently, a substantial body of research, comprising hundreds of studies, has demonstrated that pricing decisions are often systematically and substantially different from those predicted by the standard economic model. Recognizing the principles of cognitive processing and the heuristics likely to be prominent in users' evaluations of price changes will assist in adopting prices that will not arouse negative reactions.

Central ideas that emerged from the research program of three decades ago were widely incorporated into the pricing policies of leisure agencies. In many cases, this did not occur because of direct exposure to the material. Rather, it was a result of the informal sharing of procedures, ordinances and policy documents that is a corollary of professional life in the public sector. Irrespective of their communication route, it has been satisfying to see the positive practical outcomes from that effort. If this book has a similar impact, the endeavor of writing it will have been well worthwhile.

About the Author

John L. Crompton is a University Distinguished Professor, a Regents Professor and a Presidential Professor for Teaching Excellence at Texas A&M University. He received his basic training in England. His undergraduate work was in physical education and geography at Loughborough College. After teaching high school for a year, he attended the University of Illinois, where he completed an M.S. degree in Recreation and Park Administration in 1968. In 1970, he was awarded another M.S. degree from Loughborough University of Technology, majoring in Business Administration. In 1974, Dr. Crompton came to Texas A&M University. He received his doctorate in Recreation Resources Development in 1977.

He is author or co-author of 18 books and a substantial number of articles that have been published in the recreation, tourism, sport and marketing fields. He is the most published scholar in the history of both the parks and recreation field and the tourism field.

He has conducted many hundreds of workshops on Marketing and/or Financing Leisure Services; has lectured or conducted workshops in many foreign countries; and has delivered keynote addresses at the World Leisure Congress and at Annual National Park and Recreation Conferences in Australia, Canada, Great Britain, Japan, New Zealand, South Africa, and the United States. He has received numerous awards from Texas A&M, professional societies and community organizations recognizing his excellence in research, teaching and public service.

Dr. Crompton was a member of NRPA's Board of Trustees for 9 years and is a past president of four professional bodies: the Texas Recreation and Parks Society, the American Academy of Park and Recreation Administration, the Society of Park and Recreation Educators, and the Academy of Leisure Sciences. He is a Board member of the National Recreation Foundation.

In 2006, the city of College Station named a new 16-acre neighborhood park, John Crompton Park. Dr. Crompton served 4 years as a city councilman for College Station from 2007–2011 and was Mayor Pro Tem in 2010–2011.

Chapter 1

Introduction

- What is price?
- Price's role in the financing paradigm
- Focus on revenue streams or the mission?
- Pricing's central conundrum: Reconciling the Benefit and the Ability to Pay Principles
- Involvement of staff in pricing decisions
- The liability implications of pricing
- Pricing: A science and an art
- Summary

Parks, recreation, arts and culture (leisure services) evolved as social services. The rationale for using tax funds to develop facilities and operate programs was rooted in the mandate of governments to provide for the "health, safety and welfare" of their residents. There were some exceptions. For example, in the case of national parks,[1] some state park systems[2] and libraries,[3] the intent was that government's role would be limited to capital investment and user fees would be sufficient to cover their operating expenses. However, around 1920, it was widely accepted that operating costs in these services should be covered by tax funds. The prevailing view was expressed by the chair of the House Interior Committee in Congress with reference to national parks: "The American idea is not that there is going to be somebody with a collection box every time you turn around in a publicly owned enterprise."[4]

This perspective endures today in only a small number of jurisdictions. Thus, the director of a leisure agency in one of those communities observed:

> We service all people. The imposition of a fee is as bad as the imposition of a tax. We shouldn't just look around for something that's popular and then charge for it. If we charged $10 each time a policeman or fireman showed up at your door, there might be a lot fewer emergency calls, but is it what we want? Park users have already paid for the parks once, why should we make them pay again? We're not talking about

wealthy communities where virtually 100 percent of the people can afford to pay. We're talking about cities. Do we really want to say to these people, "Only those who can afford to pay can play?" (p. 3)[4]

In today's political environment, many elected officials are likely to regard this viewpoint as anachronistic and non-tenable. Two major factors account for this shift. First, government entities at all levels have taken on many more responsibilities. This increase in the number or range of services and the level of benefit each is required to provide has required higher levels of taxation to pay for them. This led to the "tax revolt" of the late 1970s and early 1980s, which was a backlash against higher taxes. It radically and enduringly changed the political climate and was the second factor stimulating user pricing.

Most elected officials are now under relentless pressure from their constituents to lower, or at least not to raise, taxes. The mantra that guided leisure agencies after the tax revolt was: Do more with less. Initially, this was pursued by robustly cutting costs. In most agencies, costs have now been pared to the bone. A complementary mantra that subsequently emerged was: Do more with more, which meant raising prices to create self-generated revenue. This recognizes that support from elected officials for new services is likely to depend on them being self-sufficient.

This revised mantra is reflected in the emergence of the term "net budget," which is defined as the tax-supported portion of an agency's budget. During budget discussions, if a director reports no increase in the net budget, it is likely to meet with approval. The gross budget may increase, but if the increases are funded by program-generated revenues, elected officials are unlikely to be concerned. Hence, the future mantra of this field is likely to be: Do more with more (but not tax funding).

Annual reports published by the Census Bureau on the expenditures and revenues of local governments show that in 1964/65 local government parks and recreation services generated $115 million in non-tax revenue. By 1999/2000 35 years later, this had increased to $514 million in inflation adjusted dollars;[5] hence, when the influence of inflation is removed, self-generated revenue increased by 450 percent. By 1999/2000, it accounted for 34 percent of local parks and recreation departments' operating costs, indicating that for every $2 of tax funds they received, agencies generated $1 from users of their services. The authors of this study concluded:

These data have equity implications. The park and recreation field initially was regarded as a welfare service, concerned with ensuring that opportunities for the economically disadvantaged would be improved. Over time, this compensatory approach was gradually replaced by notions of equality under which all residents received equal emphasis in the allocation of resources. These data suggest to the authors that in the past decade the field has moved more towards a market equity model, under which more fee-based programs have been introduced, higher prices have been imposed, and residents buy as little or as much of a service as they can afford at the given price. (p. 131)[5]

Similar trends emerged in a longitudinal analysis of the finances of all 50 state park systems. Self-generated revenues rose consistently, so they now account for approximately 40 percent of state parks' operating expenditures.[6, 7] This share has remained roughly constant since the mid-1990s. It is the largest source of state parks' funding, exceeding the 34 percent and 20 percent shares derived from general and dedicated funds, respectively.[7]

Within these mean averages for local and state agencies, there are wide variations reflecting not only differences in community philosophy, but also diversity in the bundles of services that parks and recreation agencies deliver. For example, agencies that have extensive class programs, athletic programs, campgrounds, and recreation centers are likely to generate more revenue than natural resource–based agencies without such programs.

At the federal level, user pricing was accentuated by the 2004 Federal Land Recreation Enhancement Act. This authorizes the National Park Service (NPS) and other federal land management agencies to charge higher prices and to keep the revenues rather than sending them to the national treasury. This act allows each facility to retain 80 percent of its receipts, while the remaining 20 percent can be allocated elsewhere within the agency at the director's discretion. Before this act was passed, revenue from user fees typically accounted for approximately 3 percent of the NPS budget. Ten years after it was passed, almost $300 million of the agency's $2.5 billion budget (12 percent) came from this source.

WHAT IS PRICE?

Price is popularly perceived as the amount of money users are charged to engage in an activity by a leisure agency. It has a diverse nomenclature: Fees, charges, permits, rentals, registrations, and licenses are all synonyms for price. These terms refer only to monetary payments. However, from a user's perspective, price comprises multiple other ingredients. It is the totality of what is given up or sacrificed[8] when these ingredients are aggregated; their totality constitutes a user's composite price.[9] While agencies' revenue goals invariably cause them to focus narrowly on monetary price, when users make a purchase decision, they are likely to consider all the resources they invest, that is, the much broader all-embracing composite price. The ingredients of composite price can be classified as either fixed or variable.

Fixed ingredients may include investments in major equipment, clothing and footwear and in an annual membership or a season pass. Such investments are incurred only irregularly. They are considered to be sunk costs because they cannot be reclaimed once they have been made. As ingredients of composite price, they are likely to influence participation decisions. The nature of this influence is discussed in depth in Chapters 5 and 12.

The variable ingredients of composite price are the resources users invest each time they engage in an activity. These are summarized in Figure 1-1. They may be classified as monetary and non-monetary. Monetary prices are paid for the following:

- Participation in a program.
- Transportation to and from a facility. The challenge of overcoming the "friction of space" is most obvious when substantial distances are traveled, for example, to a state or national park or to a special event. However, substantial effects have been reported for travel times of 30 minutes or less, especially among the economically disadvantaged, older adults, and people with disabilities.[10, 11]
- Ancillary purchases of food, drink, accommodations, equipment (balls, tees, paints etc.) or rentals (carts, bikes, canoes etc.).
- Temporary assistance to take over a user's conflicting responsibilities (e.g., babysitter).

The composite price comprises the following non-monetary resources:

- Opportunity costs of resources. That is, the activities that are given up because monetary and non-monetary resources have been committed to a leisure program. These will include time spent in preparation (i.e., searching for information) and in organizing a schedule to create the time block needed (e.g., find a babysitter, change existing commitments); traveling to and from a facility; queuing; engaging in the activity; and subsequent "cleaning" of equipment, clothing etc.

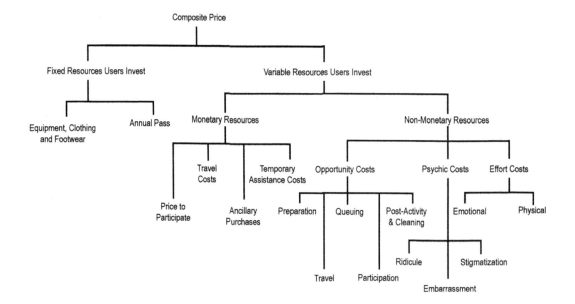

Figure 1-1. The Ingredients of Composite Price

There is an intrinsic difference in monetary and time opportunity costs. Because money is storable, it can be used at multiple times and for many other purposes at some point in the long-term future. For example, the (say) $80 fee for a series of art classes is likely to be weighed against other potential uses of that money over the next (say) 3 months. In contrast, time cannot be stored. It is perishable, which makes its opportunity cost context specific. That is, what are the alternate options for using that time during the scheduled hours the art class will meet?

- Psychic costs such as ridicule because of lack of skill or knowledge; embarrassment from inappropriate somatotype, etiquette or behavior perhaps associated with cultural or language differences; and stigmatization from having to prove eligibility for discounted or free admission.
- Effort costs that make up the emotional energy committed to surmounting the frustrations that may arise and in completing the arrangements; and the physical energy needed to handle the stresses of traveling and participation, and the physiological wear and tear that accompanies physical activities.

The concept of composite price has three important implications for managers. First, the magnitude of its aggregated variable and fixed costs is likely to influence the acceptance or rejection of a monetary price increase. This concept of price elasticity of demand is discussed in Chapter 5. At this point, it is sufficient to note that if people invest (say) $1,000 and 6 days in traveling to visit Grand Canyon National Park, the high composite price makes it unlikely they will be perturbed if the entrance price is increased by $5. However, if the admission price to a local swimming pool is increased by $5, there is likely to be an outcry because this constitutes a large proportion of the composite price.

The second managerial implication of composite price is that its components are substitutable. If value is added by reducing non-monetary costs, monetary price can probably be raised without increasing composite price. For example, some will pay a premium monetary price for a reservation because the time saving is more valuable to them than the premium. Consider the following scenario:

- The cost of offering a class that meets for 2 hours once a week for 5 weeks is $500. The class has to be self-sustaining, so it is priced at $50 predicated on 10 people registering for it. At the end of the registration period, there are only six registrations. What actions should managers take?

Unfortunately, the tendency for some would be to notify those who registered that the class was canceled because of insufficient numbers. The concept of composite price suggests that is an inappropriate response given the investment in search and travel time, travel costs, arrangement of personal schedules to accommodate the class, and perceptions of minimal psychic costs. Accordingly, the approach should be to contact the six registrants; explain the situation; point out that if it can be made to work with fewer in the class, they will receive more personalized instruction; and offer alternatives. For example, see if they would accept the class meeting for 1 hour instead of 2 hours (so costs would fall to $250), or be prepared to pay $84 instead of $50, or pay $65 for five 1.5-hour classes.

A third implication is that more is not necessarily better. For many middle-income users, time is their most scarce and valuable resource. Therefore, it is the most important ingredient of their composite price. As a result, in some instances, longer participation times or a longer series of classes may make the composite price too high for them to participate.

PRICE'S ROLE IN THE FINANCING PARADIGM

Figure 1-2 shows a conceptualization of the relationship between a leisure agency and users of its services. It is a voluntary exchange in which something of value is offered to users who reciprocate by exchanging something else of value. An agency delivers services that provide benefits that users seek. Users provide support to the agency through the monetary price they pay, the opportunity costs they incur by participating, and their psychic and effort costs. Some of the components of composite price are not shown in Figure 1-2 because they are paid to entities other than the leisure agency (i.e., payments for transportation; ancillary purchases; temporary assistance; clothing, footwear and equipment). These payments by participants are excluded from the conceptualization of the exchange relationship in the figure because, for the most part, they cannot be influenced by leisure managers. This exchange is analogous to transactions in the private sector.

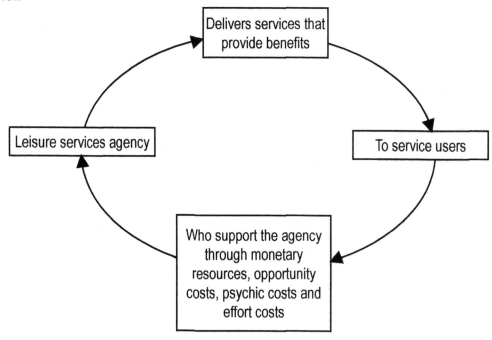

Figure 1-2. The Voluntary Exchange Relationship

In the public sector, however, this exchange has to be embedded within a more comprehensive financial paradigm because most leisure agencies' primary source of funding is taxes, not self-generated revenues. Taxes are fundamentally different from prices in that people are mandated by law to pay them. They have no choice in the matter. In contrast, paying a price is a voluntary decision—people can elect to do it or not. (There are some situations in which the payment is a hybrid. For example, boaters are legally required to pay to register their craft. The legal requirement ostensibly indicates this is a tax, but the choice as to whether to own a boat suggests it is a price. In these cases, the term "specialized taxes" may be most appropriate.)

The comprehensive public financing paradigm shown in Figure 1-3 recognizes that users and non-users pay taxes to a jurisdiction's general fund. The legislative body with responsibility for the general fund redistributes these funds among departments, one of which is leisure services. The agency uses these resources to pay for (subsidize) services that are perceived to benefit the whole community. This paradigm retains the elements of the exchange in Figure 1-2, showing the price paid by users to the agency for services from which they directly benefit. However, it expands that model to incorporate the role of taxes, and it shows revenues collected from users by the agency in most cases are passed through to the general fund.

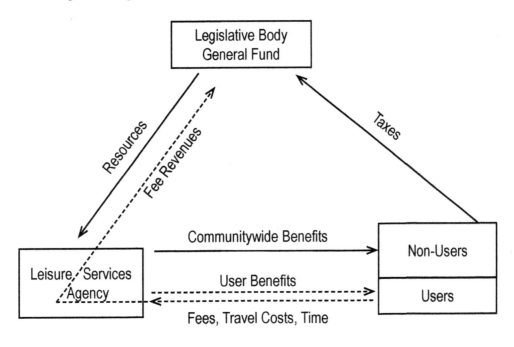

Figure 1-3. The Public Financing Paradigm

The exchange relationship in Figure 1-2 is misleading in that it implies a leisure agency operates in an open system like a private company does. This suggests its managers have sufficient independence to respond directly and quickly to the needs of service users and changes in the environment in which they operate. However, in reality, they operate in a closed system in which their actions are constrained and proscribed by an elected legislative body that limits managers' discretion by its political philosophy, distribution of tax allocations, service priorities and campaign commitments.

FOCUS ON REVENUE STREAMS OR THE MISSION?

A corollary of the ongoing pressure to increase revenues and decrease tax subsidies is that revenue streams may dictate and drive the mission instead of contributing to it. This is manifested by subsidized services being reduced, ignored or terminated, while those which are self-sustaining flourish, even though the former is more important to accomplishing the agency's primary mission. It is illustrated in Figure 1-4, which suggests the priorities manifested by those responsible for managing public lands are sometimes guided by revenue streams rather than by long-term ecological best procedures.[12]

There is no doubt that revenue streams associated with user groups have significantly affected how land managers view their jobs. A familiar example with a very long history is state fish and game agencies, which are heavily funded through the sale of hunting and fishing licenses. As a result, agencies have traditionally focused their efforts not on all wildlife and all fish but on those that hunters and anglers favor. Rather than seeking to maintain healthy ecosystems that support natural biodiversity, the fish and game agencies have sought to maximize the pounds of huntable wildlife and catchable game fish. This often has led to the reduction or removal of wildlife that prey on big game and the introduction of exotic fish. In Montana, for instance, the Fish and Game Commission has opposed both the return of the wolf to its historic habitat and the listing of the grizzly bear as an endangered species. The agency's revenues flow from only certain wildlife, and its wildlife management strategy reflects this fact.

The powerful effect that revenue streams can have on management decisions worries many who would like to see public lands better managed to reflect a broader range of concerns about biodiversity and ecosystem services. If agency decisions primarily seek to serve the interests of users of public lands who are responsible for the largest flow of revenues, land managers may be hesitant, for instance, to control or regulate motorized recreation, including off-road vehicles, or mineral extraction activities that are seriously damaging the land and wildlife. The problem is created by the fact that it is easy to associate revenues with certain on-site activities but difficult to associate revenues with a much broader range of ecosystem services because of their public good characteristics and the complex and not fully understood natural processes that produce them. In this setting, an increasing reliance on locally generated fees from users of public lands to fund public land management may lead to destructive results (pp. 24–25).

Figure 1-4. An Illustration of the Influence of Revenue Streams on Management Decisions[12]

In the U.K., the expressed priority of central and local government was to improve access of disadvantaged groups to public sector sports and leisure centers. However, from an analysis of comprehensive national participation data, it was concluded: "The implication is that stronger cost recovery will cause weaker performance in low socio-economic groups' access" (p. 139).[13]

If an agency is myopically focused on reducing subsidies and raising revenues, this can easily be accomplished by targeting only responsive, middle-class clienteles and ignoring the economically disadvantaged, unskilled and disinterested target markets that are much more costly to access and are either unable or unwilling to pay a break-even price. These clienteles are not provided with leisure programs by the private sector and thus are part of the *raison d'être* for a public agency.

This trade-off between equity and efficiency is discussed in detail later in the book. The point here is to recognize that managers are responsible for making elected officials aware of the trade-off. However, if prioritizing efficiency is a purposeful policy decision reflecting the political platform on which they were elected rather than an unforeseen consequence, then it will occur. Alternatively, if elected officials want to avoid compromising an agency's traditional mission in this way, they should ensure that managers' performance evaluations include metrics beyond subsidy reductions that hold them accountable for serving less responsive clienteles.

PRICING'S CENTRAL CONUNDRUM: RECONCILING THE BENEFIT AND THE ABILITY TO PAY PRINCIPLES

The tension between revenue generation and the mission is a manifestation of the central conundrum in public-sector pricing debates, which is how to reconcile pricing's two guiding concepts optimally: the Benefit Principle (sometimes called the User Pay Principle) and the Ability to Pay Principle. These two broad macro principles were prominent in the thinking of Adam Smith in 1776 when he wrote his foundation treatise on capitalism:

> The subjects of every state ought to contribute towards the support of the government, as nearly as possible, in proportion to their respective abilities; that is, in proportion to the revenue which they respectively enjoy under the protection of the state. The expense of government to the individuals of a great nation, is like the expense of management to the joint tenants of a great estate, who are all obliged to contribute in proportion to their respective interests in the estate. (p. 825)[14]

In these two sentences, Smith recognized the two concepts of fairness that remain the contemporary principles for guiding decisions on equity in taxation and in pricing. First, each taxpayer or service user's contribution should reflect the benefits he or she receives from the service. Smith observed: "It seems scarce possible to invent a more equitable way of maintaining such works" (p. 725).[14] Second, the price or amounts of tax to be paid should reflect people's different ability to pay. The Benefit Principle is analogous to Smith's "invisible hand," the market mechanism used to allocate goods and services in the private sector whereby people must pay for the services they use. Pricing is a superior mechanism to any form of taxation for operationalizing the Benefit Principle as it requires users to bear the financial responsibility for a service's cost. However, in situations in which benefits are perceived also to accrue to a large proportion of non-user residents, the Benefit Principle directs that costs associated with that proportion of the benefits should be borne by a community's tax revenues.

Elected officials frequently position themselves as "fiscal conservatives." They proclaim their intent is to keep taxes low. The primary strategy enabling them to meet that obligation without reducing the quality of services is to ensure users pay for them rather than taxpayers. Hence, the Benefit Principle is the core of fiscal conservatism. The Ability to Pay Principle recognizes a community's obligation to provide opportunities equally to all residents. It directs that as far as possible, no residents should be excluded from participating because they lack the funds to do so.

The challenge for public decision makers in arriving at a price that is perceived to be "fair" is how best to reconcile these two principles. Hence, in the first section of the book, (Chapters 2 to 4) the implications associated with operationalizing the Benefit Principle are identified and explained, while the second section (Chapters 5 to 8) discusses the discounts and premiums, which are the differential pricing mechanisms that are available to reconcile the Benefit Principle with the Ability to Pay Principle.

INVOLVEMENT OF STAFF IN PRICING DECISIONS

The success of a revised pricing policy will be strongly influenced by the extent to which an agency's front-line staff embrace it. They will be directly exposed to questions and complaints related to it. If a revised policy is foisted on staff as a *fait accompli,* they will likely be resistant, or at best disinterested, resulting in them being unwilling and unable to respond constructively and positively to negative reactions from their clienteles.

If a revised policy requires a substantial shift in philosophy toward more emphasis on revenue generation, it becomes a new "phenomenon" that changes their relationship with their clienteles from that of *giver* to that of *seller.* Some may feel threatened by this because it is inconsistent with their personal value system and/or they do not possess the management skills required in their new role. Thus, it may disturb, disrupt and cause upheaval in their working lives.

Further, front-line staff have conflicting loyalties. Their duty requires allegiance to the elected policy makers who represent the public they are paid to serve. However, they often feel an emotional connection and empathy with their clienteles. If they perceive a new pricing policy will result in some of their users withdrawing from a program, they will be tempted to bad-mouth the policy and reinforce negative reactions from users.

These factors make it imperative that all staff understand the reasons for changing the pricing policy and have the opportunity to give input into development of the revisions. The intent is to give them a sense of ownership of the changes and an understanding of the rationale and principles on which the revisions are based. This foundation should enhance their ability to articulate, explain and justify the revisions and their willingness to be public advocates for them. If staff have reservations and have no opportunity to verbalize them, then senior management has no opportunity to eliminate that resistance. The following action is illustrative of the strategies that might be used to equip front-line staff to handle a major change in pricing policy:

Front-line staff were issued 4"x10" cards that described the new fee structures and the reasons for the changes. Staff were able to use these cards as "crib sheets" to help them answer user questions. These cards were also distributed to visitors while they waited in line at main-entry points. In this way, the visitors were fully informed of the changes in fees before they were asked to pay those fees. (p. 100)[15]

THE LIABILITY IMPLICATIONS OF PRICING

Pricing decisions have implications for an agency's exposure to negligence liability claims for personal injury. The doctrine of sovereign immunity traditionally has protected government entities from such liability. However, this protection only applies when an agency's services embody a government's fundamental legal obligation to preserve its residents' general public health, safety and welfare.

When agencies engage in "proprietary functions" (i.e., act like a private business), even though they act on behalf of their own citizens, they can be held liable for negligence as if they were a private corporation. The distinctions between proprietary and governmental functions are fluid and have become increasingly blurred as agencies have focused more on generating their own revenues to reduce the tax support needed for their budgets.[16] Prices are likely to be a significant factor when courts determine whether a service is an immune governmental function or a proprietary function subject to negligence liability.

Almost all states have sought to clarify the distinction between governmental and proprietary actions by passing a state recreational use statute. Most of them are based on the Federal Tort Claims Act. With minor jurisdictional variations, these statutes generally provide that landowners (which in some cases include public agencies) who open their land for public recreational use, *free of charge,* owe no legal duty to guard, warn or make the premises reasonably safe for such public recreational use. Accordingly, under these statutes, if landowners meet the free-of-charge criterion, there is no liability for ordinary negligence. However, the owner may still be liable for willful or wanton misconduct that causes injury to recreational users. This is characterized by outrageous behavior that demonstrates an utter disregard for the physical well-being of others.[17]

Many state and federal courts have applied the free-of-charge criterion on an equal basis to public and private entities. However, some courts have denied it provides recreational use immunity to public entities. In these decisions, the courts have narrowly construed the legislative intent of the statutes to encouraging *private* landowners to allow public recreational use. Such decisions mean that charging a price has no meaningful effect on liability, as even without the price, a public agency receives no protection from these statutes.

The determining role of price in liability decisions was illustrated in a case when a player was injured on a softball field during an official, city-sponsored league softball game. The Arizona courts ruled this was a non-immune proprietary use, so the city was liable because the team's entry fee gave the team exclusive use of the ball field for that time. This transformed it from being freely available to all residents to being a proprietary use.[18]

In apparent contravention of the general rule that any price is sufficient to classify a service as proprietary, some courts have ruled that the magnitude of a price defines the issue. For example, the Connecticut Supreme Court ruled a municipality may "charge a nominal fee for participation in a government activity and it will not lose its governmental nature as long as the fee is insufficient to meet the activity's expenses." However, the court determined it is engaged in a non-immune proprietary function "if it derives revenue in excess of its costs from the activity."[16]

This criterion of covering an activity's expense, albeit using in-kind contributions rather than cash, appears to have guided the South Dakota Supreme Court. It ruled that when a city gave priority use of its ball fields to a non-profit softball association for $1 and "other good and valuable consideration," it lost its sovereign immunity. The "other consideration" included administration of a softball league open to the public, maintenance of the general grounds, responsibility for mowing the fields, and all electrical bills. The court concluded: "Clearly, the lease of the fields conferred an economic benefit or consideration upon the city."[18]

This brief overview suggests price increases may increase an agency's liability exposure. However, the effects will vary according to the facts of a specific case, specific language in recreational use statutes, and the courts' criteria and interpretations of what constitutes a proprietary function.

PRICING: A SCIENCE AND AN ART

Pricing is one of the most technically difficult and politically sensitive areas in which leisure managers have to make decisions. Pricing decisions are influenced by myriad ideological, political, economic and professional arguments. However, the debate accompanying this diversity of perspectives should be focused on sound principles. In the past, when only relatively nominal prices were charged, the underlying rationale of a price structure was not as likely to be challenged. That has changed as prices have become more substantive and demands for greater transparency in government have grown. Managers and elected officials are now more likely to be required to justify price increases.

During the past 30 years, a substantial number of researchers in the fields of behavioral economics, welfare economics, psychology, marketing and political science with an interest in pricing have engaged in theoretical explanations, observations and empirical experiments. As a result of their efforts, there is now an impressive systematically organized body of knowledge related to pricing. This provides a strong scientific base from which leisure managers can draw to inform their decisions.

Unfortunately, for the most part, this body of knowledge remains untapped in the leisure field. As a result, many good managers and elected officials make poor pricing decisions. Too often, their decisions are based on "the squeaky wheel" syndrome, or "the way we've always done it." Perhaps the most widespread approach is to raise (or not) prices by an arbitrary amount or percentage each year. Such incremental price increases imply the original price was appropriate. Generally, this is a false assumption. An agency's current prices are often the cumulative result of arbitrary *ad hoc* decisions made from time to time over many years. If the initial price was arbitrarily derived, then subsequent incremental increases lead to an arbitrary price that is unlikely to ultimately reflect either an agency's objectives or its clienteles' best interests.

Agencies tend to make major price changes reactively in response to an emergent financial or political imperative. Strategic pricing, in contrast, requires proactively developing a policy. A proactive approach that embraces the science of the past three decades is needed to ensure the *right* prices are charged for services so decision makers do not expose themselves to a backlash from self-inflicted wounds.

The science base provides a strong conceptual scaffolding upon which to construct an effective pricing policy, but it does not prescribe a formula that will lead to the "one right answer":

> There is no one right way to determine price. Pricing simply cannot be reduced to a formula — there are too many interacting factors. Successful pricing requires considering all internal and external factors and adapting to changes as they occur. Successful pricing is adaptive pricing. (p. 623)[19]

This leads to a recognition that pricing is also an art because the application of the knowledge requires skill, experience, courage and imagination. Price decisions are context specific, so they cannot be formulistic. A one-size-fits-all approach cannot work. A pricing policy that has proved successful in one community may be entirely inappropriate in another. Community perspectives are different, and the expectations of stakeholders vary. Hence, adapting prices to shifts in political, economic and competitive conditions requires local knowledge and understanding. Timing, a sense of what will be an acceptable price, and the ability to influence participants' acceptance of changes are all part of the art. Nevertheless, knowledge of the science base reduces the uncertainties, is likely to prevent egregious errors, and will provide the justification required of agency managers and elected officials to demonstrate their pricing decisions are neither arbitrary nor inequitable:

> Pricing is an art. It depends as much on good judgment as on precise calculation. But the fact that pricing depends on judgment is no justification for pricing decisions based on hunches or intuition. Good judgment requires that one ask the right questions and comprehend the factors that make some pricing strategies succeed and others fail. (p. 9)[20]

SUMMARY

Most public leisure services were established as heavily subsidized social services. However, after the Depression, governments took responsibility for an increasing number of services, and taxes were raised in order to finance them. In the late 1970s and early 1980s, a backlash emerged. This was the start of enduring and relentless political pressure to generate income from user pricing, which continues unabated. The initial political demand was, "Do more with less." This led to inexorable cost cutting and, despite the mantra, inevitable reductions in services. Subsequently, it was complemented by efforts to do more with more, recognizing leisure services often can be improved and expanded if revenues generated from users are forthcoming.

Price has multiple synonyms: fees, charges, permits, rentals, registrations and licenses. However, from the users' perspective, the total sacrifice that constitutes their price comprises more than money paid to an agency for a service. The total sacrifice is the composite price. It comprises fixed and variable ingredients. Fixed elements include investments in major equipment, clothing and footwear and in annual or season passes. Variable elements may be monetary, which comprises payments to participate in a program; travel to and from a facility; auxiliary food, drink or equipment; and temporary assistance to take over users' conflicting responsibilities; or non-monetary sacrifice, which comprises opportunity costs, psychic costs, and effort costs.

The concept of composite price has three important implications for managers. First, price elasticity of demand suggests the aggregated magnitude of fixed and variable costs will influence acceptance or rejection of a monetary price increase. Second, the composite price ingredients are substitutable. Third, more is not necessarily better because it may raise the time and opportunity cost.

Price is the voluntary reciprocal that users pay in exchange for the benefits derived from a program. This relationship is analogous to transactions in the private sector. However, in the public sector, it is embedded within a more comprehensive financial paradigm that recognizes the primary source of funding for most leisure agencies is taxes, not self-generated revenues.

The pressure to increase revenues and decrease tax subsidies may result in revenue streams driving the mission instead of contributing to it. This tension is a manifestation of the central conundrum in all public-sector pricing decisions, which is how to reconcile pricing's two guiding concepts optimally: the Benefit Principle, which states each user's contribution to costs should reflect the benefits he or she receives from the service, and the Ability to Pay Principle, which directs that residents should not be excluded from participating because they lack the funds to do so.

The effectiveness of price increases will be strongly influenced by the extent to which they are embraced by front-line staff. If staff do not understand or accept the legitimacy of reasons for the changes, they will be resistant, or at best disinterested, when implementing them. If they are unwilling or unable to respond constructively and positively to negative reactions from their clienteles, political controversy may flourish. This means staff must be fully engaged in the development of revised prices and their input solicited.

Pricing decisions have implications for an agency's exposure to negligence liability claims for personal injury. They invariably are a significant factor when courts determine whether a service is an immune governmental function or a proprietary function subject to negligence liability. The greater the magnitude of a price, the more likely it is the courts will make an agency liable.

As prices have become more substantial and demands for greater transparency in government have grown, managers and elected officials have been required to justify their price increases. During the past 30 years, a substantial body of knowledge has emerged to facilitate this task, but it remains untapped by many leisure managers. A strong conceptual and scientific scaffolding upon which to construct an effective pricing policy is provided in this book, but a formula is not proscribed that will lead to the "one right answer." Pricing is also an art requiring managers to adapt the principles to the unique, context-specific, political, economic and competitive conditions that prevail in their community.

REFERENCES

1. Macintosh, B. (1983). *Visitor fees in the National Park System: A legislative and administrative history.* Washington, DC: History Division, National Park Service, Department of the Interior.

2. Crompton, J. L. (2007). *Twentieth century champions of parks and conservation: Volume I.* Champaign, IL: Sagamore.

3. Drake, M. A. (1981). *User fees: A practical perspective.* Littleton, CO: Libraries Unlimited.

4. Harnik, P. (1998). *Paying for urban parks without raising taxes.* San Francisco, CA: The Trust For Public Land.

5. Crompton, J. L., & Kaczynski, A. T. (2003). Trends in local park and recreation department finances and staffing from 1964–65 to 1999–2000. *Journal of Park and Recreation Administration, 21*(4), 124–144.

6. Crompton, J. L., & Kaczynski, A. T. (2004). State governments' expenditures on parks and recreation 1989/90 through 1999/2000. *Journal of Park and Recreation Administration, 22*(2), 101–116.

7. Walls, M. (2013). *Paying for state parks.* Washington, DC: Resources for the Future.

8. Zielhaml, V. (1988). Consumer perceptions of price, quality, and value: A means-end model and synthesis of evidence. *Journal of Marketing, 52*(3), 2–22.

9. Gratton, C., & Taylor, P. (1985). From economic theory to leisure practice via empirics: The case of demand and price. *Leisure Studies, 14,* 241–261.

10. Prottas, J. M. (1981). The cost of free services: Organizational impediments to access to public services. *Public Administration Review, 41,* 526–534.

11. Pearlman, R. (1975). *Consumers and social services.* New York, NY: Wiley.

12. Anderson, T. L., Huggins, L. E., & Power, T. M. (2008). *Accounting for Mother Nature: Changing demands for her bounty.* Stanford, CA: Stanford Economics and Finance.

13. Taylor, P., Panagouleas, T., & Kung, S. P. (2011). Access to English public sports facilities by disadvantaged groups and the effect of financial objectives. *Managing Leisure, 16,* 128–141.

14. Smith, A. (1976). *An inquiry into the nature and causes of the wealth of nations.* R. H. Campbell & A. S. Skinner (Eds.). Oxford, England: Clarendon Press. (Original work published in 1776)

15. McCarville, R., Sears, D., & Furness, S. (1999). User and community preferences for pricing park services: A case study. *Journal of Park and Recreation Administration, 17*(1), 91–105.

16. Kozlowski, J. C. (2013, November). Traditional municipal immunity for local parks. *Parks and Recreation, 48*(11). Retrieved from http://www.parksandrecreation. org/2013/November/Traditional-Municipal-Immunity-for-Community-Parks/

17. Kozlowski, J. C. (2011, August). Vehicle fees may impact recreational use immunity. *Parks & Recreation, 46*(8). Retrieved from http://cehdclass.gmu.edu/jkozlows/ lawarts/artlist.htm

18. Kozlowski, J. C. (1998, July). Sport league fees: Exception to recreational use statute immunity. *Parks & Recreation, 33*(7), 46–51.

19. Monroe, K. B. (2003). *Pricing: Making profitable decisions.* New York, NY: McGraw-Hill.

20. Nagle, T. T., & Holden, R. K. (2001). *The strategy and tactics of pricing: A guide to profitable decision-making.* Englewood Cliffs, NJ: Prentice Hall.

Section 1

Multiple Dimensions of the Benefit Principle

The Functions of Price in the Public Sector

Invariably, the primary question elected officials and managers ask when they discuss pricing, especially during times of fiscal austerity, is: How much additional revenue will proposed changes in price produce? This question is discussed in Chapter 4. However, a necessary prerequisite to that discussion is an understanding of the role of the other functions of price, which are addressed in Chapters 2 and 3, respectively: facilitating equity and facilitating efficient allocation of resources. They are termed "invisible" in the chapter titles because they are rarely overtly considered in pricing decisions.

This is unfortunate because this will likely have negative consequences and lead to acrimony. If they are ignored and the focus in pricing decisions is exclusively on revenue production, users of the service are likely to vociferously oppose the proposed price increases. In contrast, if these invisible functions are considered and formally incorporated into pricing policies and procedures, increases in price will likely arouse little controversy.

An exclusive focus on generating additional revenue reflects a private sector mindset, consistent with the naïve mantra that agencies should act like a business. A business identifies target markets that are likely to be responsive to its offerings and then develops a marketing mix (service/product, distribution, promotion and price) strategy that it anticipates will produce the maximum financial return on its investment. However, a public agency has much broader objectives. It is required to be inclusive. Its mandate is not to serve only responsive target markets, but to offer services that *equitably enhance* the health, safety and welfare of *all* the residents of a community.

This concept of *equity*, which is discussed in Chapter 2, is the core element that differentiates marketing in the public and private sectors. In simple terms, equity is concerned with how benefits are distributed. It questions whether the allocation of services in a community is fair. Every time a service is expanded or contracted, and every time a price or tax is increased or decreased, an equity decision has been made. Equity revolves around the question: Who gets what? In the context of pricing this becomes: Who ought to pay for what? Because an agency's economic resources are finite, the allocation of leisure services to one community, neighborhood, or clientele group means that others must be deprived of the use of these resources. Similarly, because the agency's resources typically come from non-user taxpayers as well as from service users, non-user residents are deprived of discretionary income. These equity issues undergird much political debate.

Unfortunately, decision makers seldom consider the relationship between who pays for, and who benefits from, public services. Tradition and emotion are frequently more powerful influences on pricing decisions than is rational economic thinking. Too often, "the squeaky wheel gets the grease"; that is, those who are most vociferous and persistent succeed in persuading elected officials to subsidize the services from which they receive a disproportionate amount of benefit.

Price *facilitates the efficient allocation* of an agency's resources. This role has two dimensions, which are discussed in Chapter 3. The first is economic. A basic problem confronting leisure managers is how to allocate their finite resources in the most efficient way to people with unlimited desires. In the private sector, this is usually done by the price mechanism, which regulates and creates a balance between supply and demand.

Pricing makes it likely that those service users place a relatively high value on it. Zero price or an unreasonably low price means that a subsidy will be needed. This has three potential negative outcomes: (i) an opportunity cost, as these funds cannot be used to deliver other needed services or to reduce the tax burden on residents; (ii) increased numbers, which may result in congestion and overcrowding, so the quality of the leisure experience and/or the resource base will be eroded; and (iii) a reduction in the leisure services available to residents because subsidies preclude non-profits and businesses from charging prices that will generate the revenues necessary for them to offer the services.

The second dimension of using price to facilitate the efficient allocation of resources is behavioral in that it may encourage more positive attitudes and behavior by users and stronger accountability among managers.

While the efficiency role of price is important, it is secondary to equity considerations, as they reflect a community's value system. Efficiency is focused on aggregate benefits and costs. It does not consider their distribution among individuals or purport to address the principle of inclusion. If an agency's mission is subsumed to a preoccupation with revenue production, efficiency is likely to prevail over considerations of equity. It has been argued that in such a situation:

> The question becomes: "How well is the agency doing?" (in terms of reducing costs) rather than "How well is the public function being served?" This masking is exacerbated by the current use of business metaphors like "customer satisfaction," which push public agencies toward a private-like conception of themselves. It has been

pointed out that a customer is a person who buys something from someone who owns it. This reverses the situation with respect to public lands where the public is the owner, not the customer. The lands are managed by the agencies in trust of the public and not for agency benefit. (p. 239)[1]

This revenue focus is inappropriate for a public agency. The issue is further illustrated by the following vignette:

Trading Equity for Efficiency

The primary focus of a 15-acre park located proximate to a busy highway in a major city was a large outdoor lido pool constructed by the Works Progress Administration in the Depression years of the 1930s. The pool was open for 4 months in the summer. The neighborhood had changed from middle to lower income residents, and in recognition of this, prices were kept low. Although it now looked "tired," average daily attendance over the past 5 years was 200–300. The combination of high maintenance costs on the old equipment and low prices resulted in the pool losing around $400,000 a year. The city was approached by a company who wanted to lease the site and build a water park on it. They offered a lease fee of $500,000 a year for 12 years. The council accepted the offer, noting that removal of the loss and the lease fee meant a net gain of $900,000 a year.

In terms of efficiency, this was obviously a prudent action. But what about equity? It seems likely that those willing to pay $20 for admission to the new water park would be different from those who were paying $2–$3 to use the pool.

Serving the economically disadvantaged is often expensive because subsidies are needed; their levels of leisure literacy are lower; and the challenges of communicating with them are greater. This means that gains in efficiency can be achieved relatively easily by shifting the target market from lower income groups to higher income cohorts. However, those revenue gains often come at the expense of underserving low income groups.

Trade-offs between efficiency and equity are inevitable, so some efficiency will be sacrificed for equity, and vice versa. Some view the pricing of public leisure services with suspicion and apprehension as they associate price with market forces. They suggest this is inappropriate and that trade-offs associated with public resources should be established through the political process. However, price does not usurp the trade-off decisions. Rather, it is the vehicle for implementing the outcome of the political process.

REFERENCE

1. More, T. A. (1999). A functionalist approach to user fees. *Journal of Leisure Research, 31*, 227–244.

Chapter 2

Facilitating Equity

The First "Invisible" Function of Price

- Alleviating inappropriate income redistribution
- The Benefits Continuum
- Summary

In this chapter, the two primary issues in facilitating equity are discussed: using price to alleviate inappropriate income distribution and operationalizing the Benefit Principle so costs of a service are allocated fairly among those who benefit from it.

ALLEVIATING INAPPROPRIATE INCOME REDISTRIBUTION

General Principles

Income redistribution occurs in the provision of every government-supplied service—unless everyone receives benefits proportionate to the amount he or she pays in taxes. The key question is: Is the redistribution congruent with, or in conflict with, generally held social and ethical values? In the U.S. and other advanced economies, these values have led to the development of tax systems that were designed to collect resources from wealthier individuals and then redistribute them as public services to the economically disadvantaged. The intent was that the economically disadvantaged should not be excluded from public services because they cannot afford to pay.

Concern for the economically disadvantaged underlies the frequent contention with which leisure managers are confronted that raising user prices will impose hardship on poor people. However, in this section, it is pointed out that break-even pricing is not incompatible with social justice. If used appropriately, it can facilitate it. In many instances, providing subsidized services instead of charging user prices may not achieve the antici-pated redistribution results. Indeed, *in some cases, low income groups are better off when user prices are charged.*

The principle of those with higher incomes paying a higher percentage in taxes as their income increases is termed "progressive taxation." It is consistent with the Ability to Pay Principle in that those who have more income make a larger contribution to services financed by the government. It is embedded in income tax structures used by state and federal governments in the U.S.

The federal income tax rates shown in Table 2-1 exemplify a *progressive* tax. The table shows that a single person earning (say) $95,000 a year will pay 10 percent in tax on the first $9,075; 15 percent on the $27,842 between $9,025 and $36,900; 25 percent on the $52,449 between $36,900 and $89,350; and 28% on the residual $5,650 between $89,350 and $95,000.

Table 2-1

Federal Income Tax Brackets and Rates

Rate	Single Filers	Married Joint Filers	Head of Household Filers
10%	$0 to $9,075	$0 to $18,150	$0 to $12,950
15%	$9,076 to $36,900	$18,151 to $73,800	$12,951 to $49,400
25%	$36,901 to $89,350	$73,801 to $148,850	$49,401 to $127,550
28%	$89,351 to $186,350	$148,851 to $226,850	$127,551 to $206,600
33%	$186,351 to $405,100	$226,851 to $405,100	$206,601 to $405,100
35%	$405,101 to $406,750	$405,101 to $457,600	$405,101 to $432,200
39.6%	$406,751+	$457,601+	$432,201+

Note. Every year, the IRS adjusts these brackets for inflation. This is done to prevent "bracket creep." This is the phenomenon by which people are pushed into higher income tax brackets be-cause of inflation instead of any increase to real income. The IRS uses the Consumer Price Index (CPI) to calculate the past year's inflation and adjusts income thresholds accordingly.

Income taxes are the federal government's main source of revenue, whereas local and state governments rely primarily on property and sales taxes, respectively. On average, local governments receive 74 percent of their resources from the property tax and much of the rest from a sales tax.[1] At the state level, sales taxes on average provide 22 percent ($340 billion) of states' revenues, a further 15 percent comes from income tax, and 37 percent is received in transfers from the federal government.[2]

The property tax is sometimes rationalized as meeting the Ability to Pay Principle in that real property serves as a proxy for income. However, it has long been recognized that the correlation between income and real property is often not strong. For example, in a classic treatise published in 1895, the author criticized the use of property taxes by pointing out that government services have a direct relationship with people, not property: "Every civilized community professes to tax the individual according to his ability to pay . . . But is property the true test of ability?" (p. 54). His emphatic response to his own question was, no, it is *income* that determines ability to pay[3]. Despite the long-established repudiation of the contention that the property tax is progressive, it has endured as the primary source of revenue for local governments.

Unlike income taxes, property and sales taxes in almost all cases are *regressive;* that is, they require those with lower incomes to pay a higher percentage of their income in taxes, so they are inconsistent with the Ability to Pay Principle. These differences are shown in Figure 2-1.[4] The figure shows that states' income taxes are progressive as their proportion of household income consistently increases with income level, so, on average, households in the lowest 20 percent income cohort pay only a tenth of the income tax paid by the wealthiest families.

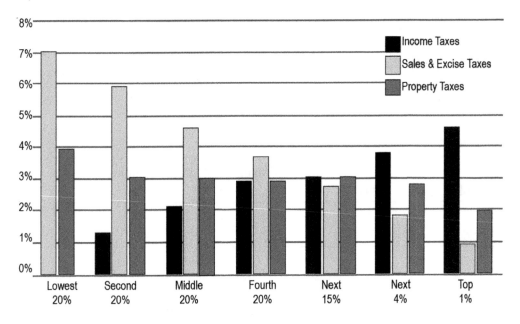

Figure 2-1. Comparing Types of Taxes: Averages for All States

Figure 2-1 shows that sales taxes are the most regressive element in most state and local systems. It shows that while the poorest 20 percent of families pay 7 percent of their income in sales taxes, this falls to 4.6 percent and 0.9 percent for the middle 20 percent and wealthiest taxpayers, respectively.[5] Because sales taxes are levied at a flat rate, and because spending on services and goods as a proportion of income declines as income rises, sales taxes take a larger share of income from low and middle income families than from the more affluent. This is illustrated in Table 2-2.

Table 2-2

Illustrating the Regressive Nature of Sales Taxes

Cost of a new washer and dryer	$2,000
State and local combined sales tax rates	7.5%
Sales tax paid	$150
Person A: Sales tax paid as a percentage of $20,000 annual income	0.75%
Person B: Sales tax paid as a percentage of $100,000 annual income	0.15%

Similarly, property taxes are regressive and distort the principle of income redistribution. On average, low income homeowners and renters pay a higher proportion of their incomes in property taxes (almost 4 percent) than any other income group, while the wealthiest taxpayers pay the least (2 percent). This principle is illustrated in Table 2-3. The table shows two households with homes of the same value, but with different household incomes. They both pay the same property tax rate of 2 percent of their property's appraised value (for city, county, school and special district taxes), but the lower income family pays a higher proportion of their income in taxes.

Table 2-3

Illustrating the Regressive Nature of Property Taxes

Household	Home Value	Property Taxes at 2%	Annual Household Income	% of Income on Taxes
Household A	$200,000	$4,000	$40,000	10
Household B	$200,000	$4,000	$100,000	4

As shown in Figure 2-2, the regressive nature of sales and property taxes is endemic among U.S. states, irrespective of their dominant political philosophy. The most populous state, California, is predominantly Democratic, while Texas, the second most populous state, is predominantly Republican. Nevertheless, as illustrated in Figure 2-2, their sales and property taxes are similarly regressive.[4]

The Role of Price in Alleviating the Impact of Regressive Taxes

Some elected officials invariably are opposed when higher prices are proposed because they believe it would impose hardship on lower income groups. However, this is predicated on the assumption that substantive numbers of those who are economically disadvantaged are heavy users of leisure services, and in most communities, this assumption is false. Use tends to be heavily weighted to the middle and upper income segments of the public, most of whom would be unlikely to forgo these public offerings if a break-even price was charged.

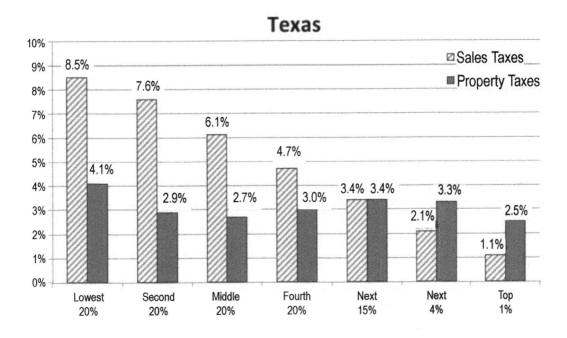

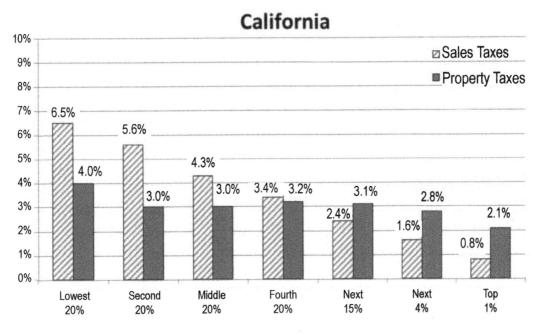

Figure 2-2. A Comparison of Shares of Family Income Expended for State and Local Sales and Property Taxes by Non-Elderly Taxpayers in California and Texas

The findings of an analysis of the regular users of a metropolitan leisure center were typical.[5] The 10,000 users represented 4 percent of the jurisdiction's population, and only 300 of them were low income users. Prices were low because an explicit political objective was to reduce the cost barrier to access. As a result, the annual subsidy for the center was $3.5 million. If 300 low income users were the rationale for the $3.5 million subsidy, each of them received a subsidy of almost $12,000. The opportunity cost of these funds is likely to be significant: either to subsidize other services that would deliver greater aggregate benefits to the economically disadvantaged or to reduce the regressive property and sales taxes, which hurt them the most.

Surveys of users at cultural facilities, such as libraries, art galleries, zoos, aquariums, boat marinas, and museums, have consistently shown similar findings. For example, "It has been repeatedly documented that library users are predominately middle and upper-middle class, middle to upper-middle income, white collar, professional, managerial, better-educated individuals" (p. 16),[6] leading to the conclusion:

> It is clear that, by their financing and operation, public libraries actually redistribute income from the poorest to the more affluent strata of the community . . . The conclusion we cannot avoid is that the poor do not get their money's worth from the public library . . . The public library is not simply neutral in regard to the disadvantaged whom it serves poorly; it is an integral part of the burden resting on those least able to bear it. (p. 352)[7]

Similar observations have been made about public parks:

> By and large, the supply of free public parks in the United States is less adequate in crowded city areas where people are poor, than it is in suburban and higher income residential areas where the people concerned are more nearly able to pay for their own outdoor recreation. On a state or national basis, the discrepancy is even worse: The really poor people do not own the private automobiles which are necessary to get to most state parks and to all national parks and national forests, nor can they in most areas afford the travel costs of such visits. The argument that free public parks help the poor is almost wholly myth. (p. 322)[8]

As pointed out in this observation, for the economically disadvantaged, the substantial cost of overcoming the distance and time constraints involved in getting to state and national parks means subsidizing these facilities constitutes subsidies to the wealthier elements of society for whom the constraints are not such a substantive barrier.

The data in Table 2-4 are typical of the recreational use patterns among different income groups.[9] They were collected in a probability survey of households sponsored by a large metropolitan parks and recreation department. They show that at every facility except basketball courts, participation increased with income. Since provision of these facilities was subsidized, and as the subsidy came from regressive property and sales taxes, income was redistributed toward greater inequality. This typical finding caused a respected state parks director to comment:

Clinging to the feel-good philosophy underwriting the 90% so as not to be blamed for the 10%'s absence helps no one … For generations we built the quantity of public use by subsidizing users who could afford to pay. How relevant is a profession that continues to insist on such subsidies in the face of deteriorating park conditions and declining quality of experiences? (p. 5)[10]

Table 2-4

The Proportion of Residents in Each of Four Household Income Categories Who Use Selected Facilities at Least Once a Month

Facility	Less than $25,000 %	$25,001–$45,000 %	$45,001–$75,000 %	Over $75,000 %
Parks and Playgrounds	22	30	38	40
Tennis Courts	6	10	13	19
Swimming Pools	10	12	13	15
Golf Courses	2	4	3	6
Racquetball/Handball Courts	7	9	11	14
Recreation Centers	8	8	11	11
Fields for Organized Sports	8	11	20	22
Bicycle Trails	8	11	21	20
Basketball Facilities	10	11	12	14
Beaches	29	37	49	46
Marinas or Boat Ramps	5	5	9	15
Jogging Trails	8	10	15	19

Providing services in which the wealthier segments of society are supported by those at the lower end of the income scale has been termed "a distorted price system."[11] It results in a perverse income or benefit redistribution. The distortion is illustrated by the "line of incongruity" in Figure 2-3. It shows the primary beneficiaries of a tax subsidy, which ostensibly is justified because it assists the economically disadvantaged, are higher income groups. The serrated lines in Figure 2-3 indicate that low income groups should receive a subsidy in accordance with the Ability to Pay Principle, while other groups should pay for the benefits they receive in accordance with the Benefit Principle. As well as being inequitable, a distorted price system is wasteful and inefficient as subsidies are given to middle and upper income users who do not need them.

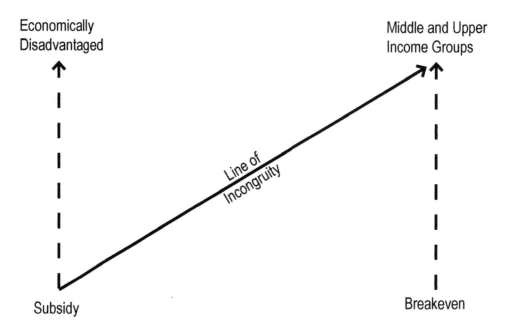

Figure 2-3. A Distorted Price System

This distortion leads to the conclusion that *if a break-even price is charged, it allevi-ates some of the financial burden on those with low incomes,* **provided** *they are not users of the service.* As only 6 percent of the low income cohort report they play tennis, as shown in Table 2-4, it means 94 percent of that cohort who pay regressive taxes and do not use the facility will be better off if a break-even price is charged. Hence, the appropriate policy is to charge the break-even price and meet the Ability to Pay Principle by giving discounts to low income users rather than offering the service to all at a reduced price regardless of income (mechanisms for doing this are discussed in Chapters 6 and 7). This gives lower income groups the option of whether they want to use a service rather than requiring them (and non-users in all other income cohorts) to pay for a service they do not use through the regressive tax system.

The fallacy of basing pricing decisions on emotions rather than on rational analysis was highlighted over 50 years ago:

The social objections to charging – particularly that the poor cannot pay – are the most difficult to discuss rationally because they are advanced for emotional as well as logical reasons. It is easy for the opponents of charging to make themselves seem to be on the side of the angels; compassionate, caring, concerned for the poor, the halt, the lame, the sick, the blind, the fatherless, the deserted, the neglected, the bashed and in general the down-trodden, the under-privileged and the disadvantaged. Con-versely it is easy to make the advocates of charging appear cold, callous, unfeeling, hard-hearted. (p. 231)[12]

It is important to recognize that public resources are finite, not infinite, so an opportunity cost is associated with revenues that are forgone and taxes used to subsidize a given service. It is unreasonable to advocate for satisfying recreation needs fully unless the resources invested could not be put to better use in subsidizing housing, health, first responders (i.e., police and fire), food or whatever. In many cases, failure to price leisure services at break-even level will effectively penalize poor people, because there are no funds available to facilitate their access to other services they may deem to be more desirable. This issue was pithily addressed 30 years ago, but it seems equally appropriate today, even though "free" is likely to have been replaced by "heavily subsidized":

> If we have a goal of providing free recreation to all citizens, then we will be destined for failure and frustrating careers. The statement, "If we charge fees, only those who can afford it will have recreation and those who can't won't" offers a conclusion contrary to what we hope to accomplish by assessing fees. Charging those who can afford to pay for recreation allows subsidization of a greater number of people who cannot. Striving to subsidize everyone hinders the opportunities for people who are poor. (p. 59)[13]

Empirical support from survey findings for this policy has been available for a long time. For example, when a national probability sample of 800 households were surveyed 40 years ago, it was reported:

> Respondents typically accept user fees as a reasonable method of paying for outdoor recreation activities. Most citizens also feel that recreation services should be on more of a pay-as-you-go basis. This attitude was shared by all demographic groups, for all regions of the country. The greatest support for user fees came from the elderly, the low income, and rural residents. Often these characteristics corresponded to persons with low rates of participation (non-users). Lesser support for user fees (although supporters are still a majority in all cases) came from the young, high income and college educated groups. Often these characteristics corresponded to persons with high rates of participation (users). (p. 12)[14]

In another study undertaken three decades ago, the authors reported results of surveys in three U.S. cities and stated:

> One conclusion evident from the study results is that the *implied* service priorities of agencies today, appear to be dramatically different from the historical service orientation of public recreation agencies. The recreation movement in this country began as a response to the wretched living conditions of the urban poor, largely comprised of black and immigrant minority ethnic groups. The data indicated that a major, perhaps unconscious, transformation has occurred. Low income groups were found to consistently underutilize public park and recreation resources, with non-use figures exceeding 80 percent for all facilities except parks and playgrounds. Conversely, the primary clientele of all three municipalities were upper and middle income groups. Significantly, that segment of the population which this field was born to serve – the poor and the disenfranchised – is apparently no longer the focus of service delivery. (p. 48)[15]

There appear to be three reasons why these price distortion inequities have prevailed for so long. First, the contention that raising prices will reduce the financial burden on the economically disadvantaged is ostensibly counterintuitive. Second, price changes are frequently incremental, building on existing historical prices, so inequities from past decisions related to who benefits and who pays are never addressed and thus are perpetuated.

Finally, there is the political reality that anytime a substantial price increase is proposed, users who will be adversely affected by it may protest sufficiently vigorously that elected officials and managers are dissuaded from pursuing such an action. Whatever the reason, many agencies clearly have potential for prices to be raised to alleviate the inappropriate income redistribution created by a distorted price structure.

A Caveat

While the role of price in correcting inappropriate income redistribution is conceptually sound, its impact on alleviating inequity is likely to be minuscule in a macro societal context because government tax spending policies combine to redistribute more than $2 trillion from the top 40 percent of families to the bottom 60 percent annually. This is illustrated in Figure 2-4, which shows that the typical family in the lowest 20 percent, about 26 million households with incomes between $0 and $17,104, pays an average of $6,331 in total taxes and receives $33,402 in funds from all levels of government.[16] Thus, the average amount of redistribution to a typical family in the bottom quintile is $27,071, so it receives $5.38 worth of government spending for every $1 paid in total taxes. Middle income families receive $1.48 in total spending per tax dollar. The top quintile pays $87,076 more in taxes per family than it receives in government spending, which is 29 cents return on each $1 paid in taxes. The majority of the redistribution benefit comes as a result of federal policies and programs, such as Medicaid, Medicare, Social Security, housing assistance, food stamps and unemployment insurance. This caused one respected analyst to conclude:

> Generally, it is considered desirable if local governments concern themselves with providing goods and services and allow the federal government to worry about income distribution and stabilization. Local governments should regard effects on income distribution and stabilization as being incidental. (p. 273)[17]

This caveat does not mean local elected officials and managers should not be concerned about distorted pricing policies in programs over which they have control. These policies should be avoided as much as possible because the issue is emotionally compelling. A political reality is that many in a jurisdiction are likely to expect that pricing will not be regressive. In these situations, adherence to the principle is important rather than the magnitude of its impact on the economically disadvantaged.

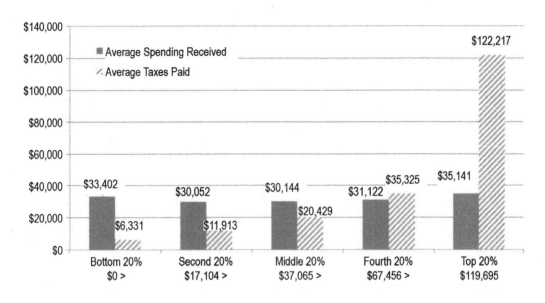

Figure 2-4. A Comparison of How Much Families Paid in Total Taxes with How Much They Received in Total Government Spending in 2012

THE BENEFITS CONTINUUM

Evolution of the Continuum

The Benefit Principle requires the cost of a service be apportioned among stakeholders in proportion to the benefit they receive from it. In the 1950s, economists developed an elegant framework to accomplish this, classifying goods and services into three categories: public, merit (sometimes termed "club" or "mixed") and private.[18, 19, 20]

When the tax revolt of the late 1970s and early 1980s resulted in substantial increases in prices, users, elected officials and taxpayers demanded leisure agencies provide a rationale that justified their prices. At that time, decision makers seldom considered the relationship between who pays for and who benefits from public leisure services. Tradition and emotion often were more powerful influences on pricing decisions than rational economic thinking. Too often, "the squeaky wheel got the grease." That is, those who were most vociferous and persistent succeeded in persuading decision makers to subsidize the services from which they received a disproportionate amount of benefit. However, financial constraints forced a reexamination of traditional irrational approaches, generated greater criticism of emotional rhetoric and required justification of taxation subsidies and the user prices adopted.

This environment led to the public–merit–private continuum being introduced to the field and being adopted by many leisure agencies as the central element of their pricing policies.[6, 9, 21, 22, 23] However, it became apparent that the economists' conceptualization and definition of these terms and the nomenclature they used needed to be modified to better fit the context and needs of the leisure field. It had three major limitations.

First, economists used a service's characteristics to differentiate among public, merit and private services. They presented the framework as a technical, objective method by which the three types of services could be differentiated. For example, public goods or services had four technical characteristics that defined them: (i) non-exclusivity, meaning exclusion of people from receiving benefits from a service is not possible, even though they do not pay for it; (ii) all members of the public jointly share benefits from the service equally; (iii) users cannot choose the amount of it they purchase; and (iv) non-rivalness, meaning one person's consumption of the service does not lower the quantity or quality of it enjoyed by others.

Services widely cited as meeting these criteria were national defense, police protection and mosquito extermination, but in the context of leisure, examples were elusive. Such technical criteria did not reflect the real-life context in which leisure professionals worked. In this milieu, the categories are not defined by technical parameters, rather they are socially constructed.[24] For example, national and state parks have a century of tradition of not charging for interpretation programs. It is possible to exclude people; all do not share equally in all benefits; users can choose the amount of the service they desire. Nevertheless, tradition has created a reference price or widespread expectation (this concept is explained in Chapter 9) that, as in public education, the community as a whole benefits from users being better educated on ecological and historical issues, so interpretation programs should be free.

A second limitation was that reliance on technical definitions of services was incompatible with the emerging awareness among leisure managers in the 1980s and 90s of the importance of focusing on the benefits users sought rather than on the services per se:

> People expend their money and time resources with the expectation of receiving benefits, not the delivery of the services themselves. *People don't buy programs or services; they buy the expectation of benefits. Programs themselves are not marketable. Only their benefits have a value.* (p. 311)[25] [Italics in the original]

Third, the meanings of the terms "public," "merit" and "private" were neither self-evident nor immediately obvious to a leisure agency's non-economist constituents. For example, many incorrectly assumed that the public and private service designations were synonymous with the public and private sectors, which led to confusion and misunderstanding.

The evolution of the benefits continuum shown in Figure 2-5 incorporates how real-world people think and act. It assumes an objective is to price each service at a level that is fair and equitable to users and non-users and recognizes that price changes are political decisions involving (often competing) value systems rather than technical issues that can be resolved by adhering to objective criteria promulgated by economists. Residents' perceptions (or those of their elected representatives), not economists' technical rules, determine how the benefits continuum will be operationalized. This was recognized over 40 years ago by a leading scholar of public finances:

The citizens of a community define what is public and what is private, and within the public sector they also define what may be sold and what is free. Regardless of the theorizing on the nature of public goods or devising methods to allocate costs, it is what people expect of their local political system that limits the official's choice of a good for user-charge financing . . . the case of user charges is too often viewed as a problem of connecting burdens and benefits, as a technical question of allocating costs and dividing benefits. (p. 270)[16]

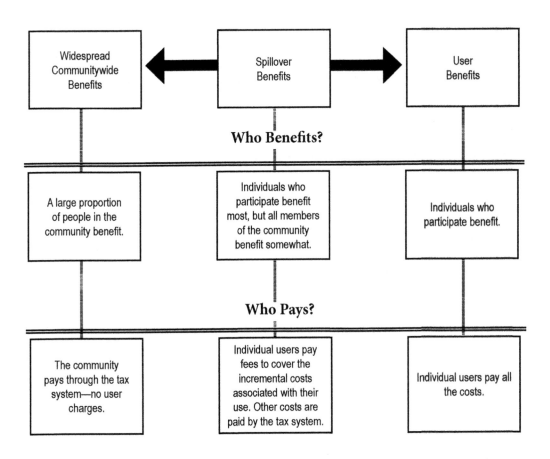

Figure 2-5. The Benefits Continuum

Characteristics of the Continuum

The primary characteristic of services at the *user benefit* pole of the continuum in Figure 2-5 is that benefits are received almost exclusively by participating individuals rather than the rest of the community. A list of potential user benefits is given in Table 2-5.[26] When individuals receive most of the benefits from a service, it is fair they should pay a price that covers the cost of supplying it. Many would categorize adult athletic programs; facilities such as skiing centers, equestrian stables, and marinas; and public library services such as copying and printing as examples of amenities for which benefits accrue almost exclusively to users.

Table 2-5

Potential Benefits Sought by Individuals from Participating in Leisure Services

---

- Social interaction with friends and family kin.
- Social interaction with previously unknown others.
- Ethnic and cultural identity.
- A gain in prestige; social recognition; status. The mastery of particular skills may be regarded as a form of "conspicuous consumption," which brings forth peer group recognition.
- Excitement; an adrenaline rush; exhilaration.
- Ego-satisfaction of achievement and accomplishment; a desire to be successful.
- Security; to be part of a group that gives a sense of belonging, connectedness to others, and a sense of affection.
- The feeling of being important and having responsibility; growth of self-worth and self-confidence.
- Fantasy; illusion; offering temporary escape from the realities and routine of everyday life.
- Relaxation and alleviation of stress and tension, which may be obtained from hard or no physical effort.
- Catharsis from "flow" to alleviate negative tensions, anxiety, anger and unwanted adrenaline.
- Acquisition of knowledge; satisfaction of curiosity.
- Feeling of well-being and vitality derived from exercise and physical fitness and from mental alertness.
- Regression; the desire to "let your hair down" and act in a puerile, adolescent way.
- Aesthetic enhancement derived from being in an attractive natural environment.
- Challenge and risk, which lead to self-exploration, self-discovery and self-development and may be obtained from sailing or skydiving or from acting, dancing or fly-fishing.

These transactions are somewhat analogous to those in the private sector in that prices are voluntary payments and they are set to cover costs. This caused economists in their original conceptualization of the continuum to term them "private goods." However, there are obvious differences: Public agency user prices are usually intended to cover costs and do not include a profit margin, and the costs they cover generally exclude capital expenditures.

At the other end of the continuum shown in Figure 2-5 are communitywide benefits, indicating that a large proportion of a jurisdiction's residents benefit from a service rather than only a small number of users. The aggregate benefit to a community is perceived to be large enough to justify a program's cost, but the benefit to any one individual is not high enough to induce that individual to provide it. As Smith noted in 1776, such services:

May be in the highest degree advantageous to a great society, but are of such a nature that the profit could never repay the expence to any individual or small number of individuals and which it, therefore, cannot be expected that any individual or small number of individuals should erect or maintain. (p. 723)[27]

In economists' terms, these are "collectively consumed" services. Because all or a majority of residents share the benefits (in a democracy this presumably means 51 percent), the cost of these services is borne by taxes from a community's general fund rather than by revenues paid by individual users.

Facilities such as urban parks are typically perceived to deliver widespread community benefits because not only do a relatively large population of residents tend to use them, but they also contribute benefits to residents who do not directly use urban parks, such as reducing the "heat island effect," alleviating rapid stream water runoff, ameliorating air pollution and enhancing real-estate values.

In some instances, such as a public library, it is possible to levy a user price, but communities elect not to do so because, as with grade school education, they perceive libraries to be an investment in human capital from which everyone in society benefits:

The library creed repeated over more than a century is clear: democracy is desirable; it depends on an educated populace; libraries provide the means for educating members of society to pursue both personal and social goals . . . it makes available information necessary for a citizen to participate in an informed way in the political process. (p. 171)[28]

Viewing services as opposite poles of a user–communitywide benefits continuum is helpful in understanding the essential differences between them, but most public leisure services lie somewhere between the two poles. Fundamentally, they are services that deliver benefits to individual users, but spillover benefits also accrue to non-participants. Although it is possible to levy user prices for these services, it is not reasonable to expect users to cover all costs because of the spillover benefits that accrue to the whole community. The perception of some collective benefits justifies subsidizing users to the extent that benefits are perceived to accrue to the whole community. This rationale was articulated 70 years ago by Secretary of the Interior Harold Ickes in the context of the national parks:

Those who actually visit the national parks and monuments should make small contributions to their upkeep for the services those visitors receive which are not received by other citizens who do not visit the parks that are available to them, but who contribute to the support of these parks.[29]

This means participants are likely to make more use of the service, than if they had to pay a price that covered its costs. Thus, it may be perceived that a tax subsidy and the resultant lower prices will encourage greater participation in leisure activities, which is justified because the community also benefits through, for example, reduced health care costs, fewer work days lost to illness, and increased productivity.

Types of Externalities

Externalities refer to the communitywide and spillover benefit categories shown in Figures 2-6 to 2-9. These benefits are perceived to have consequences for the community as a whole beyond those derived by users.

Economic development is widely viewed as being central to a community's economic prosperity because it is viewed as a means of enhancing the tax base. The enhancement is perceived to provide additional tax revenues, which governments can use either to improve the community's infrastructure, facilities and services or to reduce the level of taxes that existing residents pay. It is seen also as a source of jobs that provide income, which enables residents to improve their quality of life. Leisure agencies can be a central contributor to economic development. That role may take the form of the following:

1. **Attracting Tourists:** The major factor that tourists consider when making a decision about which communities to visit on a pleasure trip is the available attractions. In most cities, those attractions are dominated by facilities and services operated by leisure agencies and their non-profit partners (parks, beaches, events, festivals, athletic tournaments, museums, historical sites, cultural performances, etc.). Without such attractions, there is no tourism.

2. **Attracting Businesses:** The viability of businesses in the highly recruited high technology, research and development, company headquarters and services sectors in many cases depends on their ability to attract and retain highly educated professional employees. The deciding factor of where these individuals choose to live is often the quality of life in the geographic vicinity of the business. No matter how quality of life is defined, leisure opportunities are likely to be a major component of it.

3. **Attracting Retirees:** A new clean growth industry in America today includes the growing number of relatively affluent, active retirees. Their decisions as to where to locate with their substantial retirement incomes is primarily governed by climate and recreational opportunities.

4. **Enhancing Real-Estate Values:** People are frequently willing to pay more for a home located close to a park or natural area than for a comparable home elsewhere. The enhanced value of these properties results in owners paying higher property taxes to governments, reflecting the benefits they receive from their proximate location. When the incremental amounts of property taxes attributable to the park are aggregated, they are likely to be sufficient to pay a substantial proportion of the debt required to retire the bonds used to acquire, develop or renovate the park.

5. **Reducing Taxes:** There is a prevailing myth that development is the highest and best use of vacant land. Consequently, growth is perceived to be the key to enhancing the tax base and keeping property taxes low. The reality is that while residential development is likely to generate significant tax revenue, in most cases, the cost of providing services and infrastructure, especially schools, to the development is likely to exceed the tax revenue emanating from it. So the taxes of existing residents will increase. Creating parks and natural areas is likely to be a less expensive alternative to taxpayers than residential development.

6. **Stimulation of Equipment Sales:** Manufacturers and retailers of recreational equipment and others who sell related services (equipment repairs and leasing, outfitters, etc.) depend on the availability of recreation facilities at which people can use the equipment. This creates jobs and income for residents and sales tax revenues for government.

Figure 2-6. Externalities Leisure Agencies Could Deliver to Enhance a Community's Economic Prosperity

Parks and natural areas enable nature to perform environmental services cost effectively that otherwise would require costly investments in infrastructure and technology to provide. These services include the following:

1. **Protecting Drinking Water:** Development of watersheds brings degradation to aquifer and surface sources of drinking water. The degradation emanates from runoff from septic and sewer systems; lawn and garden chemicals; and rooftops, parking lots and highways. In addition, the development removes the natural processes that filter pollution. Keeping water clean by acquiring or preserving watersheds as natural areas is almost always less expensive to taxpayers than having to invest in the expensive equipment needed to clean them after they have been polluted. The impervious surfaces created by development redirect runoff from water aquifers into culverts and drainage ditches, so in addition to adversely affecting its quality, development may result in reduced quantity of drinking water.

2. **Controlling Flooding:** When flooding occurs, it is testimony that the efficient and effective drainage system created by nature has been abused either by the overdevelopment of watersheds or the infilling of floodplains. Controlling flooding involves substantial cost in dredging, channeling, concreting and building dikes and levees. This is expensive, tends to deflect the flooding to downstream areas rather than resolve it, and periodically fails in times of atypical storms with disastrous consequences. Creating substantial park and open space areas in watersheds and preserving floodplains as greenways helps in managing the flow of the runoff more effectively and less expensively than concrete sewers and drainage ditches.

3. **Cleaning Air:** Air pollution threatens the health of those with asthma and other respiratory diseases, contributes to heart and lung disease, and increases the risk of cancer. Trees and vegetation improve air quality by removing from the atmosphere (i) ozone, other gaseous pollutants and toxic chemicals; (ii) particulate pollutants; and (iii) carbon dioxide. Urban areas have especially high concentrations of these pollutants from traffic, boilers, generators and other sources, and trees are a relatively inexpensive way to mitigate these pollutants.

4. **Reducing Traffic Congestion:** A complementary strategy for cleaning air is directed at reducing traffic congestion. Automobile travel can be reduced by providing hike and bike trails to encourage people to walk and ride rather than to drive. In addition to alleviating air pollution, diverting people to trails reduces the magnitude of investment

needed in highways and encourages people to exercise and embrace a healthier life-style.

5. **Reducing Energy Costs:** The urban heat island effect is caused by the dark surfaces of rooftops, roadways and parking lots in urban areas absorbing the day's heat and radiating it at night. As a result, cities cool less at night than surrounding rural areas, and they remain hotter during the day. The shade and evapotranspiration provided by trees act as natural air conditioners to help keep individual homes and cities cooler, reducing the amount of energy and cost needed to do this.

6. **Preserving Biological Diversity:** Gene pools of species and ecosystems may be essential for future human survival. Species yet unknown or unresearched may hold the key to future food, medicine and fiber sources. Preserving natural areas and creating conservation corridors to connect them are important in preserving genetic diversity.

Figure 2-7. Externalities Leisure Agencies Could Deliver to Enhance Environmental Sustainability in a Community

From a societal perspective, issues identified in this category of benefits are effectively summarized by the mantra: Pay now or pay later. A failure to invest resources in delivering services that will preempt the potential social problems is likely to result in society paying a much higher cost at a later date to resolve the problems when they have escalated to a more serious level. If people are exposed to more than one or two of these social problems so they become mutually reinforcing, they may reach the chronic problem level, which is embraced by the term "social exclusion." Often, the challenge is to assist vulnerable groups, frequently young members of ethnic minorities, in becoming employable and in engaging in civic life and civil society. It involves bringing marginalized residents into the mainstream to strengthen community cohesion. Leisure is potentially a strong vehicle for facilitating this social process of enhanced connectedness.

1. **Reducing Environmental Stress:** Environmental stress may involve psychological emotions, such as frustration, anger, fear and coping responses, and associated physiological responses that use energy and contribute to fatigue. Many who live or commute in urban or blighted areas experience it daily. Parks in urban settings have a restorative effect that releases the tensions of modern life. Evidence demonstrating the therapeutic value of natural settings has emerged in physiological and psychological studies. The cost of environmental stress in terms of workdays lost and medical care required is likely to be substantially greater than the cost of providing and maintaining parks, urban forestry programs and oases of flowers and shrubs.

2. **Community Regeneration:** Regeneration involves improving the physical, social, community and environmental aspects of an area. Effective regeneration is unlikely to be forthcoming if leisure services are not an integral part of it.

3. **Cultural and Historical Preservation:** Without a cultural history, people are rootless. Preserving historical remnants offers lingering evidence to remind people of what they once were, who they are, what they are and where they are. It feeds their sense of history and often is critical to community identity.

4. **Facilitating Healthy Lifestyles:** Growing recognition exists that the key to curtailing heath care costs lies in preventing illness so people do not have to be treated by the expensive medical system. Many health problems are caused by people making bad lifestyle decisions. Engagement in physical exercise is a function of personal and social factors, behavioral change programs and the physical environment. Traditionally, leisure agencies have focused on programs. Evidence suggests that the extent to which the physical environment is "activity friendly" is a central factor because it makes it easier to elect to exercise.

5. **Alleviating Deviant Behavior Among Youth:** Strong evidence exists demonstrating the effectiveness of recreation programs in preventing at-risk youth from engaging in deviant behavior. These programs are likely to be most effective when their characteristics include being carefully structured to provide interactions and relationships with adult leaders, leadership opportunities for youth, intensive and individualized attention to participants, a sense of group belonging, engagement in challenging tasks and activities, youth input into program decisions and opportunities for community service. The return on investment of such programs is substantial compared to the costs of incarceration.

6. **Raising Levels of Educational Achievement:** There has been a movement to increase the amount of time that children are involved in educational activities beyond regular school hours to enhance their educational achievement levels. Recreation has proved to be an effective "hook" for persuading many to participate in after-school programs. Children are permitted to engage in the recreation activities only after they have completed the educational enrichment components of the program.

7. **Alleviating Unemployment Distress:** Leisure agencies can contribute in two ways. First, they are extraordinarily well positioned to create meaningful construction, renovation, repair, and maintenance projects that can absorb relatively large numbers of people who are unemployed. Conservation and park work is relatively labor intensive. It offers many opportunities for unskilled people to enter the workforce and subsequently to develop vocational skills that expand their employability options. Second, agencies can develop leisure programs targeted specifically at this group and designed to provide compensatory benefits that were previously obtained in the workplace.

Figure 2-8. Externalities Leisure Agencies Could Deliver to Alleviate Social Problems in a Community

Sometimes it is assumed that a corollary of the Benefit Principle is that nonusers invariably dislike subsidizing users: "Why should I pay for your recreation?" The letter writer in Figure 2-11 illustrates this perspective. While this may reflect the attitude of some, many studies have shown that others support such subsidies not only for the externalities described in Figures 2-6, 2-7, and 2-8, but also because the subsidy ensures "availability opportunities." Three reasons underlie this phenomenon: "recognizing the existence," "maintaining the option," and "bequesting the future."

Recognizing the existence derives from the satisfaction of merely knowing that a leisure facility exists. Some people may have no children or grandchildren, yet derive a great pleasure (which has an economic value) from services being available for other people's children or for their role in preserving wildlife habitat. Some have called this a nurturance rationale: "Just as good parents want their children to have a variety of rich experiences, so may a society want its 'children' (citizens) to have such experiences."[30] Some people who perceive they are no more likely to visit an Alaskan National Park than they are to ride on a space shuttle still derive pleasure from knowing they are there. They read about them in magazines and watch television specials on them:

> They may wish to protect wildlife in its natural habitat not because they currently wish to see or hunt or pet those animals. They may simply wish to keep (say) the bald eagle in existence in just the same way others might want a medieval cathedral or a pueblo dwelling preserved. Not because they plan to use the eagle or cathedral or pueblo, but because the survival of that thing is important to them. (p. 59)[31]

Maintaining the option is self-directed in that it retains the possibility of using a service in the future. The option to visit national parks in Alaska is still there if people aspire to go there at some future date. Early in life, some people may not use golf courses; nevertheless, they may have aspirations to play golf in the future and thus perceive such facilities have an economic value to them.

Bequest value is the pleasure and satisfaction associated with providing for future generations' well-being.

Figure 2-9. Externalities Derived from Residents' Perceptions of Availability Opportunity

A comprehensive set of 20 externalities that public leisure agencies could deliver is classified into four categories in Figures 2-6, 2-7, 2-8, and 2-9: economic prosperity, environmental sustainability, alleviation of social problems and availability of opportunity. This set is intended to be complete. The rationale and empirical evidence documenting the field's role in delivering each external benefit is documented elsewhere.[26]

Conflicting Stakeholder Interests in Pricing Decisions

Much of the debate about whether a user price should be charged, and if so at what level, revolves around the classification of the service. Because the category boundaries on the benefits continuum are socially constructed[23] and defined through political processes, they shift with social currents. A service's position on the continuum may ebb and flow with changes in community values. For example, a tennis complex assigned to one category may be shifted to another when there is a change in elected officials and philosophy on a city council. Further, an identical complex located in three communities may be perceived to have communitywide benefits in a low income community where elected officials believe the whole community benefits from the provision of healthy activities for residents; from improving quality of life in the area, which raises the value of everybody's property; or from the psychological satisfaction of knowing that the less wealthy are being provided with recreational opportunities that they could not otherwise afford. In a second community, similar benefits may be perceived, but decision makers could argue users receive incremental benefits that do not accrue to non-users and so should pay a price that covers part of the costs. In a third community, benefits may be perceived to be confined exclusively to users, so they are required to pay a price that covers all costs of delivering the service.

Because tax subsidy can only be justified if collective benefits are accruing to a majority in the community, user groups in a community typically seek to shift perceptions of their activity of interest as far as possible away from the user benefits end of the continuum toward the communitywide benefits end, as shown in Figure 2-10, to persuade the agency and the community to pay more of the costs out of taxation revenues and reduce user prices. These user groups are often vociferous and politically active in their efforts to preserve their benefits.

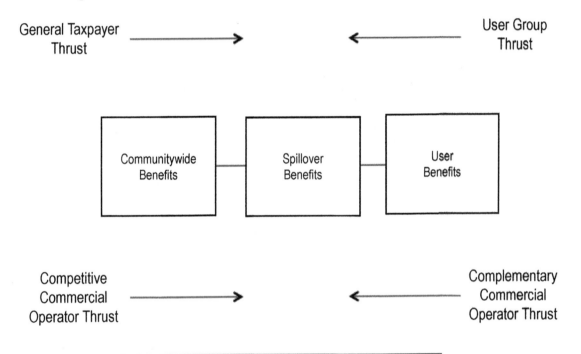

Figure 2-10. Conflicting Stakeholder Thrusts to Influence Pricing Decisions

In the past, reductions in general taxes brought about by the revenues accruing from any specific user price were so small that the average benefiting citizen was disinterested. Hence, user groups frequently prevailed in retaining the price *status quo*. However, as the letter in Figure 2-11 suggests, the general public and their elected representatives now are likely to be more active in demanding that higher user prices should contribute significantly to reducing general tax burdens.[32] Hence, they more frequently seek to shift services away from the communitywide benefits end toward the user benefits end to make participants pay for the benefits they derive from the services they use. The point on the continuum at which a particular service is located will depend upon the relative size and political strength of these groups.

> In the February and the March issues there were comments about the Texas park system needing more money. Why shouldn't the park system support itself? Let those that use the parks pay for them. Charge whatever it takes to operate the parks. Why should someone that never uses the parks pay for someone else's usage? We don't pay for someone to go to the movies do we?

Figure 2-11. A Letter Writer Asks, "Why Shouldn't the Park System Support Itself?"

Elected officials are familiar with pleas from all sections of the community not to raise prices and to improve the quality of services from which they benefit. Unfortunately, some of these same people are also prominent in their criticism of the tax increases and the expansion of government activity in general. They are in favor of tax reductions, but if that results in lowering the quality or elimination of services they use, or in price increases for them, they are likely to oppose such changes. The fictitious discussion among council members in Figure 2-12 illustrates this duplicity.

The role of a commercial business offering similar services in this debate is likely to vary. In situations in which entrepreneurs are in competition with the public agency, their support will be with those seeking to make users pay a higher price because higher prices provide more opportunities for the entrepreneur to compete. For example, increasing user prices at a public marina will make it more viable for private marinas to operate in the area. However, in other situations in which the service is complementary rather than competitive, entrepreneurial support is likely to be with user interest groups because lower prices may mean a larger number of participants frequenting their commercial service. For example, a concession operator at an aquatic arena would probably oppose increases in the admission price because it may lead to fewer visitors using the concession.

> A major controversy has arisen in the city of Laughville concerning the subsidy of recreation and culture. Laughville has a population of 60,000 and is located 60 miles west of the Moonshine Metroplex area. At last month's council meeting, three councilmen suggested that the city include a $6 million recreation center in its new proposed bond referendum. This would be the city's first recreation center.
>
> Two of their colleagues were outraged by this suggestion. Ben Blower, who is now retired and who has been a council member for 14 years, stated:
>
>> Since when is it the proper domain of government to provide luxury items for the public? We have tremendous needs with regard to roads and education in this city, and it's not the proper business of government to spend millions of dollars on recreation facilities. Laughville has prospered without a recreation center for the last 100 years and is likely to do very well without one for the next 100 years. This center will cost $100 for

every man, woman and child in Laughville just to build and goodness knows how much to run each year. If we wanted the amenities of a recreation center and the high taxes required to pay for it, we would have moved to the Moonshine Metroplex. I can't afford to live there, and now I soon may not be able to afford to live in Laughville.

Of course, the proponents claim we will receive all sorts of benefits by taxing ourselves to build a recreation center. But if the benefits are as great as the proponents claim, why do we have to be forced into paying for this recreation center via taxes? Why wouldn't we just heap all those benefits upon ourselves voluntarily?

The proponents could have chosen to raise the funds to build the center through charitable voluntary donations, but that would have taken time, hard work and community spirit. Instead, the proponents have chosen to try and use force to build their recreation center. It doesn't sound too neighborly to me.

Fred Feisty supported Blower by pointing out that just 5 miles down the road in Plainsville is Fitpersons Health Club, which is a commercial facility:

If we build a recreation center in Laughville, it will hurt the Fitpersons business. With the tax-exempt status that goes with a city facility and the lower prices we would charge, they couldn't compete. It's not fair for us to drive a private business into bankruptcy.

The leading proponent of the recreation center is Ms. Myra Hamilton, who reacted angrily to Blower's outburst:

You are a major supporter of the arts and have no problem with proposing each year that the city provide $80,000 to support the arts. But you define the arts narrowly to fit only your interests. Classical music and opera qualify in your mind as "arts," but not rock music. Why not? It is more socially significant, just as artistic and is of interest for more young people. Why not support our kids in bands, a local alternative music radio station and an alternative music concert series? Those who enjoy "the arts" as you define them are a privileged minority who are in the upper educated and income group. Subsidies to the arts have not changed that reality. You, and others like you in this community—the older middle-class folks, enjoy the arts, but we've also got to look out for those who are younger and poorer, who have different interests. It's time you supported something that's going to provide a great deal of enjoyment for the younger people in this city.

She went on to discount Feisty's arguments:

It's obvious there is a need for such a center in our city that is not being met by the Fitpersons facility. What we need here is affordable recreation facilities, conveniently located for our kids. We won't be able to offer the same level of individual attention that people can get at Fitpersons. We'll probably finish up feeding people into their business after they've had some introductory experience at our facility.

Ron Grunt is one of Hamilton's allies in supporting the recreation center. His strategy to remove Blower's opposition appears to be to threaten the subsidy given to the arts:

What are we doing subsidizing the arts? They are basically private pleasures and pursuits. The benefits go primarily to the individual artists and small art groups that receive the grants and to their very small audiences. Community benefits are meager.

Suppose someone proposed the council give grants to a rodeo. Grants would go to individual rodeo riders ("to foster bull-riding skills") and to rodeo shows ("to make rodeos more available to the public"). Questions would arise. Why do rodeo riders and fans merit special treatment? Do they create some community benefit?

It's considered uncouth to ask similar questions of community support for the arts, but what justifies the subsidies? The idea that the community's artistic future depends on council handouts to free artists from commercial pressure falters on two counts. It overlooks the complexity of creative motivation and ignores the corrupting influences of government grants. Mark Twain did not need a public grant to write; Winslow Homer did not need public support to paint. Art consumers benefit from the council's grants because their ticket or purchase prices are indirectly subsidized. But these are mainly higher income people who deserve no subsidy. No great (or even minor) harm would occur if we axed these arts subsidies. The money saved could be used for more legitimate public needs, such as looking after the poor in our community and providing amenities such as a recreation center for them to use.

Figure 2-12. The Subsidy Controversy in Laughville

SUMMARY

In the U.S. and other advanced economies, the intent in designing the tax system was that it should be progressive. That is, resources should be collected from wealthier individuals and then redistributed as public services to the economically disadvantaged. While the income tax, which is the federal government's primary revenue source, is generally consistent with this objective, local and state governments rely primarily on property and sales taxes, respectively. These are regressive; that is, they require those with lower incomes to pay a higher percentage of their income in taxes.

Even though the economically disadvantaged are not major users of most public leisure services in most communities, they are required to pay for them through the regressive tax system. This creates a line of incongruity, that is, a distorted price system in which the wealthier segments of society are supported by those at the lower end of the income scale. This is an inappropriate income redistribution. If low income households are not major users of a service, charging a break-even price will leave them better off. The Ability to Pay Principle should ensure they are not excluded from use by providing them with discounted access.

While this role of price in removing inappropriate income redistribution is conceptually sound, the caveat is that its impact on alleviating inequity is likely to be minuscule in a macro societal context. However, this does not mean elected officials and managers should disregard this line of incongruity in programs over which they have control. Many in a jurisdiction are likely to expect that pricing will not be regressive. Hence, adherence to the principle is important rather than magnitude of its impact on the economically disadvantaged.

The Benefit Principle requires the cost of a service be apportioned among stakeholders in proportion to the benefits they receive from it. In the 1950s, economists developed a framework to accomplish this, classifying all goods into three categories along a continuum: public, merit and private. This continuum has been adapted so its focus is on benefits rather than goods, so the three categories are now communitywide, spillover and user benefits. Concomitant with the adaptation is a recognition that positioning services on the continuum is a social/political decision, rather than a technical decision made by adhering to objective criteria promulgated by economists.

There are likely to be conflicting views in a community on where along the continuum a service should be positioned. Often the views reflect self-interest, so user groups seek to shift perceptions to the communitywide benefits pole by stressing societal gains associated with their program to reduce the user price and justify tax subsidy. In contrast, non-participants may seek to emphasize user benefits and dismiss societal benefits with the intent of raising user fees and decreasing tax subsidy.

REFERENCES

1. U.S. Census Bureau. (2013). Local property taxes as a percentage of total local tax revenue. In U.S. Census Bureau (Ed.), *Statistical abstract of the United States.* Washington, DC: Department of Commerce.
2. Malm, L., & Kant, E. (2013). *The sources of state and local tax revenues.* Washington, DC: The Tax Foundation.
3. Seligman, E. R. A. (1985). *Essays in taxation.* New York, NY: Macmillan.
4. Davis, C., Davis, K., Gardner, M., Heimovitz, H., McIntyre, R. S., Phillips, R., . . . Wiehe, M. (2013). *Who pays? A distributional analysis of the tax systems in all 50 states* (4th ed.). Washington, DC: Institute on Taxation and Economic Policy.
5. Holmes, G., Christie, M., & Higgens, L. (2000, July). Is the price right? *Leisure Manager, 2000,* 14–16.
6. Crompton, J. L., & Bonk, S. (1980). Pricing objectives for public library services. *Public Library Quarterly, 2*(1), 5–22.
7. Weaver, F. S., & Weaver, S. A. (1979). For public libraries the poor pay the most. *Library Journal, 104,* 325–355.
8. Clawson, M., & Knetsch, J. L. (1966). *Economics of outdoor recreation.* Washington, DC: Resources for the Future.
9. Crompton, J. L., & Lamb, C. W. (1987). Establishing a price for government services. *Journal of Professional and Services Marketing, 2*(3), 67–82.
10. LaPage, W. F. (1995). Parklands as paradox: The search for logic in the public's parklands. *Journal of Park and Recreation Administration, 13*(4), 1–12.
11. Thompson, W. (1986). The city as a distorted price system. *Psychology Today, 2*(3), 28–33.
12. Seldon, A. (2004). Introducing market forces into "public" services. In C. Robinson (Ed.), *The collected works of Arthur Seldon* (Vol. 4). Indianapolis, IN: Library Fund.

13. Ellerbrock, M. (1982, January). Some straight talk on user fees. *Parks & Recreation, 17*, 59–62.

14. Economics Research Associates. (1976). *Evaluation of public willingness to pay user charges for use of outdoor recreation areas and facilities.* Washington, DC: Superintendent of Documents.

15. Howard, D. R., & Crompton, J. L. (1984). Who are the consumers of public park and recreation services? An analysis of the users and non-users of three municipal leisure service organizations. *Journal of Park and Recreation Administration, 2*(3), 33–48.

16. Prant, G., & Hodge, S. A. (2013). *The distribution of tax and spending policies in the United States.* Washington, DC: The Tax Foundation.

17. Meltsner, A. J. (1971). *The politics of city revenue.* Los Angeles: University of California Press.

18. Samuelson, P. A. (1954). The pure theory of public expenditure. *The Review of Economics and Statistics, 36*, 387–389.

19. Samuelson, P. A. (1955). Diagrammatic exposition of a theory of public expenditure. *The Review of Economic and Statistics, 37*, 350–356.

20. Musgrave, R. A. (1959). *The theory of public finance: A study in public economy.* New York, NY: McGraw-Hill.

21. Crompton, J. L. (1981). The role of pricing in the delivery of community services. *Community Development Journal, 16*(1), 44–54.

22. Crompton, J. L. (1984). How to establish a price for park and recreation services. *Trends, 21*(4), 12–21.

23. Crompton, J. L. (1981). How to find the price that is right. *Parks and Recreation, 16*(3), 32–39, 64.

24. Malkin, J., & Wildavsky, A. (1991). Why the traditional distinction between public and private goods should be abandoned. *Journal of Theoretical Politics, 3*(4), 355–378.

25. Howard, D. R., & Crompton, J. L. (1980). *Financing, managing and marketing recreation and park resources.* Dubque, IA: Wm. C. Brown.

26. Crompton, J. L. (2007). *Community benefits and repositioning: The keys to park and recreation's future viability.* Ashburn, VA: National Recreation and Park Association.

27. Smith, A. (1976). *An inquiry into the nature and causes of the wealth of nations.* R. H. Campbell & A. S. Skinner (Eds.). Oxford, England: Clarendon Press. (Original work published in 1776)

28. Gell, M. K. (1979). User fees 2: The library response. *Library Journal, 104*, 170–173.

29. Mackintosh, B. (1983). *Visitor fees in the National Park System: A legislative and administrative history.* Washington, DC: History Division, National Parks Service, Department of the Interior.

30. Driver, B. L., & Baltic, T. (n.d.). *Equity in the distribution of public leisure services.* Fort Collins, CO: Rocky Mountain Forest Range Experiment Station.

31. Powell, T. M. (1996). *Environmental protection and economic well-being.* New York, NY: Armouk.

32. Wilson, C. (2000, April). Funding for parks. *Texas Parks and Wildlife, 2000*, 9.

Chapter 3

Facilitating the Efficient Allocation of Resources

The Second "Invisible" Function of Price

- Efficient regulation of the supply of services
- Rationing use: Trade-offs between monetary price and other options
- Encouraging the private sector to deliver services
- Enhanced accountability
- Summary

The efficiency objective of price is concerned with ensuring a community derives the maximum possible benefit from the services offered and from the scarce resources used to finance those services. This chapter describes how price encourages efficiency by (i) regulating the supply of services, (ii) rationing their use, (iii) expanding the range of leisure opportunities available by encouraging the private sector to invest in them and (iv) enhancing accountability by discouraging users from engaging in inappropriate or deviant behavior and holding managers more accountable for their wise use of scarce resources.

EFFICIENT REGULATION OF THE SUPPLY OF SERVICES

The Fallacy of the "Need" Argument

Justification for subsidizing leisure programs is sometimes based on an emotional appeal that everyone "needs" them. It is argued that leisure opportunities are "essential for a healthy and happy existence." Some suggest this is inherent in the "pursuit of happiness," which is one of the three examples (i.e., life, liberty and the pursuit of happiness) of "inalienable rights" that government entities are mandated to protect in the Declaration of Independence. From this perspective, it follows that (i) if large numbers participate, an agency is best serving society and (ii) these services should be heavily subsidized from tax resources and be charged at zero or a nominal price.

However, this line of argument fails for four reasons. First, the Declaration of Independence guarantees the right to the pursuit of happiness, not the attainment of it: "It is not an inalienable right for everyone to visit Yosemite. People have a right to visit Yosemite if they can get there and pay the entrance price" (p. 62).[1] Second, as suggested in Table 2-4, most households do not use public recreation services. Hence, residents' behavior is incompatible with the contention that leisure services constitute a societal need.

Third, this position implicitly assumes that the population's need for leisure services must be fully satisfied. This has been deemed "a very heroic assumption and completely inconsistent with the way we view other goods and services in our economy, even food" (p. 49).[2] People pay a price for food, and they have to compromise on their desires and preferences (e.g., hamburger instead of steak) to accommodate their budget.

Fourth, this tenet perpetuated by advocates that all people "need" leisure services "is not unusual at all. In fact, nearly all professions have a similar one" (p. 47).[2] Such a perspective is myopic because it ignores opportunity cost. Government revenues from taxes are finite, so their allocation has an opportunity cost. "You can't have your cake and eat it too" is a fundamental principle of economics. Producing more of one service means using resources that could be devoted to something else. Thus, every dollar spent to subsidize a leisure service is a dollar that cannot be expended on another service that may be more of a "need." Unfortunately, most citizens do not consider the effect of subsidies on forgone opportunities because they are not obvious:

> If we had to discharge a teacher or policeman every time we built another boat dock or tennis court, we would see the real cost of these public services. But in a growing economy, we need only not hire another teacher or policeman and that is not so obvious. In general, then, given a binding local budget constraint — scarce tax money — to undertake a local public service that is unequalizing or even neutral in income redistribution is to deny funds to programs that have the desired distributional effect, and is to lose control over equity. (p. 29)[3]

Mechanisms for Determining Priorities

The number of programs sought by different beneficiary groups that a leisure agency could provide invariably exceeds the resources it has available. Hence, decisions have to be made about which programs should be given priority. Two prioritizing mechanisms are available. The first is price. When users pay break-even prices for services, their actions signal shifts in demand more quickly and flexibly than can be accomplished through the alternative, which is the inherently cumbersome and less objective administrative and political process. Price gives people an effective way to vote their priorities.

It makes it likely that the limited resources at the disposal of an agency are allocated to those programs for which users are prepared to make the most sacrifice. It has been suggested:

> We are too reluctant in the recreation profession to use the most efficient mechanism ever devised for distributing limited resources: the price system. When consumers are charged the cost of production, they become the ultimate decision makers in society by demonstrating monetarily which goods they most prefer. (p. 60)[1]

The alternative administrative and political process mechanism too often results in services being over- or under-resourced, so priority is given to the wrong services in the wrong quantities. Subsidies are likely to result in people demanding an unreasonably high supply of a service for two reasons. First, many who use the service would not do so if a break-even price were charged. Second, those who benefit from a program correctly perceive that increasing its supply occurs at little or no cost to themselves:

> The principle of fiscal equivalence — that those receiving the benefits from a service pay the costs for that service — must apply in the public economy just as it applies in a market economy. Costs must be associated with benefits if people are to have any sense of economic reality. (p. 31)[3]

Thus, pricing provides "discipline" against excessive claims of beneficiaries and keeps their competing claims in check.

If this efficiency role of price is embraced, it leads to the following radical conceptual proposition: Unless it can be demonstrated that leisure facilities will serve the economically disadvantaged or will offer spillover or communitywide benefits, they should not be built if they require subsidy because residents are communicating that the value of such facilities is not commensurate with their cost.[4] Absent those two conditions, only when prices are high enough to generate break-even revenues should facilities or programs be developed. Certainly, most resistance by elected officials to new programs or facilities stemming from fiscal barriers will be removed if the new offerings are shown to be self-financing.

An artificially large demand induced by an inappropriately low price will often be accompanied by "cries of alarm" that there is a shortage of supply. On occasion, leisure managers may be supportive of these claims because they are emotionally vested in their clients' interests, or perceive that expansion of services for which they have responsibility is a vehicle for "growing their empire." It has been observed:

> The absence of appropriate user prices ultimately results in increased political pressure from benefitting groups for expansion of the services. The natural desire to obtain more subsidized services traditionally has united with the equally natural desire of politicians to be popular (and re-elected), and of managers to be part of a growing organization enhancing their power, prestige and influence. These forces form a powerful upward pressure on the level of government spending. It has been argued that the most important role of pricing for public services is to restrict demand rather than simply to expand supply. (p. 334)[5]

The distortion of demand created by inappropriate subsidies makes it difficult to evaluate the legitimacy of one service's claim on resources compared to the claims of alternate services. The issue has been illustrated by an analogy:

> Suppose that a city decides to finance all steak consumption through general taxes rather than to allow butcher shops or supermarkets to operate in the private market. Individuals would consider steaks to be "free"; they would try to secure as many as possible. The result would be the immediate appearance of a serious "shortage." If the government tries to respond to this "shortage" by supplying more steaks, far too many resources will be drawn into this line of investment relative to its alternatives. (p. 453)[6]

Substantial subsidies are likely to result in one of three inefficient outcomes: (i) there will be a serious shortage of the service with congestion resulting; (ii) relatively too many resources will be allocated to expanding the service to alleviate the perceived shortage; or (iii) if capacity constraints do not limit demand, the relatively large number of users results in low quality service. In regard to this latter condition, when California dramatically lowered fees at state parks by over 50 percent, the annual number of visitors increased from 72 million to 93 million, but no additional resources were provided to serve them. Thus, campgrounds in most popular parks were cleaned less often, public safety calls increased 39 percent and more damage of the parks' ecosystem was reported.[7]

If efficient prices are established, they provide the basis for decisions on the quantity and quality of service that should be offered. For example, if admission price to a community's swimming pools is $2 because they are heavily subsidized and admission to its fitness centers is $8, which is the break-even price, all else equal, participant numbers in the pools will be substantially greater. This may translate to strong political pressure for future investments to prioritize pools over fitness centers. If the price structures were reversed with a $2 charge at fitness centers and $8 at pools, the participation numbers and pressures for prioritizing future investments would likely be reversed.

This distortion caused by different levels of subsidy occurs when residents are surveyed and asked to prioritize future expenditures on facilities. They are unlikely to consider the subsidies of each option because they will be unaware of them. Thus, they are likely to prioritize allocations to those services for which there is a perceived shortage—often reflecting those that are the most heavily subsidized.

RATIONING USE: TRADE-OFFS BETWEEN MONETARY PRICE AND OTHER OPTIONS

The scenario described in Figure 3-1 illustrates the challenges that confront leisure managers at peak times.[8] Many facilities are used intensively during a brief time and moderately or lightly at other times. The intensive use creates either overcrowding or congestion.

Parking lots can be full or overflowing. Lines can be long, and waiting for service can be irritating and stressful. Traffic patterns and flows can resemble urban area rush hours and occasionally result in gridlock. Busy telephones can make contacting site managers for information impossible. Once at the site, direct contacts with area personnel can be nonexistent or limited. Limited and overworked staff unable to deliver quality service can result in unhappy customers and employees alike. Campgrounds and other sites are often full by midmorning, and many people are turned away. Competition among vacationers and squabbling over available sites can give visitors the impression that chaos is the normal style of operation.

Restrictions on recreation activities, party size, equipment, length of stays, pets and other aspects of an outing can make trip planning a major challenge. The need for reservations, advance bookings for some activities, fees and limitations on numbers of vacationers allowed through the gate inconveniences or discourages some visitors to the point that they stay home—or at the least it forces them to cope if they do venture into the great outdoors. Increasingly, it has become obvious that use of many sites exceeds their design capacity—congestion and potential crowding threaten to impact not only the quality of the visitor experience but also the integrity of biophysical and cultural resources.

Figure 3-1. Negative Consequences of Crowding and Congestion at State and National Parks[8]

Overcrowding is a social construct in which the number of people encountered exceeds an individual's normative standard for a satisfying experience. Figure 3-2 shows a typical reaction to overcrowding. Initially, the presence of others may enhance an experience, but at some point overcrowding occurs. If a rationing mechanism is not introduced, the quality and value of the experience decline.

In contrast, *congestion* refers to the physical conditions that occur when infrastructure and services are seriously stressed:

> Under such conditions there is often a lack of available parking spaces and visitors spend much time driving around looking for places to park, there is competition among visitors to access facilities and services, water and sewage systems are near capacity, campgrounds and picnic areas are near of more than 100 percent occupancy, and reservation and quota systems are full and some visitors are turned away. (p. 697)[8]

When natural resource areas are involved, the mandate to conserve the ecological and cultural attributes is paramount because if they are eroded, the enjoyment of future users is compromised.

Value

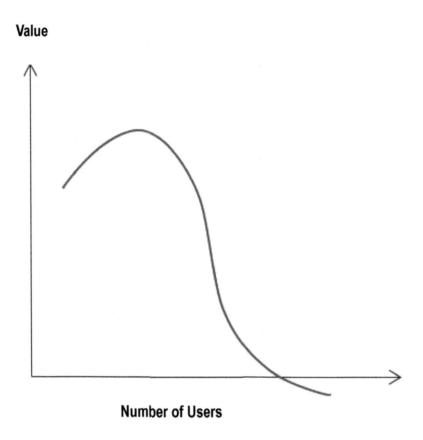

Number of Users

Figure 3-2. The Influence of Overcrowding on the Quality of a Leisure Experience

The policy question confronting managers is how best to equitably allocate peak time access to a service at times when demand for it exceeds its social or physical carrying capacity. There are four primary options:

(i) People apply in advance, and a lottery allocates access for individuals, for groups or for times.

(ii) People apply in advance, and reservations are accepted on a first-come, first-served basis.

(iii) Queuing (waiting in line) allows individuals to trade their time rather than their money for the desired service. Ostensibly, allocation by time may appear to be fairest because time is evenly distributed. However, queuing discriminates against people with a high opportunity cost of time.[9] Leisure time is not evenly distributed, but rather it is probably U-shaped with relatively more available during youth and retirement. Although queuing requires people to pay for a service with their time, no one benefits from this form of price payment. When individuals pay a monetary price, their loss is the agency's gain. When they give up time, it is not available to anyone else, but is lost forever.[10]

(iv) Charge a premium price that is enough to cause those less willing or able to pay to forgo the opportunity. This allows the agency to capture the price of the rationing program, rather than it being lost, as is the case with time pricing. However, it may discriminate against the economically disadvantaged.

When the National Park Service (NPS) commissioned a survey in which a national probability sample of 5,757 respondents was interviewed, it was found a large proportion preferred the first two options and there was little support for the premium price options.[11] In a survey of state and federal river managers, it was similarly reported that premium price was the least preferred among these options for rationing access to rivers.[12] A similar reaction was forthcoming when respondents were asked the fairest way to ration tickets for a sport event when demand exceeded supply (see the vignette in Figure 3-3).[13] The premium price introduces a discriminatory element. These results reaffirm the American empathy for egalitarianism in the realm of public services (i.e., a tendency to prioritize equity over efficiency).

> The opposition to price as a rationing mechanism is illustrated in the responses of residents in Vancouver, Canada, who were asked the following question in a telephone survey:
>
> A football team normally sells some tickets on the day of their games. Recently, interest in the next game has increased greatly, and tickets are in great demand. The team owners can distribute the tickets in one of three ways. (1) By auction: the tickets are sold to the highest bidders. (2) By lottery: the tickets are sold to the people whose names are drawn. (3) By queue: the tickets are sold on a first-come, first-served basis. Rank these three in terms of which you feel is the most fair and which is the least fair: the auction, the lottery, and the queue.
>
> Resources to this question are given in the following table:

Allocation Method	Most Fair (%)	Least Fair (%)
Auction	4	75
Lottery	28	18
Queue	68	7

> In terms of economic efficiency, the three procedures are ranked from the auction, which would allocate the good to the customers willing to pay the most for it, down to the wasteful method of queuing. The inverse ordering prevails when the allocation procedures are ranked by their fairness.
>
> Rationing by time rather than money through queuing is inefficient, but is perceived as being more equitable because it is believed that time is more equally distributed than money. In addition, the money cost of time is presumed to be higher for those who are more wealthy.

Figure 3-3. Reactions to Options for Rationing Tickets to a Sport Event[13]

Event venues sometimes elect to use queuing rather than higher prices to ration tickets for popular events, so people wait in long lines for hours or even camp out for days. The intent is that this will screen out those with the least enthusiasm for the event. The enthusiasm of those who obtain the tickets is likely to enhance the experience for all, which will be reflected in their support for future events. Those who endure wait time in the queues will also likely be inclined to buy performers' albums or branded equipment, T-shirts, posters, and other paraphernalia sold inside the venue (probably at inflated prices). Indeed, it is not unreasonable to expect that the lower the ticket prices and the longer the queues, the greater the prices of the products sold after admission.[14]

Notwithstanding this lack of public support for rationing through price, economists suggest an important advantage of using price is that it prioritizes access by "high-value users" (i.e., those who most value the service), while "low-value users" will elect to come at a different time or to do something else.[15] For example,

A night's developed camping may be worth $25 to a family that enjoys camping, but only $5 to a family with marginal interest . . . In this way pricing assures an efficient allocation of resources, awarding them to people who value them most. (p. 229)[16]

However, this ostensibly rational argument disregards equity implications:

A wealthy family with an annual income of several hundred thousand dollars might find $15 for a night's camping to be negligible. But a working-class family making $30,000 is likely to view the situation differently: that is, a night's camping might be equally desirable to both, but the choice is much more difficult for the family with limited means. And factoring in ability to pay makes it easy to imagine situations that exclude "high-valued users" but include "low-valued users." . . . The key point is that the argument from efficiency is valid only if you assume that one dollar has the same meaning to everyone. (p. 236)[16]

ENCOURAGING THE PRIVATE SECTOR TO DELIVER SERVICES

From an efficiency perspective, communities should encourage private sector suppliers of leisure services for two reasons. First, the presence of fair competition may stimulate the agency to improve performance in terms of responding to user demands and of minimizing costs. Second, most public agencies are unable to satisfy fully all of the demands expected of them. If the private sector can meet some of these demands, agency resources can be redirected to meet other priorities. This explains why most public agencies have a policy (often unwritten) of not competing with the private sector.

Despite their avowed intentions to the contrary, communities too often take actions that discourage private sector leisure suppliers. The vignette in Figure 3-4 illustrates how this occurs.[17, 18] The financial advantages of public agencies include paying no property, sales or income taxes; being self-insured; financing improvements with tax-exempt funds rather than borrowing money at commercial rates; not being required to cover debt charges with operating revenues; not being required to cover operating expenses with revenues; being exempted from many regulations; and receiving free advertising from the agency. The potentially devastating impact of them providing subsidies is illustrated by the following examples:

- Lafayette, Colorado, had a population of 15,000. The city built a $4 million sports and fitness facility with three pools, steam rooms, a whirlpool, dry saunas, racquetball courts, a gymnasium, an indoor track, a fitness center with free weights and cardiovascular equipment, and babysitting services. When it opened, three private fitness clubs operated in Lafayette. After 1 year, one had gone out of business; a second saw its membership decline from 500 to 250; and the third, an aerobics studio, was unable to maintain the numbers it needed to justify proceeding with an expansion to which it had previously committed.[19]

- Gore Mountain Ski Center, a public facility operated by the state of New York, received an annual tax subsidy of $50,000 each year and was constructed with tax-free bonds. It applied for $246,000 in federal grants to help fund a $2.87 million capital extension that involved installing snowmaking machinery and other equipment. The balance of the capital was raised by issuing tax-free bonds. With these advantages, Gore Mountain charged $400 for a family season pass. The four commercial resorts in the area charged an average of $1,125 for the same pass because they had to pay commercial prices for investment capital and received no assistance from federal grants. They also had to show a reasonable return on their investment. Thus, the publicly operated state project gradually forced the commercial operation out of business. An editorial in the *Wall Street Journal* commented: "By a sort of Gresham's law of competition, we have noticed that state enterprises in the mixed economy tend to drive out private enterprise."[20]

- The Marine Command at Camp Pendleton, California, saw nothing wrong with a base recreational program that included sail-boat rentals, a diving school, whale-watching cruises, and sport-fishing trips. However, these competed with local businesses that could provide these activities for the 37,000 marines and their 10,000 dependents on the base. The base refurbished a surplus harbor tugboat for diving, fishing, and whale-watching trips. As a result, boat operations in nearby Oceanside lost nearly 100 trips each year that the marines and their dependents used to charter from them. Camp Pendleton charged $11 per person, including tackle, for a 1-day fishing trip, whereas local operators typically charged $29 per person. However, the U.S. Marine Corps got its boat for free, did not have to pay $10,000 to $15,000 each year to insure it and was not required to make a profit.[21]

Let's say you own a small, neighborhood grocery store. You have owned your store for many years, dutifully paying taxes and contributing to the community in a variety of ways. Suddenly, you find out that you will have new competition in 6 months. Another grocery store will open down the road.

"Fair enough," you say. "My customers like my store because the prices are fair, the store is clean and my employees are friendly. I may lose a few customers, but having good, clean competition is part of doing business. Besides, this may help me find new ways to appeal to my loyal customers." But wait a minute . . . You find out that the new store will look exactly like yours (only newer). The new store claims that selling food is a service to the community and that it will sell healthy food, which promotes a sound mind and body. Because the store will "benefit the community as a whole" and "promote health," the money to buy the land and build the store will come from tax-exempt bonds redeemed by public tax dollars. You pay thousands of dollars every year in interest on the money you borrowed to buy the land and build your store. The competition won't be paying for anything

Not only does the new store avoid paying debt charges, but because it "promotes health" and wants to encourage as many residents as possible to take advantage of its healthy foods, and because its annual operating costs are subsidized by taxpayers, it is also not required to break even. Further, since it is owned and operated by the public sector, it does not have to pay property, sales or income taxes, which you are required to do. Finally, it receives free advertising and promotion from agency brochures, literature and articles and has signs on surrounding highways informing travelers of its existence and location. In contrast, you have to pay for your promotional vehicles.[17]

Given these advantages, the new grocery store is able to price its food products at half the prices you are charging. How can you compete with it? This scenario occurs repeatedly in the sphere of leisure when public sector and non-profit organizations offer similar services in the same geographic area as those offered by commercial suppliers. Consider the following example:

> I operate two clubs. They are 16,000 square foot facilities with swimming pools, which occupy 4,000 square feet of the total. The North Clackamas Parks and Recreation District will locate its 80-acre Regional Park complex costing $16 million, precisely between my two clubs. The new indoor complex will be a 60,000 square foot aquatic center with five pools under one roof. My combined square footage for swimming is only 8,000 square feet. The projected costs of users of the huge regional complex who purchase monthly passes will be one-third to one-half the cost that my business charges. My business caters to middle class families, but not upper-income wealthy individuals. The regional complex will market their facility to this same group. Clackamas County orchestrated a sophisticated marketing and advertising campaign in order to sell this idea to the voters, with the assistance of three highly compensated full-time staff who worked on this project for 18 months prior to advancing the concept to the voters.[18]

Figure 3-4. Discouraging Private Sector Leisure Service Suppliers

These competitive actions by the public sector not only adversely impact existing businesses in a specific area, but also may dissuade other entrepreneurs from establishing new recreation services everywhere because of a fear that a public agency may open near them and drive them out of business by charging substantially lower prices. New recreation and fitness centers that public agencies construct have emerged as a primary focus of the unfair competition debate as they have evolved beyond basic gymnasia and pools to incorporate a higher quality level of provision in response to citizens' expectations of an increased level of sophistication. Private health and fitness club owners allege that many proposed new recreation centers are indistinguishable from their facilities and serve only to drive them out of the marketplace. Some of their more extreme spokespeople ask: "Why should government build public recreation centers, when they don't build public food stores or pharmacies?" Others more reasonably ask: "Is the city going to build and operate its own movie theaters and bowling centers as well as recreation centers since they are also recreation facilities?"

If public offerings are subsidized, the private sector is effectively excluded from supplying a similar service: "We cannot give away cake and expect people to rush into the bakery business at the same time." Efficiency is achieved if a private non-profit or commercial entity delivers a service because it enables a public agency (i) to withdraw resources from that program and reallocate them to another service that will enhance the range or quality of offerings to the community or (ii) to return funds to taxpayers. This has long been recognized. For example, in 1962, the Outdoor Recreation Resources Review Commission stated: ". . . [prices] will serve to stimulate provision of similar services by private operators, who will not be faced with competition from free government facilities" (p. 169)[22]; in the same year, the Secretary of the Interior testified to the U.S. Congress: "The application of user fees for recreation on Federal lands would be a great stimulus to recreational investment by private enterprise" (p. 31).[23]

Many public agency managers may regard pricing analogies with the private sector as inappropriate because the private sector does not have to consider equity. Nevertheless, the purposeful adoption by businesses of penetration or predatory pricing strategies serves to illustrate the unintended consequences of subsidizing public leisure services.

If a business decides on a *penetration price,* the price is set below economic value. Its goal is to attract and hold a large customer base. This strategy is sometimes called stay-out pricing because it discourages competitors from entering the marketplace. Consider the following illustration:

- The potential sales in a community are projected to be 50,000 widgets a year. The manufacturer sells them to large retailers for $5. Retailer A decides to offer them for sale at $5.50. This low 10 percent markup generates $25,000 toward overhead costs and profit. When Retailer B explores the implications of selling the widgets, to break into the market, it will have to price them lower, say a 5 percent markup at $5.25. However, given the inertia/loyalty of existing buyers with Retailer A, it likely will attract no more than half the market. If it captured half the market, its return would be only $6,250, which is too small to cover overhead. Thus, the initial penetration price enables Retailer A to capture and retain the whole market.

This effect is exacerbated by the sunk cost effect. Retailer A (or the leisure agency) has constructed capital assets in facilities and equipment to manufacture the widgets. However, these are now sunk costs; that is, they cannot be recouped. Hence, economists argue they should be disregarded and the focus should be confined to the return on future costs, which the company controls. In contrast, Retailer B will include these fixed costs in its return-on-investment calculations, ensuring its prices will be higher.

A *predatory price* "involves lowering prices to an unreasonably low (usually below-cost) or unprofitable level in a market in an effort to weaken, eliminate, or block the entry of a rival" (p. 87).[24] The focus is on imposing losses on other firms rather than on garnering gains for themselves. In many states, this practice is illegal as they have passed "sales below cost" statutes or minimum markup laws in which below-cost pricing is *prima facie* evidence of anticompetitive practice. Nevertheless, it has been found that predatory pricing is pursued by some

> business managers seeking to maximize their own career opportunities . . . Below-cost pricing can result in dramatic changes in market share, which, if employed as a criterion for evaluating managerial performance, may motivate some business managers to engage in such pricing decisions for nonpredatory purposes. (p. 96)[24]

While it is unlikely that public leisure agencies have purposefully adopted penetration or predatory pricing strategies, their substantial subsidizing of services means they have often been inadvertently embraced. In many communities, subsidized prices are a primary reason why public agencies effectively have a monopoly on leisure services. If they raise prices sufficiently to permit private or non-profit enterprises to recover the capital they invest, the presence of competition may significantly improve the efficiency of the public agency. Conventional wisdom sometimes suggests that provision of similar services by others leads to duplication of effort, which is wasteful and inefficient. However, duplication of services is a necessary condition for competition. It is the basis for the attendant incentives for efficiency inherent in the private sector market system. In a competitive market economy, the price system encourages economic efficiency by yielding rewards to, or by imposing losses upon, those who cater to the demands of individuals. Break-even user prices could have a similar effect on leisure service delivery by subjecting public managers to the competitive challenges of private service suppliers.

While competition with commercial operators may generate significant philosophical, ethical and political debate, agencies are not required legally to refrain from such competition. Under the general power authorizing them to provide leisure opportunities for citizens, if agencies choose to do so, they can legally provide facilities and programs similar to those offered by private businesses. The courts generally have rejected suits brought by businesses alleging unfair competition, confirming that agencies have no obligations to businesses that suffer from such actions.[25]

To address this issue, some government entities have enacted "Competitive Neutrality" ordinances designed to eliminate competitive advantages that arise solely through the public sector status of an agency. They aim

> to promote an economically efficient use of resources by increasing the extent that public sector providers of goods and services are exposed to competition. . . .
>
> An objective of competitive neutrality is to achieve an efficient allocation of resources between public and private businesses. This requires fair pricing and the elimination of resource allocation distortions. For government business activities, this means offsetting any net competitive advantages that arise simply as a result of public ownership.

Typically this means factoring into the price of a good or service an allowance for the following:

- taxes that may not be paid by the government business, but would be paid by the private sector competition;
- the cost of capital; and
- any other material costs not borne by the government business purely as a result of its government ownership status. (p. 6)[26]

Thus, in addition to covering the costs incurred by the agency, these guidelines require managers to incorporate into a price their estimates of additional costs the agency could incur if it were in private ownership. These types of ordinances typically apply only to services for which the benefits are confined to individual users. They do not govern services that are perceived to offer spillover or communitywide benefits.

The state of Colorado responded to concerns that recreation special districts were developing facilities that were traditionally the domain of the private sector by passing a statute that stated:

No district shall construct, own, or operate any bowling alley, roller skating rink, batting cage, golf course on which the game is played on an artificial surface, or an amusement park which has water recreation as its central theme, unless the board of such district receives approval for such project from the board of county commissioners of each county which has territory included in the district.

The statute required county commissioners to disapprove a facility or service unless it could be shown it was not adequately provided in the district by private suppliers.

The role of price in expanding the array of leisure opportunities available in a community is consistent with the contention that elected officials should consciously separate the policy or *provision* decision that determines what should be provided from the subsequent *production* decision of who should provide it. The role of the agency is seen as being analogous to that of an orchestra conductor:

The conductor himself does not play an instrument. He need not even know how to play an instrument. His job is to know the capacity of each instrument and to evoke optimal performance from each. Instead of being the "performer," he has become the "conductor." Instead of "doing," he leads. (p. 219)[27]

This philosophy views government as being the provider of last resort, which directly delivers a service only if there are no other competent suppliers in the community with which to contract to provide it efficiently.

ENHANCED ACCOUNTABILITY

More Responsible Behavior Among Users

Higher prices may encourage more responsible behavior by users, which increases efficiency in two ways. First, a higher price is likely to attract those who have a relatively high regard for the service and discourage those whose interest is marginal. It may enhance a user's feelings of responsibility and "ownership" toward the service. This is perhaps why managers have reported reductions in abuses such as graffiti, littering, vandalism and theft of flora or artifacts after prices have been increased:

- When policy at two Corps of Engineers parks located on the same reservoir shifted in successive years from uncontrolled access and no entrance fee to controlled access through manned entrance gates and an entrance fee, it provided an opportunity to evaluate the impact of charging on safety and security in these areas. Data were collected during the same 4-month summer period in the year before the policy shift and in the following year when the change was implemented. The data comprised crime and incident reports from area law enforcement agencies and park managers and responses to structured on-site interviews undertaken with a probability sample of park users. The authors concluded, "A comparison of visitor-reported crimes and visitor-perceived safety and security problems shows a significant reduction in both actual and perceived problems after the parks' conversions" (p. 22).[28]

Concerns about pilfering and graffiti are especially prominent among managers of historical and heritage sites. Charging a reasonable price, rather than authorizing free admission, to their facilities "sends visitors a clear signal about the significance and worth of the property or site they are visiting, encouraging them to be more respectful of it"(p. 213).[29]

- Hueco Tanks State Historical Park near El Paso in West Texas protects Indian rock paintings. After some of the 1,000- to 2,000-year-old pictographs were defaced with logos and insignia of El Paso street gangs by spray paint and marking pens, admission fees were raised. Each visitor now has to pay an annual fee of $25 to visit the park, whereas the previous price had been $3 per carload per visit. The agency's intent is to "protect the rocks from vandalism and still allow appropriate visitor access."[30]

The Director of the National Park Service, testifying at a Congressional Hearing, stated:

At Cape Canaveral, for example, from January 1 to April 20 last year we had $21,000 in felony losses. Now we have established an entrance kiosk and a fee charged there, the felony cost for the same period of time this year dropped to $2,369. I think that is true throughout the system, as I have discussed this with various superintendents. Where we are charging a fee the felony costs have gone down and we are finding that the people are not littering the park as much as they did in the past. It seems to have a psychological effect on people. When they go through an entrance kiosk and know there is going to be somebody there when they come back out again, there is less vandalism, less littering of the parks, and a much better attitude with regard to the use of the facilities (p. 48).[31]

A second dimension of responsible behavior is that higher prices encourage greater commitment to a service. In some cases, such as recreation classes, or music or art performances, the price may be paid before the program is delivered. Besides helping the agency make an efficient decision concerning allocation of resources to the program (staffing, equipment and facilities), advanced payment provides increased incentive for participants to commit to the program. The clientele are likely to feel more pressure to use a service fully after they have paid a higher price for it. If a price is too low to encourage this commitment, classes or performances may draw participants who do not make the effort to attend all the sessions. Others who make the effort may be turned away if full capacity is reached. A user price can help resolve these problems of marginal commitment. This link between price and level of commitment is elaborated upon in Chapter 12 in the discussion of the sunk cost effect.

Enhanced Managerial Accountability

For managers, a consequence of higher prices is clienteles' raised expectations of service quality. An aphorism in the private sector says: A poor salesperson sells on price, whereas a good salesperson sells on the quality of the product. Too often, clients use a leisure service either because no alternative is available in the community or because it is inexpensive, rather than because they are satisfied with the quality of the service. Price is perhaps the most potent tool available for fostering increased accountability among elected officials and agency personnel for raising the quality of service offerings.

Funding from tax sources often makes agency managers less sensitive to the needs of their clients than when they are directly dependent on client revenues for their programs' continued viability. A respected state park director observed:

> User fees are nothing less than an expression of support given in trust of parks. They express much more than the visitor's "willingness to pay" for value received; they are truly votes in support of assumed goals, votes that must be constantly re-earned by building confidence in the system's ability to convert revenue efficiently into meaningful accomplishments. (p. 51)[32]

If participants pay a direct monetary price at the point of service, they are more likely to insist on a higher standard (e.g., cleaner facilities, better equipment and better trained staff). In contrast, when services are funded indirectly from taxation, users often regard them as free, assume that responsibility for their quality lies with "the city" and thus accept lower delivery standards. It is not easy for users to assess what the level of service quality should be if they are not aware of its cost. A price that closely reflects the cost of delivering a service enables a participant to better judge if the quality of the service is appropriate. User pricing may also encourage elected officials to maintain or increase service quality. When a direct price is paid, the expectations of users are likely to be higher, so more pressure is on elected officials to allocate the resources necessary to ensure these expectations are met.

Pricing provides evidence that visitation numbers which managers report are valid. Numbers are a ubiquitous measure of accountability and performance evaluation among leisure agencies. In some cases, they are used for allocating resources, while in others they may be used to provide an indication of an agency's success in meeting constituents' needs. They are the basis of efficiency ratios, such as subsidy per user or number of participants per employee hour. Unfortunately, such metrics mean some managers may be tempted to inflate their participation numbers. In the parks field, for example, this potential for abuse has long been recognized:

> Although attendance data are a readily available quantitative measure, the use of these statistics is based on the assumption that they have been accurately reported. Unfortunately, it is a simple matter for agency personnel to inflate attendance data by spinning the turnstile, running park vehicles across traffic counters, or by counting several trips associated with a single visit as so many different attendances. Since attendance is used for evaluation and is frequently considered as a factor in the budgetary decision making process, there is incentive for managers to abuse the system. (pp. 317–318)[33]

When a price is charged, it makes two contributions to enhancing the credibility of visitation numbers. First, for the numbers to receive widespread acceptance, they have to be consistent with the revenues collected. For example, one park reported an average monthly attendance of around 40,000. However, the admission price was $3 and the monthly revenues were approximately $3,000, which suggests only about 1,500 visitors per month (making allowances for annual pass holders). Clearly, the attendance numbers were unreasonable.[34]

A second dimension of this enhanced credibility is that it ensures visitation numbers are reflective of a service's intent rather than incidental to it:

- A large art gallery prominently sited in the center of the city, for which no admission was charged, reported an annual attendance of 240,000. A research class from a local university surveyed almost 1,000 visitors over 6 weeks to identify major features that attracted them to the gallery. The students found that the two primary features people reported were to use the clean restrooms (no other public restrooms were available in the city center) and to have their lunch in a nice environment (numerous office towers were located in the proximate area). Clearly, the zero price distorted the meaningfulness of the numbers. The study's authors suggested if even a nominal price were charged, these primary users would disappear, resulting in a decline in numbers of approximately 30 percent.

SUMMARY

Appropriate prices encourage more efficient delivery of leisure services in three ways. First, they regulate the supply of services. Advocates sometimes argue that everyone "needs" public leisure services, so they should be heavily subsidized. Such emotional arguments are not defensible because they induce unreasonable and unsustainable opportunity costs and are not supported by people's behavior (i.e., only a relatively small number of households use them).

Two prioritizing mechanisms are available for determining which services should receive an agency's limited resources. Price is the most efficient because it gives people an effective direct vote. The alternative administration/political process mechanism too often results in services being over- or under-resourced, so priority is given to the wrong services in the wrong quantities.

If some services are subsidized more than others, all else equal, those that are subsidized the most will likely report the most visitation. This may lead to three inefficient conditions: (i) There will be a perceived shortage of the service with congestion resulting; (ii) relatively too many resources will be allocated to expanding the service to alleviate the perceived shortage; or (iiii) if capacity constraints do not limit demand, the relatively large number of users will result in low quality service.

A second potential contribution of price to efficiency is its rationing effect. Four primary strategies are available for rationing use: selection by lottery; advance reservation; first-come, first-served; and premium pricing. Consistent with the prioritizing of equity over efficiency, the least public support is likely to be for premium pricing. Nevertheless, economists suggest that in contrast to other options, premium pricing gives priority to those who most value the service. However, this also may have negative implications for equity as it assumes users have equal amounts of discretionary income, when actually a $10 price to low income participants may constitute a greater sacrifice than a $20 price to those who are more affluent.

A third dimension of price's efficiency role is that it encourages the private sector to deliver more leisure services. Efficiency is achieved if a public agency is able (i) to withdraw resources from a service and reallocate them to another service to enhance the range or quality of its offerings to the community or (ii) to return funds to taxpayers. Too often, public leisure agencies inadvertently adopt penetration or predatory prices that effectively preclude the private sector from complementing their offerings.

In addition to these economic mechanisms, pricing may induce more responsible behavior among users and enhanced accountability among managers. Among participants, it may reduce deviant and illegal behaviors and encourage greater commitment to a program, which reduces wasted capacity. For managers, a consequence of higher prices is raised expectations of service quality (e.g., cleaner facilities, better equipment and better trained staff). Prices also enhance perceptions of the validity of participation numbers, which are the basis for several evaluation performance metrics used in many leisure agencies. The numbers have to be consistent with the revenues collected from pricing, and price ensures the numbers are reflective of a service's intent rather than incidental to it.

REFERENCES

1. Ellerbrock, M. (1982, January). Some straight talk on user fees. *Parks & Recreation, 1982*, 59–62.
2. Chappelle, D. E. (1973). The need for outdoor recreation: An economic conundrum. *Journal of Leisure Research, 5*(3), 47–53.
3. Thompson, W. (1986). The city as a distorted price system. *Psychology Today, 2*(3), 28–33.

4. Ostrom, V., & Ostrom, E. (1977). Public goods and public choices. In E. S. Savas (Ed.), *Alternatives for delivering public services*. Boulder, CO: Westview Press.

5. Crompton, J. L., & Lamb, C.W. (1986). *Marketing government and social services*. New York, NY: John Wiley.

6. Buchanan, J. M. (1970). *The public finances*. Homewood, IL: Irwin.

7. Lucas, G. (2001, November 5). Visitors flood parks after user fee cuts: Understaffed rangers find resources stretched thin. *San Francisco Chronicle*. Retrieved from http://www.sfchronicle.com/news/article/Visitors-flood-parks-after-user-fee-cuts-2860934.php

8. Lime, D. W., McCool, S. F., & Galvin, D. P. (1995). Trends in congestion and crowding at recreation sites. In J. L. Thompson, D. W. Lime, B. Gartner, & W. M. Sames (Eds.), *Proceedings of the Fourth International Outdoor Recreation and Tourism Trends Symposium and the 1995 National Recreation Resource Planning Conference, May 14–17, 1995*. St. Paul: University of Minnesota College of Natural Resources and the Minnesota Extension Service.

9. Shelby, B., Danley, M. S., Gibbs, K. C., & Peterson, M. E. (1982). Preferences of backpackers and river runners for allocation techniques. *Journal of Forestry, 80*, 416–419.

10. Stankey, G. H., & Baden, J. (1977). *Rationing wilderness use: Methods, problems, and guidelines* (Research Paper INT-19). Ogden, UT: Intermountain Forest and Range Experiment Center.

11. National Park Service. (1986). *1982–1983 nationwide recreation survey*. Washington, DC: U.S. Government Printing Office.

12. Wikle, T. A. (1991). Comparing rationing policies used on rivers. *Journal of Park and Recreation Administration, 9*(3), 73–81.

13. Kahneman, D., Knetsch, J. L., & Thaler R. H. (1986). Fairness and the assumptions of economics. *Journal of Business, 59*(4, Pt. 2), 285–300.

14. McKenzie, R. B. (2008). *Why popcorn costs so much at the movies*. New York, NY: Springer Science + Business Media.

15. Rosenthal, D. H., Loomis, J. B., & Peterson, G. L. (1984). Pricing for efficiency and revenue in public recreation areas. *Journal of Leisure Research, 16*, 195–208.

16. More, T. A. (1999). A functionalist approach to user fees. *Journal of Leisure Research, 31*, 227–244.

17. IHRSA. (n.d.). *The case for fair competition*. Boston, MA: Author.

18. Testimony of M. Jennifer Harding to the Oregon House of Representatives concerning HB 3513. The Unfair Competition Bill, which would have prohibited public sector organizations from providing goods and services that are already provided by private businesses.

19. Martinsons, J. (1994, May). The new kids on the block: Park and rec. departments. *Club Industry, 1994*, 20–26.

20. Mike Brandt's competitors. (1975, September 12). *Wall Street Journal*, p. 4.

21. Jacobs, S. I. (1985, October 14). Local firms say a marine base has stolen their customers. *Wall Street Journal*, section 2, p. 17.

22. Outdoor Recreation Resources Review Commission. (1962). *Outdoor recreation for America: A report to the President and to the Congress.* Washington, DC: Superintendent of Documents.

23. Udall, S. L. (1962). Testimony to the U.S., Congress, House, Committee on Interior and Insular Affairs, *Land Conservation Fund, Hearings on H.R. 11172 et al.,* 87th Congress, 2d Session, July 11–12 and Aug 8, 1962, pp. 31–32.

24. Guiltinan, J. P., & Gundlach, G. T. (1996). Aggressive and predatory pricing: A framework for analysis. *Journal of Marketing, 60,* 87–102.

25. Kozlowski, J. C. (1993). Authorized public recreation may legally compete with private facilities. *Parks and Recreation, 28*(9), 36, 44.

26. Neale, I. (2001). *Guidelines for pricing of user charges.* New South Wales, Australia: Office of Financial Management Publications Office.

27. Drucker, P. F. (1969). *The age of discontinuity.* New York, NY: Harper Row.

28. Fletcher, J. E. (1984). The effect of controlled access and entrance fees on park visitor safety and security. *Journal of Park and Recreation Administration, 2*(4), 13–24.

29. Fyall, A., & Garrod, B. (1998). Heritage tourism: At what price? *Managing Leisure, 3,* 213–228.

30. Abram, L. (1992, November 26). Steep fee aimed at keeping Hueco Tanks vandals out. *Houston Chronicle*, p. 42A.

31. Mott, W. P. (1987). *Testimony before the subcommittee on Public Lands, National Parks and Forests on HR 1320.* Washington, DC: Superintendent of Documents.

32. La Page, W. (1996). Fees as dedicated park income: Linking user fees to system costs and objectives. In A. L. Lundgren (Ed.), *Recreation fees in the National Park Service: Issues, policies, and guidelines for future action* (pp. 51–56, Minnesota Extension Service Pub. No. BU-6767). St. Paul: Cooperative Park Studies Unit, Department of Forest Resources, University of Minnesota.

33. Howard, D. R., & Crompton, J. L. (1980). *Financing, managing, and marketing recreation and park resources.* Dubuque, IA: Wm. C. Brown.

34. Kaczynski, A. T., Crompton, J. L., & Emerson, J. E. (2003). A procedure for improving the accuracy of visitor count at state parks. *Journal of Park and Recreation Administration, 21,* 140–151.

Chapter 4

Revenue Production

Establishing the Base Price

- Positioning services on the Benefits Continuum
- Enterprise funds for services delivering exclusively user benefits
- Identifying costs
- Adjusting a cost-based price to reflect the going rate
- Summary

The process for establishing an equitable base price is described in this chapter. The Benefits Continuum is used as a vehicle for operationalizing in monetary terms the relationship between who benefits and who pays. The positioning of services on the continuum defines the appropriate level of taxpayer subsidy and the proportion of costs that user prices should be designed to recover. The base price is a point of departure. It is likely to be subsequently amended to reflect the "going rate," the Ability to Pay Principle (Chapters 5 to 8) and behavioral factors (Chapters 9 to 12). Thus, at this first stage, ability to pay is not considered in the positioning decision. Reconciling the base price based on the Benefit Principle with the Ability to Pay Principle is a subsequent task.

One weakness associated with deriving a cost-based price in this manner is that it is assumed client groups will be willing to pay it. This is most likely to occur if it is consistent with the price of a similar service offered by others. Hence, the chapter concludes with a discussion of methods to find the going rate that other public and commercial suppliers are charging.

The key contribution of this first step in establishing a price is that it provides a target cost recovery amount on which to base price. If there is a gap between the desired and existing cost recovery ratios, a strategy for reducing costs and/or raising prices can be developed. Closing this gap is always challenging because of adverse psychological factors. As discussed in Chapters 9 to 12, the reaction of users is often irrational because of historical expectations, analogous experiences, emotion or self-interest. These behavioral factors will temper what can be accomplished.

Nevertheless, this rational process for establishing a base price starting point contrasts with the approach that many leisure agencies adopt, that is, raising all prices by some arbitrary percentage each year. They have made few attempts to discover who is benefiting, who is paying, and the level of benefits and costs associated with each service. Even if incremental price increases are based on some acceptable criterion, they assume the original price was appropriate. However, if the initial price was arbitrarily derived, subsequent incremental increases will result in an arbitrary price.

The approach described in this chapter enables managers to communicate clearly to their stakeholders the rationale for adopting a given price. The approach will not always be immediately convincing to elected officials. However, if a rational approach is not presented to elected officials, this will encourage continuation of irrational pricing using whatever personal or arbitrary criteria they care to adopt. Unfortunately, the dominant criterion in such cases is often "the squeaky wheel gets the oil."

POSITIONING SERVICES ON THE BENEFITS CONTINUUM

The Benefit Principle recognizes that those benefiting from a service should bear financial responsibility for its cost. The Benefits Continuum provides the foundation upon which to build a user price. It assumes the objective is to price each program or service at a level that is fair and equitable to participants and non-participants. Conceptually, the proportion of costs that should be subsidized is dependent on the extent to which non-users benefit from a user utilizing a service. As the benefits that accrue to non-users increase, the proportion of costs met by pricing should decrease, while the proportion met by tax subsidy should increase.

Figure 4-1 shows that services perceived to provide *communitywide benefits* should be fully subsidized from taxes so a price is not charged for them. At the other extreme, when all benefits accrue to users, a price should be set that covers all of its costs. The magnitude of spillover benefits that a community receives varies among services, so three position points are shown on the continuum, reflecting services where benefits accrue primarily to the community (25 percent cost recovery), equally to users and the community (50 percent) and primarily to the users (75 percent.)

Figure 4-1 shows an example of where the leadership in one community positioned its services on the continuum. It was noted in Chapter 2 that these positions are not located by an objective formula, rather they are socially constructed. Because perspectives and values are different among and within communities, it is inevitable that a given service will be positioned differently on the continuum by (i) different communities and (ii) by the same community at different points in time. Because positions are community specific at a given time and are not generalizable, those shown in Figure 4-1 are merely illustrative. For example, it was noted in Chapter 2 that a tennis facility in a high income neighborhood may be perceived as having exclusively user benefits, so cost recovery should be 100 percent, while an identical tennis facility in a low income, high crime neighborhood may be perceived as benefiting the whole community through alleviating deviant behavior so no prices would be charged.

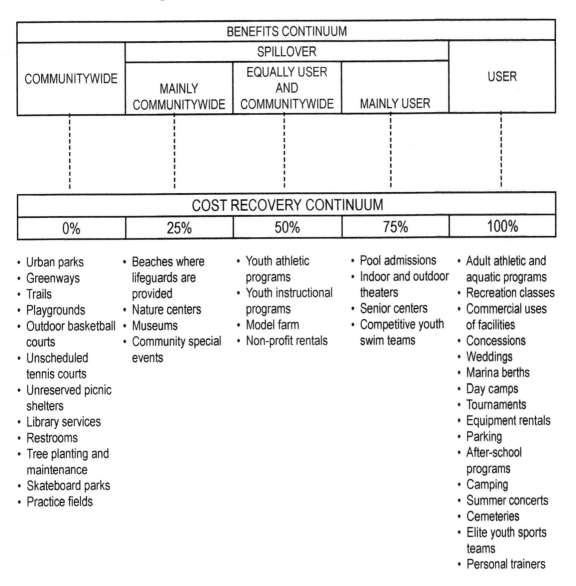

BENEFITS CONTINUUM				
COMMUNITYWIDE	SPILLOVER			USER
	MAINLY COMMUNITYWIDE	EQUALLY USER AND COMMUNITYWIDE	MAINLY USER	

COST RECOVERY CONTINUUM				
0%	25%	50%	75%	100%
• Urban parks • Greenways • Trails • Playgrounds • Outdoor basketball courts • Unscheduled tennis courts • Unreserved picnic shelters • Library services • Restrooms • Tree planting and maintenance • Skateboard parks • Practice fields	• Beaches where lifeguards are provided • Nature centers • Museums • Community special events	• Youth athletic programs • Youth instructional programs • Model farm • Non-profit rentals	• Pool admissions • Indoor and outdoor theaters • Senior centers • Competitive youth swim teams	• Adult athletic and aquatic programs • Recreation classes • Commercial uses of facilities • Concessions • Weddings • Marina berths • Day camps • Tournaments • Equipment rentals • Parking • After-school programs • Camping • Summer concerts • Cemeteries • Elite youth sports teams • Personal trainers

Figure 4-1. Relationship between Perceived Benefit Recipients and Cost Recovery Ratios

The subjectivity of positioning services suggests the process should be reviewed periodically (say) every 3 years. During this period, changes in political leadership and philosophy and/or changes in economic conditions may result in a desire to adjust some of the programs' positions on the continuum.

While elected officials will be the ultimate adjudicators of a service's position, they are likely to receive recommendations from staff and citizen groups. Because staff are responsible for explaining the rationale for price changes to participants, their widespread engagement is needed to secure their ownership, commitment and understanding of it. Similarly, the wider the involvement of citizen groups, the more extensive the understanding of the process in the community.

It could legitimately be argued that all of the services listed as providing communitywide benefits in Figure 4-1 offer users increments of benefits that do not accrue to non-users. Hence, they should be more appropriately positioned in one of the other four categories. For example, it is incontrovertible that those who use public urban parks benefit more than those who do not. However, urban parks are likely to be used by a larger proportion of residents than is any other facility a leisure agency operates; probably offer more of the external benefits listed in Figures 2-6 to 2-9 than does any other service; and have traditionally been free of charge, so any attempt to restrict access and to charge admission to them would likely arouse contempt and outrage. These factors have resulted in urban parks almost universally being positioned as communitywide assets.

Sometimes, services assigned to the zero cost recovery category are there by default. That is, it is recognized that users receive increments of benefit that do not accrue to the community, so the service should be assigned to one of the other four categories. However, it is impractical, it is too costly or tradition is too strong to establish a system to identify and charge the users. Even though a user price might be warranted on equity and efficiency grounds, widespread public resistance to paying it may become the overriding consideration. Consider the reaction to a proposal by Los Angeles County to require trail users to purchase a $23 annual permit or pay a fine of $100 if caught on park trails without the permit:

> The intent seems to be to raise revenue. So why single out bikers and other trail users? How about a "Buck-a-Duck" program for seniors who enjoy feeding waterfowl at county lakes? How about instituting "Pay-per-View Scenic Viewpoints" along Mulholland Drive and the Pacific Coast Highway? Creeks are an untapped source of revenue, say, $2 to cool your heels, $10 to skinny dip. . . .
>
> Should the county stick to its policy of sticking it to hikers, how will the permit process be enforced? Along the 12-mile Puente Hills Skyline Trail, for example, there are dozens of places to join the trail. Will the county erect a forest of signs to explain at each junction that hiking without a permit is verboten? A hiker traveling the Backbone Trail through the Santa Monica Mountains could pass through city, county, state and federal land during a day's journey. What if other park agencies, following the county's example, required the purchase of trail permits?
>
> Who will patrol the pathways? During the more than 20 years I've hiked county parks, I've never spotted a county employee on the trail. (p. 14)[1]

In Figure 4-1, the community assigned its skateboard parks to the zero cost recovery category, even though almost all those engaged in the positioning process believed benefits accrued exclusively to users, so 100 percent cost recovery should be the goal. However, a state law related to skateboard parks mandated that the city had only nominal liability exposure if it was an open access, free facility. However, if it was programmed, access was restricted or a price was charged, the city had a full "duty of care" obligation and no protection from liability. The cost of insurance in that case was sufficiently high that it could never be covered by user fees. Assigning it to the zero cost recovery strategy was the least-cost option for the city.

Potential *spillover benefits* were identified in Figures 2-6 to 2-9. Positioning services in one of the three spillover benefit categories (25, 50 and 75 percent cost recovery) recognizes it is practical to levy a user price for them, but users should be subsidized to the extent that benefits to the whole community occur. There is a challenge not only in identifying spillover benefits, but also in measuring their magnitude, which is a subjective task. If the user price is set too high, individuals may choose to make less use of the service than is considered desirable by the community. If the price is too low, there will be a consumers' surplus (Chapter 5) and an unnecessarily high level of tax support.

The following is a typical pricing policy statement for services whose benefits are perceived to be confined exclusively to *individual users*:

- While a primary mission of government is to satisfy community needs, many services solely benefit specific individuals. It is the general policy of the City Council that the public at large should not subsidize activities of such a private interest through general tax revenues. Therefore, the City has established user fees at a level that ensures those who use such a proprietary service pay for that service. With few exceptions, such as those services provided for low income residents, fees have been set to enable the City to recover the full cost of providing those services.

ENTERPRISE FUNDS FOR SERVICES DELIVERING EXCLUSIVELY USER BENEFITS

Enterprise funds are fiscal entities that are self-financing. They are independent of the general fund and ideally they receive no tax support. They can be viewed as businesses engaged in by a jurisdiction that closely mirror how private companies operate or as subsidiary companies of a parent company, that is, the government entity. They exemplify the direct relationship between an agency and its clienteles shown in Figure 1-2 rather than the more complex traditional relationship displayed in Figure 1-3 in which the intervening legislative body plays a central role.

It is not uncommon for advocates to persuade governments to provide additional leisure facilities and services by assuring them that operation and maintenance expenses will be covered by user revenues (i.e., they will be financed through an enterprise fund approach). Unfortunately, such assurances often prove optimistic, and a tax subsidy is needed. Some of the most cherished leisure services in the U.S. followed this pattern:

- The first public library in the U.S. opened in 1787, but as the idea spread across the country, libraries were primarily financed by the people who used them. Either they were proprietary or they were funded through subscriptions—essentially an enterprise fund. Subsequently, libraries evolved into a tax-supported system, as their advocates successfully positioned them as extensions of free public education and the school system.[2]

The formative years of the National Park System (NPS), which similarly was initially conceived as an enterprise fund operation free of tax subsidy, are described in Figure 4-2.[3] While the enterprise fund had a short life in the NPS, Congress subsequently authorized vestiges of this approach. For example, acquiring land to expand the National Wildlife Refuge System was the major reason for passing the Migratory Bird Hunting and Conservation Stamp Act of 1934, which required purchase and possession of a "duck stamp" by those who hunted migratory waterfowl. The same rationale backed the levying of a federal sales tax on hunting and fishing equipment under the 1937 Pittman–Robertson and 1950 Dingell–Johnson Acts. All of these laws require that user payments be expended on facilities that those users frequent—a key element of enterprise funds.

Ferdinand V. Hayden and other Yellowstone proponents assured members of Congress that the first national park, established in 1872, would require no appropriated funds. Concessioner rents were envisioned to provide the income necessary for Yellowstone's administration. Nathaniel P. Langford, the park's first superintendent, generally agreed. He advocated leasing to concessioners the major points of interest and granting leases for toll roads; the lessees would provide protection for the park. However, Langford saw the need for an initial appropriation to mark boundaries and institute protective measures, and in 1878, the park began to receive federal funds.

The ideal of self-supporting parks continued to receive rhetorical homage and was achieved at various times in particular areas. Yosemite made a profit, primarily from concessions, in 1907, for example, and Yellowstone's receipts exceeded expenditures in 1915 and 1916, the first years when automobiles were admitted. The 1916 automobile permits for admission to Yellowstone ($10), Yosemite ($8), and Mount Rainier ($6) were equivalent to approximately $160, $120, and $96, respectively, in 2014 dollars.

Thus, when the NPS was established in 1916, Stephen Mather, its first director, stated that park entrance fees and other revenues would eventually be sufficient to pay for all NPS operations and maintenance costs and that the Congress would have to appropriate funds only for construction projects and acquisition of additional lands. In his report to the Secretary of the Interior, Mather wrote:

It has been your desire that ultimately the revenues of the several parks might be sufficient to cover the costs of their administration and protection and that Congress should only be requested to appropriate funds for their improvement. It appears that at least five parks now have a proven earning capacity sufficiently large to make their operation on this basis feasible and practicable. They are Yellowstone, Yosemite, Mount Rainier, Sequoia, and General Grant (now part of Kings Canyon/Sequoia National Park). Accordingly estimates have only been submitted to Congress for appropriations for improvements of these parks.

In accordance with this policy, revenues from NPS fees were held until 1918 in an enterprise fund where they could be spent for park purposes without congressional appropriation. As a result, the NPS was highly motivated to levy and collect fees. However, Congress viewed this arrangement as circumventing its prerogatives and, beginning in 1918, required fee revenues to go to the general treasury. Inevitably, this reduced the service's incentive to collect fees.

Today, none of the 400 NPS units generate sufficient revenues to cover their operation and maintenance expenses, even though these revenues increased substantially after passage of the 2004 Federal Land Recreation Enhancement Act, which created vestiges of enterprise funds at each unit, enabling the units to retain 80 percent of the revenues they collected.

Figure 4-2. The Fledging National Park Service Enterprise Fund[3]

As these illustrations indicate, the technical definition of enterprise funds as being self-financing is frequently qualified by leisure agencies. In some cases, elected officials may approve transfer of money from the general fund that is dedicated to subsidizing economically disadvantaged users of an enterprise service to address the Ability to Pay Principle. In other cases, the enterprise fund may limit the costs that are to be covered, so the mandate to be "self-sufficient" is interpreted loosely.

Hence, in many leisure agencies, the self-sufficiency definition is replaced by recovery ratios that are lower than 100 percent. In the next section of the chapter, five categories of costs are identified, and few leisure agency enterprise funds cover all of them. In cases in which only some costs are covered, revenues are supplemented with general fund taxes. The intent is to secure the flexibility and efficiencies offered by the enterprise fund approach, even though full self-sufficiency is not a reasonable goal. For example, several state park systems have enterprise funds, but they are supplemented by tax appropriations.[4] New Hampshire has the only state park system that fully covers operating costs with park-generated revenues.

In most government entities, appropriated dollars from the general fund are the primary source of funding for leisure services, and elected officials usually require self-generated revenues to be deposited there (Figure 1-3). The result is a disconnect between money spent and money earned, making revenue maximization and cost control abstract concepts rather than fiscal imperatives. Enterprise funds establish a link between suppliers and users of services.

The advantages of using an enterprise fund will dissipate if surplus revenues that exceed the target cost recovery ratio are returned to the general fund, or if tax support for the following year is reduced by the surplus amount. There is no escaping the natural tendency for elected officials to yield to this temptation, and if they do, the enterprise fund will lose much of its potency to enhance efficiency because it will be disheartening to managers and discourage them from committing to robust revenue generation.

At a national level to ensure self-generated revenues are used to supplement the resource rather than to offset it, the National Park Service has long worked with non-profit cooperating associations to manage some of its revenue-generating operations, such as gift shops, concessions and educational offerings. They are independent entities, not managed or controlled by the National Park Service, so their contributions to the parks derived from the profits are not subject to congressional reviews. In essence, they serve as surrogate enterprise funds because their profits remain in the park to fund other services rather than going to the federal government's general fund.

By definition, enterprise funds are limited to leisure services that have a substantial revenue stream. Typical examples are golf courses, marinas, recreation programs, athletic complexes, campgrounds and cemeteries. For example, the city of Plano, Texas, operates its golf courses and recreation centers out of enterprise funds; these operations are described in Figure 4-3.

Golf

The city has a management services agreement with a golf professional who is an independent contractor. He manages the golf course; operates the pro shop, clubhouse and food and beverage concessions; provides teaching programs; and provides carts and clubs for rent.

The city's responsibilities are to maintain the course and facilities except the clubhouse and pro shop buildings, including paying for utilities. The city sets the rates for green fees. It receives all green fee revenues, together with 5 percent of gross revenues or $30,000, whichever is greater from services provided by the golf professional. The enterprise fund showed:

Green fees and percent of gross		$1,000,000
Operating expenses	$873,000	
Transfer to the general fund	$50,000	$923,000
Surplus for reinvestment into the course		$77,000

The 5 percent transfer to the general fund is a contribution to overhead costs.

Recreation Revolving Fund

This fund supports recreation and aquatic classes and adult sports (youth sports in the city are primarily operated by non-profit organizations). The revenue from fees must cover the direct cost of the programs and the "program support fees," which cover costs of computer hardware, software maintenance, credit card fees, advertising/promotional costs for classes, support for the financial assistance program, and 10 full-time employees' salaries and benefits. The enterprise fund showed:

Program fees		$3,860,000
Expenses	$3,410,000	
5% transfer to general fund	$193,000	$3,603,000
Surplus for reinvestment into the programs		$257,000

The 5 percent transfer to the general fund is a contribution to overhead costs. In addition to this transfer amount, a user charge of $4 for residents and $8 for non-residents is levied on each participant, which yields $301,000 annually. These charges go directly to the general fund each month. They are not credited to the enterprise fund, but are effectively a transfer payment. Thus, the fund's total general fund contribution is $494,000 ($193,000 + $301,000).

The city has 30 full-time employees in recreation centers and aquatics. The 10 in the enterprise fund deal exclusively with programs, as opposed to facility operation, and the remaining 20 are supported by the general fund. The number in the enterprise fund has grown over the years. In times of fiscal uncertainty when people are terminated because of lack of resources in the general fund, the department has been able to transfer them to the enterprise fund.

Figure 4-3. Enterprise Funds for Golf and Recreation in Plano, Texas

A few agencies have expanded the concept so it embraces more than a narrow set of activities. For example, Johnson County Park and Recreation District, which services suburbs of Kansas City, Kansas, operates its recreational, educational and interpretive programs within an enterprise fund. This has an annual budget approaching $15 million. Its revenues cover not only all five costs identified in the next section (Figure 4-4), but also the debt charges associated with financing its facilities with revenue bonds. The first director of their enterprise fund offered insights into the reasons for its success:

Much of the success of Johnson County's program can be attributed to the attitude of the staff who are responsible for it. Three training sessions a year are held for staff on such topics as salesmanship, program changes and information, image development, job enrichment, etc. All members of the staff are under the clear awareness that the support for their job is dependent upon the fees which clients bring into the programs which are in their domain. If they are unable to develop programs which are sufficiently attractive that clients will pay for them, then they will be out of a job. This atmosphere creates hustle.[5]

The recreation division in Johnson County now offers 2,000 classes that service over 450,000 participants in seven areas of recreation: fine arts, performing arts, senior adults, special services (including special populations and preschool programs), recreational sports, aquatics and a corporate division.

A leader in the museums field made similar observations about enterprise funds:

For the people who work in public museums, it doesn't much matter if their exhibitions are wildly popular, or hardly anyone comes at all: Their salaries, their pensions and their security aren't going to suffer . . . But money is a great motivator to imaginative thinking and goes hand-in-hand with a business-like cost-conscious approach, helping to raise productivity and staff morale. The necessity of attracting and pleasing their customers forces enterprise fund museums to develop lively, intelligible forms of presentation and interpretation. (p. 43)[6]

In addition to this potential for strengthening staff's commitment to generating revenue and producing relevant high quality services, the enterprise vehicle has three other advantages. First, if, for example, golf courses are removed from the general fund to an enterprise fund, it undercuts lobbying efforts by golfers to resist price increases and retain subsidies, or to upgrade the quality of facilities, or to build additional courses with taxpayers' money rather than with golfers' money. Absent an enterprise fund, they may be abetted in these lobbying efforts by an agency's golf course staff, who may perceive they have a vested interest in supporting such efforts to enhance "their empire." In contrast, a true enterprise fund is subject to budget constraints that are not malleable. It is the only source of funds for operations, maintenance and capital renovations, so if prices are set too low, facilities will deteriorate.

Second, enterprise funds offer a "closed-loop" mechanism that provides incentives to participants and managers (Figure 1-2). For participants, it means those paying for a service can see the direct benefits from their payments. This contrasts with revenues that go into a jurisdiction's general fund, which users are likely to perceive as a total loss because there is no direct nexus between their payment and provision of the service. As the empirical evidence and discussion relating to "enterprise fund effect" presented in Chapter 12 suggest, this will reduce resistance to price increases.

For managers, the closed loop means they are directly responsible for covering their costs with revenues, so they will tend to add services that cover costs and eliminate those that do not. In contrast, when services are mostly funded by taxes, such economic realities can be ignored. When managers are asked to generate revenues that go to the general fund, inefficient decisions are likely. For example, they may close a campground to "save" money even though its revenues exceeded its costs because the revenues went elsewhere and the costs came out of their budget.

Third, revenues retained in enterprise funds can be carried forward to future fiscal years. This facilitates the reinvestment of surplus revenues to improve programs and services. For example, the Recreation Fund described in Figure 4-3 was used to rehire employees who had been terminated from the general fund in times of fiscal uncertainty. An agency that supports its recreation, aquatic and adult athletic programs from an enterprise fund listed the following reinvestments it had made in the last 2 years:

- Outdoor program equipment including tents, backpacks, sleeping bags and bike racks.
- (2) 16-seat passenger vans.
- A day camp bus.
- Recreation computer software system and associated hardware.
- A waterslide for an outdoor pool.
- Several staff salaries that were cut from the general fund.
- Development of a marketing program and funding for department special events.

Most, if not all, of these items would not have been acquired if they had been reliant on resources from the general fund. This demonstrates the value of having alternate funding streams that supplement taxes. Reliance on a single dominant revenue source is analogous to a monoculture in nature. It increases an agency's financial unreliability.

A potential downside to enterprise funds, which it was noted in Chapter 1 applies whenever the emphasis is on revenue generation, is that the imperative to attain full cost recovery results in a reduced focus on an agency's core mission, so the original purpose of a service is lost to the new imperative of fiscal self-sufficiency. Thus, the director of an agency that funds its recreation services through a revenue fund commented:

> We don't want to get so business focused that we forget why we exist. I tell the Council that if they want us to cover more of the indirect cost, they need to be prepared to understand what that looks like and the decisions that come with that. If that is their charge, we won't offer swim lessons to little kids in the evenings, because we can make more profit by offering water aerobics at that time. Both are desired activities. However, one is a lifesaving issue, but it does not create revenue surplus because of its low instructor to student ratio.

IDENTIFYING COSTS

After a service has been assigned a position on the Benefits Continuum, the second requirement for establishing a base price is identifying the cost of delivering the service. Prices based on the Benefits Continuum seek to recover a given percentage of costs. If the costs are not known, the prices are arbitrary. Costs do not determine price because they are also governed by the Ability to Pay Principle and market acceptability. Nevertheless, they are the foundation upon which an equitable price is constructed, and they determine the desirability of offering a service at a given level of subsidy.

Understanding and identifying costs is probably the most challenging aspect of pricing. Traditionally, government accounting systems were designed to focus on corruption control and to demonstrate compliance with mandated financial rules and regulations. They were not designed to meet managers' information needs and, hence, did not provide cost information.

In previous eras, there was no imperative to have such information. Prices were relatively nominal; tax-supported budgets were expanding, so prioritizing resource allocation among services was less urgent; and evaluating the cost efficiencies of outsourcing was not a common practice. This has changed. Knowledge of costs has emerged as central to decisions in multiple contexts.

Details of the intricate processes and complex rules of how to define and apportion costs appropriately are beyond the scope of this chapter. Leisure managers can seek advice on this from their budget/financial departments, whose staff possess that expertise. The intent here is limited to describing broad principles and to illustrating their potential value with examples from agencies that have developed effective systems.

How detailed the development of a system for identifying costs needs to be is likely to be influenced by factors such as size of the agency, degree of accuracy desired and magnitude of resources allocated to services. There are two approaches. The most ambitious is *cost accounting*. It involves extensive detailed cost tracking, often using relatively complex formulas, in which costs are meticulously assigned and accurately distributed among the services delivered. This is the "deluxe" model, but operationalizing it is likely to be tedious, cumbersome, frustrating and time consuming. Further, complexity is no assurance of accuracy. If the agency lacks the resources to meet the input requirements of a model, the result will be a malfunctioning and misleading system.

Given that the resources allocated to this task should be proportionate to the likely benefits accruing from it, managers have to ask: "Are the costs and effort associated with the high level of accuracy offered by an elaborate cost accounting system justified by the purposes for which the information will be used?" Their objective is not to arrive at an absolutely correct allocation of costs, but to assign to each service an approximate "fair share" of the agency's overheads. In most instances, leisure managers have concluded cost accounting is a less viable option than the alternative approach, *cost finding*. This is

> a less formal method of cost determination or estimation undertaken on an irregular basis. There may be no formal accounting entries during the year to record costs incurred in delivering specific services. Instead, cost finding usually involves taking available fund financial data and recasting and adjusting it to derive the cost data or estimate needed. (p. 346)[7]

This approach takes advantage of Pareto's Principle. That is, it is likely to provide approximately 80 percent of a cost accounting system's benefits while requiring only 20 percent of the time, effort and monetary resources needed to implement it. Once a cost-finding exercise has been undertaken, it need not be replicated for a number of years because its findings are likely to remain reasonably accurate for a time. Some agencies have adopted decision rules, such as "aim for 30 percent cost recovery" or "aim to cover operating costs," but if these costs are not reasonably accurately defined, the goals are meaningless. Prices intended to avoid subsidy for services delivering exclusively user benefits or to fix an appropriate subsidy for those with spillover benefits can only be established if costs are known.

Many agencies unintentionally subsidize services because of an inaccurate guesstimate of costs. Once elected officials and managers know the true costs and magnitude of subsidies involved, they often decide some of the subsidy levels are inappropriate. The following reaction of the director of a leisure agency in a large city after a cost-finding system was implemented is probably typical:

> The figures blew us away. There were all kinds of results that surprised us. Each person in our competitive summer swim team program was being subsidized by $20.71. The junior ice hockey players were subsidized at a similar level. In both cases, we pointed out to the parents that this was unreasonable, that they had to meet these bills, and we assisted them in forming clubs to raise funds and operate the programs at a break-even level. On average, our recreation classes had reported being 123 percent self-supporting. But we had only been including direct costs, and when supervisory overhead and building maintenance costs were included, they were only 66 percent self-supporting.

While pricing decisions are the most compelling reason for having cost information, it has become salient in at least three other decision contexts. First, it is usually central in debates as to whether routine, unskilled labor tasks, such as mowing and garbage collection in parks, should be undertaken by department employees or outsourced. Factors such as equity, control, flexibility, convenience and dependability will be considered, but much of the frequent controversy that revolves around outsourcing decisions is likely to pertain to costs.

Second, decisions relating to prioritizing resource allocations or determining which services should be terminated in response to budget reductions require ratios, such as subsidy per user, that need accurate cost information.

Related to this is a third imperative, which is to enhance transparency and accountability to the public. Many elected officials insist on widely publicizing the cost of services as a response to the public's expectations that they demonstrate accountability for authorized tax expenditures. This extends beyond services with user or spillover benefits to those having communitywide benefits for which no price is charged. In these cases, two cost-based performance ratios may need to be disseminated. The first is cost per unit of output, for example, cost per acre of grass mowed, so once a performance standard is identified, inefficiencies become apparent. The second ratio is cost per resident of the communitywide services, so residents can decide whether a service is good value for their tax money.

Types of Costs

Often when agencies claim to be adopting a policy of full cost recovery in providing a service, further analysis reveals that this is not so because some elements of costs are omitted. Five types of costs that should be incorporated when calculating the full cost of delivering a service are identified in Figure 4-4. These elements are different from those that would be included by private sector organizations in that the agency would have to incorporate the cost of debt into its pricing structure, along with a profit margin to reflect return on the owner's investment. However, in the public sector, capital expenditures for land acquisition and facility development are usually excluded unless they are financed through revenue bonds or some other self-financing mechanism. There are two reasons for this.

First, in most cases, public leisure facilities are funded with general obligation bonds approved by voters at a referendum. Because voters are aware the bonds will be redeemed with taxes, there is *ipso facto* recognition that such facilities provide communitywide benefits, so there is no rationale for expecting users to meet these costs. Similarly, if the facilities were financed by intergovernmental transfers or other grants, users would not be charged because such financing would not be a direct burden on local taxpayers.

Second, capital expenditures are sunk costs; that is, they cannot be recovered once they have been incurred. A facility cannot be "unbuilt," and the likelihood of public leisure facilities being sold for another purpose to recover the costs is small. Irrespective of how much voters may regret the investment or what use is made of the facilities, these are historical costs and the money has gone. The only costs that can be controlled are associated with operation of the facility.

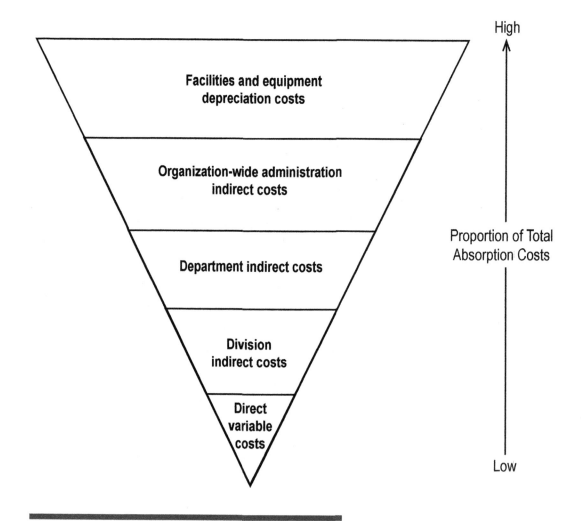

Figure 4-4. Elements Constituting Total Absorption Cost

While the original capital costs should usually be excluded from price structures, the use of a facility or major equipment will result in the asset deteriorating. Periodic renovation of facilities and replacement of equipment are inevitable. It has been argued in a private sector context that depreciation should also be regarded as a sunk cost:

Because depreciation costs reflect past decisions, they are irrelevant for pricing and other planning decisions. Unfortunately, they are often lumped in with other fixed costs and become a part of the cost that price is expected to recover. *Depreciation costs should be separated from other period expenses for the purpose of pricing.* (p. 266)[8]

However, in the public sector, this assumes funds will be forthcoming from tax sources to replace these assets when they wear out. That is a precarious and optimistic assumption, so a depreciation cost to cover these eventualities should be included.

Unfortunately, this is not required in most government accounting systems. If it is incorporated, the revenue generated should be placed in a separate account and used only for that purpose. An illustration of such an account is given in Table 12-1, with an accompanying narrative in Chapter 12. If these revenues are credited to the general fund, they will likely be appropriated for other purposes. If such funds are not created, repairs, maintenance and staffing costs will increase with deterioration, while facility quality and visitor attendance will decline.

A second source of fixed costs is indirect or overhead costs. These are not directly incurred by a service, but are necessary for the agency to function. They should be apportioned among all the leisure services offered to cover the costs of supporting them. They remain relatively constant or "fixed," regardless of the level of program participation or facility use.

Figure 4-4 shows three levels of indirect costs: organization-wide administration, departmental and division. A jurisdiction's organization-wide administration may support a leisure program by providing human resource, payroll, legal and internal audit assistance. Costs to be apportioned at the department level may include the agency's support staff (e.g., department head, office secretary, computing technical assistance), office supplies, promotional expenses and utilities. For example, if 15 percent of a department's water bill and 10 percent of its phone charges are associated with softball, these amounts should be part of softball's cost structure.

At the division level, the superintendent of athletics, her secretary, and the athletic field ground crews, for example, are indirect overhead costs. Thus, if 20 percent of their time is associated with softball, 20 percent of their salaries (including fringe benefits) should be attributed to the softball program.

The lowest level shown in Figure 4-4 is direct variable costs, the specific expenses associated with operating a given program. They vary according to the number of people using a service. For example, direct variable costs in an adult softball program include officials' salaries, equipment (softballs, bases, field striping materials, etc.), sports field lighting, trophies, scorekeepers, field maintenance staff, garbage pickup, minor equipment and other expenses that can be directly attributed to the operation of the program. These costs will increase as the number of participants increases.

Fixed costs, variable costs and total costs, which are an aggregation of fixed and variable costs, are illustrated in Figure 4-5. As the number of services or participants using a given fixed asset or indirect cost center increases, costs per service or participant decrease as they are spread among more services or participants. This is illustrated in the next section of the chapter in Table 4-3, which shows an increase of members at a fitness center from 500 to 600 resulting in a decrease in fixed costs per person and in the break-even membership fee from $564 to $477.

When all five sources of costs in Figure 4-4 are incorporated into a price structure, it is termed "absorption costing." This is the preferred approach. If costing comprises only an estimate of variable costs and a "fudged guesstimate" of (say) 30 percent for overhead, a price set to recover a given percentage of costs does not, rendering the process meaningless. Purposeful pricing that is policy driven requires that absorption costing be adopted.

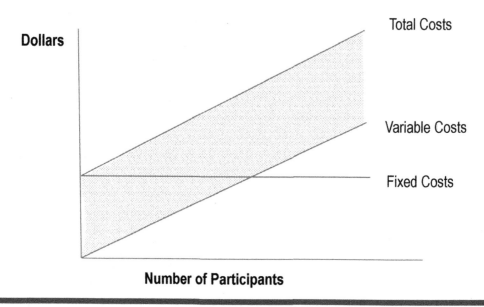

Figure 4-5. Fixed Costs, Variable Costs, Total Costs and the Potential Contribution of Discounts to Cost Recovery

Table 4-1 shows the annual budget for recreation and aquatic programs in College Station, Texas. The city elected not to incorporate depreciation costs into its pricing structure, but it did include the other four sources of costs shown in Figure 4-4. Indirect costs in Table 4-1 include apportioning 42 percent of the department's central administration costs, including personnel, and 100 percent of the recreation division's overhead costs, including personnel and utilities. Apportionment of field maintenance cost is shown as a separate item. The "G&A" stands for general and accounting charges, which are the costs associated with the central functions of the city (payroll, human resources, budget, purchasing, etc.). As a result of its cost-finding exercise, the city determined the most expeditious way to allocate these central costs was to charge them as 7 percent of the direct costs of each program.

The data in Table 4-1 illustrate the consequences of using different costing measures. For example, the first activity shown, adult softball, anticipates a loss of $135,042, a recovery rate of 55.76 percent and a per participant subsidy of $24.14. However, if only direct costs are used, a different picture emerges as the recovery and subsidy rates then become 92.6 percent and $2.43, respectively.

The type of data in Table 4-1 alerts managers and elected officials to potential policy issues. For example, in terms of equity, the per person subsidies raise two questions: Are large subsidies evidence that the Benefit Principle is being abused? and Is it fair that some participants receive much larger subsidies than those in other activities? For example, those in youth basketball programs receive a subsidy of $34 each, while the per participant taxpayer support for those in youth volleyball and youth football is $73 and $195, respectively. Similarly, in terms of efficient allocation of resources, the question arises: Could the $54,498 and the $24,499 used to fund the 80 participants in "challenger sports" and the 20 participants in water fitness, respectively, be better used elsewhere?

Table 4-1
City of College Station Budget – Recreation Programs

PROGRAM	PARTICIPANTS	REVENUE $	DIRECT COST $	INDIRECT COST $	FIELD COST $	G&A $	TOTAL COST $	% OF REV RECOVERY	SUBSIDY $	SUSIDY COST/PART. $
Adult Softball	5,595	170,225	183,826	57,574	1,000	12,868	305,267	55.76	(135,042)	(24.14)
Adult Volleyball	1,030	21,500	40,935	17,179	-	2,865	60,978	35.26	(39,478)	(38.33)
Youth Basketball	1,000	53,200	65,702	17,179	-	4,599	87,479	60.81	(34,279)	(34.28)
Youth Football	372	18,600	41,244	29,856	17,250	2,887	91,237	20.39	(72,637)	(195.26)
Youth Volleyball	500	25,000	41,595	17,179	-	2,912	61,685	40.53	(36,685)	(73.37)
Adult Kickball	1,005	20,000	28,127	27,743	6,800	1,969	64,639	30.94	(44,639)	(44.42)
Challenger Sports	80	1,200	30,426	21,023	920	2,130	54,498	2.20	(53,298)	(666.23)
Tennis	225	16,875	40,934	17,179	-	2,865	60,977	27.67	(44,102)	(196.01)
No-Fee Programs	3,200	-	24,231	362,670	256,200	1,696	644,797	0.00	(644,797)	(201.50)
TOTAL SPORTS	13,007	326,600	497,016	567,580	332,170	34,791	1,431,557	22.81	(1,104,957)	(84.95)
Extra Ed	1,600	80,000	186,291	31,979	-	13,040	231,310	34.59	(151,310)	(94.57)
TOTAL INSTRUCT	1,600	80,000	186,291	31,979	-	13,040	231,310	34.59	(151,310)	(94.57)
SW Pool	40,000	86,400	224,602	12,593	-	15,722	252,917	34.16	(166,517)	(4.16)
Thomas Pool	20,000	44,000	172,080	12,593	-	12,046	196,718	22.37	(152,718)	(7.64)
Adamson Lagoon	70,000	255,900	444,310	12,593	-	31,102	488,005	52.44	(232,105)	(3.32)
CSISD Natatorium	-	9,000	56,835	8,589	-	3,978	69,403	12.97	(60,403)	-
Splash Pads	5,000	-	20,534	11,258	-	1,437	33,230	0.00	(33,230)	(6.65)
Swim Lessons	2,500	110,000	111,872	15,262	-	7,831	134,964	81.50	(24,964)	(9.99)
Water Fitness	20	1,500	14,861	8,589	-	1,040	24,490	6.12	(22,990)	(1,149.51)
Swim Team	209	23,000	19,693	12,593	-	1,378	33,664	68.32	(10,664)	(51.02)
Stroke Clinic	110	5,500	10,750	11,258	-	752	22,761	24.16	(17,261)	(156.91)
TOTAL AQUATICS	137,839	535,300	1,075,535	105,329	-	75,287	1,256,151	42.61	(720,851)	(5.23)
SW Center-Teen	300	29,500	134,364	12,884	-	9,405	156,653	18.83	(127,153)	(423.84)
SW Center-Senior	180	10,600	105,058	11,549	-	7,354	123,961	8.55	(113,361)	(629.79)
Lincoln Center	900	47,100	366,345	20,891	-	25,644	412,880	11.41	(365,780)	(406.42)
TOTAL CENTERS	1,380	87,200	605,767	45,324	-	42,404	693,495	12.57	(606,295)	(439.34)
Conference Center	-	-	314,948	21,333	-	22,046	358,327	0.00	(358,327)	(358,327)
TOTAL CONF CTR	-	-	314,948	21,333	-	22,046	358,327	0.00	(358,327)	(358,327)
TOTAL	153,826	1,029,100	2,679,557	771,545	332,170	187,569	3,970,841	25.92	(2,941,741)	(19.12)

The data also illustrate the importance of reviewing per person, rather than absolute, subsidies. For example, Adamson Lagoon's annual subsidy is $232,000, which is substantially higher than the subsidies at SWPool or Thomas Pool. If budget reductions are needed, this may cause decision makers to reduce operating hours at Adamson Lagoon rather than at the other two pools. However, this would be a mistake because the per person subsidies at Thomas Pool and SWPool are 130 percent and 25 percent higher, respectively, than the subsidy at Adamson Lagoon. Hence, it would be most efficient to make the reductions at Thomas Pool.

Methods of Establishing a Price Based on Cost Recovery

The proportion of costs intended to be recovered by a price varies according to where on the Benefits Continuum (Figure 4-1) a service is positioned. If benefits are perceived to accrue exclusively to individual users, the goal is full cost recovery. If there are spill-over benefits, the goal changes to either partial overhead cost recovery or recovery of only direct variable costs.

A full cost recovery price is intended to produce sufficient revenue to cover the fixed and variable costs associated with the service. The formula for deriving it is shown in Table 4-2.

Table 4-2

Setting a Base Price to Recover Full Cost

Full Cost Recovery = Average Fixed Cost + Average Variable Cost

Where: $\text{Average Fixed Cost} = \dfrac{\text{Total Fixed Costs}}{\text{Number of Users}}$

$\text{Average Variable Cost} = \dfrac{\text{Total Variable Costs}}{\text{Number of Users}}$

If: Total Fixed Costs = $3,000

Total Variable Costs = $1,000

Projected Number of Users = 100

Then: $\text{Price} = \dfrac{3000}{100} + \dfrac{1000}{100}$

Thus: Price = $40

Table 4-3 shows how to determine a price that is intended to recover partial overhead costs. A price is established that meets all direct variable costs and some proportion of fixed costs. The remaining proportion of the fixed costs that it is not intended to recover represents the tax subsidy for the particular service. The amount of subsidy is dependent on the extent to which communitywide benefits are perceived to accrue. As these increase, the proportion of fixed costs met by a subsidy, rather than users, increases (Figure 4-1).

Table 4-3
Setting a Base Price to Recover Partial Overhead Costs

Partial Overhead Recovery Price = Average Fixed Cost + Average Variable Cost – Average Subsidy

Where:	Average subsidy represents the amount to which each user is subsidized out of tax funds
If:	Average Fixed Cost = $8
	Average Variable Cost = $4
	Average Subsidy = $3
Then:	Partial Overhead Recovery Price = $8 + $4 – $3
Thus:	Program Price = $9

It is important to note the anticipated per person subsidy is built into the formula. This is a different approach to the frequent practice of assigning (say) a 20 percent overhead figure to direct variable costs without identifying all the sources of fixed costs, as that arbitrary process does not indicate the extent to which individuals are subsidized.

If variable cost recovery pricing is used, the established price is equal to the average variable cost of providing a service. In this context, variable costs are direct operating and maintenance expenses. No attempt is made to contribute toward meeting fixed costs. Table 4-4 shows how to determine a price that is intended to recover direct variable costs.

Table 4-4

Setting a Base Price to Recover Direct Variable Costs

Direct Cost Recovery Price = $\dfrac{\text{Total Variable Costs}}{\text{Number of Participants}}$

If: Total Variable Cost = $2,000

               Projected Number of Participants = 200

Then: Variable Cost Recovery Price = $10

When only partial direct variable costs are to be recovered, a tax subsidy amount is subtracted from the full variable cost recovery price.

Because direct variable expenses can be relatively easily documented, basing price decisions on them is tempting. This is a popular approach with many agency personnel because when fixed costs are omitted, a relatively low price can be charged and a larger client support constituency is likely to emerge.

When participants pay for a service, their receipt should itemize the costs involved in delivering it. If that is impractical, this information should be prominently displayed at the entrance to a facility. In addition to transparency, it is pointed out in Chapter 11 that lack of awareness of the magnitude of costs, subsidies and cost recovery ratios is a primary reason why price increases are resisted. Controversy is invariably reduced when users are provided with this information.

What About Marginal Cost Pricing?

It is an established tenet of economics that price should be set to recover the marginal cost of delivering a service rather than the average cost, which is used in Table 4-2, because in the short term, maximum economic efficiency is attained when price equals the marginal cost of provision. Marginal cost is the cost of servicing "one more" participant, class or team (i.e., the incremental cost of the next unit of service). Participants then pay the additional costs associated with their use of the service. Given that fixed costs remain constant, marginal cost is the direct variable cost of serving the next participant.

The data in Table 4-5 illustrate the concept of marginal cost pricing. The projected annual operating costs of a new fitness center being considered by a community are listed. The goal is for it to be self-sustaining. It will be funded by annual memberships and is projected to attract 500 members. Fixed costs are estimated at $260,000 and variable costs at $22,000.

Table 4-5
Annual Operating Costs of a New Fitness Center (Assuming 500 Members)

Item	Fixed Cost $	Variable Cost $	Total Cost $
Equipment costs	60,000		60,000
Equipment maintenance	5,000	1,000	6,000
Equipment depreciation	6,000	1,000	7,000
Class instructors/personal trainers	60,000	18,000	78,000
Manager and assistant manager salaries	70,000		70,000
Front desk staff salaries	34,000		34,000
Supplies		2,000	2,000
Indirect administration	25,000		25,000
Total	**260,000**	**22,000**	**282,000**

Break-Even Price at Different Membership Levels

Number of Members	Fixed Cost Recovery	Variable Cost Recovery at $44 per Person	Total Price
400	$650 (260,000/400)	$44	$694
500	$520 (260,000/500)	$44	$564
600	$433 (260,000/600)	$44	$477

To achieve full cost recovery, the price of an annual membership would be $564 ($282,000/500). If only 400 were attracted, the break-even price would rise to $694, while if 600 members joined, it would fall to $477. However, if 600 were attracted, the marginal cost of servicing the additional 100 people would be only $44 per person. The fixed costs do not change. The only additional cost incurred in servicing these extra 100 members is the variable cost.

Despite advocacy by economists, marginal cost pricing is not a viable option for public leisure agencies because it is not viewed as equitable. If marginal cost pricing were to be adopted for the scenario in Table 4-5, the first 500 members to enroll would pay $564, while the last 100 participants would be charged only $44. This would likely be regarded as outrageously unfair, and it is doubtful that any elected official would support it. The probable outcome is that the average cost price of $477 for 600 members would be adopted.

The Contribution of Discounts to Cost Recovery

In some situations, it is advantageous for leisure managers to offer discounts as part of their strategy for meeting a given cost recovery goal. Those include encouraging access to economically disadvantaged groups (discussed in Chapters 6 and 7), non-peak time users (Chapter 8) and promotional prices intended to incentivize non-users to participate (Chapter 12). In these cases, the discounted price is intended to generate additional revenue by expanding the client base.

For this strategy to work, the discounts must attract only people who were previously non-participants and not permit existing users to switch from the more costly regular price to take advantage of the discount. The strategy is especially viable in situations in which fixed costs constitute a high proportion of total costs. If spare capacity can be filled by participants paying a discounted price, then *provided the price exceeds variable costs*, it makes a contribution to fixed costs. This is shown in the hatched area on Figure 4-5. The additional net revenue will mean the number of participants paying the regular price to reach the cost recovery goal will be lower than it would be otherwise. This can be illustrated using the data in Table 4-5, for which, with 500 members, the annual full cost recovery price would be $564. If an additional 100 residents who were economically disadvantaged were enticed to join by discounting the price to $240 (i.e., $20 a month instead of $47 a month), it would yield $19,600 [($240 × 100) – Variable Costs of $4,400], which would reduce the annual fee to the 500 regular users from $564 to $525.

Weaknesses of Cost-Based Pricing

Establishing a price derived from a desired level of recovery of costs yields a base price—the foundation upon which a final price structure is constructed. However, four potential limitations inherent in a cost-based price need to be addressed, making it likely changes will be made to this base price.

First, prices based on recovery of costs ignore the Ability to Pay Principle, market conditions and competitive suppliers. They assume client groups are willing and able to pay the proposed prices, whereas it would be purely fortuitous if this was the case. The more likely probability is that users will perceive the cost-based price as being too high, or their willingness to pay will be underestimated and it will be too low. It is participants, not agencies, who determine price. The sequence of actions in cost-based pricing is this:

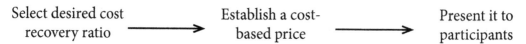

Select desired cost recovery ratio $\longrightarrow$ Establish a cost-based price $\longrightarrow$ Present it to participants

In contrast, rather than pricing "forward" from a cost recovery ratio, the sequence for establishing a price that is grounded in the context of local market conditions moves "backwards" in the opposite direction starting with participants:

Participants' willingness and ability to pay $\longrightarrow$ Cost-based price adjusted to reflect this $\longrightarrow$ Adjusted cost recovery ratio

This recognizes the desired cost recovery ratio will likely have to be compromised to reflect realities of the marketplace.

For example, if the partial overhead recovery price of $9 derived in Table 4-3 were for admission to an aquatic facility at which the existing price was $5, and if there were a similar quality pool in a neighboring jurisdiction that also charged that price, many users would likely not pay the new cost-based $9 price. For some, the inconsistency of the new price with their reference price (Chapter 9) would cause them to resist, some simply could not afford the new price, and others would consider it poor value for money and would likely travel to the neighboring pool.

A second weakness relates to projecting the number of service users accurately. The price will only recover the level of anticipated costs *if* the estimated number of service users is accurate. This number may be relatively easy to estimate if historical records show a consistent pattern of participation in a given program over a period of years. However, for a new service, there may be considerable error in the participation projection. If the projection is too high, the agency will receive less revenue than it had anticipated.

For example, the membership price based on full cost recovery at the new fitness center described in Table 4-5 was $564, which was predicated on 500 people joining. If only 400 enroll at that price, instead of breaking even, the facility would lose $56,400. Again, this illustrates the importance of the starting focus being on participants' willingness and ability to pay rather than on costs to be recovered with the accompanying hope that the requisite numbers needed to meet the goal will participate.

A third weakness of cost-based pricing is that it may encourage inefficiency. The danger is that little concern will be given to controlling costs or requiring efficient management as the costs would be directly passed on to client groups in the form of higher prices. Client groups have no interest in costs *per se*, only in price. The price they are willing to pay determines the costs that can be invested in a service. Using increases in costs to justify increases in price is unlikely to resonate unless the costs are outside the control of the agency (Chapter 11). Failing to make the frequently difficult decisions to control costs in the belief they will be absorbed by participants is hallucinatory.

The implications of this can be illustrated with the example in Table 4-2. Three quarters of the $40 price for (say) a basketball program is an apportionment of fixed costs. This may include the salaries and benefits of a manager and assistant manager of athletics that are spread across all athletic programs. If participants resisted $40, but would accept $30, an option may be to consider terminating one of these managers if this would reduce the overhead apportionment by one third from $3,000 to $2,000.

A fourth weakness is that cost-based pricing may encourage an irrational price structure and exacerbate a peaking problem. Consider the implications of the structure adopted by a year-round camp:

- The camp sought to recover all of its costs. Most of the costs were fixed, so the cost of operating the camp was about the same year-round. The prices charged were $200 per 3-day weekend in the winter months and $100 per 3-day weekend in the summer months. These prices reflected the much higher occupancy rate at the camp in the summer months, which enabled the fixed costs to be spread over more users. However, the price structure had the effect of persuading more people to come in the summer than in the winter. Hence, there were long waiting lists for the summer, but the camp had very low winter occupancy rates.

ADJUSTING A COST-BASED PRICE TO REFLECT THE GOING RATE

The parameters that govern price are shown in Figure 4-6. The price ceiling is the highest price participants are willing to pay, so consumers' surplus (discussed in Chapter 5) is minimized. The floor price is that which delivers the minimally acceptable cost recovery ratio. If the ratio were lower, the opportunity cost to the agency would be considered too high, so the service would be terminated and its resources either reallocated to another service that could deliver superior benefits or returned to the taxpayer. Within this range, the price charged is the result of interaction of counterbalancing forces. Downward pressure from the price ceiling emanates from concerns about ability to pay and being undercut by other suppliers of the service. Upward pressure from the price floor springs from the prevailing political imperatives to reduce subsidies and taxes and to avoid unfair competition with the private sector.

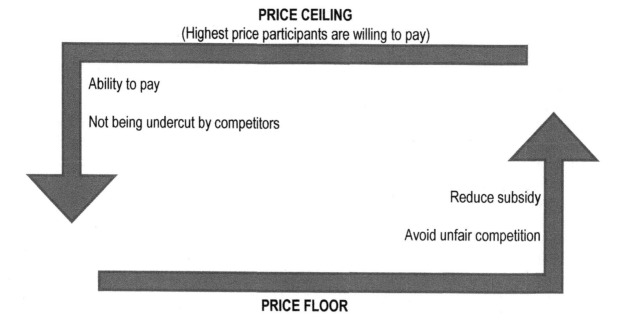

PRICE CEILING
(Highest price participants are willing to pay)

Ability to pay

Not being undercut by competitors

Reduce subsidy

Avoid unfair competition

PRICE FLOOR
(Minimum acceptable cost recovery price)

Figure 4-6. The Parameters That Govern Price

Adjusting a cost-based price so it is consistent with what users are willing to pay is done by surveying other public and private suppliers of the service about the prices they are charging. The survey provides information on the elements in Figure 4-6: the highest price participants are likely to be willing to pay and competitors' prices, which reduces the risk of being undercut by others and of engaging in unfair competition.

The survey will establish the *range* of prices that is likely to be acceptable to users. However, rarely are "apples being compared to apples." That is, services offered by other leisure suppliers and their target markets are likely to be different in format and quality, so the data need to be interpreted and allowances made for the differences. Despite these nuances, there are likely to be substantial similarities, so the results will be valuable when addressing the parameters of interest in Figure 4-6.

A further advantage of the survey is that the going rate price range can be viewed as representing the collective wisdom of professionals and elected officials in other jurisdictions. For this reason, a price within the range will probably avoid controversy and be regarded by most stakeholders as fair.

Some may challenge the value of undertaking the considerable effort entailed in positioning services on the Benefits Continuum, identifying all sources of costs associated with each service and calculating a cost-based price if after all that investment of effort the base price is then amended so it is consistent with the prices of other suppliers. Why not skip the cost-based price and simply adopt a "ballpark price" in the range defined by others?

There are three responses. First, the going rate survey is likely to reveal that prices others charge vary. Without a cost recovery goal there is no guidance as to whether the agency's program should be priced at the high or low end of the range. Second, the going rate often bears little relation to the cost of a program. Knowledge of costs provides managers and elected officials with justifications for when they are challenged by either taxpayers concerned that subsidies are too generous or users opining that prices are too high. Third, if knowledge of the magnitude of subsidy is unknown, an agency is incapable of purposefully trading off the opportunity cost of one service compared to another.

SUMMARY

The positioning of services on the Benefits Continuum defines the appropriate level of taxpayer subsidy and the proportion of costs that a user price should be designed to recover. At one end of the continuum, services perceived to provide communitywide benefits are fully subsidized from taxes, so no price is charged for them. Services positioned at the opposite user benefits end of the continuum are priced at a level that covers all their costs. The magnitude of spillover benefits varies, so three position points for them are shown on the continuum, indicating 25, 50 and 75 percent levels of cost recovery.

Enterprise funds are a special vehicle sometimes used for services from which all benefits accrue to users, and consequently, the revenue stream is substantial. They have the potential to strengthen staff's commitment to generating revenue and producing relevant, high quality services; their requirement to be self-sufficient undercuts efforts by users to lobby for taxpayer subsidies to keep their prices low; the closed loop enables those paying for a service to see direct benefits from those revenues, so their resistance to price increases is likely to dissipate; and managers are able to retain surplus funds they generate for reinvestment into these services rather than lose them to the general fund.

Because prices based on positions on the Benefits Continuum seek to recover a given percentage of costs, the costs have to be accurately identified. While the optimum approach for doing this is developing a detailed cost accounting system, the costs and effort associated with developing and maintaining such a system are often not justified. The objective is not to arrive at an absolutely correct allocation of costs, but to assign each service an approximate fair share of the agency's overheads. This can be done by cost finding, which requires a much lower level of investment. It involves taking available financial data and recasting and adjusting it to derive indirect cost estimates.

It is generally considered inappropriate to include cost of debt in a pricing structure, but five types of costs should be incorporated when calculating the total absorption cost of delivering a service: depreciation cost associated with renovating facilities or replacing major equipment; organization-wide administration indirect costs for providing services, such as human resource, payroll, legal and internal audit assistance; department-level indirect costs for the department head's office, planning, technical computing assistance and supplies; division-level indirect costs for division administrators, facility maintenance and ground crews; and direct variable costs, which are the expenses associated with operating a given program.

Economists invariably argue that averaging the costs to be recovered and distributing them equally among participants is inefficient. They point out that pricing to cover marginal costs is more efficient, that is, the cost of covering "one more" participant. However, marginal cost pricing would result in perceptions of unfairness because some participants would pay a substantially different price than others of similar economic status. For this reason, marginal cost pricing is not viable for public leisure agencies.

Discounted prices can generate additional revenues that contribute to cost recovery goals provided they meet two conditions: They must attract only people who were previously non-participants and not existing users who merely switch from the regular to the discount price, and the discount price has to exceed variable costs so it makes a contribution to fixed costs.

Cost-based pricing is a point of departure, but it has four potential limitations that make it likely that it will subsequently be amended: Price based on recovery of costs ignores the Ability to Pay Principle, market conditions, competitive suppliers and clients' emotional/psychological reactions to a price and simply assumes client groups are willing and able to pay the desired cost recovery price; it assumes the number of service users can be accurately estimated; it may encourage inefficiency in that costs can be directly passed through to client groups in the form of higher prices; and it may exacerbate a peaking problem.

The cost-based price has to be adjusted so it is consistent with what users are willing to pay. This is done by undertaking a going rate survey to review the prices other public and private suppliers of the service are charging. After it has been adjusted to conform with the going rate range, two further amendments to the base price have to be considered. Reconciling it with the Ability to Pay Principle is addressed in Chapters 5 to 8, while amending it to accommodate psychological reactions is discussed in Chapters 9 to 12.

REFERENCES

1. McKinny, J. (1993, January 12). Next: Buck-a-duck, pay-per-view. *Los Angeles Times*, p. 14.
2. Drake, M. A. (1981). *User fees: A practical perspective*. Littleton, CO: Libraries Unlimited.
3. McIntosh, B. (1983). *Visitor fees in the National Park System: A legislative and administrative history*. Washington, DC: History Division, National Park Service, Department of the Interior.
4. Walls, M. (2013). *Paying for state parks*. Washington, DC: Resources for the Future.
5. L. Younger, personal communication, June 17, 1982.
6. Hudson, K. (1984, June). Museum charges are good for the paying public. *Good Housekeeping, 1984*, 43.
7. Crompton, J. L., & Lamb, C. W. (1986). *Marketing government social services*. New York, NY: John Wiley.
8. Monroe, K. B. (2003). *Pricing: Making profitable decisions*. New York, NY: McGraw-Hill.

Section 2

Differential Pricing

Discounts and Premiums

Differential pricing is the mechanism used to reconcile pricing's guiding concepts: the Benefit and Ability to Pay Principles. Price elasticity is discussed in Chapter 5. This is the economic concept that undergirds differential pricing, which is manifested in discounts and premiums. Alternative formats, the merits and the justifications (or lack thereof) of providing discounts for the economically disadvantaged and the unemployed are evaluated in Chapter 6. This evaluation continues in Chapter 7, but the context is shifted to discounts for seniors and children that are based on age rather than on economic status. The evaluation in Chapter 7 concludes with a discussion of discounts in the form of a multi-use pass.

If discounts are not offered to the economically disadvantaged, one of two undesirable outcomes will occur: (i) Prices will be set at a level that is too high for them, so those whose need is greatest are effectively excluded, which abrogates the Ability to Pay Principle, or (ii) to preclude such exclusion, prices are set at a low level for all, resulting in a large consumers' surplus among those who could pay more, which is an abrogation of the Benefit Principle.

In Chapter 8, premiums are evaluated. In accordance with the Benefit Principle, premiums are charged to capture consumers' surplus and to cover the costs associated with meeting the demands of some users for additional increments of benefits beyond the standard offering.

Chapter 5

Price Elasticity

The Basis for Differential Pricing

- The "law" of market demand
- The concept of price elasticity
- The rationale for differential pricing
- Summary

THE "LAW" OF MARKET DEMAND

Economists describe the effects of changes in price on level of participation and revenues by the "law" of market demand. This is illustrated in Figure 5-1, which represents the visitation that would occur at each price point. It shows that, all else equal, the quantity demanded of any service falls (rises) as its price rises (falls). A demand curve is simply a statement of the amount of a leisure service that would be purchased at a specific price. Thus, in Figure 5-1, if the admission price to the swimming pool were $4, the average number of daily visitors would be 200. The curve shows that if admission were free, 400 would be attracted, while if it were raised to $9, nobody would show up. The 200 users paying $4 each would generate $800 in revenue. If $5 were charged, there would only be 160 admissions, but the total revenue would remain the same. Other potential prices below $4 or above $5 would yield less revenue.

The concept that demand will fall when price rises is predicated on two assumptions. First, buyers' actions are rational, so they always act to maximize utility (value). (Utility comprises material, physical, mental, intellectual, emotional and spiritual well-being.) That is, they will always use more of a service when the price falls because the lower price enhances the benefit/satisfaction value they derive from the purchase. However, it has been consistently demonstrated in recent decades that purchasers engage in cognitively processing multiple psychological and behavioral cues and frameworks in addition to the price, which may result in actions that do not maximize utility. The limitations and fallacies of this assumption are explained in Chapters 9 to 12.

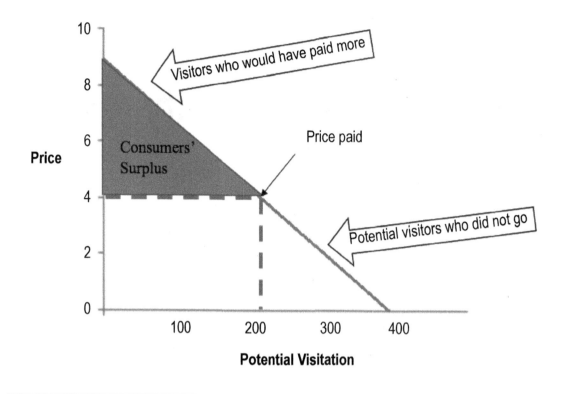

Figure 5-1. The Law of Market Demand and Consumer Surplus at a Swimming Pool

Second, price is the only, or at a minimum the most significant, determinant in a purchase decision. This assumption has not been supported in empirical studies in the public leisure field. For example, it was concluded in an experimental study of price elasticity at five recreation centers: "Price is only one, and in the majority of cases a minor, factor in the decision to participate in sport and physical recreation" (p. 19) and "Non-participants did not regard the cost of admission as a significant obstacle to participation" (p. 30).[1] Similar findings in the leisure field have been reported by others.[2-5]

In the real world, people's response to a price increase may also include consideration of changes in the attributes of a service, such as refurbishment of a facility or the equipment, changes in program leadership, how well it is delivered (reliability, responsiveness, empathy, assurance),[6] when it is available or scheduled, and convenience of its location. Beyond these features of a service, other factors influencing demand may include buyers' levels of discretionary income; the amount of promotion; accuracy of information; cost of search time; cost of participation and travel time; cost of equipment, clothing and footwear; and cost of substitute services offered by competitors.

Economists may respond to the challenges in constructing demand curves posed by these other variables in two ways. First, they may disregard them, focus exclusively on the likely impact of monetary price on demand, and proceed on the dubious premise that other factors remain constant so "all else is equal." Alternatively, they may incorporate a set of these attributes as constraints into their models. However, these variables are in a constant state of flux and are difficult to quantify. This makes the accuracy of economists' analyses notoriously tenuous. For example, the authors of an analysis of the effects of price on visitation to a set of rural park and recreation facilities observed:

> Other factors [than price] which may affect demand cause complications and, in order to isolate the influence of admission prices, we need to take account of the effect of these on visitors. To do this, it is necessary to know what the most important influences are; what effects they have; and how they change over time. In this analysis the influences of weather, incomes, gas costs, site promotion and special events are analyzed, where possible, together with a range of other variables. This is not a straightforward exercise and it has not often been attempted in the past. This has meant that previous judgments about the effects of admission prices have been greatly misleading, since they have not isolated the influence of many other factors from that of price changes. (p. 6)[7]

At this point, leisure managers may ask: "If demand curves have to be so carefully and comprehensively qualified, are they too complicated and too arbitrary to be useful in practice?"[8] This is a reasonable reaction. However, they have conceptual value because, notwithstanding these limitations and difficulties with developing and using demand curves, the basic premise that as a price goes down visitation and use will increase is appropriate in many real-world contexts. This makes the concept a useful starting point for reviewing the impact of price on different target markets.

Consumers' Surplus

When a price for a leisure service is established, groups of users will have different levels of sensitivity to it. Invariably, some would be willing and able to pay more than the price being charged. This potential revenue that is "left on the table" is termed "consumers' surplus." Consumers' surplus is the difference between the price a user is willing and able to pay for a service and the price the user actually pays.

In the hypothetical example shown in Figure 5-1, 40 of the pool users would have paid $5 if the price had been set at that level; another 40, $6; another 40, $7; and another 40, $8. Thus, the total consumers' surplus would be $400: (40 × $1) + (40 × $2) + (40 × $3) + (40 × $4).

THE CONCEPT OF PRICE ELASTICITY

Demand curves have different gradients and shapes depending on users' sensitivity to different price levels. This price sensitivity is termed "elasticity." Price elasticity of demand is defined as the percentage change in use of a service resulting from a given percentage change in its price. That is, if price is raised (or lowered) by a given percentage, elasticity is a measure of the percentage decrease (or increase) in use.

Figures 5-2 and 5-3 illustrate the difference between inelastic and elastic demand. Figure 5-2 illustrates what might be expected to occur if the price of an admission permit at Grand Canyon National Park were raised from its current level of $25 per vehicle to

$40. The permit is good for a week and may be used for multiple day visits into the park during that period. At the current fee, there are 4.4 million per person day visits. On average, there are three people in a vehicle and permit holders use the permit for 2 days. When the price is raised to $40, 4 million day visits are projected, so annual revenue would rise from $18.4 million {[(4.4/3)/2] × $25} to $26.7 million {[(4.0/3)/2] × $40}. Thus, raising the price by 60 percent would result in a day visit reduction of only approximately 10 percent and in a 45 percent increase in revenue. This target market is relatively insensitive to price increases. When the visitation declines by a smaller percentage than the price increase, demand is said to be *inelastic*.

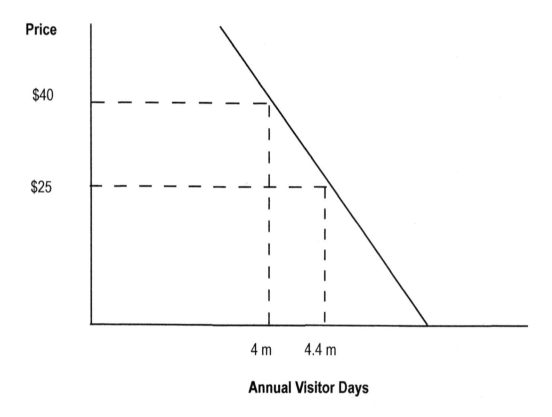

Figure 5-2. Relatively Inelastic Demand at Grand Canyon National Park

Figure 5-3 illustrates the opposite case. In this scenario, the price is for a hypothetical youth after-school basketball program at an urban recreation center. When the price was $2, there were 10,000 participant days (i.e., approximately 50 youth per day on average for the 200 school days). When it was raised to $3, the number dropped to 4,000 (i.e., approximately 20 per day) and annual revenues declined from $20,000 to $12,000. This target market was highly sensitive to the price increase. Visitation declined by a larger percentage (60 percent) than the price increase (50 percent). In such cases, demand is said to be *elastic*.

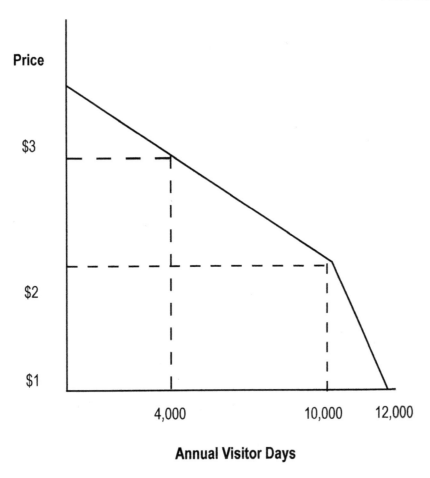

Figure 5-3. Relatively Elastic Demand at an Urban Recreation Center

The dividing line between relatively elastic and relatively inelastic demand is when changes in price are exactly offset by proportionate changes in use and total revenue remains constant. A demand curve for public leisure services is usually relatively elastic in some visitation and price ranges and relatively inelastic in others. For example, Figure 5-3 shows when the price was $1, there were 12,000 day visits. Raising it to $2 reduced visitation, but increased revenues from $12,000 to $20,000. Visitation declined by a smaller percentage (20 percent) than the price increase (100 percent), so at this part of the curve, the demand was inelastic.

Decision makers sometimes will not raise prices even when they are confident of increasing revenues because other outcomes are viewed as being more important. Thus, in the Figure 5-3 scenario, if demand were inelastic, and if the price were raised 50 percent from $2 to $3, annual day visit numbers would decline 20 percent to 8,000 (instead of 4,000) and revenues would increase to $24,000 (instead of declining to $12,000), and the price increase could still be vetoed because the agency has to decide if an increase in revenue of $4,000 is worth the potential costs to society that could result from 2,000 fewer after-school participant days and/or the loss of political or public support. In summary, the communitywide benefits may be perceived to outweigh the desire for more revenue.

Factors That Influence Price Elasticity

Four main factors influence price elasticity: proportion of the composite price making up the monetary price, availability and relative price of substitute services, users' income levels, and the existence of a strong price–quality relationship.

It was noted in Chapter 1 that the monetary price paid for a leisure service is only one component of the composite price (i.e., a user's total investment).[9] Other variable components of the composite price include travel and accommodation costs; costs incurred while participating, such as equipment rental and food and drink consumed on-site; and the opportunity cost of time, comprising preparation time, travel time to the site, time spent engaging in the activity, travel time from the site and subsequent "cleaning" time (e.g., laundry or equipment cleaning or repairing). These costs are incurred every time an individual engages in an activity. In addition, individuals incur fixed costs, such as expenditures on equipment, clothing and footwear. Total composite price comprises variable and fixed costs. However, only price changes in the variable components are likely to influence a participant's decision because the fixed costs were previously incurred. The fixed costs are "sunk costs," that is, they are irrecoverable, and as such, it is not rational to consider them in future decisions.

The illustration in Figure 5-2 suggests that increasing the entrance price at Grand Canyon National Park from $25 to $40 would likely have minimal impact on visitation. In that case, the cost of traveling to the park by automobile or airplane; the cost of accommodations, food and drink en route and in or near the park; and the opportunity cost of several days of traveling and experiencing the park may amount to thousands of dollars for many visitors. *When the price of admission is such a small proportion of the composite price, it is not likely to lead to a meaningful change in demand.*

Price elasticities may be misleading if only the admission price is considered. If other components of composite price, which constitute a larger proportion of it, such as airfares or gasoline prices, were to change by 60 percent as did the admission price in Figure 5-2, the negative impact on visitation would likely be much more substantial. These changes are completely beyond the control of leisure managers, but nevertheless they may have a substantial impact on demand.

The dominant role of composite price was empirically confirmed in a study of the contributions of economic factors to attendance declines at national parks:

- Between 1993 and 2010, visitor attendance at the 58 nature-based parks in the National Park System declined 7 percent. When allowance was made for increases in the U.S. population during this period, the per capita decline was 19 percent. An analysis of economic factors contributing to this decline demonstrated that the influence of increases in visitor entrance fees was small and demand was very price inelastic: "If simple revenue generation is a goal, the national parks probably could increase entry fees without having major impacts on visitation" (p. 162).[10]

In contrast, the impact of large increases in gas prices during this period, while household incomes had stagnated or declined, was substantial. The average entry fee at the parks was $12.77 per vehicle, while the average spending for visitor groups who stayed in motels outside the parks was $262 per day. The authors noted: "Crudely estimated then, a 10-day family trip to visit a major national park might cost over $2,600" (p. 161).[10] They observed, "The visitation impacts of fees [were] small because, for most people, the entry price is small relative to total cost" (p. 160).[10]

These findings reinforced earlier studies for which similar results were reported.[11]

A second factor that determines elasticity is the *availability and relative price of substitute services*. If another supplier offers a similar service of comparable quality, a substantial increase or decrease in the agency's price relative to the alternative supplier's price is likely to lead to a substantial change in demand for the service. The reverse situation also applies (i.e., a change in an alternative supplier's price is likely to have an impact on demand for an agency's service).

The fewer substitutes from which a participant can select, the more inelastic the demand is likely to be. More substitutes generally means participants will be more apt to resist an agency's price increases. Importantly, this refers to the number of substitutes of which participants are aware. Frequently, they have incomplete information about leisure service options available and may not know of all the acceptable alternatives.

Two other dimensions of substitutability influence elasticity. First, the more loyalty or affinity individuals feel toward other participants, program leaders or particular facilities, the less substitutable these services become. Such unique or salient features differentiate a service from competitors, making demand more inelastic. Second, even if no substitutes are available, demand can be fairly elastic if the service is not an important element of an individual's lifestyle. The more it is perceived as being necessary to well-being and quality of life, the more inelastic demand becomes.

Income level of the target market is a third factor that determines elasticity. The greater the level of affluence, the less likely a price adjustment will lead to a change in use. Participants become more sensitive to price when the expenditure constitutes a larger proportion of their budget.

A corollary of this factor is that it challenges the contention that demand curves are indicators of utility (i.e., measures of the amount of benefit/satisfaction derived from a purchase). A $5 price is a more substantial investment to someone earning minimum wage than to an executive earning $100,000 a year. The utility interpretation of a demand curve suggests the benefit/satisfaction that each receives is the same. However, it seems reasonable to postulate that because the price is a much higher proportion of income, benefit/satisfaction derived has to be higher before the minimum-wage person would be tempted to purchase a service.

A similar differential "value" is inherent in the time dimension of composite price:

Suppose both you and I have a month's vacation. During our vacations, you spend 7 days fishing while I spend 3. From this, it is reasonable to conclude that, other things being equal, you value fishing more than I do. Now, however, suppose that you have a two-month vacation, while I only have two weeks. As before, we fish for 7 days and 3 days respectively. Can we now conclude that you value fishing more than I do? I suspect that most people would be tempted to shift to a proportional scale—one that examines our participation as a function of the time we each have available. On that basis, I have actually spent a greater proportion of my available time fishing than you have; would we still conclude that you value fishing more? (p. 235)[12]

A final influence on elasticity is the existence of a *strong price–quality relationship.* This phenomenon is explained in Chapter 10. It suggests demand is more inelastic for leisure services if people use price as an indicator of a service's level of quality. In these cases, an increase in price may be viewed positively as signaling an increase in quality.

The different elasticities shown in Figures 5-2 and 5-3 are explained by these four factors. At Grand Canyon, the composite cost in time, effort and money of getting there is high compared to the admission charge; Grand Canyon is unique, there is only one, so it has no direct substitutes; surveys show its visitors are affluent; and a higher price would signal or confirm that it is a high quality attraction.

In contrast, at the urban recreation center, the entrance price is likely to represent a relatively high proportion of the total monetary costs associated with a visit, and its proximity means the opportunity cost of time will be lower; there may be several substitute opportunities available at a lower price; the target population is assumed to be relatively poor; and the clienteles are likely to have had regular exposure to it and do not need to use price to infer its quality.

Price Elasticity Illustrations

The relationship between elasticity and use is summarized in Table 5-1. Cell 1 shows that if demand is elastic, a price increase will decrease use. This occurred in New York City when the city doubled annual membership fees for adults at its recreation centers:

- The city's 35 recreation centers are "essentially city-run health clubs where New Yorkers who cannot afford memberships at expensive gyms, can work out" (p. A16).[13] Table 5-2 summarizes the outcomes when the city doubled annual membership fees for adults from $75 to $150 for centers with pools and from $50 to $100 for those without pools. The department projected a 5 percent decrease in the first year after the fees were doubled; instead, 52 percent of adults and seniors did not renew. The projected $4 million in new revenue did not materialize, but rather there was a loss of $200,000. Many of the centers' users could not afford the price increases. A council member from the Bronx observed:

  There are scores of families in my district for whom $300 for two adults is not affordable. The increases price out lower income New Yorkers, the very New Yorkers with the fewest alternatives to public recreation centers. Thirty percent of Bronx residents alone — more than 400,000 people — are living at or below the poverty rate of $23,021 per year for a family of four. The annual fair market rent of a two-bedroom apartment in the Bronx is $17,688. That leaves little more than $5,000 a year to cover all other expenses, from shoes, to school books, to food, to transportation. For these families, that extra $150 a year is simply prohibitive.[13]

Table 5-1
The Relationship between Elasticity and Use

Nature of Demand	Pricing Action	
	Raise Price	Reduce Price
Elastic Demand	1 Total use decreases by a larger percentage than the price increases	2 Total use increases by a larger percentage than the price reduction
Inelastic Demand	3 Total use decreases by a smaller percentage than the price increases	4 Total use increases by a smaller percentage than the price reduction

Table 5-2
Paid Membership at New York City Recreation Centers before and after a Large Fee Increase

Memberships	Fee Increase	Annual Members		Change in Membership	
		2011	2012	Members	Percent
Recreation Centers without Pools					
Adult Memberships	$50–$100	12,092	6,695	(5,397)	(44.6%)
Recreation Centers with Pools					
Adult Memberships	$75–$150	47,443	21,298	(26,145)	(55.1%)
Senior Memberships	$10–$25	36,153	18,055	(18,098)	(50.1%)
Child/Youth Memberships	Free	62,391	62,402	11	0.0%
Annual Paid Memberships		95,687	46,047	(49,640)	(51.9%)

Cell 2 in Table 5-1 indicates that the alternative form of elastic demand occurs when a reduction in price results in a disproportionate increase in use. Thus, in Figure 5-3, if the original price were $3 and 4,000 visits were reported, it would yield $12,000. If the price were reduced by 33 percent to $2, visitation would increase 150 percent to 10,000 visits, which would generate a 67 percent increase in revenue.

Inelastic demand in Cell 3 of Table 5-1 occurs when price is raised and the decline in use is disproportionately small:

- When the Corps of Engineers implemented fees for the first time at beaches and boat ramps at J. Percy Priest Lake in Tennessee and at Harry S. Truman Lake in Missouri, there was some expectation that use would decline. However, the visitation data in Table 5-3 indicate that, for the most part, these fears were unfounded. Demand was inelastic. Indeed, at three of the four sites, visitation increased when annual visitations in the year preceding implementation of the fees were compared with those 3 years after the fees were implemented. It was suggested: "The presence of gate attendants apparently improved the perception of safety and security." The scenario resembles that in Figure 5-2. The mean travel distances to the two lakes were 60 miles and 11 miles, respectively, so the use fees were relatively small when compared to the monetary and time costs associated with traveling to the sites. Further, users were relatively affluent, with their average household incomes comfortably exceeding the national average.[14]

Table 5-3
Site Visitation at Two Lakes before and after a Fee Was Implemented

Site	Pre-Fee Year	Fee Year	Fee Year Plus 1	Fee Year Plus 2	% Change Pre-Fee Year to Fee Year Plus 2
Truman Lake					
Site 1	48,800*	66,900	79,700	80,600	20%
Site 2	112,400	104,200	80,600	126,700	13%
Priest Lake					
Site 1	343,963	363,356	365,100	352,000	3%
Site 2	200,202	195,525	168,500	164,440	−18%

*This site was closed for part of this year, so the change comparison was made with the fee year.

Demand for the performing arts consistently has been reported as being relatively inelastic,[15, 16] so when prices are raised, demand does not fall proportionately. The findings and the reasons suggested to explain the inelasticity reported in Figure 5-4 are reasonably typical.[17]

Traditionally, the British government provided large subsidies to the country's major performing arts institutions. However, a political shift occurred and the government's fiscal philosophy was refocused on reducing taxes and public spending/subsidies. As part of this shift, major cultural organizations were directed to generate more of their own revenues by raising prices to reduce consumers' surplus.

Table A

Demand Changes and Price Increases over 10 Years for British Performing Arts Institutions

Performing Arts Institution	% Change over the 10-Year Period		
	Average Attendance (Demand)	Average Ticket Price	Total Revenue
Royal Opera House	−2	+99	+96
English National Opera	−5	+52	+46
Royal Ballet	No change	+41	+41
English National Ballet	−2	+7	+6
Royal National Theatre	−7	+38	+16
Royal Shakespeare Company	+4	+25	+29
R. Alston Dance Company	−17	+24	+3
Northern Ballet Company	+10	+61	+79
36 Provincial Repertory Theatres	−16	+32	+11
Society of London Theatres	+13	+20	+35

The data in Table A are the results over 10 years and show that demand was inelastic. Column 1 shows relatively small declines in average attendance even though the cumulative increase in ticket prices over the decade in real money terms was substantial (Column 2), with the result that revenues also increased substantially (Column 3). In the cases of the Royal Opera House and English National Opera, for example, audiences tolerated average price increases of 99 percent and 52 percent in real terms (i.e., after inflation) over the decade, with only 2 percent and 5 percent decreases in attendance, respectively.

The last line in Table A shows that the Society of London Theatres, which primarily comprises the commercial theatres in the West End of London, and which engages in joint marketing and promotion, increased prices by 20 percent and audiences by 13 percent. This produced a revenue increase of 35 percent over that decade.

The inelasticity of the institutions based in London were especially robust (the first five shown in Table A). This is explained by the four determinants of elasticity:

i. Larger proportions of London institutions' visitors were tourists, so admission price was a relatively small proportion of composite price.

ii. The reputations of the London institutions for performance excellence are among the best in the world, which confers upon them a degree of "brand uniqueness" and protects them from substitute competitors.

iii. Londoners are more affluent than those who live elsewhere in the country, and many tourists are similarly wealthy.

iv. The higher prices may reinforce visitors' perceptions by signaling confirmation of high quality, as many visitors will have no actual experience of the performance.

While demand inelasticity resulted in large revenue gains, governments have to consider other factors in their policy decisions. Accordingly, the policy was criticized by some who suspected that displacement may have occurred (i.e., that lower income attendees had been squeezed out by the higher prices and replaced by more wealthy patrons), so "cultural equity" and "access" were negatively impacted.

At the end of the 10 years, and with the large increases in revenue, these institutions still received large annual subsidies. For example, those for the Royal Opera House, English National Opera and Royal Ballet were $13 million, $18 million and $11 million, respectively. Given that this tax support comes from all residents, the central policy question is: Is it appropriate to charge high prices that effectively exclude many taxpayers from attending? The counter response to this may be: If prices are lowered, revenues are reduced, so tax support would be increased. Is it appropriate to increase the tax burden on lower income people, most of whom have no interest in these performances, to support the interests of the relatively wealthy?

Figure 5-4. The Inelasticity of Public Subsidized Performing Arts Programs[11]

Cell 4 of Table 5-1 shows that in addition to use/revenue increasing after a price increase, inelastic demand occurs when a price is reduced, but demand increases by a smaller percentage than the price reduction. Consider the following example:

- When California elected a new governor, he ordered major price cuts at its 266 state parks. He had two goals. First, to "make the parks more affordable for working families. We created the park system for all Californians and now I want to make sure our parks are accessible to all Californians." Second, to boost the economies of local communities around the parks. By lowering the price, he expected more people to visit the parks and spend money in those communities.[18]

Camping fees fell from a range of $19.50–$37.50 to $12 a night. Day use fees were cut in half and lowered to the nearest dollar. In more than 100 parks, this meant a 60 percent reduction from $5 to $2. Boat launching fees, dog fees, premium campsite fees, and higher rates for weekends and the high season were eliminated. The result was an increase in visitation in 1 year from 71 million to 93 million.[19]

Because many public leisure services are subsidized by taxes received from residents, policy decision makers, such as the California governor, are giving higher priority to increased access and participation than to revenue. The governor may have been pleased with the 30 percent increase in visitation, but technically this was an inelastic response because the price cut was approximately 60 percent and the visitation increase "only" 30 percent.

Inelastic responses to price cuts may occur when price is used to infer the quality of a program:

- A summer youth camp had charged around $100 a week for the past 3 years, and the clientele was predominantly middle class. Changes in city council members led to a directive that the price should be reduced to $20 to encourage more lower income youth to participate. However, the program failed to attract many of those participants, and the established clientele base declined. As a result of the new low price, the existing middle class clientele were concerned the day camp would no longer attract "their kind of people" and that its quality would be lower because "you get what you pay for." Consequently, they deserted the program in favor of other providers whose $100-plus price they found to be reassuring. Thus, instead of the 80 percent reduction in price stimulating increases in numbers, participation in the program declined by over 30 percent.

Estimating Elasticity

Managers can use two hands-on approaches to estimate price elasticity: review of the historical record and willingness to pay. These tools supplement rather than supplant the intuition and experience of managers.

Data are used in analyses of historical trends, but they may not accurately predict reaction to a price change because the current environmental context may be different. Accordingly, the example given below shows the review can usefully be supplemented by asking a sample of current users a few critical questions that will help guide the price change decision. The historical approach requires agencies to maintain detailed records of the impact of past price increases on use. Electronic technology makes this relatively easy to do, but many public leisure agencies have not customized the technology so it incorporates data that would facilitate such analyses.

The advantage of the willingness-to-pay approach is that information is solicited on elasticity directly from existing users rather than relying on what happened in the past. The technique's disadvantage is that respondents indicate their behavioral intentions, and their intentions may be different from their actual behavior.

Review of the historical record. This approach is used to assess the likely impact of a new price through a review of the sensitivity of users to past price changes. Figure 5-5 shows the historical reactions to price increases during a festival's 15 years of operation.[20] The figure shows the event was characterized by a remarkable level of price inelasticity. With the exception of the last price increase to $6 in Year 13, every year in which the admission price was raised, the attendance increased substantially. In Year 13, attendance declined 3 percent, but the increase from $5 to $6 represented a 20 percent increase in price. Figure 5-4 shows no price increase in Years 14 and 15. Nevertheless, the decrease in attendance in those years was substantially greater than that in Year 13, suggesting that price may not have been a prime reason for the slight attendance decline in that year. The historical evidence suggests that the festival's visitation has not been adversely affected by increases in price.

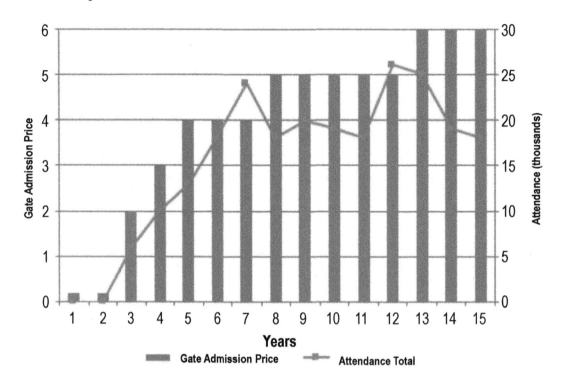

Figure 5-5. Historical Record of Attendance Total and Admission Price at a Festival

This festival was organized by a non-profit organization. It had two primary goals: to generate awareness for its mission of restoring historical properties and to raise revenue to support that mission. Given that maximizing revenue was a primary goal, managers explored the potential for raising price again in Year 16.

The historical review was supplemented with information derived from surveying a sample of visitors. The survey provided six valuable insights:

i. Forty-nine percent of attendees had not visited any other festival in the previous 2 years, while only 19 percent had been to three or more other festivals in that period. This suggests that many visitors did not perceive a direct substitute experience to be available. Further, 40 percent of those who went to another festival named the same alternative. Its admission price was $12.95, over double the existing price at the festival of interest.

ii. The survey found that 47 percent were first-time visitors, suggesting they had no firm price expectation stemming from previous experiences. Others had the $12.95 alternative as part of their expected price for admission to a major festival. Thus, the existing $6 price was unlikely to be firmly established in memory as the "expected" or "fair" price. (The importance of this is discussed in Chapter 9.)

iii. The $6 price accounted for only 8 percent of the average total trip expenditures of out-of-town visitors. It seems unlikely that an increase in admission price would deter them when it is such a small proportion of total costs.

iv. Almost 60 percent of visitors reported household incomes over $70,000, so they were relatively affluent.

v. Given 47 percent were first-time visitors, it is likely that for some a higher price was used as an informational signal confirming that this was a high quality festival.

vi. Visitors were given a 5-point value-for-money scale ranging from *very poor value* to *very good value* and responded to the following question: "Given the admission price my group paid, our experience at the festival was... ." Sixty percent reported it was *good* or *very good value*, 32 percent *fair value*, and only 8 percent *poor* or *very poor value*.[20]

These data led the organization to raise the price 33 percent from $6 to $8. Their judgment proved correct in that attendance increased in Year 16 to 21,000.

Willingness to pay. When the Corps of Engineers implemented fees for the first time at some of their reservoir parks, it surveyed a sample of visitors to identify the day use and annual pass fees they should charge. Each respondent received one of the 50 options shown in the matrix in Table 5-4. Each was asked: "If the fee was $__ per vehicle per day or $__ per vehicle for an annual pass, which of the following options would you choose?" Respondents were given three options: pay the per-vehicle per day fee, pay for an annual pass, or indicate they would not visit the site anymore.[21]

Table 5-4

Projected Revenue at Alternative Fee Levels for Harry S. Truman Lake

Annual Fee	Daily Fee				
	$1	$2	$3	$4	$5
$10	224,960	248,130	227,909	223,275	208,530
$20	289,204	343,759	313,217	255,292	210,637
$30	257,609	310,479	247,709	140,705	78,989
$40	244,128	337,019	250,026	160,927	78,989
$50	269,194	397,682	320,168	206,003	91,627

Results in Table 5-4 show that at Lake Harry S. Truman maximum revenue would be raised if the annual pass were $50 and the day fee were $2. The results show the loss of revenue associated with setting fees too high would be greater than the revenue lost by setting them too low. That is, the revenue projections in the $1 daily fee column are substantially greater than those in the $5 column across all the given annual fee options. The data suggest that the reaction of many respondents to increasing the existing price from $0 to $5 would be to cease visiting the site.

The projections in Table 5-4 are recognized as minimal estimates of revenue for two reasons. First, they reflect respondents' behavioral intentions. Some who indicated they would cease visiting would likely reconsider the decision if they failed to find an alternative substitute. Second, when asked their willingness to pay, some would likely engage in "strategic bidding." That is, they report an unwillingness either to pay the day fee or to purchase an annual pass with the expectation that this will dissuade managers from implementing the fee program, when in fact their real response is that they would pay the fee. They seek to influence the outcome by not revealing their true reaction because it is in their self-interest to give false responses.

This proved to be the case with this study at Truman Lake. Across all 50 options, almost half the visitors checked the third option; that is, they would no longer visit the site. However, as the data in Table 5-3 indicate, this simply did not occur. Indeed, 3 years after the fee program was implemented, visitation at the lake increased by 16 percent.[14]

THE RATIONALE FOR DIFFERENTIAL PRICING

A single price for all users is an imperfect compromise because users differ in their willingness and ability to pay for a leisure service and in the amount of value they attach to it. Hence, their elasticities also differ. Most agencies seek to create a price structure that aligns with these differences by offering discounts to those who are likely to have difficulty paying the regular price and by charging premiums to capture consumers' surplus from those who are willing to pay more for additional increments of benefit.

This strategy of charging different users a different price for the same service, even though there are no proportional differences in the cost of providing the service, is termed "price segmentation" in the marketing field and "price discrimination" in economics. However, both of these terms have exclusionary connotations that are contrary to the inclusiveness which is sought in the delivery of public leisure services. Accordingly, in this context, the term "differential pricing" has been adopted.[22]

Differential pricing balances the weights assigned to each of the two principles that guide all public leisure service pricing decisions. The Benefit Principle states that those who benefit from a public service should pay a price that covers the cost of delivering the service. Thus, for example, because the benefits associated with an adult softball league in a middle class suburb are likely to accrue almost exclusively to the 1% of residents who play in it, they may be expected to pay a price that covers all costs because the other 99% of residents receive no benefit from the service.

However, the Ability to Pay Principle directs that as far as possible no residents should be excluded from participating because they lack the funds to do so. In some communities in which discounts for the economically disadvantaged are proposed based on social justice arguments, there is political resistance. The source of the resistance may be ideological or pragmatic. The political reality for many elected officials is that they are unlikely to be reelected if they raise taxes. Hence, they search for areas in which tax subsidies can be reduced.

Leisure service managers are frequently exhorted by elected officials "to operate like a business," by which they mean reduce costs and increase revenues so the agency's subsidy from taxes is minimized. Typically, it is relatively difficult to communicate with disadvantaged groups, they are less leisurely literate, and they are more price sensitive.

Because these factors make them costly to service, and because they generate relatively low amounts of revenue, it is tempting to withdraw from the commitment to ensure services are accessible to them in order to appease the pressures to reduce tax subsidy.

In this climate, discounts for the economically disadvantaged are vulnerable to being discontinued. If this occurs, an agency no longer serves all residents in the community. If that issue is framed as a trade-off between financial and access objectives, the latter will often be compromised. However, if the issue is presented to these elected officials through an economic lens rather than from a social justice perspective, it is likely to be more palatable and result in discounts being supported. There are three prongs to the economic case.

First, a substantial empirical literature has verified the aphorism: You are what you were yesterday. That is, the leisure behaviors in which adults engage are learned in youth and endure throughout the life span. If people do not acquire leisure skills in their formative years, they are unlikely to participate in leisure in their adult lives.[23] Thus, discounting to encourage youth to participate is an investment in the field's future economic viability. However, this argument is unlikely to resonate with elected officials whose focus is on short-term reelection rather than on the long-term well-being of their constituents.

A second economic prong is to articulate the economic consequences of not having the economically disadvantaged engage in leisure services. These may be framed, for example, in terms of savings in health care costs from alleviating obesity. Quoting the U.S. Surgeon General: "Americans can substantially improve their health and quality of life by including moderate amounts of exercise in their daily lives" (p. 3), and "health benefits appear to be proportional to the amount of activity; thus every increase in activity adds some benefits" (p. 2).[24]

Similarly, the potential of recreation programs for alleviating juvenile delinquency was the primary rationale for establishing recreation as a public service in the field's formative years.[25] A comparison of the subsidies provided to encourage youth to engage in a leisure agency's programs with the costs incurred when they enter the criminal justice system may be used to frame the economic case.

However, the strongest economic argument is the different elasticities of users, which means that discounts can generate net revenue for agencies they would otherwise forego. Differential pricing is a market-oriented response to users' heterogeneity that enables a leisure agency to increase its revenues and the number of participants using a service. It means finding credible and sustainable ways to serve different segments at different prices.

The ultimate manifestation of differential pricing is setting a customized price, which is the maximum each individual is willing and able to pay. Clearly, that is administratively non-feasible, but it is feasible to segment users into price-sensitive groups, enabling managers to customize a price that is most appropriate for users in each segment. Establishing a range of prices that is sensitive to the maximum each group is willing and able to pay will yield the most revenue. Consider the following hypothetical example:

- A large outdoor public swimming pool that opens for the summer months charges an admission price of $7 per person for all who are 4 years of age or older. On average, the pool receives 200 visits a day. Almost all of its costs are fixed: debt charges, heating, number of lifeguards, front desk personnel, maintenance costs, etc. For the most part, these costs remain the same irrespective of whether 200 or 300 people visit the pool. For an economically disadvantaged family of five, $35 for admission is not feasible, so they are excluded. If a discounted price of $3 is made available to the economically disadvantaged, so the family of five pays $15, an additional 100 visits a day from this group would occur. That would translate to over $2,000 per week in additional net revenue the leisure agency would receive that would not be forthcoming without the discount.

This accomplishes the access goal, but uses an economic framework to make it more palatable to those who are more focused on financial outcomes. It was pointed out in Chapter 4 that most leisure facilities have high fixed costs and low variable costs. Hence, if there are no capacity constraints, as long as discounted price exceeds the variable costs, agencies capture revenues that would be forgone at the regular price.

Conditions for Effective Implementation of Differential Pricing

Three fundamental conditions must exist if differential pricing is to be effectively implemented. First, it is only politically and ethically acceptable and viable if it does not arouse antipathy or resentment from a threshold number of users who are paying the regular price, and if it is culturally consistent with a jurisdiction's normative values so there is no widespread indignation within the community. If users say: "It is unfair to charge us more than you charge them," it is untenable. Communities evaluate fairness by whether a discount is justifiable and reasonable. However, communities' prevailing normative value systems vary, so discounts to particular subgroups that are accepted in one community may not be deemed appropriate in another community.

The second condition is that those receiving a service at a lower price must not have the opportunity to engage in arbitrage, that is, to resell it at a higher price to those who are willing to pay more for it. This leads to the creation of a parallel or gray market in which consumers' surplus is captured as private gain by the resellers and the revenue does not accrue to the public agency. Unauthorized differential pricing and an arbitrage situation that was unwittingly created at Yosemite National Park illustrates the need to protect against resale:

- Large blocks of reservations for some of Yosemite's 900 campsites for peak times were being secured as soon as they were offered for sale. They were purchased for $20, but were then resold on eBay and similar sites for much as $100. Also, to protect the resource, the National Park Service limited the number of hikers ascending Half Dome to 400 per day and charged $1.50 for a permit. Again, these were resold by scalpers. Individuals were exploiting the situation for personal gain, when these funds should have been accruing to the National Park Service and the public who owned the resource.

There were two ways to resolve this issue. First, the National Park Service could have created an official differential pricing process by either auctioning or premium pricing some proportion of the reservations on eBay while meeting their mandate to be accessible by selling the remainder at the original price and auditing those who purchased them. Second, which was the approach they adopted, they could implement auditing procedures for all. Thus, Yosemite rangers subsequently required those possessing permits to show identification that matched the reservation and prohibited name changes on permits.

Similarly, a large proportion of the vast public lands in the West administered by the Forest Service and the Bureau of Land Management is leased to private ranches for cattle grazing. The federal government's lease fee is substantially below market rates. Accordingly, it was concluded: "Some permit holders were sub-leasing grazing allocations for between $4.49 and $9.26 per animal per month, while paying the federal government a grazing fee of $1.40" (p. 8).[27] It was noted that the federal fee "covers barely half the costs of federal range management programs" (p. 10).[27]

The third condition relates to the fairness with which differential prices are applied among subgroups and the consistency with which they are implemented across all the leisure services an agency provides. This condition is termed "horizontal equity," and it mandates that equals should be treated equally (i.e., users within a given category should pay the same price for the same service at the same time and location). Effectively, this condition merely applies to the basic principle of equality under the law.

Horizontal equity contrasts with vertical equity, which takes account of people's ability to pay. While vertical equity applies across income levels, horizontal equity refers to fairness at a given income level. It means addressing issues, such as the experience described in Figure 5-6.[26] The data in Table 4-1 show wide disparities in the per person subsidy of users in 23 recreation programs. Since the economic status of users in these programs is likely to be similar, is it fair that those in youth basketball programs receive a per participant subsidy of $34, while taxpayers support those in youth volleyball and football programs with subsidies of $73 and $195, respectively?

My nine-year-old daughter is a member of the local swim club, a nonprofit organization offering the only opportunities for advanced swimming instruction in the community. All active members are children. Parents administer the club. They handle hiring and paying the coaches; conduct extensive fund-raising activities; organize meets and serve as meet officials; and provide transportation for children who wish to compete in out-of-town meets.

The swim club is given the use of several lanes at one of the city pools throughout the year at times of the day that cause minimum inconvenience to other pool users. For the use of the pool, my daughter is charged $200 each year. I have no quarrel with this charge; it is reasonable. However, I sense injustice and inequity when I observe that no charges are imposed by the city on other youth recreation activities.

Little League, junior soccer, and junior softball, like the swim club, are operated by nonprofit organizations. Unlike the swim club, however, these groups are permitted to use city facilities without charge. The purpose of Little League baseball is "to provide an outlet of healthful activity and a training under good leadership in the atmosphere of wholesome community participation." This purpose is the same as the purpose of the swim club.

My daughter's friend who is the same age and lives next door plays junior soccer and junior softball. Another friend across the street plays Little League baseball and junior soccer. Neither of them is required to pay anything to the city for use of the fields. Why is my daughter charged and the other children not charged?

This year it is likely to cost my city around $70,000 to maintain, irrigate, and operate the new Little League complex, with floodlights, recently constructed at a cost of $800,000. Since there are approximately 500 children in the Little League program, the city is subsidizing each child in the program to the extent of approximately $140.

The swimming pool was built for general public use, and the swim team is given lowest priority. The sports fields were constructed exclusively for the use of the Little League club. What differentiates Little League from the swim club? Why does the swim club pay a pool user fee while the Little League club does not pay a field user fee?

This vignette illustrates the type of horizontal inequity that frequently occurs in the pricing structures of youth recreation programs. The reason for free use for Little League is probably historical. In the old days, the games were played on an undeveloped farmer's field. Parents built whatever improvements were necessary, mowed the grass, marked and dragged the fields, and performed other maintenance tasks.

Over time this situation has changed. In most cities, these functions are performed by city staff on city-built facilities and improvements. In my community, junior soccer and junior softball have been able to take advantage of the historical precedent of free use by Little League because they are similar types of activities.

An additional dimension to the inequity issue arises when my second daughter's main recreation interest—ice skating—is considered. The rink in our city is operated by an entrepreneur; the city provides no ice skating opportunities. A two-hour session costs $8.00. The city does not offer her a $140 subsidy. Why is she discriminated against because her preference happens to be ice skating rather than Little League, soccer, or softball?

Indeed, her case for a subsidy may be stronger than that of her friends who play Little League. The city did not have to invest $800,000 of taxpayers' money in building the facility that she uses. Instead, the private sector paid for it at no cost to the taxpayer. Because she receives no capital improvement support from the city, is it not equitable that she should receive a greater participation subsidy?

If horizontal equity is to be achieved, the city is faced with two alternatives. The first is to permit all organizations offering youth recreation opportunities to use city facilities without charge. This approach ensures that children from low-income families will not be excluded because of inability to pay. In the example used earlier, it is possible that low-income children are excluded from the swim club because of the requirement to pay a $200 per year pool use charge.

Consider the implications of pursuing this policy for my city. Suppose the swim club is given free use of the pool. Clearly, it is inequitable to give club members free admission and exclusive use of some lanes, while other children who do not have these privileges are required to pay. To be equitable and treat equals equally, the city must also offer free use of pools to all children who are not members of the swim club.

Because the primary swimming pool users are children whose admission represents a substantial source of revenue, cities are reluctant to initiate such a policy. Hence, the second alternative approach to achieving horizontal equity is to charge all nonprofit youth sport organizations that use city facilities comparable fees.

Figure 5-6. Inequitable Pricing of Youth Sport Activities[26]

Consistency across like subgroups raises questions, such as Is it fair to give discounts to all senior citizens irrespective of their economic status, when among the rest of the community they are given only to the economically disadvantaged? (This is discussed in Chapter 6) or Should golfers be required to pay a price that covers all costs, while tennis players are not charged for use of the courts? Consider the following complaint:

- I am a golfer. Why must the price for golf be set at a high level that ensures revenues will cover costs, when this is not done at other recreation facilities? If my taxes go to support all the other activities, why should they not also go to support the activity in which I participate? It is my feeling that the city should not discriminate against a person just because of the kind of recreation he or she enjoys.

In a broader context, consider the following conundrum:

- The U.S. Department of the Interior traditionally has leased Bureau of Land Management lands to ranchers at a heavily subsidized rate to graze their cattle. Environmentalists have long argued that ranchers should be charged a full market rate. However, national parks are heavily subsidized because admission charges cover less than 10 percent of their operating costs. Is it equitable to charge ranchers full market price while continuing to subsidize national park visitors?

In this federal lands context, the grazing fee subsidy and arbitrage described create horizontal inequity in the industry:

The current system provides benefits to a small percentage of the country's livestock producers. Of the almost 400,000 livestock producers in the 16 Western states, there are 23,000 permit holders; they represent only two percent of the nation's 1.6 million livestock producers. Most small producers are found in the Midwest and Southeast. If any livestock producers deserve a subsidy, surely it is these small producers. Why should all producers be taxed to benefit a few who are largely located in the West? Indeed, why should taxpayers in general pay to benefit an industry that receives other forms of economic protection from the government? (p. 10)[27]

Users care about the price others pay for the same service, and the online environment makes it relatively easy to share experiences and arouse resentment. The belief that others who are like you are being treated more favorably creates a sense of unfairness. Hence, segments paying different prices must be perceived by all concerned to be different. Perceived fairness will depend on the justification given for price differences. An agency's responsibility when adopting differential pricing is to explain explicitly how segments are different so the fairness of the price difference is apparent to all. The more aware people are of the differences justifying different prices, the less resistant they will be. Thus, conceptualization, rationale and information dissemination are crucial parts of the differential pricing process. These actions are consistent with the growing requirement to enhance transparency in government.

A common rejection of the requirement to treat equals equally that occurs in multiple leisure service contexts is application of the "Robin Hood" Principle. This is especially prominent in enterprise-provided services. It involves charging some users a higher price than it costs to deliver a service and using the surplus revenues to subsidize other users of that service or other services. Adam Smith[28] advocated such a policy and viewed it as a form of progress in taxation:

> When the toll upon carries of luxury, upon coaches, post-chaises, etc. is made somewhat higher in proportion to their weight than upon carriages of necessary use, such as carts, wagons, etc., the indolence and vanity of the rich is made to contribute in a very easy manner to the relief of the poor. (p. 725)

A leisure director described the Robin Hood Principle in these terms:

> A sliding scale for after-school programs is appropriate. To me, this is similar to the progressive principle of the income tax—those who are wealthy, pay more. Take, for example, the case of a widow in our program who works all day and is raising three children. We let her set her own fee. Sometimes she pays $20, sometimes $10, sometimes nothing for her three kids. The regular price is $50 per child per week, and because it's an enterprise fund, other users have to pay her share—but that's ok.

Others may argue that this strategy is inequitable and ask: "Why should users be singled out to subsidize her? If some users of a service should be subsidized, shouldn't the cost of the subsidy be shared by the whole community? Isn't it unfair to select some citizens to carry this compensatory burden solely because they happen to be users of the service?" Some agencies generate surplus revenues from golf facilities and use them to subsidize other services. Essentially, this is a premium that captures consumers' surplus, but golfers may legitimately question why they, rather than all taxpayers, should be responsible for the subsidy.

Bases for Differential Pricing

Figure 5-7 indicates that differential pricing is accomplished by using discounts and premiums and that these can be conceptualized as leverage points around the fulcrum of a regular price. The notion of a fulcrum suggests that the two approaches to some extent are counterbalancing. The discounts considered in Chapters 6 and 7 facilitate operationalization of the Ability to Pay Principle, while the six potential premiums discussed in Chapter 8 are vehicles for implementing the Benefit Principle.

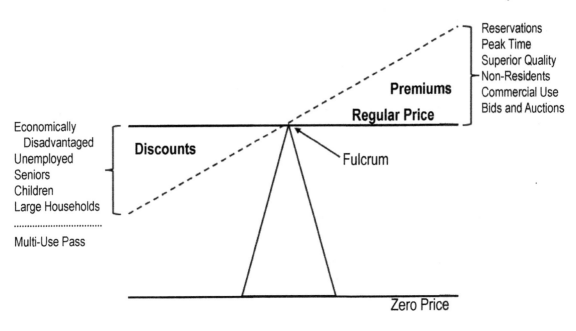

Figure 5-7. A Taxonomy of Differential Price Opportunities

Many of the discounts and premiums shown in Figure 5-7 are traditional. They have been widely accepted without question because they are long-standing cultural norms in leisure agencies. If a differential structure has been established for a long time, it becomes a cultural norm and is often expected to continue, even though the true economics of the situation suggest the differentiation is unwarranted. However, in recent years, many agencies have experienced their biggest budget cuts since the early days of the tax revolt 40 years ago. In this environment, discounts are likely to be subjected to challenge and review, while additional options for premiums are likely to be explored. The analyses offered in Chapters 6, 7 and 8 reveal inequities that are being perpetuated and opportunities missed because the assumed rationales for some discounts and premiums are mirages and myths, while opportunities for others have been overlooked.

SUMMARY

The law of market demand suggests that the quantity demanded of any service falls (rises) as its price rises (falls). However, this is predicated on the assumptions that buyers' actions are rational—so they always act to maximize utility—and that price is the most significant determinant in a purchase decision. In the real world, these assumptions are fallacious in multiple situations. Notwithstanding these caveats, the basic premise that as price goes down visitation and use will increase is appropriate in many real-world contexts.

Invariably, some users would be willing and able to pay more for a service than the price they actually pay. This potential revenue that they "leave on the table" is termed "consumers' surplus."

Users have different sensitivity to different price levels. This sensitivity is termed "elasticity." When visitation declines (increases) by a smaller percentage than the price increase (decrease), demand is said to be inelastic, whereas when visitation declines (increases) by a larger percentage than the price increase (decrease), it is elastic.

Four main factors influence price elasticity: proportion of the composite trip cost attributable to the monetary price; availability and relative prices of substitute services, but the impact of substitute services is influenced by the strength of users' loyalty or affinity to a service and the extent to which it is an important element in their lifestyle; users' income levels; and the existence of a strong price–quality relationship.

Managers can use two hands-on approaches to estimate price elasticity. Data are used in analyses of historical trends, but they may not accurately predict future demand behavior because contexts change over time. The alternative approach is willingness to pay, in which information is solicited directly from potential users. In this process, respondents indicate their behavioral intentions, and these may be different from their actual behavior.

Charging a single price for all users is an imperfect compromise because users differ in their willingness and ability to pay for a leisure service and in the amount of value they attach to it. To accommodate these differences in elasticity, leisure agencies typically offer discounts to those they anticipate will have difficulty paying the regular price and charge premiums to capture consumers' surplus from those who are willing to pay more for additional increments of benefit. This strategy of charging different users a different price for the same service, even though there are no proportional differences in the cost of providing the service, is termed "differential pricing."

Differential pricing enables the Benefit and Ability to Pay Principles that underpin all pricing actions to be reconciled. If discounts are not offered to the economically disadvantaged, one of two undesirable outcomes will occur: (i) Prices will be set at a level that is too high for them, so those whose need for the service is greatest are effectively excluded, which abrogates the Ability to Pay Principle, or (ii) to preclude such exclusion, prices are set at a low level for all, resulting in a large consumers' surplus among those who can pay more and abrogation of the Benefit Principle.

In communities where there is political resistance to discounts based on social justice arguments, the same end may be accomplished by presenting the discount as an economic response to different elasticities among potential users that enables revenues from a service to be maximized.

Three fundamental conditions must exist if differential pricing is to be effectively implemented: It must not arouse antipathy or resentment from a threshold number of users who are paying the regular price; those receiving a service at a lower price must not be able to resell it at a higher price to others; and there is horizontal equity (i.e., users within a given subgroup pay the same price for the same service at the same time and location).

REFERENCES

1. Scottish Sports Council. (1993). *The impact of variations in charges on usage levels at local authority sports facilities: Four case studies.* Edinburgh, Scotland: Author.

2. Howard, D. R., & Crompton, J. L. (1984). Who are the consumers of public park and recreation services? An analysis of the users and non-users of three municipal leisure service organizations. *Journal of Park and Recreation Administration, 22*(3), 33–48.

3. Coalter, F. (1993). Sports participation: Price or priorities? *Leisure Studies, 12,* 171–182.

4. Kay, T., & Jackson, G. (1991). Leisure despite constraint: The impact of leisure constraints on leisure participants. *Journal of Leisure Research, 23,* 301–313.

5. Taylor, P., Panagouleas, T., & Kung, S. P. (2011). Access to English public sports facilities by disadvantaged groups and the effect of financial objectives. *Managing Leisure, 16,* 128–141.

6. Parasuraman, A., Zeithaml, V. A., & Berry, L. L. (1985). A conceptual model of service quality and its implications for future research. *Journal of Marketing, 49,* 41–50.

7. Bovaird, A. G., Tricker, M. J., & Stoakes, R. (1984). *Recreation management and pricing: The effects of charging policy on demand at countryside recreation sites.* Aldershot, England: Gower Publishing.

8. Clawson, M., & Knetsch, J. L. (1966). *The economics of outdoor recreation.* Baltimore, MD: The Johns Hopkins Press.

9. Gratton, C., & Taylor, P. (1995). From economic theory to leisure practice via empirics: The case of demand and price. *Leisure Studies, 14,* 245–261.

10. Stevens, T. H., More, T. A., & Markowski-Lindsay, M. (2014). Declining national park visitation: An economic analysis. *Journal of Leisure Research, 46,* 153–164.

11. Walsh, R. G., Peterson, G. L., & McKean, J. R. (1989). Distribution and efficiency effects of alternative recreation funding methods. *Journal of Leisure Research, 21,* 327–347.

12. More, T. A. (1999). A functionalist approach to user fees. *Journal of Leisure Research, 31,* 227–244.

13. Foderaro, L. W. (2013, February 15). Public recreation centers looking to stem exodus. *New York Times,* A16.

14. Calkin, D. E., & Henderson, J. E. (1997). *Evaluation of effects of implementing day-use fees at Corps of Engineers Recreation Areas* (Technical Report R-97-1). Washington, DC: U.S. Army Corps of Engineers.

15. Heilbrun, J., & Gray, C. M. (1993). *The economics of arts and culture: An American perspective.* Cambridge, United Kingdom: Cambridge University Press.

16. Millward Brown International. (1991). *Pricing in the arts report 1990.* Warwick, United Kingdom: Millward Brown Market Research.

17. Evans, G. L. (1999). The economics of the national performing arts – Exploiting consumer surplus and willingness-to-pay: A case of cultural policy failure? *Leisure Studies, 18,* 97–118.

18. MacGregor, H. E. (2000, May 2). Governor announces plan to cut park fees. *Los Angeles Times.*

19. Lucas, G. (2001, November 5). Visitors flood parks after user fee cuts: Understaffed rangers find resources stretched thin. *San Francisco Chronicle.* Retrieved from http://www.sfchronicle.com/news/article/Visitors-flood-parks-after-user-fee-cuts-2860934.php

20. Crompton, J. L., & Love, L. L. (1994). Using inferential evidence to determine likely reaction to a price increase at a festival. *Journal of Travel Research, 32*(4), 32–36.

21. Reiling, S., McCarville, R. E., & White, C. M. (1994). *Demand and marketing study at Army Corps of Engineers day-use areas* (Miscellaneous Paper R-94-1). Washington, DC: U.S. Army Corps of Engineers.

22. Howard, D. R., & Crompton, J. L. (1980). *Financing, managing, and marketing recreation and park resources.* Dubuque, IA: Wm. C. Brown.

23. Scott, D., & Willis, F. K. (1998). Adolescent and adult leisure patterns: A reassessment. *Journal of Leisure Research, 30,* 319–330.

24. U.S. Department of Health and Human Services. (1996). *Physical activity and health: A report of the Surgeon General.* Atlanta, GA: Author.

25. Crompton, J. L., & Witt, P. A. (1999). Insights from our past. *Trends, 35*(4), 4–9.

26. Crompton, J. L. (1984, September). Treating equals equally: Common abuses in pricing public services. *Parks & Recreation, 1999,* 67–71.

27. Shannon, R. E. (1990). Grazing fees on public lands: A system under siege. *Western Wildlands, 1990,* 7–12.

28. Smith, A. (1976). *An inquiry into the nature and causes of the wealth of nations.* R. H. Campbell & A. S. Skinner (Eds.). Oxford, England: Clarendon Press. (Original work published in 1776)

Chapter 6

Differential Pricing

Discounts for the Economically Disadvantaged and Unemployed

- A caveat: Price's limited influence on participation
- Guiding principles for discounts
- Discounts for economically disadvantaged households
- Discounts for the unemployed
- Summary

It was pointed out in Chapter 5 that a convincing economic case for offering discounts to those who are economically disadvantaged can be made based on differing elasticities of demand. However, three questions are likely to arise in such discussions. The first question is: Who qualifies as being economically disadvantaged? If discounts are given to some who are wrongly assumed to meet this criterion, they are being provided with a subsidy that is not justified. Conversely, if discounts are not given to those who qualify as economically disadvantaged, revenues are being forgone and residents are being unjustly excluded from the service. The second question is: What should be the magnitude of the discount? The third question is: How should it be implemented? These three questions are addressed in the context of low income households and the unemployed, but an important caveat is discussed first.

A CAVEAT: PRICE'S LIMITED INFLUENCE ON PARTICIPATION

Many leisure facilities are expensive to construct and operate. If the private sector were the exclusive provider of leisure services, the revenues needed to cover these costs would require prices to be set at such a high level that many (perhaps most) residents could not afford to participate. Tax subsidized leisure services traditionally have been justified either by the social equity argument of an obligation to provide equal opportunities for all residents irrespective of their financial resources or on the basis of communitywide benefit, such as improved health or reduced juvenile crime, that is presumed to emanate from individuals' participation.

Those justifications have encouraged subsidized leisure services to be provided as part of a city's mandate to "protect the health, safety and welfare" of its residents. The social equity argument positions participation by the economically disadvantaged not as a privilege, but as a right. They pay taxes like other residents. Effectively servicing them is a primary justification for subsidizing leisure services. However, in Chapter 1, it was pointed out that composite price is multi-dimensional. Ingredients of it, such as transportation costs, equipment costs, organizing schedules, opportunity costs of time and psychic costs, are often sufficiently strong constraints for the economically disadvantaged that even free admission would not lead to their participation. This explains why, as highlighted in the discussion in Chapter 2 on facilitating appropriate income distribution through pricing, their participation invariably lags substantially compared to that of non-disadvantaged residents.

Discounts for the economically disadvantaged are ubiquitous in leisure agencies. The implied assumption is that price is a major obstacle to their participation. It was emphasized in Chapter 5 that elasticities are likely to be different among a population, and it is often assumed that price discounts for those whose economic status causes them to place a relatively low priority and valuation on participation will persuade them to engage.

However, this assumption has been consistently challenged in empirical findings and has been found to be overly simplistic. The decline in visitation to the major national parks between 1993 and 2010 was partially attributed to increases in the real cost of gasoline during this period, which is a major component of the composite price of visiting the parks.[1] But the authors pointed out that many other factors unrelated to price may have contributed, such as

The new fascination with all the things video (videophelia)" (p. 156)[1] . . . changes in demographics, and changes in the socioeconomic structure of the population. For example, the idea of national parks evolved in the latter half of the 19th century when the U.S. was a culture dominated by northern Europeans. Today, the country is evolving to include far more Hispanics and Asians, groups that may not share the cultural tradition of interest in the parks and the recreational activities associated with them. We are also a more urban/suburban nation today than we have been in the past, and that very urbanization could have been responsible for gradually changing outdoor recreation preferences that have begun to show up in participation patterns. Moreover, available leisure time may have declined for some people and schedules for both adults and children have become more complex. (p. 163)[1]

When probability samples of residents in three U.S. cities were presented with a list of 12 factors that could inhibit their participation in leisure activities, the results were remarkably consistent across the cities and across income categories:

Five of the top seven constraining factors could be attributed to lack of interest . . . price does not appear to be a serious barrier to participation, "It costs too much to participate" ranked close to the bottom on the overall lists of constraints, affecting the participation rate of not more than eight percent of the respondents in any of the cities. (p. 45)[2]

The authors observed:

It is important to note that the substantial underutilization of public recreation resources by low income respondents is *not* primarily attributable to monetary cost considerations. In all three communities, fewer than ten percent of low income respondents felt fees and charges levied for park and recreation services were an obstacle to their participation. (p. 40)[2]

Many who did not use public recreation facilities were not constrained or excluded by price; they simply had no interest in using them.

Similar findings were reported in several studies in the U.K. In a survey of U.K. households, only 1 percent of non-participants spontaneously referred to the expense of participation as a constraint.[3] This apparently low salience of price in the decision of whether to participate was reinforced by two studies in the U.K. focused on cultural activities. In a study of museums and galleries, attributes were examined that would attract people to attend, and it was concluded that free admission was not an important attribute—the quality of exhibits was much more important.[4]

In another investigation in the arts, it was reported:

Price was not a spontaneous barrier to attendance . . . only 1.5 percent of the 1,298 mentioned price was a reason for non-attendance [at live arts events] . . . dislike of the art form and too far to travel were the main reasons for rejection. (p. 3)[5]

When those with no intention of visiting the next year were presented with a list of factors, price-related reasons were cited by only 3 percent, while no interest (80 percent) dominated the responses. Among existing arts goers who intended to visit the arts less often in the next year, only 2 percent cited financial reasons. Much more important were general "lifestyle factors," for example, aspects of non-participants' family and work lives and the associated time constraints.[5] Overall, lack of time to participate was the largest obstacle. The combination of no time, family commitments and work commitments was referred to by more than two out of five (42 percent) respondents. In line with other studies, women were much more likely to refer to family commitments and males to work commitments.

In a study in four U.K. cities in which general household respondents were asked what inhibited them from greater participation in sport or active recreation, only 4 percent identified price as a potential obstacle. The author concluded: "In particular current non-participants do not appear to view the cost of admission as a major determent" (p. 180).[3] In a survey of facility users in those four communities undertaken after substantial increases in admission prices had been implemented, slightly higher figures were reported, with between 6 percent and 13 percent saying that price was a potential constraint that might reduce their use of a center.

The authors of another U.K. study found a relatively large proportion of their personally interviewed sample reported that "financial constraints" restricted their leisure activities. However, the activities primarily affected were going out for drinks, meals or entertainment, while only 4 percent said such constraints adversely affected their participation in sport. Further, for the most part, those who were affected found ways to surmount their constraints, so the authors concluded "financial constraints appear to be an absolute barrier for only a small minority of those affected by them" (p. 309).[6] They went on to observe: "In Britain widespread use is made of reduced-price policies as a method of increasing sports participation among low-participation groups. This study has suggested, however, that sports participation is affected much more by time constraints than by financial ones" (p. 312).[6]

It was concluded in an analysis of access by disadvantaged groups to public sports facilities in England over 10 years that despite government subsidies and substantial promotional efforts, "the evidence fails to show clear signs of improvement in the usage of these centres by disadvantaged groups (p. 134) . . . It may be sensible to not rely on price discounts to attract disadvantaged users" (p. 141).[7]

The evidence from these studies suggests price is a barrier for relatively few and that broader social and cultural factors are much more influential in explaining relatively low participation among the economically disadvantaged. Further, it has been argued that this is unlikely to change in the medium to long term because as incomes rise and obligatory expenditures are satisfied, an increasing proportion of disposable incomes in advanced societies is likely to be available to spend on discretionary items, such as leisure. In contrast, time will remain a finite resource and therefore relative to income is likely to become the more binding constraint.[8]

Despite these findings revealing the relatively small influence of price on participation, there are four reasons for agencies to provide discounts for the economically disadvantaged. First, it seems inevitable given the increasing pressures on resources at all levels of government that prices will rise as efforts intensify to capture more revenue from consumers' surplus. Demand for these services is not inherently inelastic. In this scenario, there is likely to be an increasing number of residents willing to participate, but unable to pay the regular price. Some will be priced out of the market, while others will reduce their frequency of participation. The contention that this would be negated by the expected growth in real incomes discussed in the previous paragraph is not being realized among the low income groups. Later in the chapter (Table 6-4), it will be shown that while real incomes over the past 30 years have grown substantially among the highest income groups, the change for those below the 20th percentile has been relatively small.

Second, irrespective of how small the number of people excluded by price, there is an obligation to provide them with access and also an opportunity to elicit a price elastic response from them that will enhance total revenue.

Third, there is a political imperative for elected officials to be seen addressing the social equity issue. Whenever substantive prices are considered, some are likely to argue that they will lead to exclusion. Indeed, in the past, high prices have been established with the implicit intent to deter "people who are not like us" from using a facility. This sometimes becomes a strong emotional and high visibility issue in elections. Providing discounts preempts this opposition, even though some may be skeptical that this represents a genuine effort to enhance participation. On occasion, officials may be prompted by a need to be seen addressing the issue rather than by authentic concern.

Finally, if state or federal grants have been used in financing a facility, their conditions are likely to include a requirement that it be accessible to all segments of the community:

- Lake Isle Park was a failing private country club that was purchased by the town of Eastchester in Westchester County, New York, as a public park. The site included an 18-hole golf course, five pools, eight tennis courts and a clubhouse with a large banquet hall. Part of the funding came from a grant of almost $780,000 from the Federal Land and Water Conservation Fund administered by the National Park Service (NPS). When voters agreed to issue bonds for the remainder of the funding, the referendum specified the park would be self-sufficient and not use tax revenues to support its $2.4 million budget. As a result, prices were high. The NPS alleged the club was akin to other country clubs in the area and discriminated against minority residents in the neighboring communities of Yonkers, New Rochelle and Mount Vernon. The alleged discrimination was exacerbated by non-residents of Eastchester being required to pay double the price charged to residents. The NPS spokesperson stated: "We provided funds to develop an outdoor recreation public park, not a country club." In a letter to the town, the NPS wrote:

  > Title VI of the Act states that no person in the United States shall, on the grounds of race, color, or national origin, be excluded from participation in, be denied benefits of, or be otherwise subjected to discrimination with respect to Federally assisted programs administered with the Department of the Interior. (p. B1)[9]

  The town was informed that unless it revised its prices to the satisfaction of federal officials, it could lose the federal money it receives for all its programs, not only recreation.[9]

GUIDING PRINCIPLES FOR DISCOUNTS

Six principles should guide decisions on discounts: avoid stigmatization, train frontline personnel, create widespread awareness, solicit input from the target groups, keep it simple, and offer discounted rather than free access to services.

Traditional "ask and you shall receive" approaches are unlikely to be successful in reaching the economically disadvantaged because they exacerbate *perceptions of stigma*. The barrier is raised even higher if there is extensive paperwork and bureaucratic demand for "proof" of status. It is humiliating to have to ask for a fee waiver, scholarship or "in-kind" work opportunity in lieu of paying the full price. People feel embarrassed and stigmatized: "You know, a lot of people who are on assistance . . . it is just one more piece of paper, one more person you have to tell how little money you're making" (p. 163).[10] To preserve their dignity, many will elect not to make such a request. Further, seeking this assistance requires a level of confidence that many who are economically disadvantaged do not possess.

Thus, mechanisms used to implement discounts should be discreet, automatic and preemptively offered by the leisure agency. Other participants and front-line service providers should not be able to readily identify discount recipients. Anonymity is important not only to avoid stigmatizing, but also to avoid "waving red flags" in the faces of those in a community who disapprove of special allowances to the economically disadvantaged.[11]

The term "economically disadvantaged" is nebulous and question-begging. Irrespective of their income level, most people could claim to be economically disadvantaged because there is always something they cannot afford. Long ago, it was observed:

> The poor man who says he can't afford better shoes for his children means that he and his wife would rather buy more food for them. The middle-income man who says he can't afford a holiday means he would rather keep up his smoking or motoring. The rich man who says he can't afford a boat is saying he prefers a Rolls. No one can have enough of everything. We all "cannot afford" something. (p. 234)[12]

Inevitably, this makes establishing a qualifying benchmark income level that defines who is "poor" controversial, while verifying and auditing compliance create additional layers of intrusive harassment and administrative effort. Accordingly, leisure agencies typically adopt criteria already used by others to determine who is eligible for discounts. This minimizes their administrative costs and avoids the passionate emotions and political arguments that frequently accompany such decisions. Schools, through their subsidized meal programs, and welfare and unemployment agencies are likely to have established criteria. Nurturing a collaborative relationship with each of these entities appears to be an obvious way forward because leisure discounts would complement the efforts these agencies already make to serve these groups.

As the public response to poverty is multi-dimensional and several social service agencies are involved in helping the poor, coordination with them to alert their clients to a leisure department's discounted programs would enhance awareness. Too often, these sister agencies are unaware of what leisure agencies offer. Potentially, these partners could serve as brokers, who could adopt either an active or a passive role. While legal constraints likely prevent them from releasing the names of eligible clients to a leisure agency, they could play an active role by advising their clients on how to access its offerings or by mailing out or otherwise disseminating the agency's discount passes to their clienteles. For example, one agency had the school district send an individualized letter to the parents of every child who was in the school's free meals program inviting their children to participate in a subsidized vacation day-camp program. The agency solicited corporate sponsors to fund the program. This comprehensive approach has the added advantage of creating awareness of an agency's offerings among the economically disadvantaged. If an active role is deemed not to be feasible or appropriate, a passive role would involve them serving as a conduit for disseminating information on how to receive a discount pass and about what recreation services are available.

Front-line staff should be trained to ensure they are fully briefed on the discounts and empathetic in their approach to those using them. Without such training, their responses are likely to vary. Too often, those who are poor are not made to feel welcome when they use an agency's services.[13, 14] Consider the following vignettes:

- Some front-line staff members were very helpful in assisting participants apply for and use the program, while others seemed unaware of even their own program policies intended to help these individuals. As one member noted, "I think it depends on who you get and what information you get because you get different information from different people. 'No, we don't do this,' 'Yes we can help you.'" Another noted that "Even the woman I see all the time at the community center wasn't aware of exactly what was on the card...its confusing even for people who work with it daily." (p. 166)[10]

- Users sometimes find themselves in the position of explaining that they require financial assistance. For example, one group member told a story of how staff actions added dramatically to her embarrassment over using the card. "I went and said, 'You offer help for people who are on lower incomes,' and she said, 'No I don't think we do.' I said, 'Yes you do.' There were people standing around and the [staff member] yelled, 'Guys do we offer help for people on low incomes?'" Such lack of knowledge was exacerbated by the staff member's striking lack of sensitivity. (p. 167)[10]

The potential for embarrassing people is especially prominent if discounted access requires additional paperwork:

You are standing there [applying] and the girl behind the counter goes, 'We've got to do more paperwork,' so immediately she's all put out and treats you completely differently. It's true. It's happened more than once and it doesn't matter where you go. As soon as they see the leisure access card they think, 'Oh great, here we go again.' You see it cross their faces and it's embarrassing, especially when you've got 15 people standing behind you. (p. 163)[10]

A third guiding principle is that discounts should be *well publicized* on a continuing basis. The absence of timely and relevant information about discounts, and more broadly about recreation opportunities, is a prominent factor limiting participation among the economically disadvantaged. Finding out what programs exist, their characteristics and the benefits they offer is not an easy task for this target group. Unfortunately, many agencies are passive in their approach to discounting. Once a policy has been established, they make little effort to seek out those in the community who are being targeted. If those individuals are not aware of a discount program, it literally does not exist in their minds, and the agency has failed in its responsibility to serve them. The challenge is exacerbated if some among the economically disadvantaged lack English reading skills. Indeed, recent non-English speaking immigrants are likely to be disproportionately represented among these groups, so written promotional materials will not reach them.

A fourth guiding principle is soliciting *input and feedback from the targeted groups* regarding eligibility criteria, accessing process, magnitude of the discounts, promotional strategy, duration of the pass and so forth. Invariably, this will yield insights that will elude an exclusively top-down approach.[10]

Clarity and simplicity will enhance the effectiveness of discounts. When discounts are applied to selected services and not to others, or if services have different levels of discounts, confusion and disillusionment are likely. A particular concern arises when programs are co-produced with a non-profit organization. Typically, this occurs when an agency provides the facility, but programs at it are delivered by non-profit organizations. In these cases, the discount should apply, especially if the programs are promoted by the agency:

> [The discount applied] only to programs offered directly by the city park and recreation department. It could not be used for programs offered by sport groups, not-for-profit organizations, or even selected community center programs (they were often operated by neighborhood groups). Consequently, the leisure access card could help them gain access to only limited leisure opportunities. In one case, for example, a community group controlled the hockey program so the discount was of no use to her son. She and her son were despondent over such limitations. "The kids start to feel it [disappointment over the limitations]. My oldest is ten and he is starting to say, 'Mommy, why can the other kids play hockey and I can't go play hockey?'" (p. 164)[10]

Offering *free access* to the economically disadvantaged may create control or rationing problems, and it may also have a substantial opportunity cost. Agency and city resources are finite. On average, one third of a U.S. park and recreation agency's operating budget is self-generated.[15] An opportunity cost is associated with all revenues that are forgone. Forfeiting revenue from discounts by offering free access will effectively restrict the opportunities for others who are disadvantaged, because less revenue is available to deliver other services they may desire.

Like all residents, the economically disadvantaged pay for a portion of an agency's services through taxes, so they have a right to access those services. However, by using a service, they receive increments of benefit that their non-user disadvantaged peers do not. Hence, they should be required to make an additional payment. Further, making a payment may enhance an individual's sense of self-esteem and social responsibility. Thus, the sixth principle is that *it is not appropriate to offer free access* because of the potential opportunity cost and because it would abrogate the Benefit Principle and the rule of horizontal equity, which was discussed in Chapter 5.

DISCOUNTS FOR ECONOMICALLY DISADVANTAGED HOUSEHOLDS

Measures of Who Is Economically Disadvantaged

Most of the benchmarks developed by others that leisure agencies may elect to adopt as their criteria for ascertaining who is economically disadvantaged are based on the federal government's definition of minimum poverty thresholds. Hence, to be fully informed, leisure managers need to understand how their thresholds are defined.

Thresholds were first calculated and published by the Census Bureau in 1959 and are updated each year. At the time they were developed, the official poverty thresholds represented the cost of a minimum diet defined by the Department of Agriculture multiplied by 3 to allow for expenditures on other goods and services. The methodology has remained unchanged. The threshold amounts are intended to reflect the minimum income families require to meet their basic needs.

In 2015, the poverty level for a family of two adults and two children was $24,250. This threshold was adjusted up or down by $4,160 for each child added or subtracted from this family unit. The estimate of family resources includes not only earned income, but also cash benefits from the government such as Social Security and Unemployment Insurance benefits; Supplementary Security Income; public assistance benefits, such as Temporary Assistance for Needy Families (TANF) and workers' compensation benefits.

Some argue that the thresholds are too low, stating it is unreasonable to expect a family of four, for example, to meet its basic needs with an income of $24,250. Because the thresholds are national averages, they point out this is likely to be especially challenging in areas where the cost of living is high.

This traditional poverty measure has the important virtue of being calculated in the same way for over half a century, which enables year-to-year comparisons to be made and trends to be identified. However, it has been increasingly criticized as being too arbitrary and not reflective of contemporary social and economic realities and government policy.[16]

Accordingly, in 2010, the Census Bureau established the Supplementary Poverty Measure (SPM). It is published annually and complements (not replaces) the traditional poverty measure. An alternate methodology is used to calculate poverty thresholds and to measure households' resources to assess whether they meet the thresholds. A more expansive definition of what constitutes a family is used that includes not only individuals residing at the same address who are related, but also any co-resident unrelated children who are cared for by the family (e.g., foster children) and any cohabiters and their children.

Instead of being based only on food, the SPM poverty thresholds are derived from the cost of a set of goods including food, clothing, shelter and utilities (FCSU) and a small additional amount to allow for other needs, such as household supplies, personal care and non-work-related transportation.

The SPM's definition of household resources supplements the cash income in the traditional measure with in-kind benefits that households may receive that can be used to buy the basic bundle of goods (FCSU), but also subtracts non-discretionary expenses for critical goods and services not included in the thresholds. These additional elements are summarized in Table 6-1.

Table 6-1

Components That Together with Cash Income Make Up the SPM Definition of Family Resources

Plus:	Minus:
Supplemental Nutritional Assistance (SNAP)	Taxes (plus credits, such as the Earned Income Tax Credit [EITC])
National School Lunch Program	Expenses Related to Work
Supplementary Nutrition Program for Women, Infants and Children (WIC)	Child Care Expenses
Housing Subsidies	Medical Out-of-Pocket Expenses (MOOP)
Low Income Home Energy Assistance (LIHEAP)	Child Support Paid

On the plus side of Table 6-1, SNAP (commonly known as food stamps) provides a benefits card, similar to a bank card, which is used to subsidize food purchases by low income women and their children up to the age of 5. Housing subsidies comprise rental and mortgage interest subsidies that are either project based (public housing) or tenant based (vouchers). Assistance with utility bills (LIHEAP) is provided, which may be in the form of cash payments, vendor payments, landlord payments or vouchers.

Necessary expenses subtracted from the estimate of resources a family has available to buy FCSU are federal, state and local income and social security payroll taxes (FICA), less earned income tax credits, by which on average $3,000 of federal, state and local income taxes paid by working individuals is refunded; work-related expenses, such as travel to work and purchase of uniforms or tools; expenses paid for child care while parents work; medical out-of-pocket expenses, including payments of health insurance premiums and co-payments for prescription drugs and physician visits that are not paid by insurance (including Medicare Part B premiums paid by seniors); and child support received from other households.

What the Measures Show

Trends from 1959 in the traditional poverty measure are reported in Table 6-2. The proportion of Americans living in poverty has stayed within a narrow band between 11.3 percent and 15.1 percent since 1970. However, because the nation's population has increased, more people are now living in poverty. Thus, 14.9 percent in 2014 represented 47.5 million Americans, which was the largest number in the 55 years in which this traditional measure has been calculated.

Table 6-2

Percentage of U.S. Citizens below the Traditional and SPM Federal Poverty Levels by Age

Year	All Ages %	Children Under 18 %	18–64 %	65 and Older %
		Traditional Measure		
2014	14.9	21.5	13.3	10.2
2010	15.1	22.0	13.8	8.9
2005	12.6	17.6	11.1	10.1
2000	11.3	16.2	9.6	9.9
1995	13.8	20.8	11.4	10.8
1990	13.5	20.6	10.7	12.2
1985	14.0	20.7	11.3	12.6
1980	13.0	18.3	10.1	15.7
1975	12.3	17.1	9.2	15.3
1970	12.6	15.1	9.0	24.6
1965	17.3	21.0	N/A	N/A
1959	22.4	27.3	17.0	35.2
		Supplementary Poverty Measure		
2010	15.9	17.9	N/A	15.8
2011	16.1	18.1	15.5	15.1
2012	16.0	18.0	15.5	14.8
2013	15.5	16.4	15.4	14.6
2014	15.3	16.7	15.0	14.4

The traditional measure's poverty threshold for a family of two adults and two children in 2013 was $23,624. Thresholds for the alternative SPM vary by housing tenure status. Table 6-3 shows they are higher than thresholds in the traditional measure for owners with mortgages and renters. These two groups make up approximately 76 percent of the population.[17] Proportions of the population below these thresholds are shown in the last row of Table 6-2. The SPM indicates 48.7 million (15.3 percent) of Americans were poor in 2014 compared to 47.5 million (14.9 percent) using the traditional measure. It shows lower poverty rates for children, higher rates in the 18–64 age cohort and a substantial increase in the proportion of those 65 and older in poverty.[17]

Table 6-3

Two Adult, Two Child Poverty Thresholds in 2013

Traditional Measure	$23,624
Supplemental Poverty Measure:	
Owners with a mortgage	$25,639
Owners without a mortgage	$21,397
Renters	$25,144

Emergent Inequality

Some regard such a large number of Americans below the poverty level as evidence of social inequality and injustice. In support of their argument, they point to the dramatic increase in income inequality in the U.S. during the past three decades. The 400 richest Americans now average $5 billion, so their aggregate net worth is $2 trillion. This is more than the combined net worth of the bottom 50 percent of all Americans.[18] Census data from the late 1940s to the early 1970s show that income during that period grew at nearly the same pace at all points on the income ladder.

Since that era of shared prosperity ended, Tables 6-4 and 6-5 show there has been widening inequality in average after-tax income across quintiles and the top 1 percent of the income distribution.[16] Real after-tax incomes between 1979 and 2011 grew by less than 50 percent over this period for 80 percent of households, by 78 percent for those in the 81–99 percentile and by a stunning 200 percent for those in the highest 1 percent of household income.

Table 6-4

Comparison of Household After-Tax Incomes by Quintile 1979–2011 (in 2011 dollars)

Quintile	1979	2011	% Increase
Lowest quintile	$16,300	$24,100	48
21–40 percentile	$30,700	$42,100	37
41–60 percentile	$43,600	$59,000	35
61–80 percentile	$57,000	$82,600	45
81–99 percentile	$91,000	$162,000	78
Top 1 percentile	$343,700	$1,031,900	200

Table 6-5

Comparison of Households' Shares of After-Tax Incomes by Quintile 1979–2011

Quintile	1979 %	2011 %	Increase %
Lowest quintile	7.4	6.3	−15
21–40 percentile	12.3	10.9	−11
41–60 percentile	16.5	15.2	−8
61–80 percentile	22.2	21.0	−5
81–99 percentile	34.6	35.6	3
Top 1 percentile	7.4	12.6	70

*After-tax income is defined as market income plus government transfer (i.e., cash or in-kind benefits from federal, state or local governments) minus federal income tax.

The richest 1 percent of Americans increased their share of total income from 7.4 percent in 1979 to 12.6 percent in 2011. While 80 percent of households saw their share of income decline, the shares claimed by those in the 81–99 percentile and the top 1 percent increased by 78 and 200 percent, respectively. Remarkably, these shares represent a substantial decline for the top 1 percent. In 2007 before the onset of the Great Recession, the top 1 percent share of income was 16.7 percent. Its decline to 12.6 percent in 2011 reflects declines in investment income associated with the collapse of the economy at that time. Inequality rose at the same substantial rate during this 1979–2011 period *within* each major racial/ethnic group, as richer whites, African Americans and Latinos pulled away from their poorer co-ethnics.[19]

The causes of this extraordinary growth in inequality during the past three to four decades are much debated, but it has risen from some combination of globalization, technological change, de-unionization, superstar compensation, changing social norms and a shift in public policy toward trickle-down economics.[19] This widening inequality has strengthened the arguments in many communities in support of discounts for the economically disadvantaged.

Alternate Methods of Implementing Discounts

The mechanisms used to operationalize discounts for the economically disadvantaged can be classified into three categories: means testing, proactive and reactive. Each of these is discussed in the following subsections.

Means testing. Conceptually, means testing is perhaps the most equitable mechanism for assessing the level of discount that should be given to low income households. It enables a discount to be delivered to the right people at the right level of subsidy. A sliding price scale would be used so those whose income is lowest would pay the lowest price. However, applicants would be required to provide evidence of their low income status (e.g., income tax returns), and the embarrassment and loss of dignity involved makes it likely some would be dissuaded from participating. Further, it would involve substantial administrative time and cost to implement, and those charged with that responsibility are also likely to experience personal discomfort.

An example of a recreation center where an adaptation of means testing was used to assess price is described in Figure 6-1.[20] It appeared to be successful in minimizing embarrassment to applicants and removing financial barriers to participation and did not seem to be abused. Nevertheless, the administrative burden on staff suggests that in most contexts this type of customized approach would not be feasible.

A non-profit recreation center serving a culturally and socioeconomically diverse community in a large city recognized that users differed in their ability to pay the membership fee. The membership fee was all inclusive, so it gave access to all the center's services, classes and programs. Accordingly, managers of the center initiated an approach for subsidizing fees according to the financial means of each user. In essence, it was an informal means test, but no formal thresholds or income level criteria were designated. It was believed this approach would maintain the dignity of individuals and empower staff to be responsive to each individual's needs. No proof of need was required. Honest disclosure by applicants was assumed.

The initiative enabled potential users to negotiate personally with staff a mutually acceptable monthly price for the membership. The process comprised four steps:

1. Tour the facility to ensure their needs could be met by the center's programs and services.
2. Arrange an appointment with staff to discuss their particular requirements for subsidy.
3. Complete a 20–30-minute interview with a staff member to discuss their personal situation and to develop a mutually agreeable monthly payment plan.
4. Arrange for a pre-authorized payment plan unless extenuating circumstances existed.

Six members of the center's staff were specially trained on how to conduct the negotiations and the interviews, which were intentionally informal.

Over the first six years of the initiative, total membership increased from 3,322 to 5,550. The number of non-assisted memberships remained consistent around 2,500, suggesting the assisted member policy had little impact on non-assisted participants. The increase in membership was attributable to assisted numbers whose members went from 638 (19.2 percent of all members) to 2,608 (47 percent) over the 6 years. Research showed that the assisted participants primarily comprised low income workers, the unemployed and single mother heads of households and that their participation rates equaled those of non-assisted members.

The magnitude of the subsidy among assisted members increased substantially over the 6 years. They were paying an average of 39 cents a day at the outset, but this declined to 22 cents. In contrast, the daily averages for non-assisted members increased from 86 cents to $1.01. This suggests either that assisted members were being drawn from deeper levels of the economically disadvantaged or that they were "gaming the system."

Nevertheless, total center revenues increased from $762,500 to $1,287,000 because of the increase in membership numbers.

The customized process was time consuming and emotionally demanding for all concerned. It was uncomfortable for many applicants and for the administrators who were charged with differentiating between those who were unable to pay the full fee and those unwilling to do so and with negotiating the level of subsidy. Another concern was that because this was a non-profit center with no tax subsidy, it used the Robin Hood Principle. That is, revenues from the fees of non-assisted members were used to fund the subsidies for assisted members.

Figure 6-1. Customizing Subsidies for the Economically Disadvantaged at a Recreation Center[15]

Voluntary means testing is a variation on the theme. It is a policy of "pay what you can, but you must pay something" with a "recommended" price suggested. In such cases, the user price may be called a donation. Some museums, for example, have adopted this approach. This is a participative pricing mechanism in which the price setting is delegated to users. It is not a common strategy in the private sector because the obvious risk is that users could exploit their control and pay a price well below break-even level. However, it has been adopted successfully by rock bands that invite their fans to download albums and pay as much as they want, by restaurants that allow customers to select the price they pay for food[21] and by a few professional soccer clubs in the minor leagues in the U.K.:

- Albion Rovers is a professional soccer club playing in the Scottish League Two. It reduced the season ticket price from $220 to $15, which covers the administrative cost of offering it. The club invited fans to "pay what you can." The goal was to increase the number of supporters at home games. The club's chairman said,

  > Obviously we're hoping people pay a bit more than $15 and they pay what they can afford, but we're grateful for any donations provided to us. Our hope is this initiative will be received in the true spirit it is intended and people will be fair and honest in their evaluation of what is affordable and realistic. (p. 21)[22]

The available evidence suggests that abuse of the mechanism predominantly does not occur because the normal service–price exchange relationship between a leisure agency and its users that is focused on money does not apply. The context has changed so the transaction is now governed by social exchange norms. These predict that if people abuse the process, they will be subjected to social disapproval by others and to the pangs of their conscience. For most, the benefit they receive from "low-balling" the recommended donation will be outweighed by the opprobrium associated with violating social norms or the self-loathing they experience from having acted selfishly and abrogated the social norms of fairness and reciprocity. The likelihood of abuse is especially minimal because the prices for most public leisure services are relatively low, so for most people it seems unlikely that avoiding them would be worth the costs of abrogating social norms. The price users pay is likely to be determined by the recommended donation and by their reference price (i.e., the price for the service they believe to be fair). This approach allows the economically disadvantaged to participate without embarrassment or administrative hassle. It is likely to attract more users, to increase word-of-mouth promotion and build up a positive pricing image among low income populations, and to increase revenues.[21]

Proactive strategies. Proactive strategies require a discount be given to those eligible for it without them having to ask. The three most common of these are to give discount cards to all households with children on subsidized school meals or on welfare, to use time pricing, or to use geographic pricing.

The vehicle most often used to operationalize discounts is a multi-use pass valid for a given time, usually 3 months. Typical names for it are Passport to Leisure, Leisure Access Card and Recreation Passport. Two examples of passes are shown in Figures 6-2 and 6-3. The Preston Passport to Leisure gave free admission to low income residents, residents with disabilities and unemployed residents and their dependents, and it limited the discount to off-peak times. The Wellington Passport was more extensive in that it included veterans and retirees and could be used at any time. To minimize abuse and avoid having to show an ID on each visit, a photograph was required by both programs. However, in some communities, this may cause some not to participate because of fear of being identified as undocumented immigrants.

WHO QUALIFIES FOR USE?
Any resident of the Borough of Preston who is:
a. In possession of a UB40.
b. A School leaver who has not yet received a UB40.
c. Registered Disabled.
d. In possession of a family income supplement book or a supplementary benefit book.

PLUS
their spouses and children of the above when they accompany them.

HOW DO THEY GAIN ADMISSION TO THE FACILITIES?
First you must obtain your "Passport to Leisure" Card. You apply for this at either Preston Pools, West View or Fulwood Leisure Centre and must bring with you a passport size photograph of yourself and any of your family who are to be included. There is a simple form to complete and sign. You must also produce relevant documents to prove that a) you do qualify for the Passport to Leisure in one of the categories and b) you are a resident of Preston.

WHAT DOCUMENTS WILL I NEED TO BRING?
To prove you are a resident of Preston:
a document such as a rates demand, driving licence etc. which PROVES where you live (just a letter will not do).

To prove that you belong to one of the categories:
a. If you are unemployed a UB40. For their dependants a Child Benefit Book or Form A14N or Form UB0.
b. If you are Registered Disabled a Registered Disabled green card or Invilidity Benefit Book or Form BS49.
c. If you have just left school a letter from your former Headmaster to say you have left School.
d. If you are in the low income group: Supplementary Benefit book for a Family Income Supplement book or Forms A14N or A124.

Don't forget your photographs.

YOUR PASSPORT WILL BE VALID FOR 6 MONTHS AND COSTS JUST 50p EACH TIME IT IS RENEWED.

WHEN WILL FACILITIES BE AVAILABLE?
Basically, during the daytime from Monday to Friday. You are, however, advised to check with facilities beforehand to make sure that your activity is available. There will be times when organised groups, such as schools may have priority.

WHAT TIMES WILL FACILITIES BE AVAILABLE?
Generally between 10 am and 12 noon and 2 pm to 5 pm although there will be variations in each location.

CAN I BOOK ANY FACILITIES IN ADVANCE?
Activities which are NORMALLY BOOKABLE, such as squash, can be booked by the "Passport" holders by contacting the centres after 9.30 am ON THE DAY (you must quote your passport number when making your booking).

CAN I HIRE EQUIPMENT?
Yes, you will be able to hire the equipment in the normal way but you will be required to pay the normal hire fees and deposit.

WHAT ELSE IS INVOLVED IN THE SCHEME?
It is hoped that, as the scheme grows, coaching courses will develop, so too will "come and try it" sessions where you can sample new sports.

Please note that the information contained in this leaflet is correct at the time of going to Press but is liable to immediate alterations.

Figure 6-2. Preston Passport to Leisure

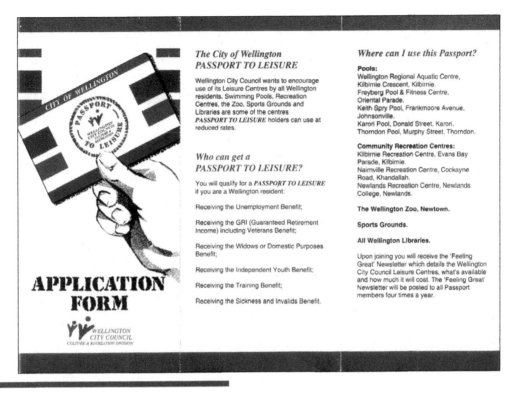

Figure 6-3. Wellington Passport to Leisure

If the *subsidized school meals or welfare criteria* are used, applications for the discount card, or the card itself, are sent to all households on these agencies' lists. For example, the city of Sacramento mails discount coupons for city recreation programs every 3 months to families who receive welfare assistance. The coupons are valid for the 3-month period. Families do not need to call or apply; they automatically receive them as long as they receive welfare assistance. The coupons offer the following:

- Half price admission to summer swim lessons, all recreation classes and all athletic programs.
- Free admission to the Art Museum, History Museum and Zoo.
- Free child admission to swimming pools and for golf rounds with a paid adult.

A traditional vehicle intended to facilitate social inclusion is to offer discounts for selected times or days. This was widely adopted in the early days of tax-supported public recreation. For example, a typical arrangement at a 19th century swimming pool might be as follows:

- Free admission on Tuesdays, Wednesdays and Saturdays.
- 15-cent fee on Mondays and Fridays.
- 25-cent fee on Thursdays.

Because 5 cents would buy a quart of milk or a pound of sugar at that time, the fees were substantive. Arrangements such as this ensured the pool could serve the whole community. However, the downside was that the fee structure segregated users along class lines. The poor had no choice but to swim on the free days, those of moderate means were likely to choose to swim on the days when the entrance price was 15 cents and the rich could afford to swim on Thursdays. A corollary of this arrangement was that the price structure would likely determine the level of crowding, so those paying 15 and 25 cents presumably would have a superior experience.[23]

Contemporary examples of this mechanism exist, but it is not widespread. For example, the National Park Service offers free admission to 133 of its sites that charge a fee on the following days:

- Martin Luther King Day (January).
- Presidents Day weekend (February).
- Opening weekend of National Park Week (April).
- National Park Service Birthday (August).
- National Public Lands Day (September).
- Veterans Day (November).

Elements of this approach are embedded in differential pricing for peak and off-peak pricing, but this is primarily intended to ration a service at peak time and to collect consumers' surplus through the use of premiums rather than to create discounts for the economically disadvantaged. Indeed, many of those with low incomes likely have less flexibility in their schedules to take advantage of off-peak prices than do those who are more affluent.

Diversity undergirds the rationale for *geographic pricing*. While descriptive statistics using averages are effective in identifying general trends, they disguise diversity. Examples abound. Thus, in 2011 per capita disposable income in the U.S. averaged $33,125, but while it was $43,734 in Connecticut, it was only $26,238 in Mississippi. Poverty levels among the states in that year ranged from 8.8 percent in New Hampshire to 22.6 percent in Mississippi. In metropolitan areas with populations over 500,000, they ranged from a low of 8.3 percent in the Washington, D.C.–Arlington–Alexandria metropolitan area, to a high of 37.7 percent in the McAllen–Edinburgh–Mission area.[24] Similar diversity occurs in income growth (Table 6-4), net worth (Table 7-3), income levels of different age groups (Table 7-4) and poverty levels among ethnic groups (Table 7-6).

Geographic pricing is a proactive discount strategy based on recognition that purchasing power and price elasticity in geographic locations are different. In the context of cities, this diversity is likely to be present among neighborhoods. For example, in New York City in 2011, 6.6 percent of households had an annual income greater than $200,000 a year, while one third of the city's population survived on Medicaid.[25] Neighborhoods tend to be relatively homogeneous. That is, residents within a neighborhood are likely to be of similar socioeconomic status (which is sometimes congruent with racial or ethnic composition). Thus, it does not appear to make sense to charge the same price for a service in all New York City neighborhoods. This was recognized by the Manny Cantor Community Center on East Broadway in New York City:

- The non-profit center has a distinguished history of community service dating back to its 19th century origins as a settlement house. It underwent a $55 million renovation and now provides a wide range of education, social service, arts and recreation programs, including a large and impressive gym for which fees are paid on a sliding scale. Families living in one of the area's many public housing projects pay $10 a month, those living in one of the neighborhood's many middle class co-op developments pay more and those living in luxury properties on the Lower East Side pay the top rate of $87 a month. Art classes at the center have a similar fee scale. As a result, about one third of the members come from each of the three groups.[26]

In the private sector, businesses with multiple outlets in a city (e.g., grocery chains, pharmacies, theaters, dental partnerships, opticians) are likely to charge different prices at each location reflecting differences in customers' income levels. Consider the following analysis:

Middle-class neighborhoods often have numerous grocery outlets serving customers with ample access to transportation (cars), which enables them to price-compare between outlets. Customers from higher-income neighborhoods place more value on their leisure time, making them less prone to price comparison; thus, they have a marginally increased willingness to pay. Meanwhile, customers in lower-income neighborhoods often suffer from lack of adequate transportation and less competition, enabling grocers to price products at a marginally higher level in lower-income neighborhoods than in higher-income ones. As such, grocery stores in middle-class neighborhoods often provide the lowest prices in comparison to those in either poorer or richer neighborhoods. While pricing products higher in higher-income neighborhoods is usually free from customer backlash, pricing products higher in lower-income neighborhoods is fraught with potential challenges. (p. 261)[27]

When city leisure agencies adopt this approach, it requires that managers price services in each neighborhood or at each center rather than set prices on a citywide basis. Some cities develop an index comprising multiple measures that defines the economic status of every neighborhood. This enables leisure managers to charge prices that are sensitive to the average income in a neighborhood. Thus, for example, tennis lessons, dance programs, adult fitness classes or after-school programs may be offered at multiple sites, but the price would vary according to the price sensitivity of the neighborhood. However, this flexibility should be accompanied by overall program revenue targets. Without this parameter, managers may overuse discounts either because of empathy with their patrons or because participation numbers are a factor in their evaluations. Occasionally, elected officials representing low income areas have protested this policy, arguing that it publicly stigmatizes residents in those areas. To protect against such protests, different names could be used for the same program in different locations so the differential prices are not conspicuous. This strategy is elaborated on in Chapter 11.

Reactive strategies. Three reactive strategies intended to provide discounts for low income households are widely used: ad hoc waivers at the discretion of agency staff;

scholarships provided by civic groups, partner businesses or welfare agencies; and "sweat equity." *Waivers granted at the discretion of agency staff* without being guided by specific criteria should be avoided. Inevitably, such a policy will result in accusations of favoritism and in inequities because of an inability to distinguish between those who are unable and those who are unwilling to pay. Managers need clear unambiguous criteria of when discounts should be provided to discourage potential abuse.

An alternative or complement to a formal discount policy is for agencies to *solicit philanthropic support* from businesses, foundations and civic groups or from partner welfare agencies to provide funds to cover the discounted amount of the price for low income individuals. The target groups are invited to apply for discounts and to provide evidence of their status. The evidence is sometimes a letter from someone who knows the family's needs, such as a school counselor, pastor or welfare organization, rather than an income tax or welfare document. Scholarships are awarded on the basis of greatest need until the donated funds are exhausted. San Francisco, for example, raises over $500,000 annually from philanthropic sources to pay for scholarships into its recreation programs. The subsidized lunch programs are used as the criterion for defining those who are eligible for the scholarships.

Sweat equity programs may be offered either in lieu of discounts or as complements to them. Those who cannot pay either the full or the discounted price have an opportunity to work for the agencies. They are paid in "Park Bucks" for their labor. These can be redeemed in payment for registrations, classes or facility admissions. Typically, the work includes non-skilled tasks, such as litter pick-up, clearing picnic table areas and grills, or assisting at special events. Participants usually have to provide the equipment or materials needed for the task, are required to sign a standard liability waiver and are required to complete a time sheet signed by a supervisor. Such programs are frequently offered only to children under age 18. If the children are very young (e.g., under 10), they must be accompanied by an adult who can help the child accomplish the assigned tasks.

DISCOUNTS FOR THE UNEMPLOYED

The U.S. Bureau of Labor Statistics calculates six alternate measures of unemployment, U1 through U6. Each measures a different aspect of unemployment. The official measure adopted by the federal government is U3, which follows that used by the International Labor Organization. It defines the unemployed as people without jobs who have actively looked for work within the past 4 weeks.

Table 6-6 shows that the U3 unemployment rate is consistently correlated with age. Among those in the 16–19 cohort, it is consistently approximately 3 times the national average, irrespective of whether overall unemployment levels are high or low, while among the 20–24 cohort it approaches double the average. Unemployment decreases consistently as age increases, so the lowest levels are always in the 55–64 age group.[28]

Table 6-6
Unemployed Workers: 1990–2015

Year	Number Unemployed	% Unemployed			
		All Ages	16–19	20–24	55–64
1990	7.0 million	5.6	15.5	8.8	3.7
2000	5.7 million	4.0	13.1	7.2	2.5
2005	7.6 million	5.1	16.3	8.7	3.2
2010	14.8 million	9.6	25.9	15.2	7.4
2015	8.7 million	5.5	18.1	9.9	3.8

The U6 measure is an often quoted, much broader alternative to U3. For the U3, only those who are unemployed and seeking full-time work are reported, whereas for the U6 measure, "marginally attached workers and those working part-time for economic reasons" are also counted. Many of these part-time workers desire full-time employment, but cannot find it. They are counted as employed in U3, but could be working as little as 1 hour a week. The "marginally attached workers" include those who have gotten discouraged and stopped looking, but still want to work. The increasingly ubiquitous adoption of robotics and electronic systems in manufacturing and service contexts, reducing the need for marginally skilled full-time workers, suggests that the U6 measure is likely to be a more accurate reflection of unemployment in the future. This measure is consistently approximately double the official U3 poverty measure. For example, in June 2015, the U3 measure showed 5.3 percent were unemployed, while the U6 unemployment rate was 10.5 percent.

It is not practical to use the U6 measure efficiently as a basis for offering discounts to the unemployed because of the challenges associated with identifying involuntary part-time workers and those who have quit searching. However, many of these people will likely qualify for low income discounts.

Implications for Leisure Managers

Unemployment is devastating to most who experience it. It often leads to deterioration in mental and physical health and, especially among the young, disruptive social behavior. In a pioneering book in which the impact of recreation programs on lives of the unemployed was evaluated, the author concluded: "Participation in recreational programs cannot be a satisfactory substitute for a job. What work removes, leisure cannot replace" (p. 158).[29] However, she went on to observe that if financial barriers are removed, recreation programs can likely partially mitigate the adverse effects of unemployment because

the losses incurred in unemployment are closely matched in typical motivations for taking part in leisure activities. Quests for identity, purpose, activity, social contacts, self-confidence, self-esteem, relaxation and physical and mental well-being — and even at the most basic level, the search for something to do — are the established stock-in-trade of the psychology of leisure. If unemployment leaves these needs unmet, leisure ought partly at least to be able to fulfill them. (p. 92)[29]

Thus, at a minimum, leisure services can fill time; offer relief from boredom; and if they are regularly scheduled, give structure, order and routine to each day. Beyond this, they have the potential to mitigate the isolation and exclusion caused by removal or disruption of social networks with work colleagues and to provide a sense of purpose and associated accomplishment that may help sustain self-esteem.

The unemployed are different from other groups discussed in this chapter as their need for financial assistance is often relatively short term. Further, their need varies widely as reported in another seminal study:

Although ability to pay may be a critical issue among unemployed adults and their families, data from this study suggest that financial needs vary widely among unemployed populations. Some respondents in the present study faced dire financial straits, whereas others were comfortable or only marginally uncomfortable. Financial need may be mitigated by the marital or partnered status of unemployed adults, the number of dependents under their care, and the housing arrangements in which they live. Unemployed adults who are supported by parents or living with roommates often get by with fewer financial resources than were necessary for individuals without such support. Others who had working partners were reasonably comfortable financially even while unemployed. (p. 180)[11]

However, the study's authors concluded that a majority of unemployed would be responsive to price discounts. As another author reported: "Income is a prime constraint on their leisure. Far from taking on new and varied leisure interests to absorb the time freed from work, financial restrictions mean that for most unemployed people, previous leisure patterns are curtailed" (p. 158).[29]

Discounts are most commonly offered through a multi-use pass entitling the unemployed to discounted access for a 3-month renewable period. Such a pass should be proactively distributed "automatically" to the unemployed. Size of the discount should be consistent with that given to low income groups. However, a payment should be required to ensure the pass is used responsibly and to mitigate the sense of it being a charitable handout.

It has been suggested that discounts for the unemployed are sometimes prompted not by authentic concern, but rather by a need to be seen being concerned. For example, in relation to the unemployed, one official observed: "The council offers free use to the unemployed as a political gesture. There has been little attempt to attack the problem of motivation of the unemployed" (p. 152).[29] This criticism could probably be generalized to other discounts for the economically disadvantaged, and it reinforces the recommendation discussed in Chapter 5 to frame discounts as a mechanism for generating additional revenue rather than in social welfare terms.

Some agencies have limited such a pass to the unemployed person, but that is myopic. Agencies should embrace the person's children and partner because all members of a family feel the adverse financial impact. Others have confined its use to off-peak times. Again, this is self-defeating because it means the person has difficulty using facilities in the evenings and on weekends with family and friends who are working.

To avoid stigmatization, leisure managers should establish working relationships with unemployment agencies that can proactively distribute passes to their clients. If extensive paperwork and bureaucratic hassle are involved, a discount program will not be effective. For children and seniors, eligibility for a multi-use pass discount is achieved by showing an ID with their age on it. A similar level of simplicity should be the goal for unemployed discounts.

SUMMARY

The assumption that price is a major obstacle to participation by low income groups is overly simplistic. At the current levels of price in most communities, it is a barrier for relatively few. Broader social and cultural factors are much more influential in explaining relatively low participation among the economically disadvantaged. Nevertheless, it is imperative they are offered because it is a social obligation; a political imperative; a potential source of additional revenue; and in some cases, an explicit requirement of state and federal grants.

Six principles should guide decisions on discounts. First, stigmatization should be avoided, so traditional "ask and you shall receive" approaches are unlikely to be successful because they exacerbate perceptions of stigma. The preferred alternative is adopting criteria already used by other agencies to determine who is eligible for discounts and proactively disseminating discount passes to those who qualify.

Second, front-line staff should be fully briefed on the discounts and empathetic in their approach to using them. Third, discounts should be well publicized on a continual basis. If low income individuals are not aware of a discount program, it literally does not exist in their minds. Fourth, input and feedback from the target groups regarding eligibility criteria, accessing process and so forth should be solicited. Fifth, clarity and simplicity will enhance the effectiveness of discounts. Finally, it is not appropriate to offer free access because it abrogates the Benefit Principle and the rule of horizontal equity.

Economically disadvantaged households are most commonly defined as those who do not meet the federal government's official minimum poverty thresholds. In 2014, 14.9 percent of Americans were in this category.

Three strategies may be used to operationalize discounts for the economically disadvantaged. Means testing is perhaps the most equitable mechanism, but is unlikely to be administratively feasible. However, voluntary means testing inviting users to "pay what you can" is a viable option in some contexts. Proactive strategies require a discount be given to those eligible for it without them having to ask. The vehicle most often used to operationalize discounts is a multi-use pass valid for a given time, usually 3 months. The three most common proactive mechanisms are to give discount cards to all households with children on subsidized school meals or on welfare; to offer discounts for participation at selected times or days; and to use geographic pricing, which recognizes that purchasing power and price elasticity in different geographic locations of a community are often different.

Three reactive strategies are widely used for operationalizing discounts: ad hoc waivers granted at the discretion of agency staff, which are likely to lead to accusations of favoritism and to inequities because of an inability to distinguish between those who are unable and those who are unwilling to pay; scholarships provided by civic groups, businesses or partner welfare agencies to provide funds to cover the discounted amounts; and sweat equity, whereby those who cannot pay the full or discounted price have an opportunity to work for the agency and pay for a program with their in-kind labor.

Discounts for the unemployed are likely to be short term. The reduction in family income makes it likely that some would be responsive to reduced prices. However, these should be extended to the unemployed person's children and partner because they will similarly be adversely affected by the loss of income.

REFERENCES

1. Stevens, T. H., More, T. A., & Markowski-Lindsay, M. (2014). Declining national park visitation: An economic analysis. *Journal of Leisure Research, 46,* 153–164.
2. Howard, D. R., & Crompton, J. L. (1984). Who are the consumers of public park and recreation services? An analysis of the users and non-users of three municipal leisure service organizations. *Journal of Park and Recreation Administration, 2*(3), 33–48.
3. Coalter, F. (1993). Sports participation: Price or priorities? *Leisure Studies, 12,* 171–182.
4. Museums and Galleries Commission. (1999). *To charge or not to charge.* London, England: Author.
5. Millward Brown International. (1991). *Pricing in the arts report 1990.* Warwick, United Kingdom: Millward Brown Market Research.
6. Kay, T., & Jackson, G. (1991). Leisure despite constraints: The impact of leisure constraints on leisure participation. *Journal of Leisure Research, 23,* 301–313.
7. Taylor, P., Panagouleas, T., & Kung, S. P. (2011). Access to English public sports facilities by disadvantaged groups and the effect of financial objectives. *Managing Leisure, 16,* 128–141.
8. Taylor, P., Owen, E., & Withnall, S. (2001). Increasing young people's attendances at the theatre: A case study in Sheffield, U.K. *Managing Leisure, 6,* 141–153.
9. Steinberg, J. (1993, August 13). Public park is too private to suit the government: Eastchester charges too much for use of a former country club, federal officials say. *New York Times,* p. B1.
10. McCarville, R. (2008). The design of financial assistance programs: Suggestions from those living in poverty. *Journal of Park and Recreation Administration, 26*(4), 157–168.

11. Havitz, M. E., Morden, P. A., & Samdahl, D. M. (2004). *The diverse worlds of unemployed adults: Consequences for leisure, lifestyle and well-being.* Waterloo, Canada: Wilfrid Laurier University Press.

12. Robinson, C. (Ed.). (2004). *The collected works of Arthur Seldon: Introducing market forces into "public" services.* Indianapolis, IN: Liberty Fund.

13. Collins, S. B. (2005). An understanding of poverty from those who are poor. *Action Research, 3*(1), 9–31.

14. Trusell, D. E., & Mair, H. (2010). Seeking judgment free spaces: Poverty, leisure, and social inclusion. *Journal of Leisure Research, 42,* 513–533.

15. Crompton, J. L., & Kaczynski, A. (2003). Trends in local park and recreation finances and staffing from 1964–65 to 1999–2000. *Journal of Park and Recreation Administration, 21*(4), 124–144.

16. Congressional Budget Office. (2014). *The distribution of household income and federal taxes between 1979 and 2011.* Washington, DC: Author.

17. Short, K. (2015). *The supplemental poverty measure: 2014* (Current Population Reports P60-254+). Washington, DC: U.S. Census Bureau.

18. Kroll, L., & Dolan, K. A. (2013, September 16). The Forbes 400: The richest people in America. *Forbes.*

19. Putnam, R. D. (2015). *Our kids.* New York, NY: Simon & Schuster.

20. Emmett, J. L., Havitz, M. E., & McCarville, R. E. (1996). A price subsidy policy for socio-economically disadvantaged recreation participants. *Journal of Park and Recreation Administration, 14*(1), 63–80.

21. Kim, J. Y., Nather, M., & Spann, M. (2009). Pay what you want: A new participative pricing mechanism. *Journal of Marketing, 73,* 44–58.

22. Press Association. (2014, May 8). Albion Rovers offer "pay what you can" season ticket from as little as £10. *The Guardian.*

23. Wiltse, J. (2010). *Contested waters: A social history of swimming pools in America.* Chapel Hill: University of North Carolina Press.

24. Bishaw, A. (2012). *Poverty: 2010 and 2011—American community survey briefs.* Washington, DC: U.S. Census Bureau.

25. Meier, A. (2013, July 28). Can't anyone here play this game? *New York Times Magazine,* 24.

26. Bellafanta, G. (2014, February 27). A community center for all income levels. *New York Times.* Retrieved from http://www.nytimes.com/2014/03/02/nyregion/a-community-center-for-all-income-levels.html

27. Smith, T. J. (2012). *Pricing strategy.* Mason, OH: South-Westson Cengage Learning.

28. U.S. Census Bureau. (2012). Unemployed workers: 1990–2010 Table 622. In U.S. Census Bureau (Ed.), *Statistical abstract of the United States.* Washington, DC: Department of Commerce.

29. Glyptis, S. (1989). *Leisure and unemployment.* Milton Keynes, England: Open University.

Chapter 7

Differential Pricing

*Discounts for Seniors and Children
and the Multi-Use Pass*

- Senior citizen discounts
- Discounts for children
- Large household discounts
- The multi-use discount
- Summary

Leisure agencies have traditionally offered discounts to seniors and children as well as to the economically disadvantaged and the unemployed. The conceptual distinction between these two groups is that while the criterion for the economically disadvantaged is financial need, the discount criterion for seniors and children is age. The implied assumption is that children and seniors have different price elasticities that merit discounts because their age cohorts are relatively economically disadvantaged. The extent to which that assumption is valid is examined in this chapter, first for seniors and then for children, and actions are recommended based on the analyses. This is followed by a discussion of the merits of discounts for large households, which, in effect, are a special form of children's discount. The fallacies and merits of multi-use discounts, which are analogous to quantity discounts in the private sector, are discussed in the last section.

SENIOR CITIZEN DISCOUNTS

In 2015, 47.8 million U.S. citizens were aged 65 or older. They accounted for 14.9 percent of the U.S. population. The number is projected to increase dramatically to 56 million by 2020 and to 82 million by 2040, at which time they will make up almost 22 percent of the population (Table 7-1).[1] Table 7-2 shows that over 60 years, the median average duration of retirement essentially doubled from 10.9 to 21.3 years for men and from 12.5 to 25 years for women.[2] The lengthening retirement period means that increasingly large time blocks are available for leisure pursuits. It has obvious implications for leisure agencies in that seniors will be a growing target market to be served.

Table 7-1
Projected Growth in Number of Seniors Over 65

Year	Millions	% of Total Population
2000	32.6	11.6
2010	38.6	12.5
2015	47.8	14.9
2020	56.4	16.9
2025	65.9	19.0
2030	74.1	20.6
2040	82.3	21.6
2050	87.9	22.1

Table 7-2
Life Expectancy at Age 65 and Age at Exit from the Labor Force (Medians)

Year	Age at Exit from the Labor Force		Life Expectancy at 65	
	Males	Females	Males	Females
Early 1950s	66.9	67.6	77.8	80.1
2013	61.6	60.5	82.9	85.5
	5.3	7.1	5.1	5.4

The image of a frail elderly person struggling to survive on a fixed pension perhaps supplemented by a meager interest income from modest savings is disturbing. Although such an image reflected reality for a large proportion of the elderly 40 years ago, it is misleading today. Poverty remains a problem in the United States, but as shown in both poverty measures in Table 6-2, those over 65 years of age are now on average no more likely to be poor than those in any other age group.

The increasing time blocks reported in Table 7-2 have been accompanied by remarkable changes in seniors' financial status. Their financial transformation has been one of this country's great national achievements in the past half century. In the traditional poverty measure, 14.9 percent of U.S. citizens in 2014 lived in poverty, but this dropped to 10.2 percent among seniors, which was far below that of children or non-senior adults (Table 6-2). In 1959 when the federal government first published this measure, 35.2 percent of seniors were below it. President Johnson's Great Society program helped change that status. By 1985, the proportion of seniors living below the poverty level for the first time (12.6 percent) was lower than that for the population as a whole (14 percent), and it has remained that way.

Seniors' income comes from four main sources: Social Security (35 percent); earnings (34 percent); private pensions (17 percent); and assets, such as interest, dividends and rents (11 percent).[3] These four sources have grown in recent decades.

The major contributor is *Social Security*. It contributes 90 percent or more of the income of 36 percent of seniors.[3] In 2015, the average monthly social security payment to retired workers was $1,328, while their spouses received on average $664. If Social Security payments were not available, the 2014 percentage of those over 65 below the supplementary poverty measure (SPM) poverty level would have increased from 14.9 percent to 51.0 percent.[4]

The Cost of Living Index, to which Social Security payments are linked, has risen faster than average wages primarily because of the relatively heavy weighting it gives to housing. Because many seniors own homes and do not take out new mortgages, their cost of living is unaffected by rises in housing costs. Even without the exaggerated cost of living benefits created by this indexing, Social Security has given seniors considerable bonus benefits. Current retirees generally receive much more in benefits than they paid in Social Security taxes during their working life. In effect, this represents a substantial subsidy to retirees from the working population.

Figures 7-1 and 7-2 show increasing proportions of seniors are remaining in the workforce and benefiting from the resultant *earned income*. In 2014, 20.8 percent of those over 65 were in the labor force and 44 percent of them were working full time, year-round.[5] This trend is likely to escalate given the abolition of mandatory retirement ages, the rising age for full Social Security benefits (now 66, rising to 67 in 2027), the need to finance more years of retirement (Table 7-2) and the improved health of the elderly. In addition, for many, the desire to continue working is motivated not by financial security concerns, but because they (i) feel "at the top of their game" and enjoy tackling the intrinsic challenges their work provides, (ii) enjoy their workplace friendships and social connections or (iii) want to give back to their community of worthwhile causes.[6]

Pension coverage beyond Social Security is virtually universal among government workers, while 42 percent of private sector full-time workers aged 25–64 reported having pension coverage in their current job. However, pensions are correlated with earnings, so while 67 percent of those in the top income quintile have private pensions, in the bottom quintile, the proportion slips to 11 percent.[5]

These sources of seniors' income are substantially augmented by in-kind health care subsidization from the federal Medicare and Medicaid programs. Over 55 million seniors over 65 are covered by Medicare. Because Medicare does not cover the cost of long-term care, seniors who lack the resources to pay for this need turn to Medicaid to meet those costs.

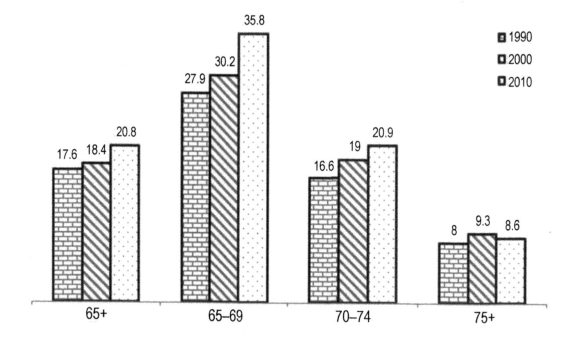

Figure 7-1. Labor Force Participation Rate for Men 65 Years and Older: 1990, 2000, 2010

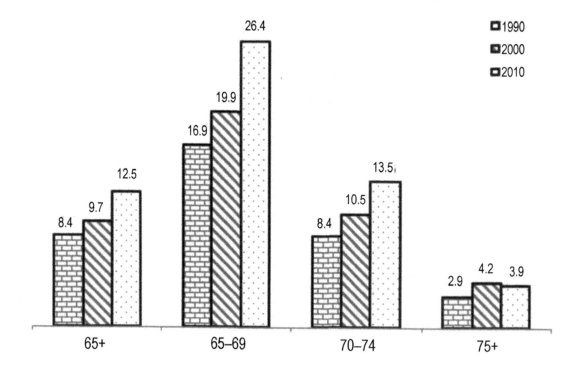

Figure 7-2. Labor Force Participation Rate for Women 65 Years and Older: 1990, 2000, 2010

Column 2 in Table 7-3 shows that the median *net assets* (total assets minus total debts) of the elderly are 2.5 times the median for the nation and that the elderly have accumulated substantially greater assets than has any other age cohort. The major component of their assets is equity investment in their homes, which is the highest of any age cohort. It accounts for 76 percent of the net worth of those over 65 (Table 7-3).[7] Assets decline in the 70–74 and over 75 cohorts, probably because they are used for financing living expenses in retirement. Clearly, assets can add to the resources used to meet basic needs. However, they are not included in the SPM poverty index because "assets can only ameliorate poverty temporarily" (p. 3).[4]

Table 7-3

Median Net Worth of Households, and Homeownership and Equity in Different Age Groups

Head of Household Age	Median Net Worth ($)	Homeownership (%)	Equity in Own Home ($)
All	68,828	66.9	80,000
Under 35	6,676	39.1	20,000
35–44	35,000	65.0	40,000
45–54	84,542	73.5	70,000
55–64	143,964	79.0	97,000
Over 65	170,516	80.5	130,000
65–69	194,226	81.6	125,000
70–74	181,078	82.4	130,000
Over 75	155,714	78.9	130,000

Table 7-4 shows income growth over the past three decades in 2013 adjusted dollars.[8] It shows that in real money terms, a general trend in all age groups was a consistent increase from 1980–2000. However, since 2000, that trend has reversed in every age group under 65, but it has continued to increase in the cohorts over 65. The percentage change over the three decades was insignificant for those in the 15–54 age range, but the median real income for those aged 55–64 increased by 9 percent and among those aged 65 and over by 51 percent.

Table 7-4
Median Income of Households 1980–2013 in 2013 Adjusted Dollars

Age of Head of Household	1980	1990	2000	2013	% Change 1980– 2013	Mean Size of Household in 2013	Per Capita Income in 2013
15–24	34,213	31,103	37,669	34,311	0	2.82	12,167
25–34	52,047	52,454	60,079	52,702	1	2.85	18,492
35–44	63,594	66,625	72,724	64,973	2	3.35	19,395
45–54	67,615	72,432	77,973	67,141	−1	2.81	23,894
55–64	52,612	55,920	60,673	57,538	9	2.18	26,393
65 and over	23,635	29,122	31,225	35,611	51	–	–
65–74	N/A	35,060	38,080	44,426		1.91	23,259
75 and over	N/A	22,720	25,450	27,322		1.60	17,076
National average	**47,668**	**51,735**	**56,800**	**51,939**		**2.55**	**20,368**

Despite these dramatic improvements, advocates for the elderly frequently note that household income for the elderly remains relatively low. For example, in 2013, their median household income of $35,611 was only 68 percent of the $51,939 median of all U.S. households. This was lower than all other cohorts except those aged 15–24. However, many argue this is deceptive because, on average, elderly households are much smaller than typical American households. Table 7-4 shows that when viewed on a *per capita* basis, the median income of those in the 65–74 cohort exceeds the national average by 14 percent, while among the over 75 age group it is 84 percent of the national average.

Seniors' costs of living are generally lower than those of non-seniors, which reinforces their income and net asset gains. A majority have neither child-rearing expenses nor work-related expenses, such as commuting costs. Table 7-3 shows over 80 percent are homeowners, and most are likely to have paid off their mortgage by age 65, so their accommodation expenses are limited to taxes and maintenance.

Further, an increasing number of local jurisdictions have enacted legislation that freezes the property taxes paid by seniors on their homes at the amount paid when they reach age 65. In these communities, seniors remain unaffected, while the inevitable future year increases in tax rates and appraised values (at a minimum to cover higher costs of services caused by inflation) result in all other property owners paying higher taxes. There is no economic justification for such legislation, but rather it reflects seniors' disproportionate political influence and effectiveness in enhancing their self-interest.

Twin Drivers: Empathy and Political Influence

Seniors' improved financial status is attributable to widespread empathy among all age groups and to their political influence. The broad support of non-seniors probably reflects their desire to act on behalf of family members who are currently or potentially in need of financial assistance. The increased longevity reported in Table 7-2 means there is a concomitant increase in the number of adults who have living parents. Their natural inclination is to support maximum income for their parents. A corollary of this is that if income is insufficient to maintain their standard of living, adult children may feel obligated to provide supplementary resources from their own households' resources. Non-seniors may also view support for enhanced senior benefits as an investment in their own futures. Unlike other special interests, seniors make up a group that all adults expect, or at least hope, to join eventually.

Gray power is a political reality. The prognosis is that it will continue to gain in strength with the substantial increase in the number of seniors and their growing proportion of the total population. Table 7-1 shows their impressive increase in the early decades of the new millennium is only the beginning. Their growing power will stem not only from their numbers, but also from their high level of engagement in the political process. At the federal and state levels, seniors fund well-resourced lobbyists through their membership in the American Association of Retired People (AARP). Further, they have the time to invest in lobbying elected officials. In many jurisdictions, a preponderance of elected officials is in the senior age cohort, which makes it likely seniors have relatively strong personal networks with these people and that these officials fully empathize with their concerns.

Table 7-5 shows the percentage of seniors who reported voting in congressional elections is greater than that of any other age group.[9] In the high profile presidential election years, the 18–24 cohort typically votes at approximately two thirds the level of seniors. In non-presidential election years, the difference is especially prominent. Only 17.1 percent of the 18–24 cohort reported voting in the 2014 election, whereas proportions in the two oldest age groups were 49.6 percent and 59.4 percent—approximately treble that of the youngest group. This latter scenario is reflective of the situation in local elections in which the lack of high profile campaigns results in disinterest among many younger voters, while seniors vote in disproportionately high numbers. A monitoring organization reported: "In many cities, mayors for example are elected with a single digit turnout. In recent elections in Dallas, Charlotte and Austin they were elected by a turnout of 5 percent, 6 percent and 7 percent, respectively."[10] Such low turnouts make it easier for seniors to dominate local elections.

Table 7-5

Percentage of Citizens in Each Age Cohort Reporting They Voted in Congressional Elections

Age	Presidential Election Years			Congressional Election Years			
	2004	2008	2012	2002	2006	2010	2014
Total	58.3	58.2	56.5	42.3	43.6	41.8	41.9
18–24	46.7	48.5	41.2	19.3	22.1	21.3	17.1
25–44	60.1	60.0	57.3	38.9	36.9	37.1	32.5
45–64	70.4	69.2	67.9	58.1	57.6	54.4	49.6
65 and over	71.0	70.3	72.0	62.7	62.5	60.8	59.4

Who Is Defined as a Senior?

Traditionally, 65 was the age at which people were defined as senior citizens because it was the age at which full Social Security payments could be obtained. For well over half a century, the Census Bureau has used it to define seniors. This suggests that when the Social Security age for full payment was raised to 66 in 2009 and when it will be raised to 67 in 2027, leisure agencies' definition of seniors would also be raised, but no such linkage has occurred.

The data in Table 7-4 show the per capita median income in the 65–74 age cohort is 14 percent above the national average, while among those 75 and over it falls to 84 percent and is lower than all other age groups except the 15–24 cohort. This suggests if senior discounts are to be retained, the eligibility age should be 75.

The case for using an older age to define seniors is reinforced by the aphorism: It is not how old you are, but how old you feel that is important. There is a large gap between the perception of the elderly by the non-elderly and the reality of the elderly. Cultural perceptions of the elderly do not often mirror the way they think about themselves. Research and experience indicate that the elderly feel younger than they are.

Typically, the gap in samples of elderly between felt age and chronological age has been found to be between 10 and 15 years.[11] For example, it was reported in a Pew Research Center poll:

> Nearly half of those over 50 say that they feel at least 10 years younger than their chronological age. As people age, the gap between felt and chronological age increases. Among those aged 65–74, one-third said they feel 10 to 19 years younger than their actual age, while over one-sixth say they feel at least 20 years younger than their actual age. (p. 22)[12]

When the potential problems related to old age are listed, Figure 7-3 shows the share of non-elderly adults who reported expecting to encounter them is much higher than the share of seniors who reported experiencing them. This perhaps explains why many seniors prefer to use leisure services ostensibly designed for everyone, but that "just happen" to meet the needs of the elderly, rather than those labeled senior programs.

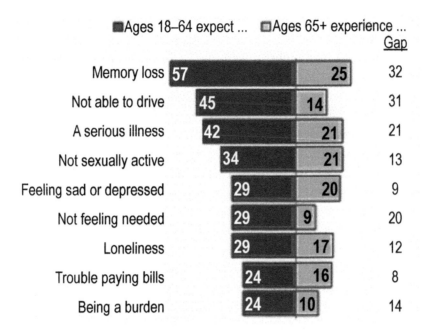

Figure 7-3. Challenges of Aging: It's Not as Bad as Younger Adults Think

While these data suggest the rational decision would be to raise the eligibility age from 65 to 75, few, if any, leisure agencies have done this. But rather the inequity has been exacerbated by many agencies reducing the eligibility age. In some instances, 62 has been adopted because this is the earliest age at which people can elect to initiate their Social Security payments if they are prepared to accept 80 percent of what they could claim at 66. Other common definition ages are 60, which reflects when withdrawals can be made from 401(k) retirement plans without penalty; 55, which is a common age at which retirees from the military, police, fire and those with union-negotiated contracts can retire with full pension and health benefits; and 50, which is the age for membership in the American Association of Retired People (AARP).

What the Averages Obscure

Five caveats qualify and modify the encouraging statistical trends presented related to the economic well-being and longevity of seniors. The first two caveats are derived from the criteria/assumptions on which the indices are based. For the latter three, the average measures obscure the reality that the elderly are not a homogeneous group and among them are cohorts that have not shared in the general enhanced well-being of seniors.

First, in the traditional poverty measure, 10.2 percent of seniors were below the poverty level in 2014, while the SPM was less positive, showing that 14.4 percent were below that threshold (Table 6-2). This suggests that 6.4 million, rather than 4.0 million, seniors live below the poverty threshold. The substantially higher proportion reported in the SPM is caused by the inclusion of out-of-pocket medical expenses in that index. These are much higher for seniors than for non-seniors. In contrast, many of the in-kind benefits included in the SPM (Table 6-1) are not targeted at seniors and do relatively little to improve their status. Most benefits to seniors are in cash and are captured by the traditional measure as well as the SPM.

Private pensions have been a central contributor to the improvements in seniors' economic status. The second caveat to the generally favorable statistical trend is that some believe this positive trend is changing and will be reversed in the future. While 42 percent of private sector full-time workers aged 25–64 reported having pension coverage in their current job in 2011, this was a decrease from the 50 percent who had coverage in 1979.[13] Currently, 55 percent of current workers do not have employment-based savings, while others end up with grossly inadequate 401(k) balances.[14]

Many current seniors have defined-benefit retirement plans that guarantee workers a steady income after retirement. Among new and future retirees, only 10 percent can expect income from defined-benefit programs. In the past two decades, most employers have switched to defined-contribution plans. In doing so, some employers reduced the funds they allocate for employees to invest for their pensions. An additional concern is that many, especially the lower educated, will fail to manage their 401(k) funds wisely. These changes suggest that increasing proportions of future retirees will face a decline in private pension income at the end of their working lives.[13]

A third caveat pertains to the data in Table 7-2 that show on average people are living much longer. These data are weighted by large increases in longevity among relatively affluent and well-educated Americans. Those with lower incomes and less education have, at best, seen hardly any rise in life expectancy at age 65; indeed, those with less education have seen their life expectancy decline. Even within races and ethnic groups, the impact of education (and its correlates income and wealth) is pervasive. Among white, black and Hispanic males, the differences in longevity between those with a college degree and those whose education did not extend beyond high school were 12.9, 9.7 and 5.5 years, respectively. The authors of these analyses concluded:

> Differences in longevity between subgroups of the U.S. population are so pernicious and systemic that it is now reasonable to conclude that at least two Americas have formed, with notably different longevity prospects. The two are demarcated by level of education and its socioeconomic status correlates, and related to race or ethnicity. (p. 1806)[15]

A fourth exception to the generally strong financial status of seniors is shown by the data in Table 7-4, which indicate a marked difference between the "young-old" 65–74 households and the "old-old" 75 and older cohort. The needs and expenditure patterns of these groups are different. The old-old are likely, for example, to have higher expenditures for health and housing as a result of chronic illness and institutionalization. Clearly, the economic status of that cohort is substantially inferior to that of seniors under 75 and continues to lag behind the national average.

Finally, the data in Table 7-6 show the poverty rates among black and Hispanic seniors are almost 3 times higher than those among whites.[16] These data were reported in the traditional poverty measure, but they were mirrored in the SPM.

Table 7-6

Percentage of U.S. Citizens below the Federal Poverty Level by Age and Race

Year	% Children under 18			18–64			65 and Older		
	White	Black	Hispanic	White	Black	Hispanic	White	Black	Hispanic
2013	10.7	38.3	30.4	9.9	23.9	20.2	7.4	17.6	19.8
2002	9.4	32.3	28.6	7.5	19.9	18.1	8.3	23.8	21.4

Implications for Leisure Managers

The economic status of seniors does not support the continued subsidization of leisure programs for seniors. Notwithstanding the caveats in the previous section, for the most part today, seniors' standard of living and their economic well-being are at least equal to that of the non-elderly. The majority of elderly persons are not poor. The U.S. still has a poverty problem, but it is pervasive across all age groups and is not selectively concentrated among seniors. Hence, the ultimate goal of leisure agencies should be to end discounts for adults that are defined by age and offer them to all the economically disadvantaged. To offer price discounts to the non-poor elderly is unfair to the non-elderly and to the low income elderly. It requires all of these groups to reach into their wallets so seniors who are not economically disadvantaged may save money, when there is no economic rationale to support this requirement.

The perceived inappropriateness of such undiscriminating subsidies is heightened when the source of the subsidy is property or sales taxes, which make up most of the general fund revenues in local jurisdictions. These are regressive taxes, meaning that low income people are hurt most by them.

Confronted by these data, advocates frequently revert to three emotional arguments to support retention of senior discounts. First, it is suggested that many seniors have income marginally above the poverty level and should also be considered economically disadvantaged. However, an equal number of non-seniors are similarly classified. Irrespective of the level at which the threshold is set, some folks will always be marginally above that level.

Second, it is argued that most seniors are "on a fixed income." However, it was noted earlier that all four primary sources of seniors' income have grown in recent years. Indeed, their primary source of income, Social Security, is adjusted upwards annually to reflect increases in the cost of living, and it was pointed out that the formula used to make these annual adjustments is overly generous to seniors. A heavily weighted component of it is the cost of housing, and it was indicated in the earlier discussion related to Table 7-3 that most seniors own homes and have paid off the mortgage, so they have minimal accommodation expenses.

Third, it is sometimes stated: "Because people have been paying full prices and taxes all their life, they should be given a break when they get older" (p. 69).[17] It must be presumed, however, that they were recipients of the services provided with revenues from those prices and taxes. This case could only be legitimate if there was evidence of some inequity, that is, if for some reason they had not received benefits commensurate with the price and tax payments made.

The demise of a rationale for senior discounts in this field was noted 30 years ago:

> The transformation of senior citizens has been one of the great national achievements of this country over the past two decades. Recreation and park departments, however, have failed to change their pricing policies to reflect this transformation. It is the author's contention that most senior citizens should be required to pay full price, and that the discounted or free use of services should be offered only to the small minority who are unable to pay in the same way as they are offered to those who are unable to pay in other age groups. (p. 4)[18]

Nevertheless, as the example in Figure 7-4 illustrates, this continues to be an issue three decades later. Its resilience is testimony to the magnitude of the challenge senior discounts present.

The federal government offers an especially egregious example of inequitable discounts given to seniors. It offers American citizens and permanent residents aged 62 and over a lifetime pass for $10 that gives free admission to the pass holder and all other occupants in the same non-commercial vehicle to 2,000 recreational areas managed by five federal agencies: National Park Service, U.S. Forest Service, Bureau of Land Management, Bureau of Reclamation, and Fish and Wildlife Service. It also entitles pass holders to a 50 percent discount at all these sites on amenity fees for activities, such as camping, boat launches, swimming and parking. These discounts were first authorized in 1972 when the lifetime passes were called The Golden Age Passport. In 2007, their name was changed to America the Beautiful National Parks and Federal Recreation Lands Interagency Senior Pass.

Many have pointed out that the cost of traveling to these sites is often substantial. They have asked: "Are seniors who can afford (say) $500 to travel to a site sufficiently economically disadvantaged that they should receive free admission and a 50 percent discount on camping fees?" The question is especially poignant when the discounts are compared to the Interagency Annual Pass, which entitles non-senior holders to multiple visit access at the same 2,000 sites. It is an annual (not lifetime) pass and costs $80 each year. It is not transferable, but each pass can have two "owners." Like the senior pass, it covers all passengers in a non-commercial vehicle. However, it applies only to entrance fees and does not offer the 50 percent discount on amenities that the seniors' lifetime pass provides.

If the discount comparison is extended to vehicles that do not contain a pass holder, it appears even more unreasonable. At the Grand Canyon, for example, the regular entrance fee is $25. The fee covers multiple visits to that park for the next 7 days, but its cost is more than double the cost of a senior lifetime pass.

Figure 7-4. Inequity in the Price of Passes to National Parks and Other Federal Recreation Areas

The challenge is exacerbated by recognition that seniors are likely to be central to the future viability of leisure agencies not only because of their political strength and changes in their time availability and financial status, but also because of the concomitant changes in their levels of leisure literacy. A substantial leisure literature has empirically verified the aphorism: You are what you were yesterday. That is, the leisure behaviors in which adults engage were learned in their youth and have endured throughout the life span. For the most part, people's leisure interests and skills are established by the time they leave high school or college.[19] Older seniors who reached adolescence before the 1960s generally have limited skills and interests because they had few opportunities to acquire them in their youth. The level of leisure literacy among baby boomers is much higher because they were exposed to many more leisure opportunities in their youth. This means the desire among those now attaining senior status for a wider range of active recreation opportunities is much greater than that of seniors a decade ago.

The increasing centrality of active leisure in the lifestyles of seniors means that providing these opportunities is integral to the economic development strategy of many communities that are trying to attract GRAMPIES (growing numbers of retirees who are active monied people in excellent shape) to relocate there. These communities have recognized that an annual inflow of 100 retired households with $40,000 annual income would equate to a new $4 million annual payroll in the community.

This income is relatively stable and not subjected to the vicissitudes of economic business cycles; seniors stimulate housing, retail and especially a community's health care industry, but do not put pressure on either the local job market or the school system; and they provide a volunteer pool. The key requirements for attracting new GRAMPIES and retaining those currently in a community are ambiance, together with amenities that facilitate socialization and an active lifestyle. Such activity friendly neighborhoods are exemplified by attractive landscaped streets, trails and recreation opportunities.

Most leisure agencies have traditionally served seniors, but in many communities, the numbers involved have been small compared to those participating in activities such as youth sports, adult sports and aquatics. However, the future viability of agencies is likely to be influenced by their ability to change this situation, by moving seniors from being a relatively small fringe target market to being a central focus of their services.[20]

Their large number, growing longevity, time availability, enhanced economic status and higher levels of leisure literacy make seniors the largest and fastest growing target market for many leisure agencies. The emergence of seniors as a central, rather than a peripheral, target market adds a sense of urgency to removing the pricing inequity. While alienating seniors may have short-term negative consequences, continuing with large discounts makes it likely there will be adverse impacts that are more severe on agencies' viability in the future and the burden on all other residents will be greater.

Seniors are susceptible to being more price sensitive than other users because their greater amount of leisure time enables them to invest more effort in comparing prices. Nevertheless, airlines, cable television companies, resorts, movie theaters and other private sector providers of leisure services that used to give senior discounts have recognized these new realities and no longer do so. Those that still do tend to offer relatively small discounts, typically 10 percent, so they meet patrons' expectation of a discount, but only at a minimum level. Further, many businesses (e.g., hotels) do not advertise such discounts and give them only if requested. General acceptance by seniors of the private leisure sector's actions suggests it is time for public agencies to make similar changes to their policies toward senior discounts.

The task may be aided by erosion of the widespread public empathy seniors have enjoyed in the past. In the 1990s, the concept of generational accounting was introduced.[21] Its use spread quickly, and it became a staple of public discussions about government budgets. Its results suggest to many that the elderly receive too many government resources at the expense of the young, and it popularized the notion of intergenerational conflict. For example, while 41 percent of the federal budget is allocated to seniors, only 9.9 percent is allocated to children.[29] As a result, typical questions raised in the media include: Are young people, especially children, being shortchanged by excessive public spending on older people? Are the age groups now in conflict? Will conflict intensify in the future? Such discussions suggest that empathy from non-seniors may gradually be replaced by resentment of their growing share of public resources.

Strategies for Reducing Senior Discounts

The economic case against senior discounts is clear and unequivocal. Many elected officials and leisure managers are familiar with it, but having the political and administrative will and skill to remove the discounts is another matter. Senior discounts became part of the marketing lexicon in the 1950s. They made commercial sense in the private sector and equity sense in the public sector because at that time over one third of seniors were below the federal poverty level (Table 6-2). Further, most recreation opportunities prior to the mid-1970s were widely viewed as providing communitywide benefits (rather than spillover or user benefits) for which no charge should be made. This long tradition has created a strong reference point. As a result, seniors expect that they will receive a discount and that such discounts are "fair," and hence, removing them is unfair and an attack on their "rights." In the case of new services, the obvious strategy is to avoid the problem by not offering senior discounts in the beginning so no reference point or expectation is created.

When participants experience a radical change in price, there is often a participant adjustment period (Chapter 10). Immediately after a substantial price increase is imposed, there is resistance. The negative reaction is likely to be motivated as much by outrage or pique at its "unfairness" as by perceived inability to pay the new price. Over time, however, the perceived unfairness of the increase evaporates as the new price slowly evolves into a new norm that most people accept. In users' minds, it gradually replaces the old price as the established reference point and the price they expect to pay.

It is often observed that "timing is everything in politics." The disproportionate influence of seniors at the polls makes their support critical at bond referendums for leisure projects. Thus, in the short term, the danger is that eroding senior discounts may result in relatively small gains, compared to their loss of support for the relatively large dollars at stake in a referendum. The optimum "window of opportunity" for addressing the issue may be soon after a referendum, so any angst among seniors caused by erosion of the discounts will dissipate over (say) the 5 or 7 years before the next referendum.

Two options are available for phasing out discounts. First, the discount could be removed at a single point in time. This is likely to precipitate the most opposition and the longest customer adjustment period because it most aggressively violates users' existing reference price. However, it confines the angst to a relatively short time, after which the issue is resolved. The alternative is to have an incremental phase out over time. It recognizes people are likely to accept price changes that do not vary widely from the reference point and that are within their latitude of price acceptance (Chapter 9). This is the range of prices around a reference price within which users have reduced price sensitivity. Thus, if a 50 percent discount were reduced (say) by 5–10 percent a year, user resistance would likely be low because the annual incremental increase in cost would be relatively small and within an acceptable range. The downside of this approach is that it takes 5–10 years to remove the discount, and it assumes the political will to pursue this strategy will be maintained throughout this period.

The most effective strategy for changing seniors' contention that removing their discounts is "unfair" is to reframe the context in which they are viewed (Chapters 9 to 12). This can be done in three primary ways: providing detailed financial information, comparing an agency's discounts with those other leisure service providers offer and shifting seniors' participation to off-peak times.

A well-developed information campaign could pose some variation of the following question: On average each time seniors use the service they pay $5, whereas all other adult users on average pay $12. This means that taxpayers, most of whom on average have less income than seniors, are heavily subsidizing their use. Is this fair?

Along with the question, four pieces of *financial information* should be provided: the net assets and income status of age cohorts described in Tables 6-2 and 7-4, costs of providing the service, amount of subsidy seniors and non-seniors receive, and data showing the agency's need for increased revenues. Users of a leisure service are likely to have little knowledge of either an agency's delivery costs or the proportion of costs of a given program that revenue from pricing recovers. Indeed, most users probably do not recognize that a subsidy is involved because it is an issue to which they are unlikely to have given conscious thought. When awareness of this is aroused, the context within which they perceive the magnitude of a price increase is likely to change. Empirical evidence of the effectiveness of this approach is presented in Chapter 11.

Comparing a program's discounts with others' discounts involves doing a going-rate survey of leisure providers in the community and/or a survey of other public agencies in the area. The intent is to change the context by creating external reference points that can be used to reframe the issue by asking: "Because others offered either no senior discount or only 10 percent, isn't it equitable for the agency to set its discount at a similar level (or abolish it)?"

The *time* available for leisure activities among those in the workforce is typically relatively tightly circumscribed: before 7:30 a.m. and after 6 p.m. on weekdays, and at weekends. Hence, these tend to be the peak use times for many agency services. Figures 7-1 and 7-2 show that approximately 80 percent of people over 65 are not in the labor force, which suggests they have more flexibility in deciding when to engage in leisure pursuits.

Thus, discounts sometimes are offered to seniors as incentives to persuade them to utilize spare capacity at off-peak times because their more flexible lifestyle enables this. For example, restauranteurs frequently offer a price discount to seniors willing to dine between late afternoon and early evening as a vehicle for increasing capacity at times when the facility is relatively empty. These incentive discounts are not stimulated by an obligation to the Ability to Pay Principle, but rather they are a sales promotion strategy to optimize revenue.

If seniors elect to participate at peak times, they may reduce the opportunities available to the non-elderly. Thus, for example, one agency that offered senior discounts for golf and did not restrict the time they could be used reported: "Over 100 golfers per week during the playing season are turned away from playing courses on weekends because of crowded conditions." In such cases, seniors should pay the full price; otherwise, the non-elderly are being unfairly discriminated against. This strategy of shifting their use to off-peak times removes the need-based discount and effectively changes it to a sales promotion designed to fill off-peak spare capacity.

DISCOUNTS FOR CHILDREN

The economic status of children is different from that of seniors. The family is the chief source of their support, followed by government programs, such as education and welfare. The deteriorating economic status of children reflects an erosion of support from within the family and a lack of political support for government expenditures on them.

Erosion of Family Support for Children

It was pointed out in the earlier discussion of senior discounts that empathy for them stems from many voters having living parents. One likely implication of this is a reluctance to advocate for increases in government support for children if the cost is an equivalent decrease in resources allocated to seniors. A second implication is that families that have to provide resources to elderly parents have fewer resources to support their children. As life expectancy increases, more middle-aged people tend to have parents who are still alive. Further, women are having children at later ages, so their parents are older, but their children are still young. Those who are simultaneously giving support to elderly parents and dependent children are known as the "sandwich generation."[22]

The demographic group most impacted is 45–56-year-old women. Table 7-7 shows the percentage of this cohort who have 0–4 living parents (including own parents and parents-in-law) and 0–4 or more dependent children. The modal number of both children and parents is 2,[22] which is indicative of the divided loyalties of this group.

Table 7-7

Percentage of 45–56-Year-Old Women with Specified Number of Living Parents and Children Under 18

	0	1	2	3	4 (or more)
% of Women	18.4	30.1	30.0	14.2	7.4
% of Children	16.6	14.5	31.9	17.9	19.1

A second factor that has eroded family support for children is the earthquake that has shaken the family structure and fractured it in the past half century. It suddenly collapsed in the 1970s. Premarital sex lost its stigma, shotgun marriages virtually disappeared, divorce became epidemic and the number of children living in single families began a long steady ascent.[23] The deterioration of children's economic well-being has been a consequence of this collapse.

Figure 7-5 shows out-of-marriage births to college-educated women remain under 10 percent and have risen only slightly since the 1970s. In contrast, they have risen sharply in the last 40 years among high school–educated females, so in 2007 they made up 65 percent of births in their group. This rise is partially explained by the increase in cohabitation. While cohabiting unions accounted for 41 percent of births to unmarried mothers, this increased to 58 percent by 2012. However, the average cohabitation period is about 14 months and typically does not end in marriage.[23] Table 7-8 shows that in 1960 only 9 percent of children were living with a single parent, but by 2012 this had increased to 29 percent.[24] A large majority of these households are headed by females, and a substantial proportion of fathers accept little or no enduring responsibility for those children.

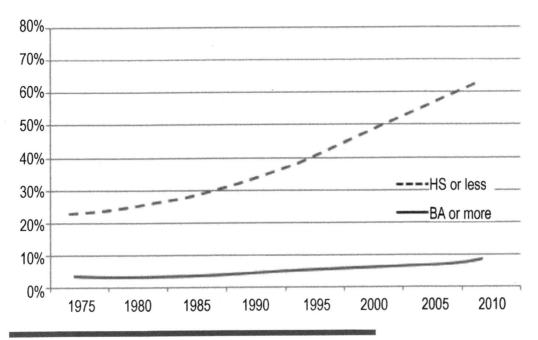

Figure 7-5. Birth to Unmarried Mothers by Education, 1977–2007

Table 7-8

Living Arrangements of Children under 18 Years Old

Year	Total Number of Children (thousands)	Living with:			
		2 Parents	Mother Only	Father Only	Other
2012	73,817	68	25	4	3
2010	74,718	69	23	4	4
2000	72,012	69	22	6	3
1990	64,137	72	22	3	3
1980	63,427	76	18	2	4
1970	69,162	85	11	1	3
1960	63,729	88	8	1	3

Increase in the number of single parent families primarily reflects dramatic growth in the proportion of children born to non-married parents (Figure 7-6). When the War on Poverty was launched in the 1960s, only 6 percent of U.S. children were born out of wedlock, but by 2010 this had increased to almost 41 percent of births.[25] However, un-married mothers are no longer typically in their teens; contrary to popular conventional wisdom, the birthrate among adolescent girls has dropped by nearly half since 1991 and was at an all-time low in 2012.[26] A public health triumph attributed to better sex education and birth-control methods. Most unmarried mothers today are in their 20s and early 30s.

The single parent increase is exacerbated by parental separation through divorce, which many children born to married couples will experience. The probability that a first marriage will end in divorce before the 10th wedding anniversary is 30 percent for men and 32 percent for women. This increases to 44 percent and 48 percent, respectively, by the 20th anniversary.[27] Again, this increases children's financial challenges. While the divorce rate peaked in 1981 and then began to taper off, it has remained relatively high. Further, this average pattern conceals significant discrepancies. While the divorce rate fell significantly among the college educated after 1980, it continued to rise among those with no college education. By 2010, the ratio of divorced to married people was 14 per 100 among college graduates, but 28 per 100 among other Americans.[23]

The negative relationship between single family homes and child poverty is shown in Table 7-9. It illustrates that children under 18 living in families headed by single mothers with no spouse present are especially at risk of being poor. In 2010, 23 percent of children lived in female-headed families (Table 7-8), but Table 7-9 shows children in such families accounted for 53.5 percent of all child poverty.[28]

One of the most dramatic social trends in recent decades has been the out-of-wedlock birthrate—the percentage of all births that occur to non-married women. Throughout most of U.S. history, out-of-wedlock childbearing was rare.

When the War on Poverty began in the mid-1960s, only 6 percent of children in the U.S. were born out of wedlock. Over the next four and a half decades, the number rose steadily. In 2010, 40.8 percent of births in the U.S. occurred outside of marriage. In 2010, there were 4.25 million births in the U.S. Of these, 2.53 million children were born to married couples and 1.72 million were born outside of marriage.

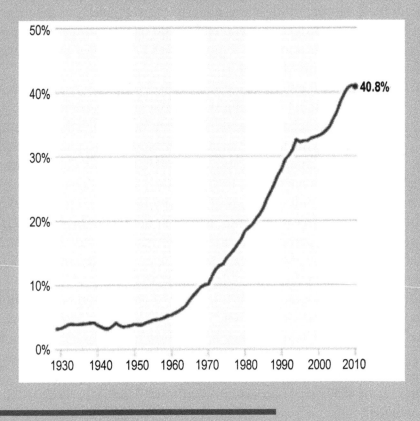

Figure 7-6. Percentage of Children Born out of Wedlock

Table 7-9

Family Living Arrangements: Where Poor Children Live, 2009

Married-couple families	35.3%	
Never married, female head	29.5%	
Separated, spouse absent, female head	12.1%	53.5%
Divorced female head	10.6%	
Widowed female head	1.3%	
Male-headed families, spouse absent	7.0%	
Live apart from parents with other relatives	4.2%	

Relatively Low Government Support

The main vehicle other than the family for transferring resources to children and the elderly is the state. Governments allocate a much smaller proportion of their budgets to the young than to seniors. The two poverty measures shown in Table 6-2 indicate that in 2014 between 15.8 million and 12.1 million children (21.5 percent and 16.7 percent of 73.6 million) lived in poverty compared to between 4.53 and 6.5 million seniors (10.2 percent and 14.4 percent of 44.5 million). In 2012, the share of the federal budget allocated to children was 9.9 percent, and this was projected to fall to 8 percent in the next decade. In contrast, 41 percent of it was allocated to the elderly. Public spending per child on federal and state programs averaged $11,300 over the course of a year, with the largest expenditures on education. For seniors, it was $24,800 per person, primarily for Social Security, Medicare and Medicaid.[29]

In earlier discussion of the status of seniors, it was recognized that their political power was influential in enhancing their allocations from the government. In contrast, the constituency for children is relatively weak. They cannot vote. Further, the empty nester and senior cohorts are growing faster than any of the younger cohorts, and they are least supportive of spending on children because they receive no direct benefit from it. It has been suggested: "Americans have never had any strong sense of collective responsibility for other people's children only private responsibility for their own" (p. 448).[30] If this is the case, children's only source of influence is parents acting on their behalf. However, it was noted earlier that even parental priorities are likely to be divided between their children and the elderly because at every stage in the life cycle most families will likely have more surviving parents than they do children under 18.

In addition to age demographic self-interest, two other factors may inhibit support for government expenditures on children.[30] First, reliable contraception gives people a high degree of control over whether they have children. Because children are now the result of a private decision rather than of chance, some people argue that parents should bear all the costs of child rearing.

A second factor that may suppress altruism toward other people's children is that disproportionate numbers of poor children are from minority groups with whom some in the majority may have trouble identifying (Table 7-6). Thus, out of the 67.3 million children identified as white, black, or Hispanic, 13.7 million were below the traditional federal poverty measure. However, only 30 percent of them were white.[16]

Implications for Leisure Managers

The data presented in the previous sections show that a relatively large proportion of children will likely have difficulty paying the full price because they are from economically disadvantaged households. There are two other rationales for supporting substantial discounts for children. First, some argue that leisure literacy is as important to a satisfying life as reading, writing and numerical literacy. As such, teaching and developing leisure skills are as much a societal obligation as educational expenditures on other forms of literacy. It is contended that the absence of such skills in some cases will lead to deviant behavior that inflicts greater costs on society.

It was noted earlier that to a large extent adults' active leisure participation reflects the leisure skills they learned in their youth.[19] Hence, a second rationale for discounts is that by investing in youth, leisure agencies are nurturing their future clienteles. From a political perspective, widespread involvement of children results in a wider base of political support from parents of the children. In addition, when these children become adults, they may recall the benefits they received from youth recreation programs and consequently be more likely to support tax expenditures on recreation services.

The U.S. Census Bureau defines children as those under 18. This is consistent with the legal definition of a child in the U.S., the age when most graduate from high school, and the age at which they become eligible to vote and serve in the armed forces. However, Table 7-4 shows the 15–24 age group is the poorest of all age cohorts with a median per capita income that is barely half of the national average. This suggests discounts should be extended beyond the age of 18. Some agencies have recognized this. For example, membership in New York City recreation centers is free for those under 18, $25 for those under 25 and over 65, and $150 for all other adults.

Extending discounts to those over 18, however, is the exception. The norm is to yield to the pressures to generate more revenue by reducing the age of eligibility for discounts and their magnitude. Four decades ago, under 18 was the eligibility norm and half price for children was the expected discount. These parameters survive in relatively few jurisdictions today. Their erosion follows the aggressive actions of commercial theme and water parks. Typically, they limit free admissions to those under 3, give 10 percent discounts to children aged 3 to 8 or 10, and charge full adult price for those over 8 or 10. Their actions have made it easier for public leisure agencies to reduce the eligibility age and discount size because they have changed the reference expectancy of many.

Among agencies that have maintained substantial discounts for youth, debate often shifts to whether they should be free. There are strong arguments against this. Children are likely to require more careful supervision and inflict more damage on a facility than are adults, so the costs associated with servicing them are often greater than the costs of servicing adults. Further, children's use of a service is likely to be contingent on their parents', rather than their own, ability to pay. It is argued that if parents are not prepared to demonstrate their support by at least partially offsetting a program's costs, it is unreasonable of them to expect people without children in the program to recognize it as worthy of subsidy through the tax system.

It is sometimes suggested that because youth recreation programs contribute toward leisure literacy and society fully subsidizes other types of education through the public school system, youth recreation programs should also be offered free and fully subsidized. This analogy has two weaknesses. First, while all children are required to participate in education offered by the schools, only a select group of children elect to participate in programs offered by leisure agencies. If only a select group of children receives benefits, it is difficult to make the case they should be fully tax supported by other citizens. The inequity becomes even more pronounced if the select group is from middle or high income families rather than from low income families, which is often the case in activities such as Little League, soccer, swimming and softball. In these situations, poor people are required to subsidize a program, usually through property or sales taxes, even though their children do not benefit from it. These taxes are regressive and hurt poor people most. The second weakness with the education analogy is that many schools already offer basic instruction in the leisure activities, and many of the programs offered by leisure agencies are for more advanced practice of those skills and competitive opportunities.

LARGE HOUSEHOLD DISCOUNTS

The family that plays together stays together is a cherished aphorism of leisure agencies. Traditionally, agencies have offered a family pass because larger families have more expenses to meet, so if all else is equal, *ipso facto* larger families are disadvantaged compared to smaller families.

Two emergent trends have resulted in the definition of "family" becoming increasingly amorphous and challenging to operationalize. First, an expanding number of permutations are now included under the rubric of family. Consider, for example, the following description of one family: "An uneasy ensemble of two sons from her two previous husbands, a daughter and son from his second marriage, ex-spouses with varying degrees of involvement, the partners of ex-spouses, [and] the bemused in-laws."[26] Second, a related issue is that relatives other than immediate family are being included, so a single pass may be used by 10 or 15 people.

In response to these challenges, the discount has been reconceptualized as a household, rather than a family, pass, recognizing that all members should reside full time in the same household. Three variations of the household pass are widely used: (i) It is limited to no more than two adults and two children, but additional children can be added at (say) half the price of a regular children's pass; (ii) the pass may include up to (say) six people who live at the same physical address; or (iii) those who are included must be listed as dependents on income tax returns.

THE MULTI-USE DISCOUNT

The multi-use discount is a form of differential pricing because it enables different users to pay different prices for the same service. However, this discount is different from those discussed previously in that it is *not* targeted at the economically disadvantaged. Rather, it is analogous to a quantity discount commonly offered in the private sector to encourage purchasers to buy a large quantity of a service or product.

This is a staple pricing option that almost all leisure agencies offer and has long been part of the field's conventional practice. Such discounts most commonly offer annual, seasonal or multi-use access to facilities, such as swimming pools, golf courses and art complexes. However, the rationale for offering a quantity discount for public leisure services is unclear. When managers are asked why multi-use passes are offered, typical responses are "I am not sure I know why we do it except that it has always been done here," or "We do it because every other leisure agency does it and it is expected of us." In short, their adoption of this discount often appears to be attributable to tradition and inertia.

In the private sector, quantity discounts are intended to reduce costs and to stimulate demand. The cost savings to businesses may include the following:

- Savings in production costs. Larger orders may result in larger production runs, resulting in lower per unit costs.
- Improved cash flow because a relatively large up-front payment is made.
- Reduced costs associated with the logistics of transportation because there will be fewer orders to process, ship and invoice.
- Reduced inventory and storage costs because costs of storage, financing inventory and carrying stock are transferred from seller to buyer.
- Reduced selling expenses. Many expenses, such as billing, order filling and the salaries of salespeople, are about the same whether the seller receives an order totaling $10 or $500.

None of these cost savings are likely to apply to public leisure agencies.

In some communities, public leisure facilities offer residents a "membership," which is a synonym for the multi-use pass. This choice of nomenclature is misleading because it connotes exclusivity, which is appropriate for private organizations but seems antithetical to an agency's mandate to be inclusive and open to all.

The intent in this section is to provide principles and rationales that may serve as guidelines so the adoption of multi-use discounts is purposive and goal directed rather than arbitrary. Clearly, those who purchase a pass would not do so unless they believe it will save them money. However, an agency is the steward of scarce tax resources entrusted to it by the citizenry and is expected to treat non–pass users equitably, so it has an obligation to consider the perspectives of these stakeholders as well as those who purchase a multi-use discount pass.

Are Multi-Use Discounts Justified?

Multi-use passes are appropriate in some situations. However, as the heading to this section suggests, they frequently abrogate the Ability to Pay and Benefit Principles because the discounts are most likely to go to those who can most afford to pay and/or who receive the most benefits.

Those who purchase passes receive two increments of financial benefit that do not accrue to those who pay a per visit price. First, if a per visit subsidy is calculated by dividing costs by number of visits, frequent users receive a greater proportion of the aggregate subsidy because they have more visits. Second, pass holders pay a lower per visit fee. These points are illustrated in the following scenario:

- Annual swimming pool revenues are $250,000, while operating costs are $650,000, so the net cost of operating the pool is $400,000. Annual attendance is 200,000 visits, so each visit is subsidized by $2. An adult annual pass holder pays $200 and uses it 100 times. The regular adult admission price is $5.

In this instance, the pass holder receives an aggregate subsidy from taxpayers of $200 (100 visits × $2 per visit subsidy), while the user who visits the pool 10 times a year receives an aggregate subsidy of $20. Further, while the pass holder's per visit cost is $2, the occasional user's cost per visit is $5.

The potential revenue forgone from pass holders means either taxpayers have to provide a larger subsidy or, in the case of enterprise fund services, other users provide the subsidy by paying more. Both of these outcomes abuse the Benefit Principle because pass holders are paying less than their equitable share of the costs. No empirical research has been reported on sociodemographic differences between pass holders and per visit payers. However, it seems plausible that pass holders are likely to be relatively wealthy because the economically disadvantaged are less likely to be able to afford the substantial up-front payment needed to purchase a pass. Thus, the Ability to Pay Principle is also abused.

A not altogether facetious case can be made that the frequent swimmer should pay a higher price than the occasional swimmer, not a lower price. The primary pressure for building and operating pools probably comes from heavy users, who will be the main beneficiaries. Their heavy use indicates the activity is a central element of their lifestyle, and as such, their demand is likely to be much more price inelastic than that of occasional users. Because they are the primary source of the operating deficits, it may be argued that given their relative price inelasticity, they should pay more per visit, not less. Consider the following case:

- A large $45 million public aquatic and recreation center attracts 1.05 million visits annually. Of these, 745,000 (71 percent) are accounted for by members who purchase an annual pass. The 11,000 members account for only 2.4 percent of the 450,000 population, so the majority of use is by a small proportion of the population. Multiple forms of membership are available, but the most popular is $1,000 a year, while a day pass is $25.

In this case, is it appropriate to offer an annual pass, which, by definition, suggests those users anticipate receiving a discount, rather than requiring all to pay the per visit price? Is it appropriate for taxpayers to fund facilities that charge such high prices, serve such small proportions of the community and presumably exclude large segments of the community who cannot afford these prices? The author of this research commented: "It is a public venue that seeks to serve everyone in the community and is not" (p. 7).[31]

There are two caveats to the conclusions drawn from this scenario. First, inequity under the Benefit Principle sometimes works against multi-pass holders because some of them are likely to make an incorrect decision. If they use it substantially less frequently than they anticipated, they may have paid more per visit than if they had opted for the per visit price. The study findings reported in Figure 7-7 suggest this is likely to be prevalent in many contexts. The issue then becomes: "Is it fair that people should pay for visits they don't use?" In a commercial context, such as that described in Figure 7-7, the response is *caveat emptor*: Let the buyer beware.[32] That is, the responsibility for the purchase outcome is exclusively the buyer's. Should this principle also apply to public agencies, whose ethical code requires them to operate transparently and equitably? Is it appropriate for public agencies to offer multi-use contracts when they are aware some proportion of users will be overly optimistic in their attendance estimates and will pay more by purchasing the "discount" pass than if they paid a per visit price?

Private health and fitness clubs typically offer three price options: per visit fee, monthly contract and annual contract. At three clubs where a study of the use records of 7,752 members was undertaken, the prices of these options were as follows:

- Per visit fee $12, or purchase of a 10-visit pass for $100.
- Monthly contract fees ranged between $70 and $85. The monthly fee was automatically debited each month to a credit card or bank account until the user canceled. Cancellation could be done in person at the clubs or by sending a written note.
- Annual contracts were 10 times the monthly fee (i.e., between $700 and $850), so users received a discount of 2 free months out of 12 in exchange for a yearly commitment. At the end of the year, the contract expired and members who wished to stay enrolled had to sign on again. The clubs sent out reminders encouraging them to do so.

It was found that 80 percent of the monthly members would have been better off had they paid per visit for the same number of visits. On average, they attended 4.5 times a month, paying an effective price of between $15.50 and $19 even though they could have paid $10 per visit using a 10-visit pass. On average, they paid 70 percent more than they would have if they had paid the per visit fee. Further, those who chose the monthly contract were 17 percent more likely to stay enrolled beyond 1 year than users choosing the annual contract despite the poor value it represented for most of them. The authors empirically explored nine possible explanations for this non-rational behavior and concluded: "In our view, the most parsimonious explanations are those allowing for over-confidence (naiveté) . . . This leads to over-estimation of attendance" (pp. 695–696).

Users had high attendance expectations when they signed up for the monthly contract. Thus, in their minds, it was the least cost option. They were also overly confident in their ability to cancel the contract if their attendance fell below the seven or eight visits a month needed for it to remain the lowest cost option. The authors suggested a supplementary contributing factor was persuasion by health club employees because the monthly contracts were profitable. This could be done by not providing sufficient information about the per visit alternative and by urging people to take the monthly contract as their least cost option.

Figure 7-7. Paying Not to Go to the Gym[32]

The second caveat is that abrogation of the Benefit Principle is at least partially mitigated by the high fixed costs and relatively low variable costs associated with facilities, such as swimming pools. This means that number of visits has relatively little impact on costs of operation. Thus, while conceptually the heavy user benefits most from the subsidy, in reality, the number of visits is not likely to influence the magnitude of the subsidy.

In the case of some facilities, such as swimming pools, public agencies are often monopolists in that they are the only providers of those services in the community. The purchasers of multi-use passes, by definition, are likely to be the most avid and committed users. Thus, given the lack of other suppliers, if a pass is not available, the probability is high that most of them would visit as frequently and would pay the regular per visit price.

From a financial perspective, the negative impact of multi-use discounts is especially pernicious if they contribute to creating congestion that sometimes occurs, for example, on public golf courses. Clearly, it is disadvantageous to have agencies squeeze out participants who are willing to pay the regular price at peak times.

In the context of parks that have an admission price and are accessed primarily by automobile, the volume discount often applies not only to the number of visits, but also to the number of individuals in an automobile. Designating the automobile as the unit to be priced rather than individuals may be administratively convenient, but it abuses the Benefit Principle and reduces potential revenues.

Per person pricing is consistent with the Benefit Principle and fairer than per vehicle admission. If the per vehicle admission price is $5 and five people are in the car, the cost is $1 per person. However, if two people are in the car, the cost to them is $2.50 per person. All else equal, the five people will likely adversely impact the resource more than the two people, but they pay a lower price. That is inequitable.

Individuals cause damage, wear and deterioration of the resource and create the need for more staffing, more regulation and more services in a park. A vehicle coming to a site is not an indication of damage or use. Further, when the price is tied to a vehicle, efforts to avoid paying it sometimes result in vehicles being parked outside the park on shoulders of highways. This creates not only a traffic hazard, but also a potential danger to vehicle occupants traversing roads when going to and from the park.

Positive Rationales

It was suggested earlier that a lack of alternative options makes it likely most pass holders will participate as frequently if they have to pay the per visit price. However, if people pre-pay for services, they will likely make more use of them than if they pay on a per visit basis because of self-pressure to get value for their money. Further, the lower cost per visit may result in passes generating additional demand from some participants. There are two potential positive outcomes for agencies if this scenario occurs. First, for better or worse, number of visits is the accountability criterion most frequently adopted by elected officials and city managers, so increases in visits may influence budget allocation decisions. Second, to earn more support from elected officials and taxpayers, some agencies are repositioning services so they better align with prevailing concerns related to health care costs. The more time individuals invest in exercising, which is a potential outcome from greater pass use, the stronger the agency's health position is likely to be in the public mind-set.

In two instances, there is a strong financial rationale for a multi-use pass. First, it may be used as a "loss leader" that induces and commits a purchaser to using the agency's service for an extended time rather than that of a competitor or alternative supplier. These situations arise when additional expenditures beyond the admission price are likely. For example, at a golf course, the multi-pass holder is likely to rent a golf cart and make purchases in the golf shop, concessions and food areas. The agency's profits from these purchases may more than offset the loss from per visit revenues.

The second instance is in contexts when revenue is maximized by aggregating different programs and charging a single price for them. This occurs when there is a difference in demand for related services, so users value them differently. As a result, a price is charged for the bundled services that is lower than the combined prices of the services priced separately. This strategy is often adopted by agencies that have programs in the performing arts. People are likely to vary in their preferences. Some may enjoy classical music rather than ballet, or Shakespeare rather than Miller or Pinter. The price they are willing to pay for individual tickets for each of the (say) five performances that make up a season is likely to vary according to these preferences. The principle can be illustrated by considering the price sensitivity of two prospective audience members for two performances:[33]

- Person A is prepared to pay $40 to watch the ballet, but only $20 to listen to the symphony. Person B holds the polar opposite view and would pay $20 for the ballet, but $40 for the symphony. Person C is prepared to pay $30 for each show. If all tickets are priced at $30, the revenues generated will be $120 ($30 from Person A and Person B and $60 from Person C). If a combined ticket is available for $55 for both shows, Person A and Person B, who were prepared to pay $60 for both shows, would buy it and so would Person C, who would save $5. Thus, the revenues from a combined pass would be $165 (i.e., $45 more than if the tickets are sold individually).

- Bundling also benefits from the psychological effects explained by prospect theory, which is discussed in Chapter 12. Because the aggregated price is lower than the summated prices of the individual programs, it is likely to be perceived as a discount, which is likely to reinforce its appeal.[34]

If a service is provided through an enterprise fund, there may be a third financial rationale for a multi-use pass in that it may be valuable to have a guaranteed cash flow at the start of a season. This may provide more time to develop strategies for resolving budget shortfalls over the rest of the season.

Recalibrating Multi-Use Discounts

Whenever additional costs are imposed or benefits are removed from a clientele group, protest is likely as users seek to protect their privileged position. It is especially probable in this context because multi-use passes have such a long heritage and are ensconced in a community's conventional wisdom. Many professionals who understand their limitations profess a desire to abolish them, but find they lack the political support necessary to do it.

Four strategies might be helpful in mitigating this difficult political environment. The first is replacing the multi-use pass with a frequent purchase card. For example, after (say) five visits the sixth is free. The second is to count single visits toward the cost of a multi-use pass. For example, if an annual pass is $100 and the per visit price is $5, the pass would be issued to users who record 20 annual visits. Both of these approaches mitigate abuse of the Ability to Pay Principle by ensuring that lower income users who cannot afford the up-front fee are not discriminated against by the pass option.

The third is to offer a minimally or non-discounted convenience pass. This would accommodate frequent users who buy a pass not for the monetary savings, but for the convenience of not having to carry cash or credit cards when they engage in a leisure activity.

The fourth is to use data to derive the price of a pass and thus remove the arbitrariness of the pricing decision. Many passes are now "swipe cards," which makes identifying the average number of visits by users easy. Alternatively, this can be done by questioning a sample of pass holders. These data can then be used to recommend a desired discount with elected officials. For example, if the per visit price were $5, the average number of visits 40, and the desired discount 25 percent, the pass would be $150 ($5 × 40 × .75).

SUMMARY

Those over 65 years of age are now on average no more likely to be classified officially as poor than those in any other age group. Senior incomes come from four main sources: Social Security; earnings; private pensions; and assets, such as interest, dividends and rents. All of these sources have grown in recent decades.

Despite these favorable changes in the financial status of seniors, it is still common for agencies to offer them substantial discounts. This can be attributed to two factors. The first is widespread empathy among younger age groups, reflecting their desire to support older family members and, perhaps, an investment in their own futures. Second, the political influence of seniors emanates from their increasing numbers, their growing proportion of the total population and their high level of participation in the political process.

Traditionally, 65 was the age at which people were defined as senior citizens. Examination of per capita median incomes among age cohorts suggests the rational age for senior discounts should be 75. However, rather than raise the eligibility age, many agencies have succumbed to political pressures and lowered it to 62, 60, 55, or 50.

To offer price discounts to the non-poor elderly is unfair to the non-elderly and the poor elderly. The goal of agencies should be to end discounts for all adults that are defined by age and offer them to all adults who are economically disadvantaged. As seniors move from being a relatively small fringe target market for leisure agencies to being a central focus of their services, removal of the discounts becomes increasingly important to optimizing an agency's revenue potential and the enhanced political viability that this brings.

Three primary strategies are available for changing seniors' contention that removing their discounts is "unfair": providing detailed financial information, comparing the discounts with those other leisure service providers offer and shifting seniors' participation to off-peak times.

In contrast to the economic status of seniors, the economic status of children has deteriorated in recent decades, reflecting the erosion of support within the family as family structures have become more fragmented and the reduced political support for government expenditures on children. Nevertheless, pressures to generate more revenue have caused most leisure agencies to reduce the age of eligibility for child discounts and the magnitude of discounts.

Discounts are often given to large families. The contemporary challenge of defining what constitutes a "family unit" has resulted in discounts being given to "household units" rather than to families and in limits on the number in a household who can use the discount.

The multi-use discount is different from other discounts in that it is not targeted at the economically disadvantaged, but rather it is analogous to a quantity discount. However, such discounts may be considered inequitable because the economically disadvantaged are unable to afford the up-front cost and therefore pay a higher per visit price. Further, taxpayers forgo potential income and give the largest per user subsidy to those who can afford the up-front cost rather than to low income individuals, suggesting that multi-use passes are regressive.

However, the lower cost per visit may result in more visits, which may contribute to society's efforts to reduce health care costs and to enhanced credibility for an agency seeking to align with that position. The multi-use discount also may be used as a "loss leader" that entices users to remain loyal to a facility at which they purchase other services, or it may be used to aggregate related services to optimize revenues when there is different price sensitivity to those services.

REFERENCES

1. U.S. Census Bureau. (2015). *Distribution of the population by selected age groups in the United States: 2015 to 2060.* Washington, DC: Author.

2. Leonesio, M. V., Bridges, B., Gesiemaria, R., & Del Bene, L. (2012). The increasing labor force participation of older workers and its effect on income of the aged. *Social Security Bulletin, 72*(1), 59–71.

3. Administration on Aging. (2015). *A profile of older Americans: 2014.* Washington, DC: Administration for Community Living, U.S. Department of Health and Human Services.

4. Short, K. (2015). *The research supplemental poverty measure: 2014* (Current Population Reports P60-254). Washington, DC: U.S. Census Bureau.

5. Kromer, B., & Howard, D. (2013). *Labor force participants and work status of people 65 years and older.* Washington, DC: U.S. Census Bureau.

6. Merrill Lynch. (2014). *Work in retirement: Myths and motivations.* New York, NY: Author.

7. U.S. Census Bureau. (2013). *Median value of assets for households, by type of asset owned and selected characteristics: 2011.* Washington, DC: Department of Commerce.

8. U.S. Census Bureau. (2015). *Age of head of household and median income 1967–2013 in 2011 adjusted dollars Table H-10AR.* Washington, DC: Department of Commerce.

9. U.S. Census Bureau. (2012). *Voting age populations – Reported registration and voting by selected characteristics: 1996 to 2012.* Washington, DC: Author.

10. Center for Voting and Democracy. (2012). *Voter turnout.* Takoma Park, MD: Author.

11. Kleinspehn-Ammerlahn, A., Kotter-Gruhn, D., & Smith, J. (2008). Self-perceptions of aging: Do subjective age and satisfaction with aging change during old age? *Journal of Gerontology: Psychological Sciences, 63B,* 377–385.

12. Pew Research Center. (2009, June 29). *Growing old in America: Expectations vs. reality.* Washington, DC: Author.

13. Krugman, P. (2013, November 21). Expanding social security. *New York Times,* p. A29.

14. Olen, H. (2014, February–March). You call this retirement? *AARP Magazine, 2014,* 42–49, 73.

15. Olshansky, S. J., Antonucci, T., Berkman, L., Binstock, R. H., Boersch-Supan, A., Cacioppo, J. T., . . . Rowe, J. (2012). Differences in life expectancy due to race and educational differences are widening, and many may not catch up. *Health Affairs, 31,* 1803–1813.

16. U.S. Census Bureau. (2012). *Poverty statistics of people by age, race and Hispanic origin 1959–2011* (Series P-60). Washington, DC: Department of Commerce.

17. Crompton, J. L. (1984, September). Treating equals equally: Common abuses in pricing public services. *Parks and Recreation, 19*(9), 67–71.

18. Crompton, J. L. (1984). The equitability of full price policies for senior citizens. *Journal of Park and Recreation Administration, 2*(1), 3–8.

19. Scott, D., & Willis, F. K. (1998). Adolescent and adult leisure patterns: A reassessment. *Journal of Leisure Research, 30,* 319–330.

20. Crompton, J. L. (2013, December). Are your seniors moving to center stage? *Parks and Recreation.* Retrieved from http://www.parksandrecreation.org/2013/December/Are-Your-Seniors-Moving-to-Center-Stage/

21. Kotlikoff, J. L. (1992). *Generational accounting.* New York, NY: Free Press.

22. Pierret, C. R. (2006, September). The 'sandwich generation': Women caring for parents and children. *Monthly Labor Review, 129*(9), 3–9.

23. Putnam, R. (2015). *Our kids.* New York, NY: Simon & Schuster.

24. U.S. Census Bureau. (2012). *Living arrangements of children under 18 1960 to 2012 Table CH-1.* Washington, DC: Department of Commerce.

25. Rector, R. (2012). *Marriage: America's greatest weapon against child poverty* (Special Report #117 on Poverty and Inequality). Washington, DC: The Heritage Foundation.

26. Angier, N. (2013, November 26). The changing American family. *New York Times.* Retrieved from http://www.nytimes.com/2013/11/26/health/families.html?pagewanted=all

27. Copen, C. E., Daniels, K., Vespa, J., & Mosher, W. D. (2012). *First marriages in the United States: Data from the 2006–2010 National Survey of Family Growth* (National Health Statistics Report No. 49). Hyattsville, MD: National Center for Health Statistics.

28. Gabe, T. (2011). *Welfare, work, and poverty status of female-headed families with children 1987–2009.* Washington, DC: Congressional Research Service.

29. Isaacs, J. B., Edelstein, S., Hahn, H., Stauerle, C. E., & Toucan, K. (2013). *Kids share: Report on federal expenditure on children in 2012 and future projections.* Washington, DC: Urban Institute.

30. Preston, S. H. (1984). Children and the elderly: Divergent paths for America's dependents. *Demography, 21,* 435–457.

31. Marriott, K. (2013, May). *Aquatic leisure venues: Do we know where we are going?* Paper presented at the 49th Annual Aquatic and Recreation Institute Conference and Trade Show, Sydney, Australia.

32. DellaVigna, S., & Malmendier, U. (2006). Paying not to go to the gym. *The American Economic Review, 90,* 694–719.

33. Smith, T. J. (2012). *Pricing strategy.* Mason, OH: South-Western Cengage Learning.

34. Kahneman, D., & Tversky, A. (1979). Prospect theory: An analysis of decision under risk. *Econometrica, 47,* 263–291.

Chapter 8

Differential Pricing Using Premiums

- Premiums for additional increments of user benefits
- Premiums to maximize the revenue from assets
- Summary

Premiums enable a leisure agency to capture more of the consumers' surplus inherent in the pricing of public leisure services. The conceptual rationale for this is twofold. Premiums for those willing to pay for increments of benefits beyond the standard offering are discussed in the opening section of the chapter. This is consistent with the Benefit Principle. In this context, premiums are appropriate for those who want to save their time by making a reservation, use a facility or program at peak times, or desire a higher quality offering than can be provided in the regular service. Peak time use and higher quality offerings are likely to impose additional costs on taxpayers beyond those needed to serve other participants. Charging all users the same price when there are differences in the costs of serving them would abrogate the Benefit Principle. Premiums rectify this inequity. Reservation options for the most part do not create additional costs, but the extra benefit increment in convenience, and the savings in time and "hassle" costs, merits a premium being charged.

In the second section of the chapter, it is recognized that agencies are taxpayers' agents in managing public assets. Thus, when those assets are not fully accessible to residents, agencies have an obligation to maximize the revenue potential of these assets. This rationale underlies the justification for premiums for non-resident and commercial use of the assets and the selective adoption of auctions or bidding to capture more consumers' surplus.

PREMIUMS FOR ADDITIONAL INCREMENTS OF USER BENEFITS

Reservation Options

The price people pay to engage in recreation includes their time as well as their money. The opportunity cost of time refers to the alternative opportunities that users forgo because their time is invested in a given leisure service. This may take the form of forgoing additional earned income, time with friends and family, or other desired activities. Time scarcity is a challenge confronting many Americans. It has been defined as "the feeling that one lacks enough time to do all the things that one would like to do"(p. 51).[1] In the context of public leisure services, time is often a scarcer resource than money, and it is consistently cited as the main reason for not participating in a leisure activity. For many potential participants, the key decision criterion on whether to participate is: "Will I give up 2 hours to travel to the activity, engage in it and travel back?" rather than "Will I pay the $5 or $10 to participate?"

In a retail context, it has been observed: "A store that wastes people's time will be committing competitive suicide" (p. 31).[2] This may be hyperbolic in the context of leisure services, but agencies have much to gain if they are responsive to people's desire to use time efficiently. Among the actions they can take are to make it more convenient for people to participate, to offer shorter and more self-directed opportunities, to provide complete information about the time requirements and to offer opportunities to make reservations.[1]

Whenever time savings can be offered by providing a reservation option, a premium can be added to a program's price. Reservations are widely offered for golf tee times, court times at tennis or basketball complexes, state park campsites and picnic shelters in local parks. However, in most agencies, the use of reservations is limited. The key role of time scarcity in participation decisions suggests that the use of reservations could be substantially expanded and that many users would be pleased to pay a premium to use their time more efficiently.

Peak Time Priority

In Chapter 3, it was recognized that monetary price can be used as a tool for rationing access to facilities or programs at times when demand exceeds supply. Charging differential prices for peak and off-peak use enables leisure agencies to manage demand relative to supply better. Anytime a facility or program is available with spare capacity, revenue is being lost. Similarly, revenue is lost when more people want to use a facility or program than can be accommodated.

Peak time pricing is the practice of charging a different price for the same service at different times. One of the most pervasive challenges confronting leisure managers is highly skewed temporal user distribution patterns. It was pointed out in Chapter 3 that peak demand creates two problems. First, it often skews decisions on amount of needed capacity. If facilities are designed with sufficient capacity to accommodate peak demand, much of this capacity remains unused the rest of the time. Further, whenever peak demand is reached and potential users are unable to participate, agencies are likely to come under pressure to add capacity. This is an inefficient use of resources. If peaks can be "flattened," less capital investment in facilities will be required. The second problem associated with peaking is that it results in crowding, which in some cases leads to a lower quality recreation experience (Figure 3-2).

The primary parameters delineating peak times are the traditional workweek and educational institution schedules and, in the case of outdoor recreation, the weather. For many potential users, these parameters dictate the times of the day, days of the week and months of the year when they can participate. However, users not constrained by these parameters (e.g., retirees, preschoolers) can still choose to participate at peak times. Even among those who are ostensibly constrained, some could adjust their schedules to participate at a different time (e.g., part-time workers, college students and the self-employed). For such groups, peak time use is a matter of convenience rather than necessity, and if sufficient incentive is available, they may be persuaded to shift to non-peak times.

If a higher price is charged for peak time use, this may provide the necessary incentive. This strategy is widely used in the private sector. For example, theaters segment their markets by offering midday matinees at substantially lower regular prices, attracting price sensitive retirees, students and unemployed workers who can most easily attend at these times, while charging a premium price at peak evening times. These price differentials would not be effective unless the premiums were high enough to represent a real savings to those who avoid them.

Peak time users are responsible for a disproportionate amount of the cost of developing a facility compared to off-peak users. Hence, they should pay a premium that covers this cost. Peak time pricing reduces excess capacity and allocates the additional cost of expanding facilities to peak time users who impose that cost on the system. At the same time, among the segments who do not have flexibility, imposing a premium price ensures those who place the highest value on the opportunities will prevail. Together, these attributes of peak time pricing maximize total user benefits and revenues.

For some people, peak time pricing at least partially counterbalances opportunity costs. When individuals participate in a leisure activity, they give up the opportunity to do other activities during that time. The most substantive of these opportunity costs are often associated with work or education. Thus, lower off-peak prices that coincide with work or education times may potentially offset relatively high opportunity costs. In contrast, the higher priced times, such as evenings and weekends, have lower opportunity costs associated with work or school schedules for many.

It was pointed out in Chapter 3 that a caveat to the use of peak time pricing in preference to lottery, reservation or queuing strategies for rationing use is its potential adverse impact on equity. Hence, the efficiencies it offers have to be weighed against an agency's social equity mandate for services in which lower socioeconomic segments are prominent users. For example, it could discriminate against lower income participants who are fully controlled by work schedules and consequently can only go to facilities in the evenings or at weekends. In contexts in which a relatively affluent clientele uses a service exclusively, this concern dissipates.

Superior Quality Increments

Superior quality increments stem from three sources: (i) variations in quality among facilities, (ii) variations in preferred locations within a facility and (iii) added service opportunities.

A leisure services system is likely to have facilities of different quality that ostensibly deliver the same service, but offer different levels of quality. Most are likely to accept that those who use a *higher quality facility or program should pay a higher price*. The higher quality is likely to require higher development and maintenance costs, so the price premiums for extra increments of benefits should at a minimum be set to cover the marginal costs of providing them:

- The city of Denver implemented a higher fee for its larger and better equipped "regional" recreation centers than for its smaller "neighborhood" centers. The larger centers were open longer hours and on more days than the neighborhood centers. Members of the smaller centers could pay a nominal daily fee to use a larger one.[3]
- Golf Course A is mature with challenging hazards designed for experienced, skilled golfers. Golf Course B is newly constructed with immature vegetation, wide fairways, minimal rough and few hazards and is designed for the inexperienced or less competent golfer. Course A is likely to be more expensive to build and maintain, so its prices should be higher.
- Similar differences occur among picnic shelters, which may range from those with kitchens, electricity and a stage to a basic shelter with a barbeque pit. In an arts context, the collections and exhibits at major galleries and museums are likely to be superior to those at local facilities. Because the expenses associated with them are likely to be higher, they are justified in charging a premium price.

If quality premiums are used, it is often advantageous to differentiate them from the regular offering by labeling them with a name that connotes their superior quality. This strategy is discussed in detail in Chapter 11. People use names as a heuristic that provides information about a service, and it has been confirmed in the marketing literature that names are a strong signal of quality.[4]

For those who want parks in their neighborhoods to be maintained and programmed to a higher level than an agency's norm, differential pricing can be facilitated through a special district. For example, Bryant Park is a dramatic 8-acre oasis in New York City comprising colorful flower beds, verdant green lawns and mature landscaping and is maintained immaculately. A substantial proportion of its $18 million renovation and $2 million annual maintenance budget is paid for by a private business improvement district. This was voluntarily created by businesses in the area that agreed to pay an annual premium of approximately $2 per square foot of their developed space and to dedicate those revenues to the park. They correctly believed that investment in these improvements would substantially increase the value of their assets.

At a concert, theater or sport event, a higher price is charged for front row seats than for back row seats. Similarly, a room in a hotel with a view of the ocean is priced higher than a room with a view of a parking lot or the back of the next building. (Interestingly, it would probably abrogate social norms and be considered unacceptable for restaurants to charge higher prices for tables with better views, but this sometimes occurs informally courtesy of the maître d'hôtel assigning the best tables to those who give the highest tips.)

In public leisure services, most *variations on preferred locations* within a facility occur in outdoor settings where landscape and topography are variable and thus inherently offer differential benefits to users. The preferred locations are easily identified—they are the most heavily used. For example, at a campsite, the preferred locations are likely to be close to a lake or river, on higher ground with a scenic view, in shady areas or at the most accessible sites. The users of these sites receive more benefits than campers on other sites. Thus, common practice at camping areas is now to offer sites at three price points reflecting their levels of perceived quality. This strategy redistributes demand over space. It has been shown to lead to a more even distribution of site use within campgrounds and to increase revenues.[5, 6]

Added services premiums are imposed to cover costs associated with extra services sought by relatively small proportions of those who use a basic offering. This leads to two-point pricing. For example, a basic admission price to a park may be charged, but additional premiums may be charged for those seeking interpretation programs, guided tours, trail permits or boat access. A membership fee for a recreation center may be augmented by additional charges for programs offered within it. In an urban parks setting, examples might include additional prices for lighting on athletic fields or tennis courts. These are clearly distinguishable augmented benefits. If the cost of these services is included in determining the regular cost-based price, basic service users will pay disproportionately more and will be subsidizing the augmented benefits users.

PREMIUMS TO MAXIMIZE THE REVENUE FROM ASSETS

Non-Resident Access

Many jurisdictions charge a higher price to non-residents than to residents. The logic for this policy is that agency budgets primarily come from general funds. Most of the money in a city's general fund originates from taxes paid by residents; consequently, residents contribute to the subsidy of these services. Non-residents do not pay property taxes. While they may contribute to the general fund through sales taxes if they shop in the community, this is a relatively small contribution. Hence, if they wish to use these services, a price premium is appropriate.

Charging non-residents a higher price than residents is discriminatory, but it is not illegally discriminatory. Thus, for example, the U.S. Supreme Court affirmed that charging out-of-state residents a hunting license fee that is 25 times that of which residents pay is legal and not in conflict with the U.S. Constitution's Fourteenth Amendment equal protection clause.[7] Generally, if a municipality can demonstrate a reasonable relationship between the differential price and legitimate governmental goals, the price will be upheld in the courts.[8] In a typical case, the court stated a city has the sovereign duty of maintaining the health of its residents:

> It owes no duty to non-residents. Residents are entitled to preference over non-residents and such action is not in contravention of the rights of non-residents. The primary purpose of a municipality corporation is to contribute toward the welfare, health, happiness, and interest of its inhabitants . . . not to further the interests of those residing outside its limits.[9]

However, because the rationale for non-resident premiums rests on those users being "free riders," it is illegal to impose the premium if the facility is funded by state or federal grants because such grants come from tax sources contributed by local residents and those from elsewhere in the state or the nation.

The rationale for charging non-residents a higher price is most compelling when demand for a service exceeds the available supply. The following cases are typical of such situations:

- The city of Palm Beach, Florida, calculated that $170 of the average household's tax bill goes toward athletic field maintenance and that 30–40 percent of participants are from other communities. As a result, city officials recommended the city raise the price for non-residents to $170.[10]

- The city's new spray pool was overwhelmed with children. Many came from outside the community in large groups. Some were teenagers whose behavior was unruly. The crowding and the lack of parental supervision, which permitted the bad behavior, led to multiple complaints to the city council. Consequently, the council restricted access to the facility. Residents could collect free season passes, but non-residents were charged $10 per child per day. Approximately, 1,000 resident passes were issued, but only 30 day passes. This resolved the overcrowding problem as attendance declined by over 50 percent.[11]

- City A (95,000) and City B (70,000) are twin cities that together form the nucleus of a metropolitan area of approximately 200,000 population. Most are unaware of where the boundaries between the two cities are located. Over 25 years, City A invested $20 million in new athletic fields, while City B invested $0 in them. As a result, residents of City B flock to play in City A's athletic leagues and facilities. The City B Council is pleased to watch this happen. It is under no pressure from its residents to develop more fields because its residents' needs are being accommodated by City A. City A not only incurs all the capital costs, but it also pays for the higher levels of maintenance associated with high levels of use. In contrast to City B, the City A Council is under constant pressure from its athletic groups to develop new fields because all the teams that want to play cannot be accommodated.

- An analogous issue arose with City A's summer day camp program. It had 400 slots available, but was flooded with 1,000 applicants on the first day of registration. Almost 50 percent resided outside the city. In many of these cases, parents worked in the city and wanted to drop and pick up their children at the start and end of their workday.

In these situations, the preferred solution is twofold. First, residents should be given priority to register/enroll before non-residents. Second, any remaining capacity should be filled with non-residents, and they should be charged a premium price that will maximize revenues generated by the service. This will reduce either the cost to residents who use it or the subsidy from taxpayers, or both.

If little spare capacity is available, the revenues can be maximized by imposing a large non-resident premium. On the other hand, if substantial capacity remains, revenues may be maximized by a relatively large number of non-residents paying a small premium or no premium. Indeed, in this case, the intent may be to attract as many non-residents as possible who are willing to pay a price that is higher than the variable cost of servicing them. Such revenues contribute to fixed costs, so the service needs less subsidy from taxpayers (Figure 4-5).

Because available space capacity and the price sensitivity of non-residents varies among services, non-resident premiums should be established for each service on an individual basis. This could entail reviewing how many non-residents participate in each program, each program's capacity, and the likely impact on demand and revenue if alternate potential non-resident premiums are imposed. Arbitrary, across-the-board premiums, such as a 50 percent higher price for non-residents for public leisure services, cannot optimize an agency's revenues. Indeed, such an indiscriminate and dysfunctional approach could result in less revenue accruing than if no premium price is imposed and could leave some programs with too few participants to be viable, and thus, residents are denied that opportunity.

The non-resident premium issue tends to be especially prominent in communities that are vacation destinations or resorts. In these cases, not only do visitors directly contribute only minimally to the taxes used to subsidize the facilities they use, but also they are likely to be less price sensitive than residents because the price to use leisure amenities for vacationers represents only a small proportion of the cost they invest in their trip.

Recognition that monetary price's proportion of composite price is a central element in determining level of elasticity leads many tourism-oriented communities to pursue a differentiated price structure:

- Ski areas in Colorado recognize monetary price for locals is likely to be a large proportion of composite price, so lift tickets available in local retail stores are priced substantially lower than those sold on-site. The on-site tickets can be sold at a premium because if tourists pay (say) an additional $25 a day for 4 days, $100 is a relatively small proportion of the aggregated $600 airfare, $600 accommodation cost, $300 for local transportation and meals, and the standard ticket cost of $200.
- San Francisco introduced an admission fee to its botanical gardens for non-residents. The 50-acre facility requires a staff of 11 gardeners. The department's budget had been reduced by $4.5 million in the previous 7 years. Visitors

make up a large proportion of the clientele. This revenue enables the quality of the gardens to be sustained.[3]

It has been suggested that this principle could be extended to international visitors in the context of national parks:

> Aren't U.S. taxpayers subsidizing foreign visitors to the parks, who benefit from the nominal entrance fees yet aren't paying any taxes at all? These international visitors, who travel when the dollar is a bargain compared to their native currencies, are among those who can best afford and are least impacted by an increase in entrance fees or changes in the fee structure. One suggestion might be to enact a two-tiered entrance fee structure-charging one rate for U.S. citizens and a higher rate for foreign visitors who do not support the parks through tax dollars. (p. 50)[12]

Such a strategy is adopted in other countries. For example, international visitors to public and non-profit attractions in Russia typically pay triple or quadruple the price charged to Russian citizens.

A contrary view is that public leisure amenities should be conceptualized as "loss leaders" in destination areas that attract visitors. From this perspective, it can be argued that the benefit from their spending at motels, restaurants and stores enhances a community's economic base, and this more than compensates for their subsidized use of amenities.

Ostensibly, it appears that premiums are relatively easy to impose because non-residents are likely to have relatively little political influence. However, sometimes such decisions are effectively challenged by the adage: We work here, we shop here, so why can't we play here? If leisure services are subsidized by sales taxes, the argument for premiums on those who reside proximate to a city but outside its boundaries is less persuasive. If they make purchases there, they have contributed sales taxes to the general fund. The debate, then, is focused on if the sales tax is a sufficiently large proportion of the general fund for their contribution to be considered equitable. In most cases, it is not.

Once a policy decision to differentiate price is made, three pragmatic decision rules have to be adopted. First, non-residents have to be defined. Are they everybody who lives outside a city's corporate limits? What about people who live outside the limits but (i) have a city postal address or (ii) own either property or a business inside the city? If school district facilities are used for many city programs, should residents include those who live outside the city but inside the school district? There is precedent for each of these definitions.

Second, athletic teams sometimes comprise residents and non-residents, so how will team entry fees be handled? Charging a premium based on the proportion of non-residents in a team would not be administratively feasible. An alternative is to define a resident team as having (say) 75% of its members who live within the defined area. Once a rule is implemented, will there be an audit process to ensure compliance, or will the honor system prevail? If it is to be audited, how will this be done?

Third, what form of identification will be accepted to verify residential status? Three types are available: (i) driver's license, automobile registration or insurance card; (ii) current telephone, gas, electric, water or cable bill; or (iii) voter registration or other government issued identification. Alternatively, an agency could issue its own leisure identification card. All verification approaches increase the irritation and harassment cost to residents and are a potential source of resentment. Many agencies simply adopt the honor system and accept its inevitable abuse by some as a reasonable cost of doing business that is preferable to the ill will created by rigorous verification. This problem does not exist when proof of residence must only be established periodically. Most states, for example, charge substantially higher annual hunting and/or fishing license fees to non-residents than to residents. In these cases, proof of residence, in the form of a driver's license or similar document, must only be provided once a year.

Commercial Use of Public Facilities

Whenever public facilities are used for commercial purposes, a premium should be charged. This transforms a facility from a public to a private good because it is no longer accessible to all and the Ability to Pay Principle is discarded. Providers of commercial services in public facilities should be required to secure a permit from the agency, which should be priced at the prevailing market rate. Such activities may include the following:

- Private tennis and basketball lessons and clinics for which public courts are taken over.
- Dog obedience classes being taught in parks.
- Private swimming lessons in city pools.
- Unauthorized, rogue athletic leagues playing on public fields.
- Sale of food or other goods in parks.
- Corporate picnics.
- Carnivals, circuses and fairs.
- Tournaments organized by commercial groups.
- Fitness "boot camps."
- Filming or commercial photography.

Hosting festivals and events promoted by for-profit entities commercializes public space, albeit a temporary transformation. Events may be accompanied by features such as large equipment containers, sponsors' enclosures, vendors, large tents and temporary car parking. In many communities, political pressure is heightened for leisure agencies to encourage commercial functions perceived to generate economic impact. However, because taxpayers own the public spaces, leisure agencies acting as their agents have an obligation to negotiate a lease, permit or rent for use of a facility that reflects the full market rate:

- Color Me Rad is a for-profit company headquartered in Utah. It organizes runs in different parts of the U.S. in which runners are doused with brightly colored corn starch. A typical run, attracting 7,000 entries, was hosted at Onondaga Lake Park close to Syracuse, New York. The county that owned the park charged the company $4,000 for use of the facility. Color Me Rad took in approximately $250,000 in registration fees. The county revised the contract the next year so it received a $40,000 fee. The deputy county executive commented: "We think taxpayers should see a little bit of relief for use of our facilities . . . it is a for-profit enterprise and we think it's appropriate to see a share of the registration fees."[13]

Failure to charge commercial suppliers the market rate adversely affects not only taxpayers who forfeit revenues, but also competitor businesses. Businesses operating on public lands without paying market rates have lower overhead than their competitors who pay those rates. For example, a fitness club owner may have debt charges, property taxes and operating expenses of (say) $10,000 a month, while a fitness boot camp operator using a park as a facility has no such overhead. Clearly, this unfair competitive advantage has the potential to damage the viability of the club owner's operation:

- Boot camp fitness classes use public parks and complement a leisure agency's mission by offering organized exercise classes. However, agencies have concerns about private instructors profiting off a taxpayer facility and sometimes flaunting posted regulations governing park usage. For example, one agency reported long streaks of torn-up turf from boot camp participants running sprints in harnesses connected to truck tires; pavilions and ramadas used as staging areas for classes; rope nettings tied to the roofs of ramadas for climbing drills; picnic tables being used as step-up platforms for cardio training; and disturbance of other users and neighbors with yelling, whistles and bullhorns.[14] Many even post calendars and schedules on their websites listing parks as class sites. Accordingly, instructors are increasingly required to have a permit that defines parameters of their use. The price of permits varies widely. Examples include the following:

  - Los Angeles County, $300 per year and 15 percent of gross receipts.
  - Henderson, Nevada, $300 and $600 for 3 and 6 months, respectively.
  - Austin, Texas, $100 per year and 45 cents per day per client.[15]

Commercial users should be required to show evidence of comprehensive liability insurance to protect the agency against lawsuits and to provide a bond to ensure the site is cleaned up and restored to its pre-use condition.

Auctions and Bidding

In contexts in which demand greatly exceeds supply, a bidding process or auction can be used to capture consumers' surplus and extract the maximum premium. This unconventional approach directly involves users in the price-setting process. Widespread access to the World Wide Web makes this relatively easy to administer. For example, if multiple teams or leagues are seeking to use athletic fields at peak times, interested parties can be invited to bid for those time slots, and the slots will be allocated to those prepared to pay the most. This is analogous to the competitive bidding process that public jurisdictions use for construction contracts and concession operators or to select other vendors from whom to buy services.

State wildlife agencies frequently use variations of this approach. For example, the Texas Parks and Wildlife Department authorizes one permit a year to harvest a bighorn ram. In a recent year, the winning bid was $152,000. This approach has the added virtue of managers not having to develop (invariably controversial) administrative decision rules to prioritize who should have access to the relatively rare resource. However, this business model ignores concerns related to equity and ability to pay.

The equity concern has led to hybrid models emerging in the form of lotteries to which all have equal access. These are used to prioritize most of a resource's use, but bids are solicited for a remaining small portion of the resource to capture substantial additional revenue and some of the consumers' surplus. In these cases, the auction component is often positioned as a subsidy to those entering the lottery. That is, without the auction revenues, entry fees to the lottery would be higher.

In the 1970s, a small group of avid sheep hunters persuaded some state game departments to donate one permit to hunt Western bighorn sheep to conservation organizations dedicated to restoring the sheep herds in the wild. The auction of these permits has largely funded one of the most successful wildlife-recovery programs in the U.S., nearly doubling their number to 45,000 animals in the following two decades. Importantly, because the auction bids are paid to a non-profit organization, they are fully tax deductible:

- In 8 years, one wealthy hunter spent $1.5 million at auctions to hunt a handful of sheep. His winning bids included $303,000 for an Arizona bighorn; $285,000 for a desert bighorn; and $281,000 for a Rocky Mountain bighorn. His other bids included $310,000 for a Montana sheep permit and $200,000 for an Alaskan Dell sheep permit, but in both cases he returned from the several week hunts empty-handed because the horns of the few sheep he saw were not sufficiently large to meet his standards.[16]

This model has been widely adopted to raise funds for managing other wild game herds:

- Prospective hunters in Vermont could purchase lottery tickets for a moose permit. Entry fees for residents were $10 and $25 for non-residents. The winners were then authorized to buy permits for $100 and $350, respectively. Over 12,000 hunters paid $170,000 to enter the lottery and 405 were successful. Those who were unsuccessful subsequently could bid on five additional permits, for which each winner typically paid over $4,000.
- In Tennessee, five elk permits were selected from entries in a lottery that hunters paid $10 to enter. An additional permit was auctioned, and the winning bid was $8,700.

If this approach were adopted for the allocation of soccer fields, for example, the process might involve the following:

- Determine the daily/weekly capacity of the fields.
- Assign off-peak, shoulder and peak prices to the available time slots.
- Conduct a lottery to decide the order in which leagues/teams select their preferred time slots.
- Allocate (say) 80 percent of the peak time slots in this way, but make the remaining 20 percent available in auction.

Revenues from the auction of hunting permits help finance the management of the herds, from which hunters benefit. In the case of athletic fields, the agency may be perceived to be gaining by unfairly exploiting its clienteles. This perception would likely change if athletic fields were financed through an enterprise fund, so revenues raised from auction of the peak time slots would reduce the amounts other groups had to pay.

For leisure managers involved with the operation of popular entertainment or sport venues, the reverse auction process pioneered by Northwestern University Athletic Department has emerged as a viable option for capturing consumers' surplus:

- The reverse auction approach was spurred by tickets for premium games being sold privately on the Web at prices far in excess of their fair value. Accordingly, prices were established for three tiers of seats and were gradually lowered over time until a tier sold out. Those who purchased at a higher price were refunded the difference between their price and the final lowest price. This process led to the highest priced tickets being sold for $190, compared to $70 before the system was introduced. An added benefit was that season tickets were more attractive because these premium games were included and a lower price was paid for them.[17]

SUMMARY

The Benefit Principle directs that those willing to pay for increments of benefits beyond the standard offering pay a premium. This occurs in three contexts. First, time scarcity is a challenge confronting many, so wherever an agency can offer time savings by providing a reservation option, a premium can be charged.

Second, charging a premium for peak time use is likely to persuade some participants to shift to non-peak times. This would alleviate crowding, which may lead to a lower quality experience, and reduce the facility capacity needed to accommodate demand. Constructing facilities for peak demand is expensive because it means some capacity is unused for much of the time. If premium pricing "flattens" peak time use, less capital investment is needed. Because peak time users are responsible for a disproportionate amount of the cost of developing a facility compared to off-peak users, they should pay a premium that covers that cost.

The third context for user benefit–related premiums is where participants seek increments of quality beyond the regular level of service. This stems from three sources: (i) If there is variation among facilities or programs, the higher quality options are likely to cost more to develop and maintain, so a price premium contributes to covering the added costs; (ii) preferred locations, especially in outdoor settings, offer a superior experience, so a premium is justified; and (iii) additional service premiums are imposed to cover costs associated with extra services sought by a relatively small proportion of those who use a basic offering.

As stewards of public assets, agencies are required, through the Benefit Principle, to maximize the revenue potential of those assets on behalf of taxpayers when this does not compromise their mandate to be fully accessible to all residents. This rationale is the justification for imposing premiums for non-resident and commercial use of the assets and the selective adoption of auctions or bidding to capture more consumers' surplus for taxpayers.

Because non-residents do not pay (or pay much lower) taxes to support the use of facilities and programs, it is appropriate they pay a premium that reflects the full market price. Similarly, whenever public facilities are used for commercial purposes, a premium reflecting the prevailing market rate should be charged. Commercial use transforms a facility from a public to a private amenity because it is no longer accessible to all and the Ability to Pay Principle is discarded. In contexts in which demand greatly exceeds supply, a bidding process or auction can be used to capture consumers' surplus and extract the maximum premium.

REFERENCES

1. Scott, D. (1993). Time scarcity and its implications for leisure behavior and service delivery. *Journal of Park and Recreation Administration, 11*(3), 51–60.
2. Berry, L. L. (1990, February). Market to the perceptions. *American Demographics, 1990,* 31.
3. Chipkin, H. (2011, September). Mastering revenue. *Parks & Recreation, 46*(9), 47–51.
4. Rao, A. R., & Monroe, K. B. (1989). The effect of price, brand name, and store name on buyers' perceptions of product quality: An integrative review. *Journal of Marketing Research, 26,* 351–357.
5. Bamford, T. E., Manning, R. F., Foreter, L. K., & Koenemann, E. H. (1988). Differential campsite pricing: An experiment. *Journal of Leisure Research, 20,* 324–342.
6. Manning, R. E., Callinan E. A., Echelberger, H. E., Koenemann, E. K., & McEwen, D. N. (1984). Differential fees: Raising revenue, distributing demand. *Journal of Park and Recreation Administration, 2*(1), 20–38.
7. Baldwin v. Fish and Game Commission of Montana, 435 U.S. 371 (1978), 56 L.Ed.2d 354.
8. Koslowski, J. C. (1982, March). Validity of non-resident and other discriminatory regulations in municipal recreation. *Parks and Recreation, 17,* 28–34.
9. McClain v. City of South Pasadena, 155 Cal. App. 2d 423, 318 P. 2d 199 (1957).
10. Doris, T. (2014, July 13). Should non-residents pay more to use city fields, parks? *Palm Beach Post.* Retrieved from http://www.athleticbusiness.com/more-news/should-non-residents-pay-more-to-use-city-fields-parks.html
11. Stamm, J. (2015, July 28). Non-resident fee eases crowding at spray park. *The Commercial Appeal.* Retrieved from http://www.athleticbusiness.com/more-news/non-resident-fee-eases-crowding-at-spray-park-br.html
12. Bailey, A. C. (1993). Disney World $34: Grand Canyon $5: A proposal for ensuring the future of our national parks. In *The American Express Annual Review of Travel* (pp. 46–51). New York, NY: American Express.

13. Coin, G. (2013, October 24). For-profit companies renting Onondaga County Parks could pay more - much more - next year. *Syracuse Post-Standard*. Retrieved from http://www.syracuse.com/news/index.ssf/2013/09/for-profit_companies_could_pay_more_--_sometimes_much_more_--_to_use_onondaga_co.html

14. Hayward, P. (2013, March). Private businesses in public parks. *Parks and Recreation, 48*, 35–39.

15. Attwood, E. (2013, April). Free-for-all. *Athletic Business, 2013*, 56–58.

16. Montaigne, F. (1998, January 9). Paying big bucks for a shot at a bighorn. *Wall Street Journal*, p. B7.

17. Seguira, K. (2014, February 11). Georgia Tech may auction tickets to Clemson game. *The Atlanta Journal–Constitution*. Retrieved from http://www.athleticbusiness.com/more-news/georgia-tech-may-auction-tickets-to-clemson-game.html

Behavioral Pricing

*Adapting Price to Fit Clienteles' Perceptions
of What Is Acceptable*

To this point in the text, much of the guiding conceptual framework has been adapted from the neoclassical economic concepts of price, demand and utility. The price–demand relationship was discussed in Chapter 5. Utility represents the satisfaction or benefits that a service user experiences. Price operationalizes it because it measures the amount people willing to pay for a given service. It is a good general principle. If the price of a service goes up, usually fewer people will use it. These concepts assume that when people evaluate a price, their thinking is logical and rational, they invariably seek to maximize utility, and they act independently on the basis of full and relevant information. In the past, economists typically have discounted behaviors that violate these principles, viewing such behaviors as idiosyncratic, unstable and atypical exceptions to the norm.

However, over the past three decades, it has been recognized that this traditional approach is incomplete. Observations of reactions to pricing decisions regularly contradict the assumption of rationality, suggesting exceptions to it are the norm rather than atypical. Hence, the focus has shifted from how economists believe people *ought* to behave to how they *actually* behave. The revised focus is now generally known as "behavioral pricing." The word "behavioral" emphasizes how real-world people act rather than prescribing how they ought to act.

The psychologist who was one of the pioneers of this focus shift acknowledged the continued relevance of the traditional economic model: "Expected utility theory, which was the foundation of the rational agent model, is to this day the most important theory of the social sciences" (p. 270).[1] He further noted, "The basic concepts of economics are essential intellectual tools" (p. 286).[1] Nevertheless, he recalled that his interest in challenging the theory's completeness was piqued when he read the opening sentence of an economist's essay: "The agent of economic theory is rational, selfish, and his tastes do not change" (p. 269).[1] He recalled his reaction:

I was astonished, my economist colleagues worked in the building next door, but I had not appreciated the profound difference between our intellectual worlds. To a psychologist, it is self-evident that people are neither fully rational, nor completely selfish, and that their tastes are anything but stable. Our two disciplines seemed to be studying different species. (p. 269)[1]

This revelation created "an opportunity for an interesting conversation across the boundaries of the disciplines" (p. 269)[1] and ultimately the emergence of behavioral economics.

It is now recognized that people often make decisions that are systematically and substantially different from those predicted by the standard economic model. Hence, in the marketing and leisure literatures, there has been a movement to supplement and enrich the neoclassical model, by embracing a cognitive processing approach that considers the reactions and behavior of individuals to a given price or changes in price.[2] Cognitive processing is the manipulation, transformation or reorganization of information.[3] The neoclassical economic principles discussed in the book to this point provide the skeletal structure for making price decisions, but understanding likely cognitive responses to price changes is central to ensuring the changes are consistent with users' expectations, thus avoiding negative reactions.

Patterns of cognitive responses to price changes have been identified. Many of them are based on heuristics. Heuristics are simple procedures that help find adequate, though often imperfect, answers to difficult questions.[1] They are cues or "rules of thumb" that offer shortcuts so users can better cope with their limited processing capacity and simplify the cognitive process of decision making. They appear to be universal; that is, they are ubiquitous and shared by a large proportion of people. The mechanics underlying heuristics are essentially automatic. Individuals do not consciously seek to control them because they are usually unaware they are operating and much of the time they work satisfactorily. However, the above definition notes they are "often imperfect," in that they are prone to error bias, which is often systematic and predictable.

The concepts of adaptation-level theory, assimilation-contrast theory, reference price theory and prospect theory provide the frameworks for explaining how these heuristics are formed, how acceptability of a price occurs and what managers can do to enhance it. The central theme of behavioral pricing is that users respond to price differences rather than to specific prices per se. It is *relative* prices that are important in judgments on the acceptability of a price.

Behavioral pricing recognizes perceptions of price are malleable. In the four chapters in this section, strategies leisure managers can use to exploit the heuristics and their biases to manipulate users' perceptions are described and illustrated. The goal is to minimize controversy and resistance often associated with price increases. These strategies move managers and elected officials away from the arbitrary and intuitive actions that have traditionally prevailed and toward the famous dictum of a "perfect" price suggested over 40 years ago:

The "perfect" price is not one where the payer gets the benefit, or where service levels are determined, or where there are no income distribution effects. For the local official, the perfect user charge may have these features but overriding importance to him or her is whether the public will resist paying for the service (p. 271).[4]

REFERENCES

1. Kahneman, D. (2011). *Thinking fast and slow.* London, England: Penguin.
2. McCarville, R. E. (1990). The role of cognitive processes in explaining reactions to price change for leisure services. *Journal of Park and Recreation Administration,* 8(3), 76–86.
3. Janiszewski, C. L., & Wyer, R. S. (2014). Context and process priming: A review. *Journal of Consumer Psychology, 24*(1), 96–116.
4. Meltsner, A. J. (1971). *The politics of city revenue.* Berkeley: University of California Press.

Chapter 9

Reference Price

What It Is and How It Works

- Defining internal reference price
- The theoretical genesis of internal reference price
- Shapers of internal reference price
- Dual process theories
- Summary

A prospective user acquires, observes or experiences price information; stores it in memory; and uses it as an internal reference against which a judgment is made regarding the acceptability of a new price. Thus, internal reference price is the primary standard against which the acceptability of a purchase price is judged.[1] Figure 9-1 shows how it is formed, and strategies are identified, which are discussed in Chapters 10, 11 and 12, that are designed either to ensure a purchase price is consistent with reference price or to reconcile prices inconsistent with reference price so they become acceptable to users.

In this chapter, reference price is defined first. The genesis of the concept springs from adaptation-level theory,[2] which suggests people judge a new price by comparing it with a benchmark level to which they have become adapted. This explanation is augmented by assimilation-contrast theory,[3] which states that the benchmark level is not absolute. Rather, there is a latitude of acceptance around it (Figure 9-1). The discussion of these theories is followed by a description of the three influences that adaptation-level theory suggests shape reference price: residual knowledge, which refers to an individual's existing knowledge; the normative equity criterion that prevails in a community; and the "value" context within which potential users perceive a service is being offered. The chapter concludes with a description of dual process theories, which explain that the cognitive processing of price-related information may be absorbed either actively and deliberately or by subconscious and non-deliberative processes.[4, 5]

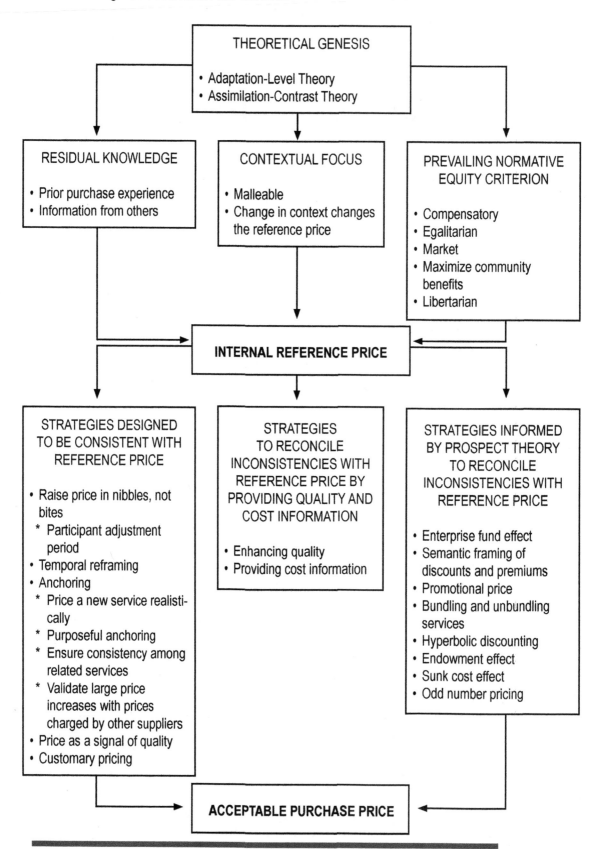

Figure 9-1. The Conceptual Framework Undergirding Behavioral Pricing Strategies

DEFINING INTERNAL REFERENCE PRICE

A common way to view internal reference price is as an expectation of what constitutes an acceptable price.[6] It is likely to be independent of the cost of offering a service because this is generally unknown to the user. Consistent with assimilation-contrast theory, there is widespread recognition that no single point can capture the internal reference price. Rather, there is a range of deviation around it. In the private sector, the *prima facie* case in support of a reference range or scale rather than a reference point is clear: "Because consumers have observed and experienced variations in prices across brands, across stores, and at different times, it is unlikely that they would have clearly defined point estimates of price for a product" (p. 257).[7] It has been suggested that the parameters of the reference range are likely to be the resistance price (upper limit) and the bargain price (lower limit below which there may be resistance because of concerns about quality).[8] These two points delineate the boundaries of the latitude of price acceptance and are discussed in the next section of this chapter.

Reference prices for and within each individual will be different because of people's different responses to contextual, residual and normative stimuli (Figure 9-1). A reference price need not correspond to any actual price. The general consensus is that internal reference price is best conceptualized as the weighted mean value of past prices to which a user has been exposed, with most weight assigned to the most recent prices.[9, 10, 11] Thus, it was concluded in a study of swimming pool users: "For those who pay fees repeatedly over time, price last paid seems to represent a parsimonious indicator of price expectations" (p. 62).[12] Certainly, prices paid on more recent occasions are likely to have a greater effect on reference price than are earlier payments.[13] When a new price is assimilated, it is averaged into the set of past prices to form a revised reference price. Evidence that changes in reference price occur with experience was provided in a study of price changes among users at five recreation centers. The authors reported: "The upper boundary of reference prices shifted as prices rose" (p. 259).[14]

Ostensibly, these definitions of reference price suggest it is actively derived through a conscious cognitive process. However, it has consistently been reported that people have only a vague idea of actual prices. In a study of reactions to price increases of between 10 percent and 70 percent at five recreation centers, it was reported that between 18 percent and 44 percent of users were not aware of the previous price.[14] Reviewers of the price recall literature concluded: "A relatively low proportion of buyers can recall accurately prices of products they had recently purchased" (p. 208).[15] Similarly, in a leisure services context, it was reported: "Respondents offered estimates of prices they believed they last paid, but most (67%) were uncertain of the accuracy of their estimates" (p. 59).[12] This uncertainty suggests a reference price is a rough estimate, reinforcing the notion that it consists of a range rather than a single point. This range (around which the latitude of acceptance discussed in the next section is constructed) represents a distribution of reference prices. Users may have a general idea of whether a price is acceptable, but their reference standard is likely to be approximate.

A relatively wide distribution of internal reference prices is likely for services that are purchased infrequently because in these cases the last price paid is likely to become vague with the passage of time. Frequent participants in a leisure service are most likely to notice price increases. Their reference price range is likely to be narrow and well defined for four reasons. First, a user may be highly ego involved. Thus, the developers of assimilation-contrast theory concluded: "The range of assimilation is inversely related to the degree of personal involvement" (p. 131).[16] Second, the agency may be the only supplier of a service in a community, so its users are exposed to few, if any, alternate reference points. Third, prices often remain stable over relatively long times. Fourth, a substantial proportion of patrons is likely to be repeat users, so their awareness of prices is likely to be relatively strong:

> Many individuals participate in recreation on a regular basis. Daily swims at the community pool, weekly exercise classes, or monthly concerts are all examples of public recreation programs that may engender definitive reference prices in the minds of consumers. As a result of the regular use of public recreation programs, consumers may be able to form definite price structures for such programs. (p. 284)[17]

THE THEORETICAL GENESIS OF INTERNAL REFERENCE PRICE

The concepts of internal reference price and of latitude of price acceptance that accompanies it have their primary genesis in adaptation-level theory[2] and assimilation-contrast theory.[3] Originally, these theories were developed to explain psychophysical phenomena related to sensory perception. Subsequently, they were recognized as having wide generalizability to other contexts, including the explanation of how internal reference prices are formed.

Adaptation-Level Theory

Adaptation is derived from the field of biology and means adjusting to the conditions under which species must live to survive. When it was subsequently embraced by the field of psychology, its general meaning was more restricted. It referred to adjusting to preceding conditions, and the perceived magnitude and effect of a stimulus depended on its relationship to preceding stimuli. That is, experience with prior stimuli creates an adaptation level or reference point, and subsequent stimuli are judged in relation to it: "Stimuli impinge upon organisms already adapted to what has gone before, and internal states depend upon previously existing internal conditions as well as external inciters to action" (p. 37).[2] Thus, a new stimulus is judged against a standard to which an individual has become accustomed: "If one has been subjected to a series of sudden, intense, sounds, another stimulus of the same kind will have less effect than if it appears against a quiet sound" (p. 228).[2] The following example provides a more concrete illustration of the theory in a sensory context:

> If a person has lived in the silence of a desert, the birds and crickets of a farm will seem noisy. But if one has lived in the hubbub of Manhattan, the same farm sounds

will seem blissfully quiet. However, after living on the farm for a while, the previous city dweller will then find Manhattan noisy. The reason is that new stimuli are incorporated into prior information so that the reference point is shifted. (p. 52)[18]

The adaptation level is the standard around which a scale of judgment of the acceptability of a phenomenon is anchored. In the context of this book, it suggests that people judge a stimulus, such as a new price, by comparing it to an existing benchmark price to which they have become accustomed.

Adaptation level is defined as "a weighted geometric mean of all stimuli impinging upon the organism from without and all stimuli affecting behavior from within" (p. 59).[2] In the context of pricing, this adaptation level is the internal reference price. It represents the pooled effect of all previous exposure to prices for a given service. This definition of adaptation level adds support to the conceptualization of reference price as a weighted mean. Because "adaptation is the adjustment of the organism to the environment," it is ongoing rather than fixed and thus "stresses changing levels" (p. 52).[2] Hence, "values assigned to an adaptation value must be regarded as mean values about which the actual value fluctuates" (p. 129).[2] New information is constantly being absorbed, and as a result, reference prices are revised. Thus, they should not be considered as fixed entities resistant to change. On the contrary, adaptation-level theory recognizes the influence of a flow of incoming information.

Assimilation-Contrast Theory

Assimilation-contrast theory (also known as social judgment theory) is based on results from a series of experiments undertaken with weights and numerical scales.[3] It was noted that subjects use two processes when making psychophysical judgments, which are termed "contrast" and "assimilation." Contrast denotes difference, repulsion and movement away from an object's anchor or position, whereas assimilation denotes likeness, attraction and movement toward the anchor. The original results were generalized in these terms:

When an anchor is introduced at the end or slightly removed from the end of the series, there will be a displacement of the scale of judgment toward the anchor and assimilation of the new reference point in the series. When, however, the reference point is too remote, there will be displacement in the opposite direction (i.e., away from the anchor). (p. 150)[19]

This theory is consistent with adaptation-level theory because it recognizes the central role of a psychological reference point and it "serves as a basis for comparison and appraisal of relevant stimulus items on subsequent encounters" (p. 13).[3] However, it extends adaptation-level theory by proposing (i) a latitude of acceptance for new stimuli that makes them tolerable, (ii) a latitude of rejection for those considered to be objectionable and (iii) a latitude of non-commitment for those not evaluated as either acceptable or objectionable. The authors observed:

The position within the [reference] scale represents [a person's] stand on the issue and serves as a major anchor in judgment. If the issue is a significant one to him, he is willing to tolerate only slight deviation [latitude of acceptance] and finds further deviation obnoxious [latitude of rejection]. (p. 13)[3]

Assimilation and contrast are viewed as complementary, not independent, processes. Thus, while adaptation-level theory introduces the notion of a reference point and explains how it is derived, assimilation-contrast theory complements it by introducing the concept of latitude of acceptance around that adaptation level.

The three latitudes or zones are shown in Figure 9-2, which transitions them from the original psychophysical context to the area of pricing. When users are confronted with a price that is different from what they expect to pay, they must decide whether the difference between the expected and the new price is significant. If they perceive the difference as insignificant, it falls within the latitude of acceptance, so they are likely to classify the two prices as similar and to behave as they have in the past. The latitude of acceptance recognizes that for a given service and quality level, people have a range of prices they consider acceptable. Hence, they have two price limits: an upper limit (resistance price) beyond which the price is perceived as too high relative to perceived quality and a lower limit (bargain price) below which the quality of the service becomes suspect. These price thresholds determine an acceptable range within which a given price should fall. A new price is assimilated and accepted only if the observed price is judged as being within that range. The range is then updated to incorporate the new information.

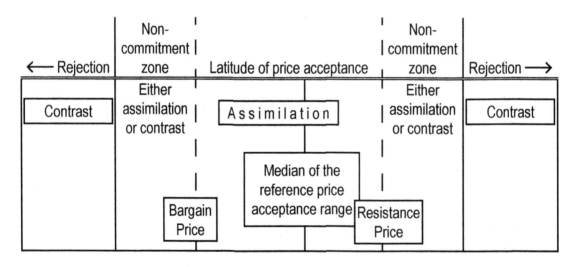

Figure 9-2. Conceptualization of the Latitude of Price Acceptance

On the other hand, if users perceive a new price to be significantly different from the expectation, a contrast effect occurs and it falls into the latitude of rejection, so the new price is considered unacceptable. The latitude of non-commitment lies between acceptance and rejection. A new price is assigned to that zone if it is not immediately accepted or rejected. From here, the price may either be assimilated and accepted or be classified as contrasting with the reference price and be rejected. Thus, while new credible prices are assimilated and used to update the internal reference price, prices that are not deemed credible are contrasted and rejected, so their influence on the reference price is likely to be minimal. Empirical support for this process emerged in a study of participants in a range of leisure services: "Recreation consumers are willing to pay within ranges of acceptable prices; those outside the acceptable range are considered objectionable" (p. 54).[20]

SHAPERS OF INTERNAL REFERENCE PRICE

The original articulation of adaptation-level theory suggests level of adaptation is determined by the pooled effect of three classes of stimuli:

- Focal stimuli: attributes of the stimulus that occupy the immediate attention.
- Contextual or background stimuli: variables that emanate from the context within which the focal stimuli are considered.
- Residual or organic stimuli: inner psychological and physiological processes affecting behavior.[2]

The potential of this theory for explaining how internal reference price is formed was recognized in the early 1970s.[1, 21, 22] It has been widely embraced by the marketing field since that time, and its component stimuli have been subject to substantial research conducted in the retailing sector. Some of the findings of this research can be adapted to the public leisure services field, but the transition requires that three substantive changes be made to the original model.

First, focal stimuli have been found to be subsumed into the contextual stimuli category.[17] This is not inconsistent with the original theory, and its author recognized this was likely in some contexts:

> The division of stimuli into three classes is largely a matter of convenience . . . What is focal at one moment may become background [contextual] or residual at the next moment . . . The particular class to which stimuli are referenced is far less important than is the determination of the contribution made by stimuli to adaptation level, regardless of what they are called. (p. 59)[2]

Focal stimuli articulated in the original theory are those to which an individual directly responds. An individual's reference price for a leisure service is based on an assumed "value package." If the price is higher than the resistance price of the latitude of acceptance zone so it is in the non-commitment zone, it may not be rejected if the contextual cues associated with the leisure service are also higher than those associated with the reference value package. Rather, the upper boundary of the acceptance zone may be shifted higher to accommodate the price. This recognizes that contextual stimuli associated with a given program can move the latitude of acceptance in either direction.

In the leisure services field, what are termed "focal stimuli" in the original theory are the on-site tangibles to which users are exposed when visiting a facility or participating in a program. The on-site stimuli may include elements such as features of the program, ambiance/atmosphere, quality of facility, dress of staff, amount of crowding and program name. In essence, these are elements of the context in which the experience will occur, so it is appropriate to classify them as contextual variables.

A second amendment is a clarification of the original theory's residual/organic stimuli category, which embraces all "within" variables comprising "inner determinants [that] have an existence more or less independent of situational factors" (p. 378).[2] In the context of pricing, the dominant "inner determinant" is likely to be the encoding of personal past experience and knowledge acquired from other sources. These create residual knowledge. They obviously vary among individuals, and this profoundly influences people's perceptions of price.[23] This was recognized in the leisure field by rejecting the amorphous, generic term "organic" in favor of "residual" to connote past experience and by more precisely defining the term: "Residual stimuli represent the relative influence of previous purchase experience" (p. 283).[17] An extended definition of residual stimuli is that they are perceptions of price derived from the internal processing of an individual's previous purchase experiences and previous information absorbed from external sources.

The third substantive change from the original articulation of adaptation-level theory is the addition of a normative stimuli category. Equity is the key element that differentiates marketing in the public and private sectors,[24] and the prevailing equity criterion in a community is likely to have a profound influence on people's acceptability of a price.

Residual knowledge is a composite of the unique life experiences that an *individual* has accumulated, whereas the prevailing normative equity criterion establishes the principles of what constitutes a "fair" price as defined by a majority of a *community's* residents. Thus, these influencers serve as anchors at the personal and community levels, respectively (Figure 9-1).

When individuals view a price as being "unacceptable," it is outside their latitude of acceptance, which reflects expectations created by the two anchors. For example, their residual knowledge may lead to rejection of a new price because "it is more than I paid in the past, than I paid elsewhere or than my friends paid elsewhere." Alternatively, the new price may be inconsistent with a community's prevailing equity criterion, for example, "I paid more than other users of similar economic status to me" (egalitarian equity); "It is too expensive, I cannot afford it" (compensatory equity); "Why should I pay so much when the community as a whole benefits from the service?" (market equity). These equity terms are explained later in the chapter.

Hence, in the leisure services field, expectations related to pricing decisions are created by the normative equity and residual knowledge anchors. Individuals' attitudes to a price (i.e., people's ways of judging its acceptability) are determined by how they perceive its context relates to those anchors (Figure 9-1). The two anchors are "givens" that leisure managers must work within and cannot manipulate. They create the expectation against which the acceptability of a price in a given context is evaluated. However, it is often possible to change people's perceptions of a context by providing additional information to stakeholders and framing it so it is congruent with their expectations. In the following subsections, an overview is provided of the characteristics of each of the stimuli that shape reference price.

Residual Knowledge

The role of an individual's past experience in serving as an anchor against which to evaluate a new stimulus was recognized in assimilation-contrast theory:

> Learning i.e., the conditions and extent of past experience with the stimulus material, is an important determinant of the nature of an individual's judgment scale and his placements of relevant stimuli. . . . Past experience in the form of practice provides the subject with an established reference scale which affects his placement of relevant stimuli. (p. 183)[3]

It also recognized the role of others' opinions in establishing the residual knowledge anchor: "The introduction of an explicit anchor in the form of another person's judgment is found to affect judgment in predictable directions" (p. 182).[3]

There is widespread acknowledgment that residual knowledge influences the extent to which consumers accept a price.[7] Such knowledge may be acquired directly based on using an existing service or by using a similar service from another leisure services agency or from another service supplier. It also may be acquired vicariously from external sources, such as others in the social group, media or promotional channels. Residual knowledge refers not only to price information, but also to information related to the quality of service associated with past purchase prices. This enables potential users to make judgments about "value for money" likely to be obtained at a given price for a given quality of service.

Confidence about the level of accuracy of the residual knowledge is likely to vary according to the number and the credibility of the information sources from which it is compiled. The degree of confidence will affect the range of the acceptable price range. As confidence in the accuracy of the residual knowledge increases, the width of the latitude of acceptance is likely to decrease. Thus, those who perceive they have relatively little residual knowledge relating to a service's price are likely to consider a relatively wide range of prices as being acceptable, and vice versa.[7]

Prevailing Normative Equity Criterion

Assimilation-contrast theory recognizes that the "formation of a reference scale [price] has to include the social setting: established norms" (p. 13).[3] All societal units have norms that are guidelines prescribing how a majority of people in that community are likely to respond to a given situation. Norms are cultural expectations—an expression of a community's values about the "right" or desirable way to act. The power of community norms was vividly illustrated in the public outcry when a $1 admission fee was proposed for a visit to the Statue of Liberty. The outcry was no less vehement when it was pointed out that "this modest charge [was] far less than fees charged by tour boat operators and parking lot managers for their services" (p. 13),[25] which visitors had to use to access the site. A senator railing against the proposal captured the public mood when he said: "Lady Liberty says at her base, 'Give me your tired, your poor, your huddled masses.' She doesn't say, 'Give me your dollars.'" (p. 13).[25] Outrage with the proposed fee occurred because it violated existing norms, and price information related to visitors' payments for boat rides and parking was not sufficiently convincing to override those norms, so it gained no traction.

Similar reactions often occur when fees are proposed for the first time for youth activities, such as Little League baseball. For many residents, their long-established normative expectation of zero price will nullify the potential influence of rational logic or any information messages designed to change their reference price. Such messages are only likely to be persuasive if they are consistent with existing norms and expectations. For example, residents in one community favored public subsidization of leisure programs for the very young and the elderly, but were not supportive of offering such support for similar programs offered to adults.[26] In that community, information messages designed to raise prices for adults engaging in programs would likely be persuasive because the appeal would be consistent with existing norms.

Norms are not right or wrong according to a generic absolute high ethical standard, and an unquestioned consensus on them is unlikely. Rather, different groups in a community are likely to have different norms and values, reflecting their different political, religious, heritage, ethnic and generational perspectives. However, a majority view will emerge and serve as the community norm until a different majority value system replaces it. The more diverse a community's population, the more rapidly the prevailing norms are likely to shift, but typically such shifts are gradual rather than precipitous.

The community norm most pertinent in the context of price decisions is the prevailing interpretation of equity. Equity is the criterion people use to evaluate fairness.[24] Notions of equity, like pricing strategies, are central to how public leisure services are allocated. The challenges associated with operationalizing equity in the context of leisure services have been expressed in the following terms:

> Equity is a pseudo-cognate term in that many who use it assume that everyone has the same intuitive definition of it. This is a fallacious assumption. Equity is not necessarily synonymous with equality, which refers to "sameness," although it can be. Rather, equity refers to fairness and justice. It addresses the question, "Who gets what?" or in normative terms, "Who ought to get what?" These questions undergird much political debate and move equity into the multifaceted realm of individuals' value systems, which makes its operationalization elusive. Not only is equity difficult to define, but invariably it is controversial when it is defined. (p. 36)[27]

Five distinct conceptualizations of equity[27] guide pricing strategies, and if the pricing strategy is not consistent with the equity norm that prevails in a community, it will be politically opposed. The implications for pricing decisions shaped by each of these equity conceptualizations are briefly discussed in the following paragraphs.

Compensatory equity "involves allocating services so that economically disadvantaged groups, individuals, or areas receive extra increments of resources" (p. 290).[28] Two pricing guidelines are commonly used to accommodate this interpretation of equity. The first is to keep all prices low so they are not a barrier to participation of the economically disadvantaged. This approach means the agency will forgo substantial consumers' surplus revenues. It was noted earlier in the book that failure to charge those who can afford to pay means fewer resources are available to subsidize more services for the economically disadvantaged. Further, if the economically disadvantaged are not major users of a service, this approach means their taxes (the alternative funding source to revenues derived from pricing) are used to subsidize wealthier participants. This creates a distorted payment system that leads to inverse income redistribution and is counter to the compensatory equity goal (Chapter 2). A second approach is to price differentially so the economically disadvantaged pay a lower price than others. It was noted in Chapter 6 that the challenge is to implement this in such a way that they are not stigmatized.

Egalitarian equity directs all residents should be treated equally. This suggests public leisure services should be priced so they "break even." This would ensure non-users are not subsidizing users. Among users, this desired equity outcome embraces horizontal equity (i.e., that equals should be treated equally).[29, 30] In Chapter 7, it was noted this means, for example, reviewing the prices of season and multi-use discount passes to see if there is any rationale for taxpayers who participate infrequently to pay substantially higher per use prices than do pass holders, ensuring that some age cohorts (e.g., senior citizens) do not pay less than other age cohorts of similar financial status (Chapter 7) and ensuring that pricing policies are consistent across different activities (Chapter 5).

Market equity is based on the Benefit Principle articulated by Thomas Hobbes, John Locke and Adam Smith in the 16th, 17th and 18th centuries, respectively. It directs that those who benefit from a leisure service should pay for the costs of delivering it and not seek tax subsidies from others. This is a bedrock principle of contemporary "fiscal conservatism."

Pricing policy designed to respond to this equity norm is governed by the Benefits Continuum described in Chapters 2 and 4 (Figures 2-5 and 4-1). The primary characteristic of services delivering exclusively user benefits is that participating individuals receive the benefits rather than does the rest of the community. Hence, in such cases, a price should be designed to recover all the service's costs. At the other end of the continuum shown in Figure 4-1 are widespread community benefits from which a large proportion of community residents benefits rather than only a small number of users. Because all or most residents share the benefits, the cost of these services is borne by taxes rather than with revenues from prices paid by individual users. Figure 4-1 shows another category termed "spillover benefits," which have attributes from each of the other two categories in that individual users receive a portion of the benefits, but some benefits also spill over to non-participants. For these services, individual users should pay a price that covers the incremental costs associated with their use, while other costs should be paid by taxes.

The *maximize community benefit* equity criterion is derived from the utilitarian philosophy of "the greatest happiness for the greatest number" (p. viii).[31] It directs that public leisure resources should be invested so they deliver the greatest net benefits to the community. It favors whatever combination of services produces the greatest total utility and is analogous to a private firm seeking to maximize profits from its investments. In contrast to the compensatory and egalitarian criteria, this norm ignores the distribution of benefits.[27]

Aggregate benefits are likely to be maximized by accruing as much revenue as possible with minimal tax subsidy because this will enable more services to be delivered with a given amount of tax funding. In many communities where there is pressure to cut taxes, or at least not to raise them, the retention or expansion of leisure services is dependent on revenue from prices.

The *libertarian equity* perspective is focused on reducing public spending: "Its advocates emphasize minimal government investment and believe that tax cuts should prevail over sustaining or increasing existing investments on leisure services" (p. 50).[27] With this criterion, public leisure services are likely to be considered "non-essential," with libertarians arguing governments should not provide them. However, if this radical view does not prevail, their alternative position is likely to be to charge the highest price the market will bear to remove as much tax subsidy as possible.

Dissonance will likely occur between a community's prevailing norm and alternate views of equity held by others. The democratic process suggests the equity norm supported by the majority will prevail, but the dissonance makes it likely that passionate feelings of anger and outrage are likely to accompany price increases that some perceive to be inconsistent with their view of equity. The contextual information changes discussed in the following subsection and the behavioral pricing strategies discussed later in Chapters 10, 11 and 12 offer vehicles for minimizing such controversy.

Context

The influence of context on perceptions and decision making is frequently demonstrated by using visual illustrations. For example, Figure 9-3 shows a black circle. When the question is: Is this circle large or small? the answer is: It depends on the context. The absence of context in the first circle means consensus is unlikely. In the second context, the response is likely to be that the black circle is large, whereas in the third context, the likely consensus is that it is small. The smaller circles in the second context make it appear large, but when placed among the larger circles in the third context, it looks to be small. Of course, the black circle is the same size in both cases, but perceptions of it are changed by changes in context.[32]

The same phenomenon is illustrated in Figure 9-4, which shows the famous Müller–Lyer illusion. The straight lines compose the "shafts" of the arrows, while the "fins" protrude from the ends of the shafts. The fins can point inwards to form an arrow "head" or outwards to form a "tail." The three shafts are of equal length, but the shaft of the arrow with two tails is invariably perceived to be longer than that of the shaft with two heads. Changing the context changes the response.

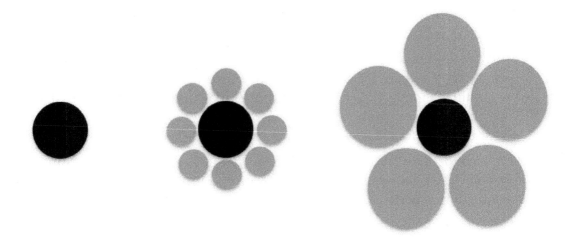

Figure 9-3. The Influence of Context on Perceptions of Size

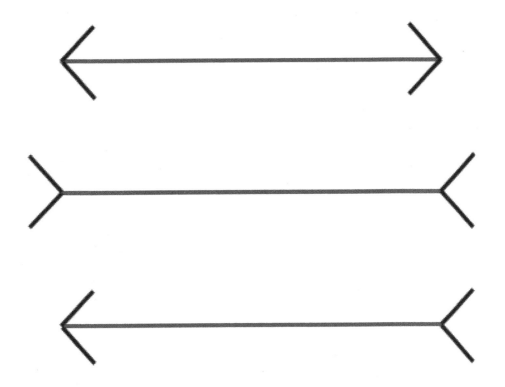

Figure 9-4. The Influence of Context on Perceptions of Length

Moving from the visual to the verbal, consider the following letter that a father received from his daughter who is in college:

- This has not been a good month. There was a fire in the dorm and I lost all my belongings. However, the good news is they believe I will regain the sight of one eye in three months time and that with the aid of crutches I should be able to walk again in a few weeks. Also, the older man, whom I have grown to love, has indicated he will stand by me when our child is born.

  P.S. None of this is true, but I wanted to provide a scenario that would ensure you retained a sensible perspective before telling you that I got an F grade in mathematics this semester.

This hypothetical anecdote illustrates that by changing the contextual focus, it is possible to change individuals' responses to a stimulus—in this case the F grade.

This principle provides leisure managers with their primary tool for alleviating opposition to substantial price increases. When confronted with a price increase, potential users ask: "Is the service still good value for money?" Value is a function of the quality-price ratio. A given price may be considered unreasonable in one context, but acceptable in another. Thus, it is inappropriate to consider price expectation without considering the context in which this expectation is generated. Essentially, the context changes the reference point.

Consider the array of contexts in which a given bottle of wine may be purchased. Its reference price in an upmarket restaurant is likely to be higher than in a low-end restaurant, but the reference price in the low-end restaurant will be higher than in a specialty store, and in turn, that price will be higher than in a discount store. Thus, the same bottle of wine may have four reference prices associated with it, which vary according to the context in which it was purchased. The key differentiating elements in this example are the features of the facility where the wine was purchased. This is also a key contextual variable in determining the quality of many leisure services.

Generic features of context that may influence quality of a service may also influence reference price. Thus, potential users will likely consider macro factors of a context, such as whether it is a public or private swimming pool. It is anticipated that users will differentiate between public and private suppliers when arriving at a reference price.[17] A taxpayer may hold strong beliefs about the role of public sector services, but such beliefs may not extend to the private sector. For example, there will be no expectation a private sector service will be subsidized, so notions of a relatively low price because of support through taxation are likely to be unique to the public sector. Other generic macro contexts of influence may include whether it is located in an affluent or deprived area of the community and whether it is in the off-peak or peak period.

It was noted earlier in the chapter that residual knowledge and prevailing normative equity are "givens"; that is, they are the personal and community shapers of price acceptability that establish parameters that managers have to accept and work within. In contrast, the contexts within which users perceive price acceptability are malleable; that is, they can be influenced and shifted by managerial action. This underlies the conclusion: "It is well understood that reference points are labile" (p. 297).[5] Shifts in users' contexts can lead to concomitant changes in their price acceptability. Often, this is done by framing pricing and program information so the outcome becomes favorable to the agency. Alternate ways of presenting the same information frequently produce different responses. It the field of psychology, it has been found that

> different ways of presenting the same information often evoke different emotions. The statement that "the odds of survival one month after surgery are 90%" is more reassuring than the equivalent statement that "mortality within one month of surgery is 10%". Similarly, cold cuts described as "90% fat free" are more attractive than when they are described as "10% fat."(p. 88)[5]

The logical equivalence of the alternative formulations of the information is transparent, but the responses are likely to be different.

Framing communications recognizes that while information about a price or program may remain the same, it may be perceived and organized differently and it may be structured differently, so it may be interpreted differently in different contexts by different people or at different times. Framing can alter people's mental representations of the information, leading to a change in their context and their decisions.[33]

It has been noted: "Large changes in preferences are sometimes caused by inconsequential variations in the wording" (p. 273).[5] Responses to framing are typically spontaneous and subconscious. This suggests that when price changes are proposed, leisure managers should view themselves as "choice architects" who can influence perspectives by being deliberative in how they present information.[34] A choice architect can organize and design the frame and the context in a way that influences people's decisions and choices. Several of the strategies discussed in Chapters 10, 11 and 12 invite managers to reframe and design price information effectively so the context within which a price is viewed is changed and their desired outcome is achieved. In adaptation-level terms, information that reframes the context in which a service is considered may cause stakeholders to judge a price against the new scenario created by the information and adjust their perceptions of price acceptability accordingly.

Figure 9-1 shows three broad reference-related strategies to implement changes in price. First, a set of strategies, discussed in Chapter 10, can be used to keep a price change close to the existing reference price so it falls within the latitude of acceptance. Users are generally likely to accept these price changes. The second set of strategies, discussed in Chapter 11, is designed to reconcile discrepancies between reference price and a new purchase price outside the latitude of acceptance by providing additional information about a service's quality and about the cost of delivering it. In Chapter 12, a third set of strategies that reconciles the discrepancies based on prospect theory is discussed.

DUAL PROCESS THEORIES

Several two-process theories of reasoning recognize that people operate with parallel processors of information. They differ somewhat in their details, but all agree on the general features of the two systems. The variations of dual process theory most widely adopted in the context of pricing are the Elaboration Likelihood Model (ELM)[4] and the Fast, Slow Thinking Model (FST)[5].

The ELM postulates two distinct routes to persuasion. The "deliberative" or "central route" involves effortful cognitive activity wherein the person draws upon prior experience and knowledge to reflect upon and evaluate the merits of arguments incorporated in a message. During this elaboration process, the message recipient reflects on the arguments in the message, develops counterarguments, forms new beliefs or alters old beliefs. This is an active process during which new thoughts are generated and belief structures are changed, which is why it is called the elaboration element of cognitive processing.[35]

The alternative is the "peripheral route" in which the response is variously described as passive, subconscious or non-deliberative and is absent of any active cognitive processing. This route is taken when people have low motivation to process the information. In this case, in lieu of active cognitive engagement, simple heuristics and cues that reflect prior experience and existing biases serve as decision rules for interpreting information. An existing reference price is the most influential of these simple cues, but they may also include the credibility of a message's source as well as comparisons and associations. This route recognizes that much human behavior is instinctive and passive and does not involve the systematic information processing of the central route.

The FST model embraces the same principles as the ELM. However, the ELM is directed to explaining how information is absorbed or inputted to memory, whereas emphasis of the FST model is on describing how information is retrieved and outputted. The FST model's two styles of processing are characterized as fast thinking (or automatic System 1), which relies on intuition, and slow thinking (or reflective System 2), which is distinguished by a focus on reasoning.

System 1 operates automatically, instinctively and quickly with little or no effort: "Knowledge is stored in memory and accessed without intention and without effort" (p. 22).[5] It emanates from a network of learned associative patterns and operates in "normal" situations for which a routine response is needed. Reactions to new price increases when System 1 is used are intuitive and not controllable. It has been observed: "One of psychology's fundamental insights is that judgments are generally the products of nonconscious systems that operate quickly, on the basis of scant evidence, and in a routine manner" (p. 167).[36]

In contrast, System 2 is a much slower and more self-conscious process. It requires effortful mental activity and conscious reasoning to make deliberative choices among options. It is activated when a "surprise", non-routine stimulus is detected that violates the "normal" situations to which System 1 responds. In System 1 processing, people are only conscious of the outcome decision, whereas when System 2 operates, they are also conscious of the process in which they engaged to arrive at the outcome. It has been suggested that the differences between the routes are manifested in the distinction between remembering and knowing because this contrasts the capacity for conscious recollection of a past price with non-conscious retrieval of it.[15]

If a price change stays within the latitude of acceptance, it will be perceived as being "normal," that is, consistent with reference price and likely to be processed passively by stakeholders by the System 1 or peripheral route without conscious attention being given to it. In contrast, when a price increase is outside the latitude of acceptance, it becomes a "surprise," non-normal event that arouses attention. Accordingly, stakeholders will process it by the central route or System 2 mechanism.

The more emotionally attached users are to a service, the more likely they are to actively process a price change: "When personal relevance is high, people are motivated to scrutinize the information presented and integrate it with their existing beliefs, but when perceived relevance is low, messages may be ignored or processed primarily with peripheral cues" (pp. 95–96).[4] Thus, if a price change is outside the latitude of acceptance and managers proactively disseminate persuasive messages explaining and repositioning the large price change by altering the context in which it is viewed, emotionally attached users are likely to arouse their central route or System 2 processing mechanisms and make the cognitive effort needed to evaluate the merits of those arguments.

If the messages are vivid and salient, they are much more likely to activate System 2 than if they are merely statistics and abstract: "Attention is a scarce resource. Vivid, salient and novel presentations trigger attention in ways that the abstract or familiar never can" (p. 83).[37] This explains why anecdotes and testimony are likely to be more persuasive than statistics.

Most of the strategies suggested for mitigating resistance to price increases in Chapters 10 and 12 will use the System 1 peripheral route, whereas those in Chapter 11 are likely to involve the System 2 central route.

SUMMARY

It is now widely recognized that client groups and elected officials do not always respond rationally to pricing decisions, because the rational person assumption inherent in neoclassical economic theory does not accommodate individuals' residual knowledge, prevailing community equity norms and differences in the contexts in which leisure services are delivered. Economic theory provides a useful skeletal framework on which to build pricing decisions, but it is incomplete. In the political arena, emotion and compromise, for better or worse, invariably trump rationality. There has to be constituency support and/or minimum stakeholder opposition before changes to the *status quo* are likely to be made. The key to meeting these conditions is that any change in price must be viewed as "fair." Stakeholders have an expectation of an acceptable price, and if they perceive a suggested price to be dissonant with that expectation, they will likely be resistant.

Internal reference price is the benchmark criterion used to evaluate whether or not a new or revised price is acceptable. The process is primarily explained by adaptation-level theory. This states that experience with prior stimuli creates an adaptation level or reference point, and subsequent stimuli are judged in relation to it. The key to minimizing resistance is to ensure a proposed price is perceived to be consonant with reference price. Adaptation-level theory is extended by assimilation-contrast theory, which explains that there is a latitude of acceptance around an internal reference price. If price changes remain within that latitude of acceptance, they will meet with little resistance.

The three shapers of internal reference price, which were derived from adaptation-level theory, are residual knowledge, the prevailing normative equity criterion and context. Managers cannot influence residual knowledge because it is the sum of potential users' past experiences. Similarly, they cannot influence equity norms, which are an expression of a community's values about the "right" or desirable way to price delivery of services. Norms are manifested in five perspectives of equity that will strongly influence a community's decisions on acceptable levels of subsidy and pricing: compensatory equity, egalitarian equity, market equity, maximizing community benefit and libertarian equity. There is likely to be dissonance between a community's prevailing equity criterion and alternate views of equity held by others in the community whose perspective does not prevail. Nevertheless, adopting an approach to pricing consistent with the prevailing view is likely to minimize controversy.

The context shaper of internal reference price gives managers the most opportunities to influence reference price and to influence price elasticity of demand. Two strategies (discussed in Chapters 10, 11 and 12) are available to managers when implementing price change: those used to stay within the latitude of acceptance and those designed to reconcile differences between reference price and a new purchase price. In both cases, managers can accomplish the goal by changing users' perceptions of context.

There are two distinctive cognitive processing routes. The central or System 2/slow route is deliberative and involves effortful cognitive activity and thoughtful reflection. In contrast, the peripheral or System 1/fast route is subconscious and non-deliberative, relying on heuristics and cues established from prior experience. The managerial strategies described in Chapters 10 and 12 primarily use the peripheral route, while those in Chapter 11 mainly rely on the central route.

REFERENCES

1. Monroe, K. B. (1973). Buyers' subjective perceptions of price. *Journal of Marketing Research, 10,* 70–80.
2. Helson, H. (1964). *Adaptation-level theory: An experimental and systematic approach to behavior.* New York, NY: Harper & Row.
3. Sherif, M., & Hovland, C. I. (1961). *Social judgment: Assimilation and contrast effects on communication and attitude change.* New Haven, CT: Yale University Press.
4. Petty, R. E., & Cacioppo, J. T. (1981). *Attitudes and persuasion: Classic and contemporary approaches.* Dubuque, IA: Wm. C. Brown.
5. Kahneman, D. (2011). *Thinking fast and slow.* London, England: Penguin.
6. Zeithaml, V. A., & Graham, K. L. (1983). The accuracy of reported reference prices for professional services. In R. P. Bagozzi & A. M. Tybout (Eds.), *Advances in consumer research: Volume 10* (pp. 607–611). Ann Arbor, MI: Association for Consumer Research.
7. Rao, A. R., & Sieben, W. A. (1992). The effect of prior knowledge on price acceptability and the type of information examined. *Journal of Consumer Research, 19,* 256–270.

8. Janiszewski, C., & Lichtenstein, D. R. (1999). A range theory account of price perception. *Journal of Consumer Behavior, 25,* 353–368.

9. Briesch, R. A., Krishnamurthi, L., Mazumdar, T., & Raj, S. P. (1997). A comparative analysis of reference price models. *Journal of Consumer Research, 24,* 202–214.

10. Della Bitta, A. J., & Monroe, K. B. (1974). The influence of adaptation levels on subjective price perceptions. In S. Ward & P. Wright (Eds.), *Advances in consumer research: Vol. 1* (pp. 359–369). Ann Arbor, MI: Association for Consumer Research.

11. Kalyanaram, G., & Winer, R. S. (1995). Empirical generalizations from reference price research. *Marketing Science, 14*(3), 1–2, G161–G169.

12. McCarville, R. E. (1996). The importance of price last paid in developing price expectations for a public leisure service. *Journal of Park and Recreation Administration, 14*(4), 52–64.

13. Mazumdar, T., Raj, S. P., & Sinha, I. (2005). Reference price research: Review and propositions. *Journal of Marketing, 69*(4), 84–102.

14. Gratton, C., & Taylor, P. (1995). From economic theory to leisure practice via empirics: The case of demand and price. *Leisure Studies, 14,* 245–261.

15. Monroe, K. B., & Lee, A. Y. (1999). Remembering versus knowing: Issues in buyers' processing of price information. *Journal of the Academy of Marketing Science, 27,* 207–225.

16. Sherif, M., & Sherif, C. W. (1968). Attitude as the individuals' own categories: The social judgment-involvement approach to attitude change. In M. Sherif & C. W. Sherif (Eds.), *Attitude, ego-involvement, and change* (pp. 105–139). New York, NY: John Wiley.

17. McCarville, R. E., & Crompton, J. L. (1987). Propositions addressing perceptions of reference price for public recreation services. *Leisure Sciences, 9,* 281–292.

18. Maxwell, S. (2008). *The price is wrong: Understanding what makes a price seem fair and the true cost of unfair pricing.* New York, NY: John Wiley & Sons.

19. Sherif, M., Taub, D., & Hovland, C. I. (1958). Assimilation and contrast effects of anchoring stimuli on judgments. *Experimental Psychology, 55,* 150–155.

20. Howard, D. R., & Selin, S. W. (1987). A method for establishing consumer price tolerance levels for public recreation services. *Journal of Park and Recreation Administration, 5*(3), 48–59.

21. Monroe, K. B. (1971).The information content of prices: A preliminary model for estimating buyer response. *Management Sciences, 17,* B519–B532.

22. Monroe, K. B. (1971). Measuring price thresholds by psychophysics and latitudes of acceptance. *Journal of Marketing Research, 8,* 460–464.

23. Thaler, R. H. (1985). Mental accounting and consumer choice. *Marketing Science, 4,* 199–214.

24. Crompton, J. L., & Lamb, C. W. (1986). *Marketing government and social services.* New York, NY: John Wiley.

25. Nobel, K. (1987, June 13). Congress votes to bar $1.00 admission fee at Statue of Liberty. *New York Times,* p. 13.

26. Wicks, B. E., & Crompton, J. L. (1986). Citizen and administrator perceptions of equity in the delivery of park services. *Leisure Sciences, 8,* 341–365.

27. Crompton, J. L., & West, S. T. (2008). The role of moral philosophies, operational criteria, and operational strategies in determining equitable allocation of resources for leisure services in the United States. *Leisure Studies, 27,* 35–58.

28. Crompton, J. L., & Wicks, B. E. (1988). Implementing a preferred equity model for the delivery of leisure services in the U.S. context. *Leisure Studies, 7,* 287–303.

29. Crompton, J. L. (1984). The equitability of full price policies for senior citizens. *Journal of Park and Recreation Administration, 2*(1), 3–8.

30. Crompton, J. L. (1984). Treating equals equally: Common abuses in pricing public services. *Parks and Recreation, 19*(9), 67–71.

31. Mark, P. (1969). *A Bentham reader.* New York, NY: Pegasus.

32. Ariely, D. (2009). *Predictably irrational.* New York, NY: HarperCollins.

33. Soman, D. (2004). Financing, loss aversion, and mental accounting. In D. J. Koehler & N. Harvey (Eds.), *Blackwell handbook of judgment and decision making* (pp. 379–398). Malden, MA: Blackwell.

34. Thaler, R. H., & Sunstein, C. R. (2008). *Nudge: Improving decisions about health, wealth, and happiness.* New Haven, CT: Yale University Press.

35. McCarville, R. E., Driver, B. L., & Crompton, J. L. (1992). Persuasive communication and the pricing of public leisure services. In M. J. Manfredo (Ed.), *Influencing human behavior* (pp. 263–292). Champaign, IL: Sagamore.

36. Gilbert, D. T. (2002). Inferential correction. In T. Gilovich, D. Griffin, & D. Kahneman (Eds.), *Heuristics and biases: The psychology of intuitive judgment* (pp. 167–184). New York, NY: Cambridge University Press.

37. Sunstein, C. R. (2013). *Simpler: The future of government.* New York, NY: Simon & Schuster.

Chapter 10

Strategies Designed to Be Consistent with Reference Price

- Raise price in nibbles, not bites
- Temporal reframing
- Anchoring
- Recognize price may be a signal of quality
- Customary pricing
- Summary

Five primary heuristics are identified in this chapter that undergird strategies designed to ensure that participants perceive price changes as compatible with their reference prices in the immediate and long term. The heuristics are (i) raise price in nibbles, not bites; (ii) temporal reframing; (iii) anchoring; (iv) recognize price may be a signal of quality; and (v) customary pricing.

RAISE PRICE IN NIBBLES, NOT BITES

Latitude of price acceptance is the range of prices around an internal reference price within which users have minimum price sensitivity.[1] In Chapter 9, it was explained that prices within the range are assimilated and accepted, while those outside it are contrasted and rejected. In Figure 10-1, the low and high parameters of the latitude of price acceptance are shown as the bargain and resistance points, respectively. Conceptually, they can be derived by asking two questions: What is the lowest price the target market will pay while still trusting the service's quality? and What is the highest price the target market will pay?[2, 3] Concerns about the first question relate to the possibility of perceptions that low price is indicative of low quality. This relationship is discussed later in this chapter. The focus at this point is on the second question, the highest price increase the market will tolerate.

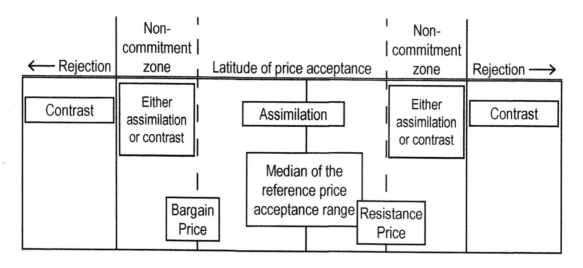

Figure 10-1. Conceptualization of the Latitude of Price Acceptance

The latitude of price acceptance zone in Figure 10-1 is shown as being asymmetrical. That is, the zone is narrower above the median reference price and wider below it. This asymmetric response to price changes is explained by prospect theory, which is discussed in Chapter 12. Prospect theory recognizes that users are more sensitive to prices above a reference point (perceived loss) than to prices below it (perceived gain).[4] Accordingly, they tend to perceive a reduction in price below an internal reference price to be smaller than it is. In contrast, when a price revision is higher than the internal reference price, the increase is perceived to be larger than it is.[5, 6]

Figure 10-1 shows "non-commitment" zones adjacent to the bargain and resistance points. These zones recognize the boundaries of the latitude of price acceptance are not fixed, but can be extended if contextual cues (e.g., knowledge of cost, improved perceptions of quality) suggest good reasons for moving them. Thus, prices falling in the non-commitment zone may be (i) assimilated and accepted or (ii) contrasted and rejected depending on the strength of the accompanying contextual cues. If a new price in the non-commitment zone is assimilated, this adaptation will result in an incremental shift in the median of internal reference price. Thus, the latitude of acceptance, like reference price, is a dynamic, adaptive concept that changes over time.

Types of service, target markets, prices that other suppliers charge, frequency of purchase, degrees of loyalty and nature of the existing price number all contribute to the latitude of price acceptance varying among individuals. The zone is likely to be wider for higher priced services. For example, an increase in a class fee from $10 to $15 (50 percent) may be rejected as being outside the latitude of acceptance, while raising another class fee from $70 to $77 (10 percent) is a larger absolute dollar amount, but it may be within the latitude of price acceptance. This is consistent with the Weber–Fechner law that, when adapted to the context of price, states that users perceive price differences in proportional and relative terms, not absolute terms.[7, 8, 9] The focal point is not the dollar amount of difference, but rather it is the proportionate difference. It is the percentage change in price, not the absolute amount of a price increase, that is likely to be critical. Again, this is also consistent with a primary tenet of prospect theory (discussed in Chapter 12) that states as gains or losses increase away from the reference point, people become less sensitive to the absolute magnitude of those gains and losses. Thus, the $7 loss ($70 ➤ $77) is not as painful as the $5 loss ($10 ➤ $15).

It was noted in the discussion of reference price definitions in Chapter 9 that availability of competitive suppliers and frequency of purchase are likely to be strong influences on internal reference price and the latitude of price acceptance. Recognition that its width is influenced by frequency of use is consistent with original observations derived from empirical studies on social issues made by the developers of assimilation-contrast theory. They commented on "the constricted latitude of acceptance of individuals who are strongly involved in their stands on an issue and the more extensive latitude of acceptance of individuals less deeply concerned with the issue" (p. vii).[8] Latitude of acceptance is also likely to increase with the income level of the target market. Higher discretionary income is likely to be associated with greater tolerance of price increases.

Those loyal to a program, instructor, facility or agency are likely to have a wider latitude of price acceptance. They tend to focus on the benefits of the experience offered rather than on the price. Deviations from the reference price must be large before they consider resistance. Marginal or fringe users, rather than core users, are likely to be more focused on price increases and to have a smaller acceptance zone.[1] If marginal users participate fairly regularly, their latitude of price acceptance is likely to be especially small because their frequency of participation will establish the existing price as a firm reference price from which they will notice relatively small deviations.

The nature of the existing price number is also likely to have influence. If it is a "rounded" number, such as $5, $10 or $20, it is likely to be recalled more accurately and to have a relatively narrow latitude of price acceptance. In contrast, if the price is $6.25, $9.30 or $17.45, recall is likely to be more vague, so the latitude of price acceptance is likely to be wider.[9]

While multiple variables influence the zone's width, as a point of departure, research in the marketing field suggests a discount should be between 15 and 30 percent below the regular price to trigger a purchase reaction.[10, 11, 12] If the discount is greater than 30 percent, it is likely to be below the acceptable bargain price (Figure 10-1), and prospective users are likely to be concerned either the offer is not *bona fide* or its quality has been compromised.[13, 14] Given the asymmetrical reaction to price change shown in Figure 10-1, it seems likely that price increases small enough to be perceived as being consistent with reference price generally should not exceed 10 percent in the private sector.

However, evidence in the public sector suggests the resistance point that denotes the high end of the latitude of acceptance for leisure services in some situations may be a higher percentage than studies in the private sector have reported. The tradition of subsidizing prices so they are low is likely to create substantial consumers' surplus that may facilitate acceptance of relatively large proportional increases in price. This was demonstrated by an Oregon leisure agency confronted with having either to increase prices or to reduce services. The agency's cost of providing each program was estimated, and three alternate pricing options were developed (Table 10-1). The low priced option recovered 50 percent of costs; the medium priced was the break-even point, recovering all costs; and the high priced was the highest price of a competitor supplier (public or private) in the region. A sample of participants in each of 15 program areas drawn from registration records was surveyed. The specific programs and their descriptions remained the same, but one third of respondents received only the low priced option, one third the medium priced, and one third the high priced. The authors concluded:

> Clear price threshold levels do exist for recreation activities, and they vary substantially from one activity to another . . . Decisions related to price adjustments should be made on an activity-specific basis. "Across-the-board" price hikes, in which all or a number of programs are raised by the same standard amount, do not allow for the kind of price discrimination evident among public recreation consumers. A 10 percent increase, which might be met with considerable resistance in one area, may be well below the acceptable price level in another. In either case, the decision could lead to negative consequences for the agency. (p. 58)[15]

Among the 13 recreation programs whose users were surveyed, a remarkably high tolerance for price increases emerged (Table 10-1). For example, among those paying for swim lessons, 100 percent and 76 percent reported a willingness to accept a 25 percent and 90 percent increase in price, respectively. The two user groups most resistant to substantial increases were those who purchased cross-country ski passes and resident camping passes, suggesting that the existing price for those activities was closer to the resistance price. However, even among those groups, 44 percent and 47 percent expressed a willingness to accept price increases of 60 percent and 38 percent, respectively. Clearly, price increases of this magnitude could not be sustained indefinitely in future years, but these data suggest the tolerance for price increases is likely to be higher than that reported in private sector studies if the programs are subsidized below market rates. The diversity of responses also illustrates why implementing across-the-board price increases of (say) 10 percent is a poor strategy.

Table 10-1

Acceptance of Price by Program Participants at Three Levels

Activity	Existing Price	Low (50% of Cost)		Medium (Break Even)		High (Going Rate)	
		Yes %	$	Yes %	$	Yes %	$
Swim Lessons	$8.00	100	10	92	12	76	15
Youth Swim	$0.50	94	.50	84	.75	77	1
Aerobic Fitness	$12.00	78	14	59	23	38	32
Weight Conditioning	$16.00	55	16	52	22	33	30
Youth Baseball	$10.00	69	20	72	28	44	35
Tennis Lessons	$8.00	76	13	86	15	62	20
Preschool Classes (per month)	$34.00	74	36	34	50	9	100
Photography Classes	$13.00	52	25	53	32	54	40
Adult Specialty Crafts	$15.00	50	33	36	43	42	50
Youth Dance Classes	$12.00	68	14	67	20	64	25
Cross-Country Ski	$15.00	44	24	53	34	30	45
Resident Camping	$70.00	47	97	53	121	28	125
Whitewater Rafting Trips	$18.00	60	23	22	32	25	35

Implications for Leisure Managers

The latitude of price acceptance suggests that whenever possible managers should make frequent small incremental price increases rather than infrequent large price increases—"nibbles" rather than "bites." Raising prices within the latitude of acceptance zone is perhaps the most risk-free way for a leisure agency to increase revenues. A series of small incremental increases in price over time—all of which fall within the latitude of price acceptance—is less likely to meet user resistance than is a single major increase.

Typically, leisure service agencies do not raise their prices to keep pace with increases in costs. To rectify this situation, a firm policy should be established to raise price every year as part of the annual budget review process to offset the inevitable increase in costs. If an agency, or its elected officials, decides to "hold the line" on price and rejects an annual increase, it will probably create a future problem. As shown in Figure 10-2, if no increases are authorized until year Y, a large price increase outside the latitude of price acceptance will likely be necessary, and it will probably meet user resistance.

Price

Years

—————— Within the latitude of price acceptance. No client
          resistance to these price increases.

- - - - - - Price increase at year Y meets client resistance.

Figure 10-2. Implementing Price Increases Compatible with the Latitude of Price Acceptance

Too often, leisure managers set their prices for the (say) 20 percent of potential participants who cannot afford the break-even price rather than providing a discount for those individuals and setting a regular price for the 80 percent who can afford the break-even price. This limits the immediate revenues received, but as illustrated in a later section of this chapter (Table 10-6), establishing a low reference price makes sustained revenue losses in the future likely. Too often, managers are evaluated only on number of participants and not on attainment of financial goals, which reinforces a culture of low prices.

The strategy of frequent small incremental increases may be difficult to enforce in jurisdictions in which managers have to seek authority from elected representatives to implement each price increase. To avoid this situation and to facilitate frequent small price increases, some governing bodies have authorized managers to implement price increases without seeking their prior approval. In such cases, an agency may only be required to provide details of the new prices, with full supporting documentation, to its controlling body for information. For example:

- The city of San Jose, California, approved a Pricing and Revenue Policy to establish cost recovery and affordable access goals. Within this framework, a council resolution then directed:

> The City Manager's designee shall be authorized to set all Parks, Recreation, and Neighborhood Services user fees with a goal of increasing the ability of the Department to respond to market trends and community needs, and to assist in generating optimal cost recovery levels per program while continuing to have scholarship programs available for certain segments of the population.[16]

This approach enables elected representatives to avoid controversy by deflecting criticism of new prices away from themselves to the agency head. It does not remove pricing decisions from the political arena, and elected representatives retain the authority to intercede. This low key approach, however, usually leads to intercession only in exceptional cases. It avoids extensive annual public debate of proposed price increases and thus facilitates frequent small increases within the latitude of price acceptance.

Participant Adjustment Period: A Consequence of Bites

A price that has been charged for a season or more typically becomes the internal reference price irrespective of the level at which it was set. Thus, when users are asked if a price is too high, too low or about right, 70–80 percent are likely to respond about right.[17–23] Increases from this reference point are routinely accepted if they stay within the latitude of price acceptance (i.e., they are nibbles). However, when price increases become bites—that is, they are raised beyond the latitude of price acceptance—substantial clientele resistance is likely. In these cases, the negative reaction is likely to be motivated as much by outrage or pique at its "unfairness" as by perceived inability to pay the new price.

This response is likely to be particularly pronounced if the price goes from zero to some monetary value for the first time. It has been suggested: "Zero is not just another price, it is an emotional hot button" (p. 49).[24] This was empirically verified in a study of visitors to a Corps of Engineers recreation area. Respondents who had paid admission to similar facilities during the past 12 months were compared with those who reported not doing so. The former group

> were more willing to pay a "fair day-use fee", to support fees used to maintain favored day-use areas, and to pay fees sufficient to cover maintenance costs . . . and were also more in agreement with the notion that higher fees could be charged for more modernized sites. Those who had not paid fees for similar services over the past 12 months were more likely to report that they would no longer visit any Corps day-use areas if fees were initiated. (p. 68)[25]

The authors stated that those unaccustomed to paying a price "often reported feeling victimized through the introduction of fees" (p. 74).[25] A long-established norm was changed. Those accustomed to not paying a price likely felt that any fee, regardless of its magnitude, violated their expectations. Their evaluation of fairness revolved around the issue of to pay or not to pay, whereas for those accustomed to paying a fee, the issue was: "How much is it fair for me to pay?" Implementing new fees and increasing existing fees to a level outside the latitude of acceptance are likely to evoke different intensities of adverse responses, with the former being perceived as a more radical shift in policy and, hence, as generating more controversy.

Over time, adaptation to a price outside the latitude of acceptance takes place. A bite price that is initially perceived to be unfair is likely to evolve slowly into a revised reference price norm that most people accept and no longer perceive as unfair.[26] This process represents a participant adjustment period and is illustrated in Figure 10-3. Its length will vary according to (a) magnitude of the increase, (b) availability of substitute service suppliers, (c) income level of the client group, (d) type of service offered and (e) the frequency of use.

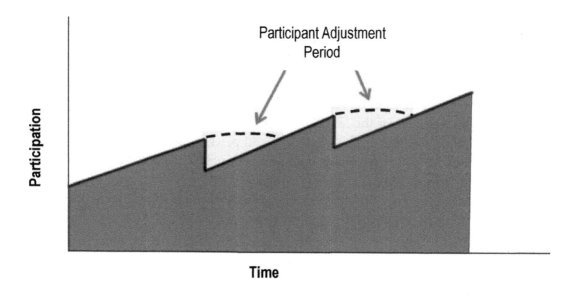

Figure 10-3. Concept of Participant Adjustment Period

When a large panel of state park visitors was repeatedly surveyed over 16 months to track reaction to substantial price increases at Texas state parks, the reduction in resistance to the price increase among per visit payers over 16 months was "narrow and limited" (p. 42).[27] There were two reasons for this. First, many users had strong internal reference prices for substitute suppliers whose prices were lower, and the new state park prices compared unfavorably to the substitute suppliers' prices. Second, per visit payers to state parks (as opposed to annual pass holders) were infrequent visitors. Hence, the traditional reference price remained strong because of the infrequent exposure to the new price. In contrast to the per visit payers, season pass purchasers experienced a substantial decay in resistance to the new prices over this time (i.e., the new prices were accepted much more rapidly).

This evidence suggests a fairly lengthy adjustment period is likely for infrequently used services because infrequent exposure to the new price means it takes longer for it to become the new internal reference price. However, for regularly used leisure services (at least once a week), the anecdotal conventional wisdom is that the adjustment period is likely to be no longer than 3 months or one season.[28]

Implications for leisure managers. Three strategies can be used to mitigate the effect of price increases outside the latitude of price acceptance and to minimize the duration of the participant adjustment period. First, if annual or season passes are involved, existing pass holders could be invited to renew them before the new prices become effective. Prospect theory, which is discussed in Chapter 12, indicates that these heavy users are likely to be the most active and vociferous and in the vanguard of objectors, and this action will preempt their objections. They are likely to appreciate being given preferential treatment, and by the end of the year or season when their renewal is scheduled, they are likely to have adapted to the new price, so it has become their reference price.

A second strategy is to provide client groups with as much warning as possible of a forthcoming price increase. If awareness of such an increase is established in clients' minds some time before implementation, at least some participant adaptation is likely to have taken place by the time the price change occurs. Thus, if prices are to be raised on May 1, they should be announced the previous December or January and be widely publicized so participants have time to adapt to the new price as the reference price.

If the facility also serves tourists, a lead time of a year may be needed. Tour companies have to accommodate changes into their own pricing structures and promotional literature to maintain their profit margins. Thus, when the Canadian Park Service makes changes in fees or fee policies, it has a list of 2,000 user companies that are notified within 48 hours, and it gives them an 18-month lead time.[29]

A third strategy, derived from attribution theory and the Principle of Dual Entitlement, which is discussed in Chapter 11, requires the agency to demonstrate to skeptical users that despite its magnitude, the increase is fair. If it is attributable to an increase in costs or improvements in service quality, the information should be provided to justify it. Thus, in early work in which reactions to a fee program at a national wildlife refuge were tracked, it was concluded: "If improvements are made at the time fees are initiated or increased, disapproval by the public is minimized" (p. 646).[30] Similarly, if a large increase is attributable to a shift in elected officials' philosophy on cost recovery, resistance is likely to be ameliorated when the rationale for the shift is explained.

The scenario reported in Figure 10-4 captures the likely outcome when a price is imposed for a service that has traditionally been free if no proactive effort is made to mitigate the outcome.[31] The obvious mistake was to create a zero reference price rather than to initiate a charge when the museum opened. However, once the decision was made to charge, a series of actions should have been launched including the following:

- Announcing the decision the previous fall (e.g., October), which would have (i) given users more time to adapt to the idea that $1 was a fair price and (ii) avoided the problem being exacerbated by the official guidebook advertising it as free.
- Widespread communication of reasons for the policy change to all impacted stakeholders. It appeared to be arbitrary and to abrogate the Principle of Dual Entitlement (discussed in Chapter 11).

- Communicating operating cost information and the subsidy per person (discussed in Chapter 11).
- Comparing the $1 price to that charged for other leisure services in the community and at similar museums in the area. The director reports she did this in response to complaints. It would have been more effective if it had been done as part of an early communication effort.

The 13,000 square foot museum was located on a back street in a resort city and so had limited visibility. Nevertheless, in the 5 years since it opened, it had built up its annual attendance to approximately 70,000. Some, 40,000 of this occurred in the months of June (11,250), July (11,400) and August (17,500).

Since it opened, admission had been free. The average visitor's stay was 1.5 hours. In March, the council changed this policy and directed that a price be imposed for adult admissions in the three summer months. They set it at the nominal price of $1, with children still admitted free, recognizing that the shift from free to any price, no matter how small, would likely meet resistance. Unfortunately, the resort's official tourist guide for the summer season had been printed and widely disseminated before this decision was made, so it advertised the museum as a "free" attraction.

Attendance in the summer months dropped from 40,000 to 16,000. Total revenue was less than $5,000, and the costs incurred in collecting the fees exceeded that amount. The museum's director reported:

The exercise was a disaster. I was prepared for some local people being reproachful; I was not prepared for their anger. I explained that it costs money to operate a museum and it was only fair to taxpayers to "spread the burden." I pointed out the price of a visit to the city's swimming pool was 50% higher and that renting a deck chair on the beach was 33% higher, but most did not want to listen.

Regular visitors who came to see each month's new exhibition made angry comments about "paying taxes" and stayed away. An adult with six children in tow (who did not have to pay) refused "on principle" to pay the $1 admission fee and ordered the children back into her expensive car. Some of the most vehemently angry were the bed and breakfast owners who, having suggested their visitors go to the museum and told them it was free, were proved wrong. The resort's tourists were irritated, questioning why they should have to pay when the locals got in free for most of the year in the non-peak months. We bungled it!

Figure 10-4. Anatomy of a Failure: Visitation Plummets When a Price Is Imposed for the First Time at a Museum

The absence of these actions meant the museum staff were required to respond to angry patrons. If the patrons had been exposed to this systematic explanatory information, many of them would likely have recognized the legitimacy of the rationales offered, so their resistance would have been ameliorated.

In contrast to the experiences described in Figure 10-4, the proactive action of managers at the Texas Parks and Wildlife Department shown in Figure 10-5 resulted in remarkably few complaints when the agency imposed a large price increase on park visitors that was outside the latitude of price acceptance:

- The admission price to Texas state parks was $2 per vehicle. The state legislature withdrew tax support from the agency and instructed it to bridge the funding gap with revenues from users. Thus, the agency shifted from a fee of $2 *per vehicle* at all parks to a *per person* fee ranging from $1 to $5 according to the quality/popularity of the park. This meant that while four people in a vehicle were previously admitted for $2, they would now pay between $4 and $20. It was to be implemented on May 1. A brochure was prepared and handed to each park visitor, starting the previous October (i.e., 7 months before the per person price increase was implemented). The brochure is shown in Figure 10-5. Heavy users were protected by being offered an annual pass at the favorable price of $50 per vehicle. The brochure stressed the Principle of Dual Entitlement, pointing out "state parks no longer receive direct support from your general taxes." It also highlighted the enterprise fund effect (discussed in Chapter 12) whereby "each park can keep a portion of all revenues generated for reinvestment," so users saw "their" park would benefit from their fee payments. Those actions resulted in fewer than 50 complaints being received from the 6 million day visits that occurred during the remaining 8 months of that year after the new structure was implemented.

TEMPORAL REFRAMING

Temporal reframing involves lengthening the time frame over which a given price is paid. A convincing body of research evidence supports the effectiveness of this strategy.[32] It works because it effectively reduces the sense of loss and changes the context in which a price is viewed. Which price is more desirable: $360 for an annual pass or only $1 a day? The price is approximately the same. However, a $360 annual pass price is a large amount that equates to a large loss of personal funds. By spreading the cost over the whole year rather than viewing it as an aggregate lump sum, the pennies-a-day reframing reduces the sense of loss.

TEXAS PARKS AND WILDLIFE

Per-Person Pricing

State Park Fee Change

An investment in conserving Texas for the future.

PUBLIC LANDS DIVISION

Is it realistic for each state park to be self-sufficient?

No, the goal of the Public Lands Division is to improve the system as a whole by working toward system-wide self-sufficiency. We realize that every park does not have the ability to become self-sufficient, but the system does.

How much will my favorite park charge per-person?

It will depend because each park manager recommends the per-person price for that park, within the range of $1.00 to $5.00. The park managers know their customers and competitors better than anyone; therefore they are best able to meet their customers' needs and determine an appropriate price. Over 76% of the state parks will have a per-person price of $2.00 or less.

Some parks will be giving a discounted entrance price to those visitors who will be camping overnight at their park. Please call your park of destination or the Information Center for specific overnight admission prices.

How does my favorite park benefit from per-person pricing?

Each park will be contributing to the parks system as a whole. Under our Entrepreneurial Budget System, each park can keep a portion of all revenues generated for reinvestment into expanding programs, products and services. Your favorite park will benefit from strengthening the entire system. Individually, a given park might not be able to operate, but, as part of a system, it can be successful.

Is an annual pass available?

Yes, a new Gold Texas Conservation Passport (TCP) will be available for $50 on May 1, 1996. It will enable vehicular entry to state parks and wildlife management areas. A new Silver TCP ($25) will gain user entry to wildlife management areas. Passports enable the holder and those in the car to enter without paying the per-person admission price.

Who should I contact for more information?

There are five sources available to assist you with questions.
1) your local park manager
2) for rates and general information call the Information Center (1-800-792-1112)
3) web site: http://www.tpwd.state.tx.us
4) for reservations call the Central Reservation Center (512-389-8900)
5) write: Public Lands Division (Pricing)
Texas Parks & Wildlife Department
4200 Smith School Road
Austin, Texas 78744-3292

TEXAS PARKS & WILDLIFE
4200 Smith School Road
Austin, Texas 78744-3292

In accordance with Texas State Depository Law, this publication is available at the Texas State Publications Clearinghouse and/or Texas Depository Libraries.   PWD BR P4000-031 (02/96)

Texas State Parks are one of the best recreational values anywhere.

They are relaxing, healthful, educational, low-priced and family-oriented, but most of all they are just a whole lot of fun!

When you compare our park prices to the cost of other types of entertainment, like a movie, sporting event or dining out, you will quickly see that a visit to a state park, state natural area or state historical park is a real bargain, especially if you are taking a family.

Questions you may have...

What is per-person pricing?

Per-person pricing is a method of charging fees on an individual basis. Each person is assessed an individual price of admission. This is the same practice as found at local movie theaters, special events and amusement parks.

Why the change to per-person pricing?

The Texas State Parks system will be changing from vehicular entry pricing to per-person pricing. (Some parks have successfully been using this pricing process since 1990.) With the new pricing change, each individual will be making a contribution to conserving and preserving the resource they are using. This will in time balance the costs associated with each individual visit. In the past, the price per car did not cover all the costs its occupants incurred. The change in pricing strategy will allow visitors to pay equally for their use on an individual basis and enable Texas Parks & Wildlife to expand and improve its products and services to you.

Who does per-person pricing affect?

Per-person pricing will affect everyone over 12 years old who visits a state park. Children aged 12 years and younger will be admitted free into the parks, except for some special tour admissions.

Here's the current situation...

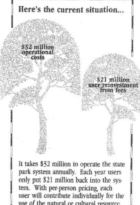

$32 million operational costs

$21 million user reinvestment from fees

It takes $32 million to operate the state park system annually. Each year users only put $21 million back into the system. With per-person pricing, each user will contribute individually for the use of the natural or cultural resource.

An example from the past...

1 car with 1 user = 1 car x $2 = $2

1 car with 3 users = 1 car x $2 = $2

An example from the future...

1 car with 1 user = 1 adult x $2 = $2

1 car with 3 users = 2 adults* x $2 = $4

*12 years and younger admitted free into parks, except for some special tour admissions.

What about senior citizen discounts, if I am 65 years old or older?

If your 65th birthday was on or after September 1, 1995 and you are a Texas resident, you may receive a 50% discount off the regular park entrance fee, rounded to the nearest higher whole dollar. Non-residents of Texas will pay regular park entrance fees.

If your 65th birthday was before September 1, 1995, or you are a veteran with at least a 60% disability, you will continue to receive free entrance into state parks. This Parklands Passport (commonly referred to as the Bluebonnet Pass) is an individual pass and is for both residents and non-residents of Texas.

When and where will per-person pricing begin?

Per-person pricing will begin system-wide at all state parks on Wednesday, May 1, 1996.

How will I benefit from per-person pricing at state parks?

We are facing over $200 million of critical repairs within state parks. Fee changes are one of many ways we are recovering costs to improve park facilities. Gradually, you will begin to see and use these improved facilities.

Don't state parks receive support from our taxes?

No, the state parks no longer receive direct support from your general taxes. In 1992, the legislature cut this support in a push for governmental cost recovery. The Texas Parks & Wildlife Department as an agency does, however, receive a percentage of the tax on sporting goods purchases, with state parks only receiving a portion of the overall agency's share.

Figure 10-5. Information Provided to Reduce the Participant Adjustment Period to a Large Price Increase at Texas State Parks

It also adjusts the reference price by changing the category of purchases with which it is being compared. When people evaluate the value for money of a leisure service, they tend to compare it with similarly priced transactions. Framing the price as a dollar a day shifts the reference category from infrequent purchases of products/services costing the large aggregate amount, such as an airline trip or a major appliance, to relatively nominal daily expenditures, such as the purchase of a coffee, a soda or a newspaper. Typically, these are perceived as trivial and affordable, so the likelihood of the price being accepted is increased.[32] Consider the following illustration:

- Some may complain about a softball league fee of $500 per team. Complaints are less likely if it is pointed out that the per person cost is $3.50 per (say) 90-minute game (assuming 12 games in a season and 12 members on a team). That is likely to be one of the best bargains for a leisure activity anywhere in the community. Further, an increase from $500 to $560 may be resisted, but if the $60 increase is framed as a per person, per game increase of 40 cents (from $3.50 to $3.90), resistance is likely to be much lower.

Other examples of temporal reframing are given in Tables 10-2 and 10-3. In Table 10-2, the public's perception may be that there is probably some "fat" in a $20.99 million budget, less in a net budget (i.e., amount of operations and maintenance funding coming from the property tax) of $9.97 million, and hardly any fat in a budget of 68 cents per resident per week. The $2 million indoor natatorium bond proposal in Table 10-3 was likely to be difficult to pass because the community already had three functioning outdoor pools. However, the new natatorium was to be constructed as part of a new middle school, and the primary mission was to teach its sixth graders to swim as a response to periodic drownings at several reservoirs in the area. Cold weather meant this could not be accomplished at the outdoor pools. Instead of a $2 million natatorium, the promotional material for the project positioned it as costing the average homeowner $1.50 a month, with the expectation that the natatorium would save children from drowning. The bond proposal passed.

Table 10-2

Change Value Perceptions

Total annual budget for parks and recreation	$20.989 million
Capital budget	5.872
Operating budget	15.117
Self-generated revenue	5.142
Annual **net** operating budget	$9.975 million
Number of residents in the community	281.382
Net **per resident** investment OR 68 cents per week	$35.45

Table 10-3

Changing Perceptions of a Bond Proposal for a $2 Million New Natatorium by Adopting a Pennies-a-Day Approach

The median home value in the community is	$150,000	
Construction cost of the natatorium	$2 million	
Annual property tax payment by an average homeowner:		$12
Annual operation and maintenance cost	$100,000	
Annual property tax payment by an average homeowner		$6
Total annual property tax payment by an average homeowner,		
which is **$1.50 per month**		$18

In most years, there are heartbreaking stories in the local news media of children from this community who have drowned in area lakes. An agreement with the ISD means that every sixth grader in the community will be taught to swim, so lives will be saved.

Invest $1.50 a month and save a child's life!

ANCHORING

The genesis of anchoring springs from the original research in psychophysics associated with the development of adaptation-level and assimilation-contrast theories. Thus, in the evolution of adaptation-level theory, it was empirically verified that it had shifted in the direction of an anchor stimulus. There was a "shift in scale values due to use of anchors outside the series range" (p. 35).[33] Similarly, the authors of assimilation-contrast theory stated: "End points defining the extremes as a scale exert greater influence than others . . . [They] may be referred to as anchorages or anchors" (p. 29).[8] The essence of their theory was derived from their observation:

> That the relative distance between the anchor and the stimulus series is a crucial determinant of displacement. An anchor placed at *either end* of a series, or even *slightly above* or *slightly below* the series, will produce an *assimilation effect*. Thus, judgments are displaced in the direction *toward* the anchor. However, if the anchor is removed progressively further from the series so that it lies *considerably above* or *considerably below* the end stimuli, a *contrast effect* ensues. Judgments are displaced *away* from the anchor. (p. 181)[8] [Italics in the original]

Anchoring came to prominence in the fields of psychology and economics as a result of a series of experiments reported in 1974.[34] The authors of those experiments reported that in many situations "people make estimates by starting from an initial value that is adjusted to yield the final answer" and that "different starting points yield different estimates, which are biased toward the initial values" (p. 1129).[34] Their work stimulated a substantial body of empirical research. It was concluded in a review of this literature that the effects of anchoring are "extremely robust" (p. 41).[35] In the context of pricing, it can be used to change people's reference price and thus ameliorate resistance to a price that otherwise would be outside their latitude of acceptance.

Anchoring is consistent with range theory, which suggests special attention should be given to revision of the lowest and highest prices within an array of similar programs because these serve as anchors. The theory posits that the two extreme values of a stimulus (price) form the psychological anchor framework for judgments: "It is primarily the end-stimuli that control the oscillations of the absolute scale. The center of the stimulus-range has no special functional significance whatsoever. It is merely a convenient numerical value: the mean of the two end-stimuli" (p. 283).[36] This is consistent with the conclusion of the authors of assimilation-contrast theory that "it is the end values of the series that ordinarily acquire an anchoring function" (p. 33).[8]

Typically, it has been found that there is poorer retention of interior numbers in a sequence relative to end numbers. Numbers at the beginning and end of a list are recalled more frequently than those in the middle of the list.[37] It has been suggested that these reactions are also related to a principle of Gestalt psychology called outstandingness,[38] which states that some phenomena have special qualities that make perception of them easier and more lasting. The visibility of end prices makes it likely they will have the most well-established internal reference prices and have the smallest latitudes of price acceptance, so revising them is likely to meet the most resistance.[38]

Given that the highest and lowest prices are likely to have more outstandingness than others in a division, participants are likely to use them as anchors against which to judge the acceptability of prices for other programs whose prices are between those anchors. Of the two ends, it has long been recognized that the lowest price is likely to have more influence on the reference price of other programs.[39] The challenge is compounded in the public leisure field because the lowest price is often zero. Range theory posits that the more frequently individuals are exposed to the extreme values, the more influence those values will have on judgments (i.e., there will be adaptation toward them). Thus, when a service has been provided free of charge for a long time, many may perceive it as a "right" and are likely to be incensed when this is changed irrespective of how nominal the initial charge may be.

Five strategies for keeping price changes consistent with reference price emanate from the anchoring heuristic and are discussed in this section. The first recognizes that when a new service is launched, its first price becomes the anchor against which subsequent price changes are measured. The second and third strategies, decoy and numeric anchors, respectively, can be purposefully used to change the context so price increases are kept within the latitude of acceptance. A fourth strategy is to ensure consistency among related services because an outlier price for one service may inadvertently serve as an anchor against which the price of related services will be evaluated. Finally, evidence is provided illustrating that the prices of other suppliers can be used as anchors to change context and reference price effectively.

Do Not Underprice a New Service

In 1935, Konrad Lorenz, who studied animal behavior, split a large clutch of graylag geese into two groups. Group 1 hatched normally, and the goslings followed their mother around. The Group 2 eggs were incubated, and he arranged it so he was the first thing the goslings saw when they hatched. From then on, they followed him everywhere.[24] Similarly, the first price of which people become aware is a stimulus (or imprint) that serves as the anchor against which subsequent price changes are compared. It is the most influential element in the formation of people's reference prices.

Managers sometimes offer a low price for a short time when a new program is introduced to induce people to try it. After the introductory period when people have experienced it, the low price is raised to a level commensurate with the program's quality and the target market's ability to pay. Essentially, the leisure agency is saying: "We are forgoing revenue now, but because we believe this is a good program that will appeal to many who are currently uncertain about its merit, we will recoup this money in the future from repeat visits." If a threshold number of marginal users are not converted to repeat visitors and/or do not influence others to participate, the agency will not recoup the initial lost revenues.

In a classic study in the marketing field, five new brands were introduced at a low introductory price in one set of stores without any indication that this was a temporary promotional price and at their regular price in a matched set of stores.[40] The discounts used for the low introductory price ranged from 8 to 56 percent. After a short time varying from 1 to 3 weeks, the low introductory price was raised to the regular price. Although the discounts varied widely, the general sales patterns at the matched stores were similar for all five brands.

Figure 10-6 shows the low introductory price was successful in the goal of attracting large initial sales. However, over the 20 weeks of the study, the total volume of sales was greater in the regular price stores, even though the sales for the first 1 to 3 weeks in those stores were much lower. The impact on revenues was even more evident because the regular price stores did not lose revenues from initial discounting. The authors concluded: "These studies indicate that introducing products at a lower than usual price is harmful to final sales" (p. 349).[40] The study confirms the adage: You can always bring the price down, but you can't easily bring it up.

Implications for leisure managers. The study has clear implications for leisure managers. It points out the most important pricing decision is the initial price that is charged because this first price is an anchor that firmly establishes the internal reference price for the service in a user's mind. Hence, it becomes the criterion to which the acceptability of subsequent price revisions is compared.

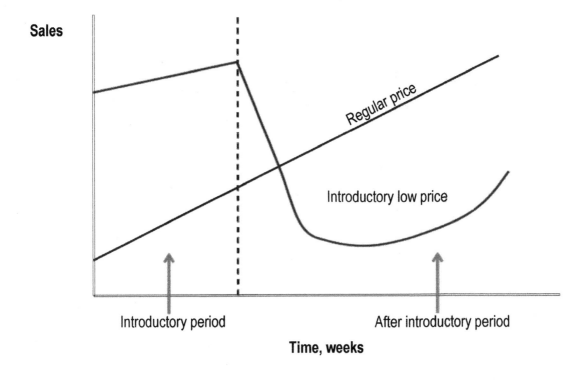

Sales

Regular price

Introductory low price

Introductory period

After introductory period

Time, weeks

Figure 10-6. The Potential Negative Impact of Introductory Price Discounts

The danger of starting with a low introductory price is that an unintended internal reference price is created. When introductory price purchasers subsequently are confronted with a big increase up to the regular price, the service is likely to be regarded as overpriced and the price viewed as unacceptable. It is outside users' latitudes of acceptable price, so it is rejected. For purchasers at the regular price, it becomes the reference price and sales of the service increase as awareness of it spreads. For example, if a city opens a new ice rink, the purpose of offering a low introductory price of (say) $5 rather than the regular price of $10 is to persuade those who have only a marginal interest and who would not go at the $10 price to try it. The anticipation is that some of the hesitant marginal users will be converted into regular users. However, the danger is that the first price becomes the reference price for core users and marginal participants. To avoid this danger, the introductory low price should be clearly positioned as a promotional price: "The price to ice skate is $10. However, to give people an opportunity to try it at our new facility, for the first two weeks only we will have a special promotional price of $5." Potential users now understand the promotional price is for only 2 weeks and the regular price of $10 is established as the reference price. This was not done in the results shown in Figure 10-6.

Consider the following situation:

- In the 1980s, a parks and recreation department launched an after-school program called Kids Klub. It was for children in Grades 1 to 5 and was available in all five of the city's elementary schools. Recreation department staff operated the program from 3:30 to 6:00 p.m. every school day at the elementary school sites, so the children did not have to travel. From the beginning, it was established as an enterprise fund operation and required no tax support. By 2012, over 1,000 children were enrolled in the program and their parents paid fees of $120 per month.

In the 1990s, the department opened a new purpose build Teen Center, which was intended to be a drop-in center for Grades 6, 7 and 8. It was located on a park site adjacent to one of the city's junior high schools. Annual membership was set at $10 a year and was not increased in subsequent years. In 2012, the cost of operating the center was $260,000 and its income was less than $3,000. Average attendance was 37 students a day. The council proposed to raise the annual fee to $100. There was outrage from parents (and by staff who surreptitiously encouraged the protests).

There was no resistance to the Kids Klub fees of $1,080 for the school year ($120 × 9 months) because break-even prices were established at the beginning of the program and raised incrementally each year within the latitude of acceptance in response to cost increases. In contrast, the massive resistance to the proposed Teen Center fee of $100 a year reflected an increase of 1,000 percent, which was far outside the latitude of acceptance.

An agency is likely to have more flexibility in the first pricing decision than in subsequent decisions because these will always be constrained by client groups relating the appropriateness and acceptability of price increases back to the anchor price. Once a low price is embodied in the public psyche, it is difficult to dislodge and overcome. Nor is there much pressure to do so until legislative bodies demand increased revenues in response to a budget crisis. By that time, the rules of the game have been set, and subsequent changes outside the latitude of acceptance are likely to invoke outrage among users no matter how vigorously the pro-poor argument of removing reverse income redistribution is made (Chapter 2). Major price changes in the future will likely incur strong opposition from those impacted by them, while only apathy or at most mild support for the increase is likely to be forthcoming from the rest of the community. Hence, there will be little managerial incentive to propose large increases.

Evidence suggests that offering a free trial rather than a low introductory price is likely to be a superior strategy for two reasons. First, there is no risk of monetary loss to the user. Second, zero price is qualitatively different from a discount. If no other similar services are offered at zero price, there will be no expectation the new offering will be free. There is awareness that this is being done for a short introductory period only, so it will not inadvertently become the reference price. When a discounted price is charged, the risk is that it will be subconsciously absorbed as a reference anchor, even when managers emphasize it is only for a short introductory period. A series of experiments on this issue led the authors to conclude: "A free promotion is more beneficial for a marketer than offering a product at a discounted price in the long term . . . Offers with low prices may lead to more devaluation, whereas a free offer may not lead to any devaluation at all" (p. 645).[41]

The constraining influence of existing prices on subsequent price revisions is illustrated by the data presented in Tables 10-4 and 10-5. These data were collected from a representative probability sample of respondents in a Texas city as part of a household personal interview survey. Respondents consisted of users and non-users of city recreational offerings. They were asked to check which of six alternate prices they considered to be the most appropriate for each of the 11 recreation services listed in Table 10-4.

Table 10-4
Perceptions of Appropriate Prices for 11 Recreation Services

Service Area	Current Average Price $	Mean Appropriate Price $	% Responding Current Average Price	Per Visit Cost of Provision $
Parks, playgrounds, greenbelts	No charge	0.00	83	4.00
Tennis	5.00	5.00	66	9.00
Swimming	2.00	2.00	72	9.00
Golf	11.00	11.00	53	19.00
Recreation centers	3.00	3.00	68	10.00
Organized athletics	3.80	3.80	62	6.00
Outdoor nature programs	2.00	2.00	67	9.00
Senior citizen programs	1.00	1.00	68	6.00
Arts facilities or programs	2.00	2.00	62	6.00
Community education programs	2.00	2.00	62	12.00
Programs for people with disabilities	No charge	0.00	90	11.00

In each case, respondents were provided with two pieces of information. First, they were informed of the current average price charged for the service (Table 10-4, column 2). Second, they were informed of the per visit cost to the agency of servicing each user (column 5). In every case, the activities were supported by a tax subsidy. Given that most respondents were non-users of a particular service, the expectation of the researchers was that perceptions of the most appropriate price would be set close to the per visit cost level (column 5) or at least at a point higher than the current average price (column 2). However, this did not occur. A substantial majority of the sample in all 11 service areas (column 4) responded that the most appropriate price (column 3) was the price currently being charged (column 2). This illustrates the strength of an existing price in formulating a reference price.

The same sample was also asked to identify the appropriate price from six alternates for two services not yet offered, but likely to be made available in the future. In these two instances, the sample was only given the estimated per visit cost to the agency of servicing each user because there was no existing price. Table 10-5 shows that without an existing price to serve as a guide, there was no consensus among respondents as to the most appropriate price. Without an existing price to serve as a cue, there was no firm reference price in people's minds. (This is analogous to the example in Figure 9-3 illustrating how context changes people's visual perceptions.) The data confirm the aphorism: A new service has no price. People showed a tendency to select the middle of the scale. This is consistent with the concept of asymmetric dominance discussed in the next section of this chapter and is a common strategy when dealing with unfamiliar phenomena. This tendency may be interpreted as representing the most comfortable "compromise" price rather than opting for the more "radical" alternatives represented by the scales' anchor points. Clearly, an agency has much more flexibility when pricing a service for the first time. In this case, managers probably could select any of the six price point options without arousing substantive opposition.

Table 10-5
Perceptions of Appropriate Prices for Two Proposed New Services

Activity A		Activity B	
Price		Price	
$	%	$	%
No charge	16	No charge	5
.75	20	1.00	19
1.25	28	2.00	33
1.75	14	3.00	25
2.25	7	4.00	4
3.00	15	5.00	14

The pernicious impact of time on initial underpricing. Underpricing a new service is likely to have a pernicious long-term impact. If a (say) 10-year forecast is made of the revenues and costs associated with a service, the results may be startling, showing the service will impose a greater burden on taxpayers every year. The effect is illustrated in Table 10-6.

Given the active opposition of users, the highest increase likely to be accepted in the political arena is one that is tied to inflation. Typically, the argument is: "Costs have gone up by 10 percent, so prices need to be raised by 10 percent." Table 10-6 shows that if admission to a new pool is set at $5 while the per person cost of servicing each user is $9, this $4 subsidy increases to $9.46 over 10 years. If there are 100,000 visits to the pool, the annual subsidy will increase from $400,000 to $946,000 over this time. The effect is especially pernicious in the case of zero-priced services because while costs will increase, zero revenues will not change.

Table 10-6

The Impact of an Initial Subsidy over 10 Years

Year	Per Person Price	Per Person Cost to Deliver the Service
1	$5.00	$9.00
2	$5.50	$9.90
3	$6.05	$10.89
4	$6.65	$11.98
5	$7.31	$13.18
6	$8.04	$14.50
7	$8.84	$15.95
8	$9.72	$17.54
9	$10.69	$19.29
10	$11.76	$21.22

While inflation means the purchasing power of the subsidy in "real dollars" will be the same in Year 10 as in Year 1, the challenge of rectifying the situation is much greater for two reasons. First, the much larger numbers in Year 10 suggest a price increase will be perceived as much higher than an equivalent increase in Year 1. For example, if a 25 percent price raise were proposed, the increase would be $1.25 in Year 1, but $3 in Year 10. Second, Table 10-6 assumes a 10 percent annual raise in price to reflect cost increases. However, the rate of increase may be smaller because of opposition from users, the empathetic bond of staff with their clienteles, and the vested interest of staff in retaining/increasing number of users if this is a primary metric in their job performance evaluation.

Purposeful Anchoring

The two types of purposeful anchors are decoy and numeric. They reflect the dual mechanisms used to process information that were discussed in Chapter 9. Decoy anchors are a consequence of the deliberative, central or System 2 route that requires effortful cognitive engagement. In contrast, the effectiveness of numeric anchors is attributable to the peripheral or System 1 processing route that is passive, non-deliberative, automatic and devoid of cognitive processing.

The implications of decoy anchors for leisure managers. The three managerial strategies associated with decoy anchors are (i) decoys may raise revenues from other services in the range, (ii) they may have an ordering effect and (iii) they can be used to frame and adjust queuing expectations.

In 1982, the results of a series of experiments were explained by "asymmetric dominance."[42] This is sometimes called the decoy effect. It occurs when a service is deliberately priced to offer inferior value to other services in the range for the purpose of increasing the sales of those other services. Effectively, the new offering is a decoy that is unlikely to be perceived as a desirable option, but can enhance the acceptability of prices and sales of other services in the range. It leads to the counterintuitive recognition that at times revenues from a division can be increased by adding a service that few have interest in purchasing. In the original study, the effect of decoys was illustrated using brands of beer:

- Subjects had the option of purchasing a six pack of premium beer for $2.60 or an alternate brand at $1.80. Only 33 percent selected the alternate brand, while 67 percent chose the premium option. When a third (decoy) option was offered at $1.60, the proportion selecting the alternate brand increased to 47 percent. When the experiment was repeated using a super premium brand priced at $3.40 as the decoy instead of the low priced option, the proportion selecting the premium option increased from 67 to 90 percent.[42]

By adding options to the high and low ends of the range that few wanted, the preferences of many were changed. In both cases, the middle priced beer benefited because it was perceived to be the safe compromise choice. The low priced brand might taste terrible, while the high priced choice might be a rip-off. The one in the middle offered the least risk.[42] The authors also provided an anecdote that is typical of findings reported in retailing:

A store owner had two camel hair jackets priced at $100 and $150 and found that the more expensive jacket was not selling. A new camel hair jacket was added and displayed for $250; the new jacket did not sell, but sales of the $150 jacket increased. (p. 95)[42]

Introducing a more expensive option raised the reference price and enhanced the value of the $150 jacket to customers.

Subsequently, the asymmetric dominance effect was explained by "extremeness aversion".[43] While losses and gains are usually defined in relation to a neutral reference point, in some situations, they are evaluated in relation to each other. If two different priced services are available, when compared to each other, their advantages and disadvantages may be perceived to be relatively large. If a middle price option is available, it will have relatively small advantages and disadvantages relative to each extreme. Thus, it becomes the compromise choice and the risk-averse action. It has been concluded that this effect is "common and robust, representing the rule rather than the exception in choice behavior" (p. 293).[43] It is likely to be most effective among users who are uncertain about the value for money of a service they are purchasing. Regular users with well-established reference prices and preferences are less likely to be influenced by this strategy. Experiments confirming the robustness of extremeness aversion have resulted in decoys becoming ubiquitous. Restaurants, for example, invariably include high priced wines on a menu because this raises the price acceptability level of their other wines. Consider the following vignettes and the experiment results reported in Figure 10-7.

- A city opened a new concession stand at its outdoor aquatic facility, which can hold approximately 700 people. It was highly successful, making sufficient profits to recover the cost of the equipment in 2 years. It sold traditional snack foods—hot dogs, hamburgers, sodas and shaved ice—but it also served the health conscious by offering chicken, Caesar salads and grilled fish. The grilled fish was an unusual item. How many mouths watered for a fish sandwich on a hot summer day? The answer was not many, and fewer than 50 such sandwiches were sold all summer. However, sales were not the objective. Fish offered a healthy choice, but also an expensive choice. They charged $6.95 for the fish sandwich, which was a lofty price for a concession stand item, but that was the point. The fish made paying $3.95 for a hamburger look like a bargain. The manager reported: "We didn't sell much fish, but it made the hamburger look cheap."

- Broadway theaters charge extreme prices for prime seats to popular shows. Five hundred dollars may seem outrageous to most theatergoers who wouldn't dream of paying that much for a ticket, but it makes whatever they do pay, say $200, seem like a deal.[44]
- Movie theater and arena/stadium operators price the super-sized popcorn slightly more than the large size so they can nudge patrons to buy the super-sized option. Its price appears reasonable when compared against the (greatly overpriced) large size, whereas without the decoy anchor, many would consider it unreasonable.[45]

The following scenario was presented to a sample of 440 student subjects:

A community recreation center offers a variety of exercise classes. All of its classes have similar features, and the costs associated with offering them are similar. They are 1 hour long, use qualified instructors and meet two times a week for 4 weeks (i.e., eight sessions). The center is starting a new yoga class. The center's managers are soliciting input on the fair price to charge participants in the new yoga class.

The sample was randomly split into five groups: a control group and four treatment groups. The price information related to the agency's existing fitness programs was provided to each group and is shown in the top half of the following table:

	T1	Control	T2	T3	T4
Price			Boot camp $110	Boot camp $130	Boot camp $250
	Pilates $85	**Pilates $85**	Pilates $85	Pilates $85	Pilates $85
	Aerobics $70	**Aerobics $70**	Aerobics $70	Aerobics $70	Aerobics $70
	Spinning $45	**Spinning $45**	Spinning $45	Spinning $45	Spinning $45
	Zumba $15				
No. of subjects	90	**123**	102	86	98
No. of usable responses	86	**100**	91	80	83
Average willingness to pay	$58.52	**$65.41**	$75.95	$70.65	$75.63

After reviewing this information, the subjects were asked:

What is the fair price to charge for a yoga class that is 1 hour long, uses a qualified instructor and meets two times a week for 4 weeks (i.e., eight sessions)?

The mean prices for the groups are shown in the last row of the table. The boot camp anchor provided to groups T2, T3 and T4 had an asymmetrical dominance effect in raising the acceptable price for the yoga class above that of the control group. However, consistent with assimilation-contrast theory, the extreme value prices for the boot camp in T3 and T4 were viewed as implausible. The results suggest that these extreme values were essentially discounted and had no more effect than the reasonable price anchor in T2. Similarly, as anticipated, the asymmetric dominance effect was present in T1, for which the addition of the low $15 anchor resulted in a lower willingness to pay than the control group.

Figure 10-7. The Influence of Price Decoys on Willingness to Pay[46]

A second strategic implication derived from decoy anchoring is potential ordering effect. Consistent with adaptation-level theory, when forming their reference prices, people apparently give greater weight to the prices they see first. Thus, users are likely to form a higher internal reference price when prices in a service line (e.g., aquatics or recreation activities) are presented to them in descending order (from high to low) rather than when they see them in ascending order (from low to high).[47-49] For example, a price of $6 is likely to be considered more favorably if it is preceded by similar service prices of $9, $8 and $7 than prices of $3, $4 and $5. The order bias is explained by anchoring on initial exposure and from loss aversion. In the descending order, each price drop is perceived to be a gain, while in the ascending order, each price increase is likely to be viewed as a loss.[49] The order bias influences communication strategies. When presenting a range of services within the same division, the highest priced services should be presented first because this will make all subsequent prices appear more reasonable.

- Assume a user has a reference price of $40 for a 10-session aerobics class. If 10-session classes for boot camp, jazzercise, yoga and spinning are priced at $100, $80, $65 and $50, respectively, and presented in that order, adaptation-level theory suggests that the aerobics $40 reference price will be raised by a greater amount than if the prices are presented in the reverse order.
- When visitors went to pay for their site in a state park campground, the ranger would respond: "It is $15 a night. Are you from out of state? Then it is $20. Do you want an electricity hookup? Then it is $22. Do you want firewood? Then it is $24." The result often was an angry camper because the first price was low, which served as the anchor, and it was then raised substantially. Rangers were instructed to reverse the offerings and start with $24. "You don't want firewood? Then it is $22. You are from in state, then it is $17."

These outcomes are consistent with the findings related to adaptation-level theory. When an experiment was conducted in which subjects were required to judge a set of weights that were presented to them in either descending or ascending order, it was reported:

> The results show that the level against which any set of weights was judged was a function of preceding stimulus levels, the ascending sets having lower adaptation levels in every case, than the descending sets. (p. 154)[33]

A final implication of decoy anchoring is that it can be used to manage customers' expectations. Because the composite price for a leisure experience includes the investment of time, decoy anchors are sometimes used to ameliorate exasperation with queues. Theme parks, for example, have signs at popular rides that say: "Wait is 30 minutes from this point." They are aware it will take 20 minutes, but by creating a decoy anchor, they hope to change customer reaction from frustration with a 30-minute wait to delight that it was "only" 20 minutes.

The implications of numeric anchors for leisure managers. The two types of numeric anchors are contextual relevant and contextual irrelevant. Their relationship can usefully be conceptualized as a continuum along which anchors are arranged according to degree of contextual relevancy. Contextual relevant anchor numbers are associated with dimensions or attributes of a program or facility, but they have no obvious influence on price. Nevertheless, in the passive processing of numeric anchors, the association with the context appears likely to endow them with more plausibility than do contextual irrelevant anchors. Results of an experiment using *contextual relevant* numeric anchors designed to influence perceptions of price are shown in Table 10-7.[46]

Table 10-7

Anchoring Admission Prices with Contextual Relevant High Numbers

The public outdoor pool is a standard 25-meter, 8-lane facility. The admission prices posted at the entrance are below:

Item	Treatment A	Control	Treatment B
Decoys			
Today's air temperature		–	30 °C
Number of staff on duty	3	–	14
Number of lifeguards on duty	7	–	–
Admission Information			
Weekend admission	$10	$10	$10
Under 16 weekend admission	$5	$5	$5
Weekday admission	$8	$8	$8
Under 16 weekday admission	$4	$4	$4
After 4 p.m. admission	$5	$5	$5
Children under 3	free	free	free
Perception of value	*3.11*	*3.28*	*3.39*

Respondents were asked:
Do you consider these prices to be (check one)

[   ]   [   ]   [   ]   [   ]   [   ]
Excellent value   Good value   Mediocre value   Poor value   Very poor value
for money   for money   for money   for money   for money

When respondents were asked their perceptions of value for money on a 5-point scale (5 = *excellent value* to 1 = *very poor value*), the group given the scenario headed by the numbers 30 and 14 reported values that were 9 percent higher than the group given the scenario headed by the numbers 3 and 7. The price structures of both scenarios were the same. The air temperature and number of staff or lifeguards relate to the context of a swimming pool, but they are irrelevant to the pricing structure. However, placing them at the top of the price list appears to have had a priming effect. A passive perusal of the list appears to result in the admission prices being perceived as either smaller or larger, reflecting the numeric anchors that were used.

Contextual irrelevant numeric anchors use numbers that clearly have no relationship to a program or its context and that are obviously arbitrary. In the marketing and psychology fields in a substantial number of empirical studies, it has been demonstrated that such implausible anchors can nevertheless be effective: "A key finding of anchoring research is that anchors that are obviously random can be just as effective as potentially informative numbers" (p. 225).[50] In the original seminal article, this was demonstrated by a famous experiment with a roulette wheel:

- A roulette wheel was rigged to stop only at 10 or 65. Subjects spun the wheel and wrote down the number on which the wheel stopped. They were then asked two questions: (i) Is the percentage of African nations among United Nations members larger or smaller than the number you just wrote? (ii) What is your best guess of the percentage of African nations in the U.N.? The average estimates of those exposed to the 10 and 65 numbers were 25 percent and 45 percent, respectively. There was no relationship between a roulette wheel number and the question of interest. Nevertheless, the numbers primed the responses.[50]

The two-stage protocol used in this experiment was widely embraced by others who confirmed the strong anchoring effect in a host of different contexts. The following examples are typical of these studies:

- Two groups were asked: Did Mahatma Gandhi die before or after the age of nine [age of 140]? And then: What is your best guess of when he died? The groups' estimates were 50 and 67, respectively.[51]
- Visitors to the San Francisco Exploratorium were asked the following questions: Is the height of the tallest redwood tree more or less than 1,200 feet [or 180 feet]? (ii) What is your best guess about the height of the tallest redwood? The average estimates were 844 and 282 feet, respectively.[50]

Typical of such studies in the context of price is an experiment in which six ordinary consumer products were used. The retail price of each was approximately $70. After the products were introduced, subjects were asked whether they would buy each good for a dollar figure equal to the last two digits of their Social Security number. After this accept/reject response, they stated their dollar maximum willingness to pay for the product. Subjects with above-median Social Security numbers stated values from 57 percent to 107 percent greater than did subjects with below-median numbers. The subjects' evaluations of the product's value were clearly biased by the first price mentioned to them, even though it was random.[52]

In all these experiments, the first stage of this standard protocol primes subjects by requiring them to process cognitively a stimulus that influences the subsequent value judgment. However, this cognitive anchor is created by an experimenter or external source and is contrived for laboratory experiments; it cannot be operationalized by leisure managers in a field situation. Any processing of a numeric anchor in the field is likely to be passive, minimal and superficial. It is unlikely to be processed into short-term memory and thus will not play a role in subsequent evaluation. This makes it unlikely that non-contextual relevant numeric anchors will be a viable tool for leisure managers.

Ensure Consistency among Related Services

Leisure agencies offer an array of services, which many will view as an inter-related, coherent set of offerings, rather than as a loose assembly of unrelated programs. Thus, the internal reference price for one of them is likely to influence, and be influenced by, the reference prices for other services that are perceived to be similar. The similarity set often comprises other programs within the same division of an agency (e.g., athletics, aquatics, recreation classes, parks, arts, recreation facilities and special events). Thus, the notion of latitude of price acceptance may extend beyond an individual program to the range of services within a division. The collective reference price may approximate the median price in the range of reference prices for all programs in the division. New programs may need to be priced within the latitude of price acceptance around that collective reference price for the prices to be accepted without resistance.[53] If one service is priced much lower than others in the division, it may be an inadvertent anchor against which the other prices are perceived to be unreasonable.

The inter-relationship of reference prices within a similarity set (assumed to be a division) directs there should be consistency of price among programs within it. For example, when the price of an aquatic program is either established for the first time or revised, users' internal reference prices for it are likely to be influenced by their perceptions of its relationship to other aquatic programs and their reference prices for those programs. Consider the following examples:

- A tanning solarium was located at a public swimming pool. The price for using the solarium was set at $10 per 30-minute session, which was the going rate for solarium use at commercial installations in the city. The intent was to use the solarium to generate funds to offset the substantial losses incurred in operating the pool without undercutting the private sector. The installation and the services associated with the solarium were high quality, but the venture was a failure. It appears the public could not accept paying $10 for a session in the solarium when admission to the swimming pool was only $2.50. The solarium's price was incompatible with the public's reference price for services offered at a public pool.
- When a community constructed a senior center, it attracted over 5,000 members to its top-of-the-line facility. It incorporated a remarkable combination of high quality aquatic, fitness, arts and social amenities. The annual membership price

for those 65 and over was $56. The popularity of this facility encouraged the council to develop an even more extensive center with similar high quality state-of-the-art elements targeted at those under 50. Membership was priced at $95. The new center's pricing flexibility was strongly constrained by the senior center's price structure because this was the anchor from which price expectations were formed. Without that anchor, if annual membership were priced at $250, there would likely have been no resistance, minimal adverse impact on visitation, but substantially enhanced revenues. However, given the $56 anchor, such a price structure for the new center would likely have aroused outrage and protest.

- A leisure agency charged $60 for a series of four art classes at its museum. It charged $20 for the same set of classes (same instructor, resources, etc.) at one of its recreation centers. Enrollments were higher at the museum than at the recreation center. Users' reference prices for the similarity set were not based on the type of class. Rather, they were derived from other offerings at the respective facilities that tended to attract clienteles with different levels of income. Inherent within this difference, it is also likely there were perceptions of a price–quality relationship, which is addressed later in the chapter.

Validate Large Price Increases by Comparing Them with Prices That Other Suppliers Charge

Simply informing people about the prices that others charge for a similar service may result in a new price being viewed more favorably. The two-step process described earlier in this section to explain the effectiveness of non-contextual numeric anchors in experimental settings similarly applies to framing new prices by comparing them with those of other suppliers. In the first stage, users are required to consider the comparative prices explicitly, while in the second stage, the comparison provides the anchor for making a comparative judgment and decision as to a new price's acceptability. Further, since other agencies have adopted them, these external prices are clearly plausible and reasonable options. Thus, given higher comparative price information, users may be persuaded to move their reference price higher and accept the new price.[19, 54, 55] For example, if the admission price to a swimming pool is increased by 100 percent from $2 to $4, there may be vigorous negative reaction. A more favorable evaluation may be elicited by comparing the new price with those charged in proximate communities: "In cities A, B, C and D, the prices are $5, $4.75, $4.50 and $4.00, respectively, so our new price is still lower than those charged by others." Alternatively, the external reference price could be that of non-profit or commercial entities in the community: "ABC health club charges $9, the university charges $7, and the YMCA charges $6, so our new price still provides residents with a relatively low cost option." Comparisons with non-substitute services may provide users with an external reference point with which to compare a service's price favorably: "For $4 you can swim all afternoon or have two large Cokes at a fast-food outlet."

The examples in Tables 10-8 and 10-9 show how the Texas Parks and Wildlife Department used this strategy to illustrate to stakeholders that the substantial price increases they were proposing to implement in boat registration, hunting and combined license prices were reasonable. The strategy was successful; there was no protest.

Table 10-8
*Comparing Boat Registration Fees with Those of
Other Suppliers*

Description	Texas	Florida	Michigan
16' and under	**$18.00**	$27.50	$10.60
16' – 26'	**$27.00**	$43.50	$60.00
26' – 40'	**$36.00**	$107.50	$162.00
Over 40'	**$45.00**	$171.50	$186.00

Table 10-9
Comparing Hunting and Combination License Prices with Those of Surrounding States

State	Resident			Non-Resident	
	Small Game	General	Combination	Small Game	General
Arkansas	$10.50	$25.00	$35.50	$65.00	$185.00
Louisiana	$10.50	$21.00	$53.00	$86.00	$160.50
New Mexico	$9.50	$43.50	$47.00	$79.00	$348.00
Oklahoma	$12.50	$44.75	$53.25	$85.00	$301.50
Texas	**N/A**	**$18.00**	**$30.00**	**$75.00**	**$205.00**
Average (Excluding Texas)	$10.75	$33.56	$47.19	$78.75	$248.75

Several researchers have investigated the influence of knowledge of external prices for comparable leisure services on changing willingness to pay a higher price. In an early study of this issue, a probability sample of 254 adult residents was asked: "What would you expect to pay for a swim at a city pool?" Those provided with the much higher external price charged for swimming at a commercial pool in the city reported a higher price expectation than those who did not receive this information. Among pool users, the commercial pool price information raised reference price by 13 percent, while among non-users, the increase was 26 percent.[56] Presumably, after being alerted to the commercial price, non-users wanted to see a higher price charged at the public pool to reduce the amount of tax subsidy they were required to provide.

The positive impact of comparative price information was reinforced soon after by similar results reported in a study of attitudes to camping fees at Maine state parks of resident and non-resident users.[17] When informed of the average fee charged at Maine commercial campgrounds offering similar facilities and services, the percentage in the two groups who thought the state park fees were too low increased from 9 to 14 percent and from 8 to 16 percent, respectively.

This pattern was further confirmed among a sample of 2,855 visitors to the Hoover Dam power plant in Nevada. The visitors were asked whether the Hoover Dam price they were charged was too low, just right or too high. Subsequently, they were given information on the entrance fees to other well-recognized attractions in the United States for which higher prices were charged and were asked the same question. Among Nevada residents, the percentage of those perceiving the price was too low shifted from 3 to 10 percent, while among non-residents, the shift was from 2 to 5 percent.[57]

The strategies of comparing prices with those of other suppliers and providing cost information, which is discussed in Chapter 11, are often alternatives. If an agency's price is high relative to other suppliers' prices, the cost information strategy is likely to be more persuasive, whereas if it is relatively low, the comparative price information may be more effective.

RECOGNIZE PRICE MAY BE A SIGNAL OF QUALITY

Leisure services are intangible. Because services cannot be touched or felt in advance, decisions by those who have no experience with a service are based on expectations and cues an agency puts forward. Price is one cue. It has to be high enough to ensure confidence in a program's quality, but not so expensive that the target market will refuse to purchase it. Thus, in some situations, price is a market signal. It has been noted: "Setting the right price in services is more than a matter of generating dollars today. It is also a matter of sending the right message about the service. Prices are evidence" (p. 104).[58] Market signals have been defined as "activities which, by design or accident, alter the benefits of, or convey information to, other individuals in the market" (p. 1).[59] Signals function as informational cues when the attributes of a service are unknown and unobservable prior to purchasing it. The void created by this information gap may be filled by price because price is observable and in most people's minds is correlated with quality.

The suggestion that purchasers can use price to evaluate quality was first mooted in 1945 when it was noted that as the array of goods available for purchase proliferated, it was no longer possible for purchasers to use their experience to evaluate quality:

> Few of us can appraise the qualities of an electric iron or of toothpaste, and the frequent introduction of new models and improvements prevents us from relying on experience. . . . More and more, therefore, the consumer of today has to judge quality by indices of quality . . . "mass observation" of one's friends and their wives shows that more often than not people judge quality by price. (p. 100)[60]

The author recognized the inherent conundrum of this phenomenon as a "double-edged weapon" in that "a commodity offered at a lower price than competing commodities will be both more attractive to the consumer on account of its greater cheapness and less attractive on account of its suspected inferior quality" (p. 101).[60]

He suggested that "it is perfectly rational" (p. 103)[60] to make this association about services whose quality is unknown before they are tried, because in most contexts a high price reflects either a high demand for superior quality or high production costs associated with high quality. This is consistent with adaptation-level theory in that users are accustomed to increments in quality being accompanied by concomitant increases in price. This was illustrated in an experimental study of differently priced campgrounds:

- Subjects for the study were drawn from a pool of state park campers. The authors examined the amenities (facilities, services) people expected at differently priced state campgrounds. Subjects were presented with one of three prices, so the three treatment groups were designed to represent a low, average and high priced campground. They were given a list of 18 campground amenities (flush toilets, wood for sale, coin-operated hot showers, etc.) and asked whether they would expect to find each at the campground they were given. The authors reported: "For a payment of $6 per night, respondents indicated they expected an average of 6.17 amenities. At $12 per night, they expected an average of 8.27 amenities. And at $18 a night, they expected an average of 10.59 amenities" (p. 88).[61]

Figure 10-8 shows a contrast of the classic backward sloping economic demand curve with the price–quality relationship curve. The principles are illustrated by using as a hypothetical example the number of registrations for a six-session bridge class targeted at a middle class clientele. The traditional curve shows that at a price of $120 ($20 per class) for the six classes, there are no registrations because the price is perceived to be too high. As the price falls, the number of registrations increases, so when it drops to $30 ($5 per class), 60 people register.

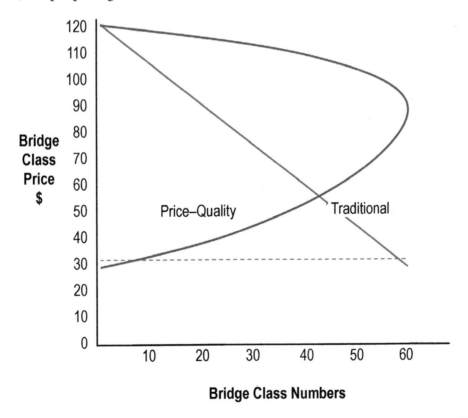

Figure 10-8. A Traditional Economic Demand Curve and a Price–Quality Demand Curve

The price–quality curve is parabolic, reflecting that the relationship operates within lower and upper boundaries.[2, 62] This also recognizes there is a latitude of acceptable prices within which it operates. Figure 10-8 shows that there are no registrations for the class when it is priced at $30 ($5 per class) or lower because prospects are suspicious that it will be low quality and perhaps that "my kind of people will not be there." As the price is raised, the number of registrations increases, so when it reaches $90 ($15 per class), 60 registrations occur. Beyond that point, the number of registrations declines because the price is perceived to be too high by increasing numbers of prospects. The figure shows that at a price of $40, 20 people register, indicating 40 prospects did not sign up because the price was too low. At a $110 price, there will also be 20 registrations, indicating 40 prospects do not sign up because the price is too high.

To accommodate the different demand curves represented in Figure 10-8, two bridge classes could be offered using different names to appeal to the different market demand elasticities. "Serious Bridge" might be priced at $90. This would offer enhanced image and prestige and would maximize participation and revenue at the high end of the market. An alternate class, "Recreational Bridge," would be priced at $50 to capture demand from those at the middle and lower ends who are more price sensitive.

The signaling power of price is suggested by the meanings associated with the words "cheap" and "expensive." In 1945, it was noted:

> The word "cheap" usually means inferior quality nowadays; and in the United States "expensive" is in the process of losing its original meaning and becoming a synonym for superior quality. Worse still, one of the largest American breweries uses the advertising slogan: "Michelob, America's highest priced brew!" (p. 100)[60]

This 70-year-old observation remains valid today. It suggests the word "cheap" should be replaced by synonyms, such as "affordable," "inexpensive," "value for money," "moderate," "modest," "economical" or "cost effective."

The rejection of low priced services is a form of risk avoidance, the risk being that inexpensive services may be less likely to give desired satisfaction. Given the investment in the opportunity cost of time, the personal energy involved, sunk costs in equipment and the travel costs incurred, many potential users may feel it unreasonable to risk using a low priced service for the relatively small monetary savings that may accrue. Long ago, the 19th century British social critic John Ruskin is alleged to have formulated the Common Law of Business Balance:

> It's unwise to pay too much, but it's worse to pay too little. When you pay too much, you lose a little money—that is all. When you pay too little, you sometimes lose everything, because the thing you bought is incapable of doing the thing it was bought to do. (p. 17)[63]

An important corollary of the price–quality relationship is that higher prices increase quality expectations. If the expectations are not met, the consequences of participants' disillusionment may be that demand for, and revenue from, a service may be lower than they would have been if a lower price had been charged.

Numerous research studies of this relationship have been reported in the marketing field. Reviews of these have confirmed general acceptance of the price–quality relationship, which is undergirded by the aphorism: You get what you pay for. However, its effectiveness is qualified by the amount of an individual's experience with a service, the nature of a particular program and the context in which it is delivered.[64]

Not surprisingly, as experience with a service increases, the effectiveness of price as a cue for quality declines. It is likely to be especially prominent when the characteristics of a service are unobservable.[65] For example, a U.S. Navy base charged officers a higher price than it did other ranks for the use of its rental cottages and golf course. The internal characteristics and quality of the rental cottages were identical, but they were unobservable. Complaints about the rental cottages came from the other ranks who assumed their lower price meant they were being allocated inferior cabins or receiving lower levels of service. There were no complaints about the different golf fees because they could visibly observe they were receiving the same experience.

If no other extrinsic cues are available, price is a relatively powerful communicator of quality. The presence of additional cues in a given context reduces the signaling influence of price. People's knowledge or impression of an agency's quality "norm" will be used to interpret the probable quality of a new service. If an agency has a reputation for delivering good quality and value—for integrity—and there is consistency in the perceived quality–price ratios across its offerings, these attributes will positively reinforce the strength of a price signal.

Other cues may include experience with similar programs offered by other leisure agencies, a program's name, the instructor's reputation, and knowledge of the cost required to deliver the program. The signaling impact of price will only be interpreted with confidence if it is consonant with these other cues. Evidence suggests the agency's reputation is likely to be the strongest of these perception cues and that multiple cues have more effect than single cues.[66]

Implications for Leisure Managers

If a leisure agency charges a low price that does not accurately reflect the quality of a program, it is devaluing the program to potential users. Consider the following illustrations:

- A summer youth day camp program was offered and priced at $10 for the week. Too few signed up for the program to be implemented. The following year, the same agency offered the same program at $50 per week, and it was fully subscribed. This suggests the targeted group took price to be an indicator of the quality of the day camp.
- A regional parks agency constructed two campsites on opposite sides of the same river. They were of similar design and quality. The agency priced them at $15 and $20 per night, anticipating that the $15 site would attract larger numbers and be relatively crowded, while the $20 site would offer a more exclusive experience. The reverse outcome occurred. The less crowded, more exclusive site was invariably the $15 site. The $20 price unintentionally signaled that site offered a superior experience, resulting in it being more crowded.

- If daily swim lessons for children in the summer months are offered in a community by four entities whose prices for a week's lessons are private club, $70; YMCA, $45; university, $40; and leisure agency, $30, many residents would elect the private club assuming that its lessons are the best because its price is highest.
- Broadway theaters have long used the price–quality relationship to their advantage. A Broadway producer explained:

  > Cheap seats don't sell. You know why they don't sell? Because if you price Orchestra or Mezzanine seats real cheap, people think there is something wrong with them: Broadway depends on tourists who have a limited time to pick a show and may have only a sketchy notion of what they're buying. They are not in a position to judge how much specific seats are worth. In assessing the value of a seat, there is not much a tourist can do except take a cue from the ticket's price. A ticket's perceived value is proportional to its price, almost regardless of what that price is. Many believe that the $450 premium orchestra seats for *The Producers* were a factor in that show's long, profitable run. Tourists figured that any show with $450 tickets must be worth seeing. (p. 14)[67]

- An annual banquet held to honor volunteers was provided free of charge. Attendance was disappointing. Many volunteers had assumed it would be a self-service, down-market, barbeque occasion, whereas it was in fact an upmarket waiter-serviced occasion. The following year, the city printed tickets with a price on them of $50, but gave them free to qualified volunteers. Attendance increased dramatically.
- The Hollywood Bowl traditionally offers tickets as cheap as $1 to its summer concerts. The Bowl is run by Los Angeles County Parks and Recreation Department, and the dollar seats are intended as a public service:

  > The trouble is that those who've never tried them assume they're awful. The Bowl is a huge place (17,376 seats), and the one-dollar seats are the farthest from the stage. But the musical experience is essentially the same because of the excellent sound system in the Bowl. The view of the sunset and the city is better from the dollar seats. Much of the time, the hundred-dollar seats are packed and unobtainable, while the one-dollar seats are empty. A lot of music lovers miss out – because the price is too *low*. (p. 15)[67]

These examples suggest that if the targeted clientele for a program is middle class, a low price may be interpreted as signaling a low quality program not intended for them and may dissuade some from participating. Thus, greater participation may be forthcoming if prices are raised. Target markets will interpret what constitutes a high or low price differently. For some, $5 for a program may be a high price and connote high quality, while for others, a $5 price may be perceived as a low price and communicate low quality.

The price–quality relationship is especially salient in the public leisure services field because of its tradition of subsidizing programs, driven by a concern for serving the economically disadvantaged. The resulting low prices, for the most part, do not reflect low quality. Nevertheless, they inadvertently communicate that message to uninformed citizens who have few other clues available to them for evaluating the agency's quality. This contributes to reinforcing negativism in the community toward the field. It suggests that whenever the economically disadvantaged are not the target audience, it would be helpful to enhancing an agency's overall image as a high quality service provider if it charged higher prices that signaled that message.

In Chapter 11, it will be noted that if the perception of quality is enhanced, prices can be raised concomitantly to reflect this. In the leisure field, there are opportunities to raise perceptions of quality by regulating the supply of a program so user demand for it is greater than the available supply. In Chapter 1, it was pointed out that investment of time is a component of composite price. Hence, the price–quality relationship can be extended to time. In this case, the cue used to deduce quality is queues and wait times rather than money. For example, if there are queues outside a restaurant, to some it is likely to communicate a superior experience because people are incurring the additional cost of their time. If the restaurant were bigger so queues were absorbed, this cue would be lost.

New movies sometimes open at a restricted number of theaters rather than being widely released. The theaters typically charge standard prices, even though they could sell out at higher prices. They believe the resulting long lines for tickets (no advance purchases are allowed) generate publicity that communicates these are must-see movies. This is worth more than the additional revenue they could collect by charging a premium price. An exemplar of this strategy is *The Mousetrap*, the longest running theater show in the world, which is described in Figure 10-9.

The Mousetrap is a run-of-the-mill murder mystery play set in Monkswell Manor country guesthouse in the English countryside. When it opened in the West End theater district of London at the Ambassadors Theatre in November 1952, its creator, Agatha Christie, predicted its run would last 8 months—it is still running! It has completed over 26,000 performances, with eight showtimes a week for over 60 years. It is by far the longest running show of any in the world.

Since the opening night, each performance has finished with one of the actors saying: "Now you have seen *The Mousetrap* you are our partner in crime, and we ask you to preserve the tradition by keeping the secret of whodunit locked in your hearts." Thus, the audience and media are requested not to reveal the identity of the murderer.

Ambassadors is one of the smallest of the approximately 40 theaters in the West End with a capacity of 450 seats. After being produced there for 22 years, *The Mousetrap* moved next door in 1974 to St. Martins Theatre and has played there since that date. St. Martins, which was planned and constructed at the same time as Ambassadors in 1913, is only marginally larger with 550 seats.

The restricted seat capacity was a key factor in creating and sustaining momentum for *The Mousetrap*. London hosts over 25 million tourists every year. One of the items on the to-do list of many of them is to see shows in the West End. The high visibility productions are likely to be sold out months in advance and are expensive, so many tourists settle for whatever is available at a more reasonable price.

Agatha Christie was a renowned mystery writer and her name recognition, together with the lower price reflecting low production costs of the play, was sufficient to attract many tourists to *The Mousetrap*. With such a small seat capacity in the theater, the show quickly sold out. To many, this communicated it must be a superior experience, even though in reality it was attributable to the theater's small size. The sold out mantra created momentum, which was sustained when it changed theaters. The creation of scarcity was further enhanced by Ms. Christie stipulating that outside the West End only one version of the play can be performed annually in the U.K., and no film adaptation can be produced until the West End production has been closed for at least 6 months.

In addition to communicating superior quality, the restricted supply also conveyed prestige on those who saw it because many were unable to do so. At some point, the source of momentum became its longevity, which conveyed legendary status. Visitors now have their photograph taken alongside the sign in the foyer proclaiming: "This performance is number 25,871 of Agatha Christie's *The Mousetrap*, the world's longest running play," thus proclaiming to their friends their place in theatrical history. *The Mousetrap*, like Big Ben and the Changing of the Guard, is now something you have to see if you visit London.

Figure 10-9. Communicating Quality by Creating Scarcity: The Case of *The Mousetrap*

Recognition that scarcity leads to an aura of exclusivity, which raises perceptions of quality and enables a higher price to be charged, has resulted in the downsizing of many sport arenas and stadiums. Traditionally, it was almost axiomatic that bigger sport facilities were better. This resulted in building many facilities that were typically half full:

> We're going back into a number of facilities and downsizing from, say, 12,000 to 8,000 seats. They're suddenly selling out games at 8,000. They're pulling more people than they've ever pulled, because the environment is just so much better. The buzz inevitably extends beyond facility walls. The old wisdom was, "Well, we always want to have a ticket for anybody who wants a ticket." But when you're experiencing sell-outs, more people want season tickets. More people buy their tickets in advance. And then there's buzz about a hard-to-get ticket. If everybody knows that they can walk up the day of a game and get a ticket, no one talks about it. (p. 144)[68]

The downsizing invariably is accompanied by an upgrading of quality. Instead of benches having seats squeezed together, seat width is increased from 19" to 20"; chair backs are added; and seat depth is increased from the old standard 24" to 33", which creates more foot room. The result is loss of only seats that could not be sold; increased difficulty in acquiring a ticket; much improved crowd atmosphere and ambiance in the facility; and higher prices for the enhanced experience, leading to more revenue.[68]

The generalizable message for leisure managers is that scarcity often enhances perceptions of quality. Consider the following:

- A campsite that is fully booked.
- A festival site that has reached capacity.
- A softball league that cannot accommodate more teams.
- A national park that closes its gates on peak days because it is deemed to be full.
- A decade long wait for a permit to raft on the Colorado River through the Grand Canyon.
- A recreation class that has reached capacity.

In these types of situations, price can be increased because scarcity is created, and with it, the perception of high quality. Price can be part of the rationing mechanism to determine who should receive the service. The presumption is that those who most desire it will be prepared to pay more for it. If the supply is increased so scarcity is removed, more resistance to higher prices is likely.

In extreme cases, prestige and status may contribute to the quality–price relationship. In these instances, being able to pay a higher price is a self-authentication of success or alternatively offers an individual the opportunity to communicate a higher social status to friends, relatives or the world in general. For example, in the art world, it is sometimes said: "If you can't sell something. Just double the price." Often the price paid for an artwork is the trophy itself. It becomes a manifestation of "conspicuous consumption" designed to ostentatiously communicate status. Indeed, the pragmatic uselessness of an artwork may reinforce this end. Some among the crowds are also likely to line up to see painting exhibitions featuring famous artists; they are motivated not by emotional affect or enjoyment associated with viewing the artworks, but rather by the ability to say to friends: "I saw that $50 million piece of art." They "bask in the robust glow of prosperity."[69]

Over a century ago, it was suggested that "conspicuous consumption of valuable goods is a means of respectability to the gentleman of leisure" (p. 75).[70] The author suggested, "The only practicable means of impressing one's pecuniary ability on unsympathetic observers of one's everyday life is an unremitting demonstration of ability to pay." He further observed, "A cheap coat makes a cheap man . . . There is probably no one who does not feel the convincing force of this maxim" (p. 157).[70]

CUSTOMARY PRICING

There are occasions when costs for a service increase by an unusual amount, when policy changes require a larger proportion of costs to be covered by revenues or when some other contingency arises that appears to make an increase beyond the latitude of price acceptance inevitable. An alternative strategy is to keep the price increase within this latitude zone and to accomplish the financial goal by cutting a program's costs. This strategy removes the need for adaptation to a new price. It has been termed "candy-bar pricing"[44] in recognition of the candy companies' strategy of keeping the price of a chocolate bar at (say) 75 cents and the packaging at the same length to perpetuate the illusion of the status quo while incrementally reducing the size of the bar. Similar examples abound in the private sector:

- In addition to candy bars, cigarettes, potato chips and cookies may keep the same price and packaging, while the size or quantity of the product is reduced.
- Telephone companies may keep the same price, but reduce the amount of calling time it buys.
- Restaurants may reduce the size of meal portions (and the size of plates on which the meals are served to "hide" the reductions) while holding down the price.

Implications for Leisure Managers

In the leisure field, the term "customary pricing" has been adopted to describe this strategy because this situation often arises when a price has been at the same level for so long that users have become accustomed to it and raising it will arouse protests.[71] It could also be termed "backward costing" because it is based on the premise that the price is fixed and managers have to work backwards and reduce the cost of service delivery to ensure there is no net reduction in the program's bottom line.

Customary prices are difficult for a leisure manager to ignore. In a sense, the existence of customary or traditional prices simplifies the pricing task. Historical precedent or custom has determined these prices, and it is up to the agency to produce programs or services that may be offered economically at those prices. The emphasis has to be on cost control, which means reducing the quantity of the service offered. Consider the following examples:

- Retain the price of a senior citizen annual pass for the golf course, but limit its use to off-peak times or to a fixed number of rounds per year, say 50, after which the regular greens fee applies. The times and number of rounds may be incrementally curtailed each year with the increments being small enough to stay within the latitude of acceptance.
- Retain the price for a softball league, a recreation class or another activity and incrementally reduce the number of games or classes the fee buys.
- The price for prime seats at a major college football stadium had been $95 for several years. There was concern that raising the price to $100 for the usually sold out games would arouse attention, be perceived as a quantum increase outside the acceptable zone, and generate negative fan and alumni reactions. The equivalent amount of revenue was raised by keeping the price at $95, but reducing the width of bench seats in the stadium from 18" to 17" so more spectators could be accommodated.

When the quantity of service offered reaches the lowest point acceptable to a client group, the price can be raised and justified by a commensurate increase in the quantity offered. Applying this strategy to a recreation class may result in the pattern shown in Table 10-10. The price in this example remains at $50, but the number of classes each year is reduced. In Year 5, the original number of classes is restored, but because this represents a 30 percent increase over the previous year, the price is increased by a similar percentage.

Table 10-10
An Illustration of Customary Pricing
Applied to a Recreation Class

Year	Number of Classes	Price
1	10	$50
2	9	$50
3	8	$50
4	7	$50
5	10	$70
6	9	$70

The cost reduction associated with customary pricing should always be imposed on the quantity of service provided, not on its quality. One aphorism states that the pain of low quality is remembered long after the joy of low price is forgotten. The adaptation mechanism ensures that price changes have a relatively short-term impact on the psyche. Memories of poor quality are much more durable, which makes it unwise to reduce quality to "hold the line" on price. The long-term viability of an agency depends on the quality of its services. If this is compromised, its reputation and image suffer and the confidence and support of users diminishes, along with that of their elected representatives.

SUMMARY

As long as price increases are *nibbles and stay within the latitude of acceptance zone,* there will be no resistance. Thus, there should be frequent (probably annual) small price increases rather than infrequent large increases. Types of service, different target markets, prices other suppliers charge, frequency of purchase, degrees of loyalty and nature of the existing price number all contribute to the breadth of the latitude of price acceptance. However, the zone is likely to be wider for higher priced services than for those at the lower end because it is the percentage change in the price, not the absolute amount of a price increase, that is likely to be critical.

When price increases become bites—that is, they are raised beyond the latitude of price acceptance—clientele resistance is likely, and is often motivated more by outrage at its "unfairness" than by inability to pay the new price. This response is likely to be particularly pronounced if the price goes from zero to some monetary value for the first time. Over time, a bite price that is initially perceived to be unfair is likely to evolve into a revised reference price norm that is no longer perceived as unfair. This process is termed a "participant adjustment period." Three strategies can be used to minimize its duration: (i) invite existing pass holders to renew before the new prices become effective, (ii) announce the price increases a long time in advance of their implementation and (iii) demonstrate the increase is attributable to cost increases or changing political or economic conditions outside the agency's control.

Temporal reframing or the pennies-a-day strategy involves lengthening the time frame over which a given price is paid. This reduces the sense of loss associated with a large price and adjusts the reference price by changing the category of purchases with which it is being compared.

Anchoring recognizes that the most distinctive and resonant price stimulus to which people are exposed substantially influences their subsequent judgments. Five strategies for keeping price changes consistent with reference price emanate from the anchoring heuristic.

The first is to recognize that the initial price charged firmly establishes a reference price in a user's mind. It becomes the criterion against which the acceptability of subsequent price revisions is compared. This makes it imperative not to underprice a new service because sustained revenue losses for the duration of the program's life are likely to result. The effect is especially pernicious in the case of zero price because while the costs will increase, zero revenues will not change.

Decoy anchors derive from the concept of asymmetric dominance. This strategy requires pricing one service at the high end of a range unreasonably high so it is unlikely to be perceived as a desirable option. However, its existence enhances the acceptability of prices and sales of other services in the range. There are two other dimensions of decoy strategies. First, people give greater weight to the prices they see first. Thus, their reference prices for services within a division are likely to be higher if they are listed from highest to lowest rather than vice versa. Finally, decoys can be used to manage customers' expectations by reducing their frustration with long wait times for a service.

While decoy anchors require deliberation and cognitive engagement, the third anchoring strategy, numeric anchors, is intended to influence non-deliberative, automatic, passive decisions. The two types of numeric anchors are contextual relevant, whereby the anchor numbers are associated with dimensions or attributes of a program or service, and contextual irrelevant, whereby the numbers have no relation to a program or its context and are obviously arbitrary. The substantial literature showing the effectiveness of contextual irrelevant numbers in a laboratory situation is not operationalizable in the leisure field. In contrast, contextual relevant numeric anchors constitute a viable strategy for leisure managers to consider.

A fourth anchoring strategy is to ensure consistency among related services. The latitude of acceptance may extend beyond an individual program to the range of services within a division. An individual reference price must be consistent with those in the range. The collective reference price may be the median price of all reference prices in a division, and the latitude of acceptance may be constructed around that median. If one service is priced much lower than others in the division, it may be an inadvertent decoy anchor against which other prices are perceived to be unreasonable.

If people are informed or reminded of the higher prices that other suppliers of a similar service charge, this comparative information may persuade them to move their reference price higher. This fifth anchoring strategy complements that of providing cost information, which is discussed in the next chapter. If an agency's price is high relative to other suppliers, the cost information is likely to be more persuasive, whereas if it is relatively low, the comparative price information may be more effective.

Many leisure services are intangible. When the attributes of a service are unknown and unobservable prior to purchasing it, price is often used as a signal from which potential users infer its quality. Some will reject a low priced service because they will infer the risk that it will not deliver the desired level of quality. Cognizance of the *price–quality relationship* is especially pertinent in the public leisure field because of its tradition of subsidizing programs. The resulting low prices for the most part do not reflect low quality, but this is the message they may communicate to uninformed citizens who have few other clues for evaluating services. In some instances, the relationship extends to wait lists and lines, which may be perceived as clues that an offering is high quality.

Customary pricing cuts a program's costs rather than raising its price to keep the price within the latitude of acceptance. However, the cost reduction should always be imposed on the quantity of service provided, not on its quality.

REFERENCES

1. Kalyanaram, G., & Little, J. D. C. (1994). An empirical analysis of latitude of price acceptance in consumer package goods. *Journal of Consumer Research, 21,* 408–418.
2. Gabor, A., & Granger, C. W. J. (1965). The pricing of new products. *Scientific Business, 3,* 3–12.
3. Gabor, A., & Granger, C. W. J. (1964). Price sensitivity of the consumer. *Journal of Advertising Research, 4*(4), 40–44.
4. Kahneman, D., & Tversky, A. (1979). Prospect theory: An analysis of decision under risk. *Econometrica, 47,* 263–291.
5. Krishnamurthi, L., Mazumdar, T., & Raj, S. P. (1992). Asymmetric response to price in consumer brand choice and purchase quantity decisions. *Journal of Consumer Research, 19,* 387–400.
6. Kaman, J. M., & Toman, W. (1970). Psychophysics of price. *Journal of Marketing Research, 7*(1), 27–35.
7. Monroe, K. B., & Lee, A. Y. (1999). Remembering versus knowing: Issues in buyers' processing of price information. *Journal of the Academy of Marketing Science, 27,* 207–225.
8. Sherif, M., & Hovland, C. I. (1961). *Social judgment: Assimilation and contrast effects on communication and attitude change.* New Haven, CT: Yale University Press.
9. Schindler, R. M., & Kirby, P. N. (1997). Patterns of rightmost digits used in advertised prices: Implication for nine-ending effects. *Journal of Consumer Research, 24,* 192–201.
10. Della Bitta, A. J., & Monroe, K. B. (1980). A multivariate analysis of the perception of value from retail price advertising. *Advances in Consumer Research, 7,* 161–165.
11. Gupta, S., & Cooper, L. G. (1992). The discounting of discounts and promotion thresholds. *Journal of Consumer Research, 19,* 401–411.
12. Marshall, R., & Long, S. B. (2002). Price threshold and discount saturation point in Singapore. *Journal of Product and Brand Management, 11,* 147–159.

13. Della Bitta, A. J., Monroe, K. B., & McGinnis, J. M. (1981). Consumer perceptions of comparative price advertisements. *Journal of Marketing Research, 18,* 416–427.

14. Mazumdar, T., Raj, S. P., & Sinha, I. (2005). Reference price research: Review and propositions. *Journal of Marketing, 69*(4), 84–102.

15. Howard, D. R., & Selin, S. W. (1987). A method for establishing consumer price tolerance levels for public recreation services. *Journal of Park and Recreation Administration, 5*(3), 48–59.

16. City of San Jose, Resolution No. 74983.

17. Reiling, S. D., Criner, G. K., & Oltmanns, S. E. (1988). The influence of information on users' attitudes towards campground user fees. *Journal of Leisure Research, 20,* 208–217.

18. Coalter, F. (2004). Reference pricing: Changing perceptions of entrance charges for sport and recreation. *Managing Leisure, 9*(2), 73–86.

19. Fix, P. J., & Vaske, J. J. (2007). Visitor evaluations of recreation user fees at Flaming Gorge National Recreation Area. *Journal of Leisure Research, 39,* 611–622.

20. Vaske, J. J., Donnelly, M. P., & Taylor, J. G. (1999). The price is "about" right: National wildlife refuge visitors' evaluations of the fee demonstration program. *Human Dimensions of Wildlife, 4*(4), 62–72.

21. Ostergren, D., Solop, F. I., & Hagen, K. K. (2005). National Park Service fees: Value for the money or a barrier to visitation? *Journal of Park and Recreation Administration, 23*(1), 18–36.

22. Lundgren, A. L., Lime, D. W., Warzecha, C. A., & Thompson, J. L. (1997). *Monitoring 1997 park visitor reactions to the National Park Service Recreational Fee Demonstration Program* (Research Summary No. 10). Minneapolis: Cooperative Park Studies Unit, University of Minnesota.

23. Duffield, J., Patterson, D., Neher, C., & Chambers, C. (2000). *Evaluation of the National Park Service Fee Demonstration Program: 1998 visitor survey* (Research Summary). Washington, DC: National Park Service Social Science Program.

24. Ariely, D. (2009). *Predictably irrational.* New York, NY: HarperCollins.

25. McCarville, R. E., Reiling, S. D., & White, C. M. (1996). The role of fairness in users' assessments of first time fees for a public recreation service. *Leisure Sciences, 18,* 61–76.

26. Kahneman, D., Knetsch, J. L., & Thaler, R. H. (1986). Fairness as a constraint on profit seeking: Entitlements in the market. *American Economic Review, 76,* 728–741.

27. Crompton, J. L., & Kim, S. (2001). Reactions to a large increase in admission price to state parks. *Journal of Park and Recreation Administration, 19*(4), 42–59.

28. Crompton, J. L., & Lamb, C. W. (1986). *Marketing government and social services.* New York, NY: John Wiley.

29. McCarville, A. E., Sears, D., & Furness, S. (1999). User and community preferences for pricing park services: A case study. *Journal of Park and Recreation Administration, 17*(1), 91–105.

30. McCurdy, D. R. (1970). Recreationists' attitudes toward user fees: Management implications. *Journal of Forestry, 68,* 645–646.

31. Evans, J. (1983). Admission charges to Woodspring Museum 1980. *Museums Journal, 82,* 241–242.

32. Gourville, J. T. (1998). Pennies-a-day: The effect of temporal reframing on transaction evaluations. *Journal of Consumer Research, 24,* 395–408.

33. Helson, H. (1964). *Adaptation-level theory: An experimental and systematic approach to behavior.* New York, NY: Harper & Row.

34. Tversky, A., & Kahneman, D. (1974). Judgment under uncertainty: Heuristics and biases. *Science, 185,* 1124–1131.

35. Furnham, A., & Boo, C. (2011). A literature review of the anchoring effect. *Journal of Socio-Economics, 40*(1), 35–42.

36. Volkmann, J. (1951). Scales of judgment and their implications for social psychology. In J. Rohrer & M. Sherif (Eds.), *Social psychology at the crossroads* (pp. 273–296). New York, NY: Harper.

37. Hinrichs, J. V., & Novick, L. R. (1982). Memory for numbers: Nominal vs. magnitude information. *Memory & Cognition, 19,* 479–486.

38. Monroe, K. B. (2003). *Pricing: Making profitable decisions.* New York, NY: McGraw-Hill.

39. Nagle, T. T., & Holden, R. K. (1995). *The strategy and tactics of pricing.* Englewood Cliffs, NJ: Prentice Hall.

40. Doob, A. N., Carlsmith, J. M., Freedman, J. L., Landauer, T. K., & Tom, S. (1969). Effect of initial selling price on subsequent sales. *Journal of Personality and Social Psychology, 11,* 345–350.

41. Palmeira, M. M., & Srivastara, J. (2013). Free offer ≠ cheap product: A selective accessibility account on the valuation of free offers. *Journal of Consumer Research, 40,* 644–656.

42. Huber, J., Payne, J. W., & Puto, C. (1982). Adding asymmetrically dominated alternatives: Violations of regularity and the similarity hypothesis. *Journal of Consumer Research, 9,* 90–98.

43. Simonson, I., & Tversky, A. (1992). Choice in context: Trade-off contrast and extremeness aversion. *Journal of Marketing Research, 29,* 281–295.

44. Blinder, A. S., Caunetti, R. R. D., Labow, D. E., & Rudd, J. B. (1998). *Asking about prices: A new approach to understanding price stickiness.* New York, NY: Russell Sage Foundation.

45. Simonson, I. (2014). Vices and virtues of misguided replications: The case of asymmetric dominance. *Journal of Marketing Research, 51,* 514–519.

46. Crompton, J. L., & Jeong, J. Y. (in press). Experiments testing the effectiveness of purposeful anchoring on reference price in the context of public leisure services. *Journal of Leisure Research.*

47. Dhar, R., & Simonson, I. (1992). The effects of the focus of comparison on consumer preference. *Journal of Marketing Research, 29,* 430–440.

48. Diehl, K., & Zauberman, G. (2005). Searching ordered sets: Evaluations from sequences under search. *Journal of Consumer Research, 31,* 824–832.

49. Suk, K., Lee, J., & Lichtenstein, D. R. (2012). The influence of price presentation order on consumer choice. *Journal of Marketing Research, 49,* 708–717.

50. Kahneman, D. (2011). *Thinking fast and slow.* London, England: Penguin.

51. Strack, F., & Mussweiler, T. (1997). Explaining the enigmatic anchoring effect: Mechanisms of selective accessibility. *Journal of Personality and Social Psychology, 73,* 437–446.

52. Ariely, D., Loewenstein, G., & Prelec, D. (2003). Coherent arbitrariness: Stable demand curves without stable preferences. *The Quarterly Journal of Economics, 118,* 73–108.

53. Petroshius, S. M., & Monroe, K. B. (1987). Effect of product-line pricing characteristics on product evaluations. *Journal of Consumer Research, 13,* 511–519.

54. Blair, E., & Landon, E. (1981). The effects of reference prices in retail advertisements. *Journal of Marketing, 45,* 61–69.

55. Urbany, J. E., Bearden, W. O., & Weilbaker, D. C. (1988). The effect of plausible and exaggerated reference prices on consumer perceptions and price search. *Journal of Consumer Research, 15,* 95–110.

56. McCarville, R. E., & Crompton, J. L. (1987). An empirical investigation of the influence of information on reference prices for public swimming pools. *Journal of Leisure Research, 19,* 223–235.

57. Schwer, R. K., & Daneshvary, R. (1997). The effect of information on attitudes regarding tour fees: The case of the Hoover Dam powerplant tour. *Journal of Travel Research, 36*(2), 37–42.

58. Berry, L. L., & Parasuraman, A. (1991). *Marketing services: Competing through quality.* New York, NY: Free Press.

59. Spence, M. (1974). *Market signaling: Information signaling and related screening processes.* Cambridge, MA: Harvard University Press.

60. Scitovszky, T. (1945). Some consequences of the habit of judging quality by price. *The Review of Economic Studies, 12*(2), 100–105.

61. More, T. A., Dustin, D. L., & Knopf, R. C. (1996). Behavioral consequences of campground user fees. *Journal of Park and Recreation Administration, 14*(1), 81–93.

62. Gabor, A., & Granger, C. W. J. (1966). Price as an indicator of quality: Report on an enquiry. *Economica, 33,* 43–70.

63. Honomichi, J. (1991, February 4). A price that's too good to be good usually is. *Marketing News, 1991,* 17.

64. Cronley, M. L., Posavac, S. S., Meyer, T., Kardes, F. R., & Kellaris, J. J. (2005). A selective hypothesis testing perspective on price–quality inference and inference-based choice. *Journal of Consumer Psychology, 15,* 159–169.

65. Gardner, D. M. (1970). An experimental investigation of the price/quality relationship. *Journal of Retailing, 46*(3), 25–41.

66. Dewar, N., & Parker, P. (1994). Marketing universals: Consumers' use of brand name, price, physical appearance, and retailer regulation as signals of product quality. *Journal of Marketing, 58*(2), 81–95.

67. Poundstone, W. (2010). *Priceless: The myth of fair value (and how to take advantage of it)*. New York, NY: Hill and Wang.

68. Steinbach, P. (2015, June). Less is more. *Athletic Business, 2015,* 144–147.

69. Gopnik, B. (2011, December 5). Why is art so damned expensive? *Newsweek.* Retrieved from http://www.newsweek.com/why-art-so-damned-expensive-65919

70. Veblen, T. (1899). *The theory of the leisure class: An economic study in the evolution of institutions.* New York, NY: Macmillan.

71. Howard, D. R., & Crompton, J. L. (1980). *Financing, managing and marketing recreation and park resources.* Dubuque, IA: Wm. C. Brown.

Chapter 11

Strategies to Reconcile Inconsistencies with Reference Price by Providing Quality and Cost Information

- Enhancing perceptions of quality
- Providing cost information
- Summary

A fundamental principle in pricing is that *price is a statement of value, not a statement of cost.* Value is measured by the following ratio:

$$\text{Value} = \frac{\text{Quality of Service}}{\text{Price Paid}}$$

Thus, in the eyes of potential users, the value decreases if the price denominator is raised, unless there is a concomitant increase in the quality of the service numerator. When a price increase is imposed outside the latitude of acceptance and quality of the service has not changed, user resistance is likely.

The evaluation process of a price's acceptability is often depicted as follows: "New price information is compared to the reference price and this determines an individual's assessment of whether the new price is too low, too high, or about right" (p. 45).[1] However, this is an incomplete explanation. Reference price assesses whether the value ratio *in a given context* makes the new price "too low, too high, or about right." In this situation, if the perceived quality is enhanced, less resistance is likely to a new price outside the latitude of acceptance.

Information dissemination strategies in leisure services have revolved almost exclusively around providing factual information on program, time, price and location. This is a lost opportunity. Users should be given information designed to enhance perceptions of quality and provided with details of a service's cost, because this will often change the context within which users evaluate a price.

In the first part of this chapter, strategies are offered for changing the context by providing additional information that will raise users' perceptions of quality (i.e., the numerator in the value ratio). In the remainder of the chapter, it is pointed out that, for the most part, neither users nor non-users are aware of the cost of delivering a service or of the magnitude of subsidy that users receive. Disseminating this information is likely to enhance participants' perceptions of the value they receive and reduce their resistance to a price increase. Providing additional information enables users to make a more informed decision and, consistent with traditional economic theory, to better optimize their utility.

ENHANCING PERCEPTIONS OF QUALITY

Traditionally, the tendency in the public leisure field has been to keep the value ratio high by charging low prices. That strategy is less viable today for two reasons. First, tax subsidies from many agencies have been reduced, and there is a growing expectation by elected officials that self-generated revenues should be increased to replace them. Second, the quality expectations of patrons in many communities have risen. The results of one agency's survey of parents of children in its youth sport programs shown in Table 11-1 are typical.[2] When parents were asked how important each of the seven factors was in the decision to enroll their children, the responses were heavily weighted toward quality issues, while price was relatively unimportant. Thus, the contemporary challenge to leisure managers is to sell their services based on quality, not on price. This reflects the aphorism: Poor salesmen sell on price; good salesmen sell on the quality of their product. Researchers investigating the influence of providing different types of information for leisure programs on reference price concluded:

> Program information alone generates low reference price levels. This finding replicates those reported in earlier research. Efforts to generate higher price expectations should not focus on basic program characteristics . . . they are ineffective in establishing appropriate price expectations. Program information must be supplemented with additional messages. (p. 127)[3]

Table 11-1

Parents' Ratings of the Relative Importance of Seven Factors in Decisions to Enroll Their Children in Youth Sport Programs

Factor	Mean
Coach's quality	4.3
Program's quality	4.3
Parks and recreation staff quality	4.1
Time of activity	3.9
Location	3.6
Price	3.1
Knowing others in the activity	2.6

Note. Ranked according to their mean scores (1 to 5 scale).

In the following paragraphs, six strategies are suggested for enhancing perceptions of a service's quality: add features to the service, describe all the attributes of a service, promote benefits, focus on quality of visible tangible components and on ambiance, change program names and create awareness of external recognitions.

A study of visitor reactions to prices at Corps of Engineers recreation facilities highlighted that the potential role of *adding features* in raising quality and price expectations:

> Respondents expected to pay more as basic services were enhanced. Price expectations for both the boat ramp and the picnic packages climbed significantly as services were added to the basic Corps product/facility . . . This suggests that as services are enhanced, prices may also be elevated to reflect improved service quality. It also suggests that an all-sites pricing policy [is inappropriate] since [visitors] expect fee level to be linked with the quality of a site. As the quality varies, so too should the price for that site. (p. 83)[4]

Often a feature can be added without substantial investment so it can be used as a rationale for a price increase that will generate revenue that exceeds the additional cost of offering it. For example, if a charge is imposed for the first time at a museum or the price of admission is increased, an additional feature, such as a conducted tour, special lecture series or a new exhibit, may enhance users' perceptions of the value of the service and foster acceptance of the price increase. Thus, it was concluded in an early work in which reactions to a fee program at a national wildlife refuge were tracked that "if improvements are made at the time fees are initiated or increased, disapproval by the public is minimized" (p. 646).[5]

A detailed description of all a service's attributes may assist in raising its perceived value. One recreation agency decided to charge a price of $4 for family uses of a beach at which there had previously been no charge. For the first time, the agency stressed 20 amenities available at the beach and pointed out that they cost only 20 cents each for a family's use for a whole day. These amenities, which included professional lifeguards, picnic tables, and barbeque pits, had been available in previous years when there was no admission price. However, no attempt had been made to make users conscious of them. By unbundling the amenities from "the beach" and specifying multiple benefits, the agency raised perceptions of value and ameliorated resistance to the $4 admission charge.

Some participants in running, cycling, triathlon and other multi-sport events rail against what they consider to be unacceptably high entry fees: $75–$100 for a 1-day running or cycling event; $100–$250 for marathons, duathlons or triathlons; and $250–$400 for long-distance ironman events. At least some of this angst is attributable to participants taking many of the benefits they receive for granted. If these benefits are listed, perceptions of quality and value would be enhanced and negative responses likely would be reduced:

- Venue use fees.
- Police for traffic control.
- Emergency medical services.
- Insurance.
- Chip timing; results promptly available and electronically accessible immediately after the event.
- Rental of P.A. and timing equipment.
- Multiple manned refreshment stations around the course.
- Portable toilets at the start/finish (2 or 3 per 100 participants) and scattered round the course.
- Recognition T-shirts and medals.
- Post-race refreshments.
- Course markings: Directions, distance markers.
- Accurately measured course distances.
- Bib numbers.
- Promotional activities arousing awareness and interest in the event.
- Sanctioning fees if the event is permitted by a national organization.
- Race officials.[6]

A similar approach is to identify the proportion of a fee that pays for each component of a service. For example, an agency informed those registered for softball that 10 percent of their fee paid for the lights, 30 percent for the umpires, 15 percent for trophies and 45 percent for field maintenance.[7] This approach was advocated in a pricing study at Corps of Engineers lakes:

Benefits should be fully explained. Price expectations may rise as a result. For example, receipts might outline how each fee is allocated within the project. The message on the receipt might be worded thus: "Thank you for your fee. We want you to know that we will be using your money to help make your stay with us even more pleasant. Sixty percent of your fee will be devoted to maintaining our day-use areas, twenty percent will buy new shelters for our picnic areas, and the rest will be used to provide staff for security patrols around the project." In this way, the user is made aware of the benefits to be enjoyed as a result of paying that fee. (p. 40)[4]

Table 11-2

Potential Benefits Sought by Individuals from Participating in Park and Recreation Programs

- Social interaction with friends and family kin.
- Social interaction with previously unknown others.
- Ethnic and cultural identity.
- A gain in prestige; social recognition; status. The mastery of particular skills may be regarded as a form of "conspicuous consumption," which brings forth peer group recognition.
- Excitement; an adrenaline rush; exhilaration.
- Ego-satisfaction of achievement and accomplishment; a desire to be successful.
- Security; to be part of a group that gives a sense of belonging, connectedness to others and a sense of affection.
- The feeling of being important and having responsibility; growth of self-worth and self-confidence.
- Fantasy; illusion; offering temporary escape from the realities and routines of everyday life.
- Relaxation and alleviation of stress and tension, which may be obtained from hard or no physical effort.
- Catharsis from "flow" to alleviate negative tensions, anxiety, anger and unwanted adrenaline.
- Acquisition of knowledge; satisfaction of curiosity.
- Feelings of well-being and vitality that derive from exercise and physical fitness and from mental alertness.
- Regression; the desire to "let your hair down" and act in a puerile, adolescent way.
- Aesthetic enhancement derived from being in an attractive natural environment.
- Challenge and risk, which lead to self-exploration, self-discovery and self-development and may be obtained from sailing or skydiving or from acting, dancing or fly-fishing.

It has long been recognized that users of leisure facilities and programs do not seek the services *per se*, but rather *they seek the benefits that those services facilitate.*[8] A comprehensive list of these potential benefits is shown in Table 11-2. Flying a kite, throwing a Frisbee, walking with friends and family, sitting under a tree or hitting a softball ostensibly appear to be unimportant, trivial activities. However, this superficial view is a misinterpretation that confuses means with ends. The activities themselves are not important. What is important are the benefits that accrue to people from engaging in those activities. If a visit to a state park or museum is framed in terms of enhancing family bonding and educational growth rather than having a picnic in a nice environment or visiting exhibits, its perceived quality and value are likely to be much higher.

Most leisure managers implicitly assume their clienteles understand the value of what they are buying. They do not! Many agencies focus on programs and facilities; list where and when they are available; describe the structures, meeting rooms, classes and amenities, but rarely do they describe benefits that emanate from this infrastructure or disseminate testimonials from their users that illustrate those benefits. Unless the agency explicitly points out the benefits of its services, participants will undervalue them and be more resistant to higher prices.

Parents who enroll their children in a youth soccer program typically go to watch the games and cheer when Jill or Dan executes a good pass, dribble, tackle or shot. Most of them are unlikely to give much thought to the benefits their children receive unless they are prompted to do so. Benefits from the soccer program may include public approbation and recognition, enhanced self-confidence, improved social interactive skills, reduced obesity, confidence from belonging to a team or greater comfort with other ethnic groups. These are important ingredients in children's evolution into fully functional adults. When a soccer program is framed in these enhanced value terms, the result is likely to be not only increased participation, but also willingness to pay a higher price and reduced resistance to price increases.

The *quality of tangible elements and the ambiance or atmosphere* at leisure facilities are key indicators of a service's quality. It is widely recognized that five elements determine the quality of a service: reliability, responsiveness, empathy, assurance and tangibles.[9] The first four of these primarily reflect interactions with personnel, but many leisure services do not require users to have much interaction with agency personnel. For the most part, agencies provide facilities (parks, swimming pools, museums, athletic fields, recreation centers, performing arts centers, ice rinks, etc.), and individuals and groups use them without much interaction with agency staff. Thus, it is the tangible elements of a service—the physical things people can observe at a site—that most frequently serve as cues from which the likely quality of experience being offered is inferred. The question for leisure managers is whether those cues tell the intended story: "Most of us unconsciously turn detective . . . processing what we can see and understand to decipher what we cannot" (p. 101).[10]

A leisure agency's parks, landscaping, buildings, equipment, furnishings, ambiance, signs, colors, art, personnel dress (does it convey professionalism and expertise?), program names and other sensory stimuli offer a plethora of clues about the likely quality of an experience, "and these clues have a disproportionate impact on customers' overall evaluation of the service. . . . In effect, [they] offer significant surrogate evidence; the facility tells a story about the service that the service cannot entirely tell by itself" (p. 5).[11] Thus, if the quality cues are upgraded effectively so the perceived quality of a service is enhanced, a higher reference price is established so a higher price becomes more palatable.

If facilities are dismal, dowdy and unattractive, they are unlikely to facilitate the benefits users seek. Consider selecting a restaurant for an evening out. Frequently, the decision is not made because of its distinctive food quality as a number of restaurants probably have similar food standards. Rather, selection is likely to be made on the basis of "atmosphere." Participants at an executive development program who were regular beer drinkers were given two versions of the following scenario:

> You are lying on the beach on a hot day. All you have to drink is ice water. For the last hour, you have been thinking about how much you would enjoy a nice cold bottle of your favorite brand of beer. A companion gets up to make a phone call and offers to bring back a beer from the only nearby place where beer is sold (a fancy resort hotel)

[a small, run-down grocery store]. He says that the beer might be expensive and asks how much you are willing to pay for the beer. He says that he will buy the beer if it costs as much or less than the price you state. But if it costs more than the price you state he will not buy it. You trust your friend, and there is no possibility of bargaining with (the bartender) [store owner]. What price do you tell him? (p. 206)[12]

Those receiving the fancy resort hotel version gave significantly higher responses than those receiving the small rundown grocery version (medians $2.65 and $1.50). Although the product (beer) was the same and the customer would be drinking the beer on the beach and not entering the hotel or store where the beer was purchased, the contexts were different and willingness to pay increased with the perceived increased quality of the supplier's facility. Presumably, the implicit belief was that the resort hotel had a higher operating cost than the grocery store. The researcher's advice to his imaginary grocer for boosting sales in this local monopoly scenario was to "invest in seemingly superfluous luxury" (p. 231). If he simply raised his price to $2.50 without changing the quality context, "he would sell little beer and would face a constant stream of expletives from unhappy patrons" (p. 231).[13]

Little things can have a major impact on the ambiance created. Negative cues about quality can be communicated by things such as overflowing garbage cans; litter; temporary or dilapidated signs; outdated posters or notices; indifferent staff manners and demeanor, or sloppy dress; and lack of cleanliness of agency vehicles. Small investments in landscaping at high visibility locations may result in disproportionate gains in perceptions of a service's quality. A leisure facility that projects an old-fashioned, rundown visual appearance can hardly be expected to inspire confidence among users that it really does offer opportunities for a high quality experience.

> *What's in a name? That which we call a rose*
> *By any other word would smell as sweet*

With these words, Juliet Capulet tells Romeo Montague that a name is an artificial and meaningless convention, and that she loves the person who is called "Montague," not the Montague name. Sometimes, however, Shakespeare got it wrong because names do matter. They have power and meaning. A name is not merely a label; it is shorthand for describing who someone or what something is.

The marketing literature has confirmed that *names are one of the strongest signals of quality.*[14] People regard names as heuristics that provide information about a service. They are dominant cues. They are usually the first, and sometimes the only, clues available to participants considering a leisure opportunity. The authors who introduced "positioning" into the marketing lexicon emphasized the importance of names:

The name is the hook that hangs the brand on the product ladder in the prospect's mind . . . the single most important marketing decision you can make is what to name the product. A rose by any other name would not smell as sweet. Not only do you see what you want to see, you also smell what you want to smell. . . . and Hog

Island in the Caribbean was going nowhere until they changed its name to Paradise Island. (p. 89)[15]

A program's name may be the only information potential users have available when evaluating the acceptability of a price, so it is a cue that should elucidate the benefits of participation. The results of a study in which three groups were provided with the same information about a fitness club facility, but the facility name given to each group was different are reported in Table 11-3.[16] Each group's members were asked what they would expect to pay for an annual membership at the facility they were given. Table 11-3 shows the Ideal Health and Fitness Club price was 46 percent and 28 percent higher than the no-name facility and the Weights N' Bikes Exercise Center, respectively. The authors concluded: "The name that focused on benefits generated higher assessments than did the other names. This was the case even though the other information provided to subjects described the facility in identical terms" (p. 25).[16]

Table 11-3

Influence of Different Names for Fitness Facilities on Price Expectations

Facility Name	Price Expectation
Ideal Health and Fitness Club	
(offering a positive assessment of the benefits provided by the facility)	$439.90
Weights N' Bikes Exercise Center	
(focusing on the facility's attributes and amenities)	$344.00
No name: "Everything you need for total fitness. Open 7 days a week."	$302.00

Consider the informational cues and connotations of quality associated with the following pairs of names, which in each case have been used to describe the same program or facility:

Tumbling	Gymnastics
Sailing	Yachting
Reservoir	Lake
Day care	Child development center
Par 3 golf course	Executive golf course
Hobby shop	Skill development center
Gym	Fitness center
Law enforcement	Visitor protection
Staff training	Career development training
Calisthenics	Aerobics
Outdoor recreation	Outdoor adventure

For most people, especially neophytes, the names on the right are likely to suggest a higher quality experience and have a higher reference price than the names on the left.

Finally, if an agency receives *outside recognitions or awards,* this can serve to raise perceptions of its quality and the value of its services in users' minds. If an agency's staff, its facilities or its programs have been recognized as outstanding by some external body, users need to be aware of this. Such recognitions should appear on letterhead, notice boards, social media and promotional materials. These awards point out to citizens the superior quality of the services being offered and make it easier for users to accept price increases.

PROVIDING COST INFORMATION

The following scenario is not unusual:

- The county maintained 200 athletic fields at 50 sites. The 50,000 participants in youth sports were members of 70 non-profit groups who leased the fields from the county at no cost. The county proposed to implement a fee of $5 per participant to raise $250,000. The user groups were outraged. One leader's reaction was typical: "We're paying to play when we're paying taxes. We're being taxed again." The county's athletic director responded:

  > It's not a tax, it's a small token payment that will almost cover the annual cost of lighting these fields. Leagues don't seem to understand the costs at our end. In addition to the $250,000 electricity bill, add the cost of labor and maintenance – trimming trees, mowing fields, building clay mounds. Soon you realize $5 doesn't pay for much. (p. 40)[17]

Users of a leisure service are likely to have little knowledge either of an agency's costs or of the proportion of costs a given program recovers from pricing. Indeed, most users probably assume the price covers the full cost and do not recognize a subsidy is involved because it is unlikely to be an issue to which they have given conscious thought:

> When he pays, the user assumes he is paying for the total cost of the service; he has no way of taking into account the subsidy from tax sources. If the public golf course green fees are only a fraction of those of the private course, the user is more likely to interpret the difference as a matter of lesser quality of service for the public course and not as subsidization by the public for the same quality. (p. 272)[18]

Perceptions of price fairness and value are distorted by this implicit cost reference point. When this is replaced by an explicit awareness of the costs and subsidy, users will likely change their perceptions of what constitutes a fair price.

Evidence in the leisure literature supporting the impact of cost information on raising reference price is substantial and convincing. In the earliest of these studies, the impact of cost information on reference price for a city's public swimming pools was investigated.[19] A probability sample of 254 adult city residents, comprising users and non-users of the pools, were asked: "What would you expect to pay for a swim at a city pool?" Those informed of the city's cost per pool visit reported price expectations 38 percent and 33 percent higher than those who did not receive this information among users and non-users, respectively.

One corollary of providing cost information to users is that non-user taxpayers also learn the magnitude of subsidies to users, and this may create a constituency to counter protests of higher prices from users. Consider the following scenario:

- There were 1,000 adult softball players in a city's leagues. They vigorously opposed the staff's suggestion to increase the team fees by 14 percent from $350 to $400 per season. They protested to the city council that such a large increase was unreasonable. However, when a cost accounting analysis showed the city's cost to provide the experience was $600 per team, the direction of the debate changed. Instead of pressuring the council to reduce the 14 percent increase, the softball players had to justify and defend why after the proposal price increase they should still receive a 33 percent subsidy. Non-users and anti-tax advocates pressured the council to make the 14 percent increase higher, arguing the subsidy was unreasonable.

This reaction was reported in an early study of pricing recreation services. A national probability sample revealed that the greatest support for user fees was displayed by elderly, poor and rural residents who the authors reported were most likely to be low or non-users of public recreation programs. They tended, therefore, to support price structures that required users to bear a greater part of the financial burden of such services.[20]

When resident and non-resident campers in Maine state parks were informed of the actual cost of providing and maintaining a state park campsite, the proportions who believed the existing subsidized prices that campsite users were paying were too low increased from 9 percent to 38 percent among residents and from 8 percent to 45 percent among non-residents.[21]

In two studies, the same lead researcher used similar protocols, but reported somewhat different results. Nevertheless, the results in both studies confirmed the influence of cost information in raising reference price. In the first study, two groups were given information about an aerobics program comprising 12 class sessions. The treatment group members were informed that the cost of providing the program was $50, while those in the control group were given no cost information. The two groups were asked: "What is the most you would be willing to pay if you were to attend all the classes?" The treatment group mean was $37.07, which was 27 percent greater than the $29.02 average reported by the control group.[22]

When the same aerobics program scenario was presented to a different sample from the same population, much higher price expectations were reported. The mean response of the control group was $40.42, while the treatment group receiving the $50 cost information reported an average price expectation of $54.91, which is an increase of 36 percent.[23]

Other researchers replicated the latter study in the context of a 10K road race.[24] The control group was given only basic information related to products and services that participants received for their entry fee, which was $14 in advance and $16 on race day. The treatment group was given the additional information that it cost the city $25 to provide each participant with the race opportunity. They were asked: "What would you be prepared to pay to enter next year's race?" The control group's average response was $16.45, while the group receiving the cost information reported an average of $19.86, an increase of 20 percent.[24]

The following information was given to 768 adult users at six recreation centers: "Local authorities keep charges for leisure activities low by subsidizing them. If this subsidy was removed, the charge for the activity which you did today might double." Between 55 and 67 percent reported they were willing to pay a higher price after receiving that information.[25]

Similarly, parents of participants in youth soccer, basketball and softball/teeball programs were asked: "If circumstances arose where the Parks and Recreation Department had to either raise fees or cancel your youth sports program, what is the maximum you would be willing to pay for a season?" Parents in these programs reported they were prepared to pay increases over the current price of 73, 68 and 63 percent, respectively.[2]

A farm park operated by a county parks and recreation department had annual operating costs of $1.2 million and revenues of $750,000. Elected officials directed staff to remove the $450,000 operating deficit so it operated at break-even level. Accordingly, staff surveyed existing patrons, giving them five information/outcome messages to test which would be the most effective communication to accompany the inevitable price increases.[26] Results of the survey are summarized in Table 11-4.

Table 11-4

The Impact of Five Information Messages on Willingness to Pay Admission Price to a Farm Park (Current Price: $3)

Information Message	Mean	Increase
The park would have to close if admission is not raised	$4.46	49%
All revenues will be reinvested in the park	$3.75	25%
Information on prices at other local attractions	$3.71	24%
Provide scholarships for the economically disadvantaged	$3.70	23%
The existing operating deficit is $450,000	$3.54	18%

The most striking result was that each of the information messages succeeded in raising patrons' willingness to pay. The most effective by far was the threat of park closure, which raised willingness to pay by 49 percent. The assurance that all revenues would be reinvested into the park, knowledge of competitive attractions' prices and use of some of the new revenue for scholarships were all effective in raising willingness to pay by approximately 25 percent. The least effective message (even though it also raised willingness to pay more) was knowledge of the operating deficit alone, presumably because some patrons saw no reason why "their" facility was required to break even when other parks were not.

Finally, the influence of cost information on reference price at Texas state parks was evaluated in two studies.[27] In the first study, 2,465 respondents over age 65 receiving free admission to Texas state parks were asked for their response to being required to pay half price. Among the control group members, 77 percent indicated a willingness to do this. When cost information was provided to a treatment group, this increased to 81 percent. Although this was a significant difference, it was unexpectedly small. The distinctive feature of these results was the large proportion of senior citizens who supported the fee increase.

In the second study, 2,688 respondents were chosen randomly from a list of those holding a current Texas driver's license, so some were park users, while others were not. A control group was given no cost information, while the treatment group was informed:

> All income from park users, including entrance fees, contributes about 60 percent of the cost of operating and maintaining Texas State Parks. Thus, about 40 percent of the costs are subsidized by various taxes paid by all residents of the state, some of whom may never use state parks. It was decided in the last session of the Texas Legislature that the Texas Parks and Wildlife Department would receive less tax support for the state park system.

The control and treatment groups were presented with an admission price for Texas state parks that was higher than the current price. They were asked to report their response to it on a 5-point scale ranging from *much too low* (1) to *much too high* (5). Among park visitors, the cost information had no influence. The control and treatment groups reported average scores of 2.9 and 2.8 on the scale. However, among non-visitors, there was a substantial difference between the groups. The control group score was 3.07, whereas that of the cost information group was 2.63, indicating that when non-visitors were aware of the subsidy, they were 14 percent more likely to believe the price was too low.[27] From the perspective of non-visitors, it is rational for prices to be raised so they do not have to provide as much support for parks through their taxes.

These studies suggest that users are generally willing to take responsibility for more of subsidized costs through paying a higher price when they are made aware of the costs and that non-users expect them to do so. However, while the cost information was consistently effective in raising the reference price, in only one of the studies described did it raise the level high enough to cover all the costs. This pattern appears to hold for non-users as well as users. This is perhaps surprising because non-users could be expected to be advocates of full cost recovery to reduce the amount of tax support they have to provide. It suggests a prevailing equity norm that there should be some level of subsidy for public leisure services.

The cost information strategy has been extended in several studies by linking it to possible outcomes. For example, in several studies guided by prospect theory (discussed in Chapter 12), it was hypothesized that outcomes focused on either losing or gaining may influence participants' perceptions. In all of them, four experimental hypothetical scenarios were developed suggesting that gain from the revenues collected may accrue either (i) to the respondent's program or (ii) to another program if fees collected exceed the program's costs and the program may be either (iii) reduced or terminated or (iv) maintained at the expense of other users if a higher price is not paid. For the most part, these studies indicate that augmenting cost information with these additional messages is unlikely to shift reference price significantly.[22–28]

Attributing Price Increases to Cost Increases

If it can be demonstrated to skeptical users that, despite their magnitude, price increases outside the latitude of acceptance are justifiable, reasonable and fair, resistance may be overcome. In this regard, it has long been established that presumptions about an agency's motives influence users' judgments of fairness. Attribution theory is central to this process. It recognizes people are likely to search for causal evaluations when confronted with a situation that is surprising and has negative consequences for them.[29, 30] A price increase outside the latitude of acceptance meets these criteria, so users are likely to want to know the cause to which the price increase can be attributed.

Attribution theory addresses how people make causal interpretations. It posits that members of a target market will cognitively infer a motive for a cost increase in an attempt to understand the rationale for it. It recognizes that people interpret behavior in terms of its causes, and these interpretations often determine how they react to the behavior. Thus, "causal attributions play an important role in providing the impetus to actions and decisions among alternative courses of actions" (p. 125).[31] The general model of attribution theory states that *antecedents* that make up consumers' beliefs toward the price increase and their suppositions about its motives lead to *attributions* as to whether the agency is acting fairly or is being unreasonably exploitive, which lead to *consequences* that result in consumers embracing or rejecting the increase.[32]

Thus, attributions explaining fairness of a price and imputations of an agency's motives for raising price are contextual influencers that can be used to shift reference price. Substantial evidence suggests that justifications or explanations for an act influence people's perceptions of fairness.[33–38] This evidence led to the recommendation that "marketers should proactively provide relevant information to influence buyers' attributions for the price discrepancies" (p. 9).[39] In the context of leisure services, it was reported: "If justifications for new fee initiatives were not made explicit, perceptions of unfair treatment seemed to be exacerbated" (p. 74).[40] Indeed, early leisure researchers urged this strategy and reported:

> [These results] suggest that a well-developed information program about the rationale or need for higher fees may be an effective way to increase users' understanding and acceptance of the increase. It may also significantly decrease complaints associated with the fee increase. (p. 216)[21]

Acceptance of the explanation is likely to be influenced by the extent to which a price increase is "controllable" by the agency or attributable to "uncontrollable" market forces. Thus, the Principle of Dual Entitlement states that when a private sector firm raises price to increase its profits, this is controllable by the company, and it is likely to be considered unfair. In contrast, an increased price is likely to be perceived as fair if it is in response to costs outside the firm's control and designed to maintain the firm's existing level of profit (i.e., the price increase was proportionate to the firm's increase in costs).[41, 42] The firm is entitled to retain its current profit, so if it faces threat of a loss, it can raise the price without being considered unfair.

This principle governs community standards of fairness. It was first developed in a landmark study in which responses were sought to approximately 30 scenarios from multiple groups of respondents.[41] The following was a typical scenario:

> A hardware store has been selling snow shovels for $15. The morning after a large snowstorm, the store raises the price to $20. Please rate this action as: completely fair, acceptable, unfair, or very unfair. (p. 729)[41]

In this case, 82 percent contended it was unfair for the hardware store to take advantage of the short-run increase in demand associated with a blizzard because such an action would violate the customer's entitlement to the reference price. The clear conclusion emerging from the full set of experiments was that if the same price increase had been induced by a $5 increase in the wholesale price of snow shovels, it would probably have been widely accepted. The authors explained: "By large majorities, respondents endorsed the fairness of passing on increases in wholesale costs and in operating costs" (p. 732).[41]

Similarly, an outcry met Coca-Cola's pilot program that on hot days raised the price of drinks sold through temperature-sensitive vending machines. The motives were interpreted as greed and exploitation. Consumers would be thirstier on a hot day, the rise in temperature inflicted no additional cost on the company, children whose parents gave them the exact coins normally required would find it was insufficient, and the Coke brand promise implies ubiquity and affordability. These factors resulted in the action being seen as unfair. The program was abandoned, even though an economic analysis would likely show the refreshment value of a cold drink on a hot day is greater and raising prices would ensure the vending machine's supply would be allocated to those who most desired the drink.[43]

In the context of public leisure services, the Principle of Dual Entitlement suggests users should be informed of the reasons for substantial increases in an agency's costs of delivering a service whenever they occur and then prices should be raised proportionally. This information is likely to raise their internal reference price and the upper boundary of the latitude of acceptable price, so a revised price reflecting those costs is likely to be accepted. For example, immediately after a large increase in gasoline or electricity prices, after a well-publicized labor contract has been signed, or after increases in the minimum wage, the additional costs can probably be passed on to users without resistance if they are attributed by an agency information campaign to these causes.

Figure 11-1 illustrates how one city used this strategy effectively. The city offered summer swimming classes that met each week for 2 weeks (i.e., 10 classes per 2-week session). In the previous year, these were priced at $42. Historically, the price had been increased by a small increment each year to stay within the latitude of acceptance. However, the aquatic managers proposed to raise the price to $56 for the forthcoming summer, which was a 33 percent increase. They produced and widely disseminated material through multiple media explaining the increased price was attributable to increases in the minimum wage and in more competition for qualified staff, both of which were outside their control. The increase was implemented in Year 4 (Figure 11-1). While the number enrolled in the classes continued in a downward trend, it was not accentuated, suggesting the justification for the large price increase was effective in removing most clientele resistance.

The minimum wage for all city employees has been raised to $8.50 from $7.25 per hour. This means increasing the salaries of all our aquatic staff. We have four levels of instructors in the program:

- Level 1: Volunteers
- Level 2: Red Cross–certified Advanced Water Safety Instructor Aides starting at minimum wage (i.e., $8.50/hr).
- Level 3: Non–Red Cross–certified instructors now starting at $9.75/hr.
- Level 4: Certified Red Cross Water Safety Instructors starting at $10.50/hr.

Supervisor and coordinator staffing positions have been similarly affected by these changes. Several years ago, our Red Cross Learn to Swim program only employed certified Red Cross Water Safety Instructors and Instructor Aides. Over the last 4 or 5 years, we have been unable to hire enough certified Red Cross instructors to meet the needs of the number of classes we want to offer. We have had to hire uncertified swimming instructors to fill the positions. The program cannot be the high quality it could be when we have many instructors who are not certified by the Red Cross.

The major reason we cannot attract Red Cross instructors to our teaching positions is because we do not pay them enough. Other nearby cities and private country clubs are competing for the same instructors. In addition, the lure of teaching private swimming lessons at $30.00 per hour is a strong incentive for swim instructors to be self-employed. Restaurants and malls offer jobs at equivalent or greater pay. The long hours of planning and teaching lessons in the heat and humidity, coupled with the low pay, result in fewer instructors willing to teach swimming lessons. There is a great demand from parents in this community who want their children to learn to swim well. We are failing them by our inability to attract high quality instructors.

Over the last 3 years, the number of people taking swimming lessons has decreased primarily because we have had to eliminate one pool from our lesson program as we could not staff it with instructors. Further, we have had to reduce the number of swimming classes offered at other pools for the same reason.

Year	Number of Swim Lessons Taught
1	2,886
2	2,635
3	2,504
4	2,326

This price increase will enable us to restore the high quality of instruction we could offer a few years ago and to expand the number of classes we are able to offer.

Figure 11-1. Justification for a Large Increase in Price for Swimming Classes

If a price increase is aligned with and proportionate to an increase in the costs of a program, users are likely to view the costs as being beyond the control of the agency. Hence, their perceptions of unfairness are likely to be attenuated and the price increase accepted when the cost information is provided to them. Indeed, it has been noted: "Dual Entitlement's basic premise that cost-justified price increases are perceived fair has not been questioned" (p. 454).[44]

In the aforementioned snow shovel scenario, the $5 increase in revenue to the company resulted in a $5 loss to the customer. If the company generated an additional $5 in profit by reducing its costs by that amount, no loss would be inflicted on its customers, so they would likely accept it as being fair. For public leisure managers, this means that an expectation by users that prices will be reduced when cost savings are made is not likely.

When demand for a major sporting, concert or cultural event is strong, ticket scalpers often emerge who take advantage of the consumers' surplus by re-selling tickets at prices that exceed their face value. The consumers' surplus is available, at least in part, because such events tend to attract marginal supporters who are enticed by the sense of occasion or celebrity and would not be regular patrons. The question arises: Why don't event managers sell the tickets for a higher price? The answer is because such an action would alienate regular patrons and damage the organization's ongoing relationship with them. Such prices would be much higher than the well-established normal reference price and thus would be perceived by regular clienteles as being exploitive and unfair because they are not justified by increases in costs. The strategy would abrogate the Dual Entitlement Principle.

Attribution theory is sometimes embraced by commercial promoters of special events who partner with public leisure agencies and high profile local charities. The partnerships offer multiple benefits to a promoter. The attributional link with the charity justifies a high price for the event because a donation will be made to the charity, it legitimizes a shift in the fee for use of public facilities from the higher commercial price to the lower non-profit organization fee and it encourages volunteers (in lieu of paid labor) to assist with production of the event. For many, the link with the public and non-profit partners results in the attribution that this is a charitable venture, and this connotation implies the financial underpinning of the event is not profit oriented. Consider the following event:

- The promoter of a half-marathon race partnered with a local charity and the city's parks and recreation agency. The race started and finished in a city park. Over 4,000 runners paid $100 each to enter. Over 400 volunteers assisted at the start/finish area and in manning aid stations and mileage points around the course. Prominent positive news coverage was given to the $100,000 donation made to a local charity. The commercial use charge for the city park was waived because of the charitable connotations of the event. Detailed accounts of income and expenditures were not available because it was a privately promoted race. However, given that $400,000 in entrance fees was collected and a number of sponsorships were sold, it seems reasonable to postulate that the promoters' profit exceeded $200,000.

If a price increase is attributable to a change in the prevailing community norm (e.g., from compensatory to egalitarian equity or from egalitarian to market equity), this is outside an agency's control and therefore likely to be accepted. Thus, a decision to raise prices to recover a greater proportion of costs that may stem from a change in elected officials or changing economic conditions is likely to be accepted, even though it may be controversial. When the social norms or rules of behavior change, the rationale for the change and the new rules of behavior should be explained.

Idiosyncratic Response to Cost Information Messages

The effectiveness of providing cost information to a target population will vary because the message is likely to be "idiosyncratically evaluated and interpreted" (p. 79) by those receiving it.[45] Thus, the price behavior of some is likely to be positively changed, while others remain unresponsive. Part of this idiosyncratic response is explained by the two distinct "routes to persuasion" discussed in Chapter 9: the active/deliberative, central or System 2 route and the passive/non-deliberative, peripheral or System 1 route.[46, 47]

Early explanations for the differential response emerged from empirically testing the utility of assimilation-contrast theory. Two main factors were identified that were influential: ego-involvement of the message recipient and credibility of the source of the communication. In this early research, it was concluded: "Individuals differentiated as to involvement do show systematic differences in their perceptions of the position presented in communication" (p. 120).[48] The more important respondents perceived an issue to be, the more likely they were to engage actively with a communication. The implications of this for assimilation-contrast theory were stated in these terms: "We conclude that the range of assimilation is inversely related to the degree of personal involvement" (p. 131).[48] This finding is embraced by the ELM and FST dual process theories (Chapter 9).[46, 47]

In the context of price, it suggests that as the level of personal involvement increases, the latitude of acceptance narrows. By definition, most users of a leisure service are likely to regard a service as important and to be ego-involved with it. Hence, if a price increase is outside the latitude of acceptance, users are likely to engage cognitively with information messages related to it.

The role of perceived credibility of an information source in explaining idiosyncratic response to information messages has generated a substantial literature dating from 1940.[49] It demonstrates that the effectiveness of information messages is influenced by a recipient's perception of the credibility of its source. Hence, if a leisure agency has a good reputation for transparency and integrity, messages regarding cost of services are likely to be effective, and the converse will similarly be true. In essence, a high level of trust by users widens their latitude of acceptance, while a low level of trust narrows that zone.

Indeed, the very act of providing users with detailed, accurate cost information is likely to enhance perceptions of an agency's credibility and trustworthiness. Support for this probable outcome is provided by signaling theory.[50] It suggests that in contexts in which users and an agency have asymmetric information (i.e., the agency has much information, while users have relatively little), if the agency "signals" information so users become fully informed, enhanced trustworthiness results and price controversy is likely to be ameliorated.

SUMMARY

If a proposed price is outside the latitude of acceptance, the challenge for managers is to raise perceived value so the reference price is increased. One of the ways to do this is by enhancing perceptions of quality. An associated level of quality is implicit in a reference price. Six strategies can be adopted for enhancing perceptions of a service's quality: adding features to the service; offering a detailed description of a service's attributes so users are aware of them; pointing out the benefits it delivers rather than focusing on the service *per se*; enhancing the tangible quality, ambiance and atmosphere of facilities at which services are offered; reviewing the names given to services because different names for a service often have different connotations of quality; and promoting external recognitions or awards the service, facility, staff members or agency has received.

Users are likely to have little knowledge either of an agency's costs or of the proportion of costs a given program recovers from pricing. Providing this information has consistently been shown to raise reference price and positively influence perceptions of fairness. A substantial number of studies have shown that users are willing to take responsibility for more of the subsidized costs through paying higher prices when they are made aware of costs and that non-users expect them to do so.

By attributing price increases to cost increases, the cost amounts provide a point of comparison for evaluating the fairness of the price increase. Resistance to price increases outside the latitude of acceptance will be influenced by users' views of an agency's motives. If the increases are attributed to factors perceived to be outside an agency's control, such as changes in costs or in political leadership that provide lower tax subsidy, the Principle of Dual Entitlement suggests they are likely to be viewed as reasonable, justifiable and fair.

The effectiveness of providing cost information will be influenced by the credibility of an agency manifested by its reputation for transparency and integrity, and by the extent of users' ego-involvement with the service which determines the degree to which they actively cognitively engage with the information.

REFERENCES

1.   Monroe, K. B., & Petroshius, S. M. (1981). Buyers' perceptions of price: An update of the evidence. In H. H. Kassarijian & T. S. Robertson (Eds.), *Perspectives on consumer behavior* (pp. 43–45). Glenview, IL: Scott Foresman.

2.   Steele, C. (1984). *Participants' willingness to pay higher fees for parks and recreation services* (Unpublished master's thesis). Virginia Commonwealth University, Richmond, VA.

3.   McCarville, R. E., Crompton, J. L., & Sell, J. A. (1993). The influence of outcome messages on reference prices. *Leisure Sciences, 15*, 115–130.

4. Reiling, S. D., McCarville, R. E., & White, C. M. (1994). *Demand and marketing study at Army Corps of Engineers day-use areas* (Miscellaneous Paper R-94-1). Washington, DC: U.S. Army Corps of Engineers.

5. McCurdy, D. R. (1970). Recreationists' attitudes towards user fees: Management implications. *Journal of Forestry, 68,* 645–646.

6. Cullins, B. (2015, March 21). Breaking down the math of event race fees. *San Angelo Standard Times.* Retrieved from http://www.athleticbusiness.com/marketing/breaking-down-the-math-of-event-race-fees.html

7. McCarville, R. E. (1992, December). Successful pricing is in the eye of the beholder. *Parks and Recreation, 27,* 36–40.

8. Crompton, J. L. (2007). *Community benefits and repositioning: The keys to park and recreation's future viability.* Ashburn, VA: National Recreation and Park Association.

9. Parasuraman, A., Zeithaml, V., & Berry, L. L. (1985). A conceptual model of service quality and its implications for future research. *Journal of Marketing, 49,* 41–50.

10. Berry, L. L., & Bendapudi, N. (2003). Clueing in customers. *Harvard Business Review, 81,* 100–106.

11. Berry, L. L., Parker, D., Coile, R. C., Hamilton, K., O'Neill, D. D., & Sadler, J. D. (2004). The business case for better buildings. *Frontiers of Health Services Management, 21*(1), 3–24.

12. Thaler, R. H. (1983). Mental accounting and consumer choice. *Marketing Science, 4,* 199–214.

13. Thaler, R. H. (1985). Transaction utility theory. In R. P. Bagozzi & A. M. Tybout (Eds.), *Advances in consumer research: Volume 10* (pp. 229–232). Ann Arbor, MI: Association for Consumer Research.

14. Rao, A. R., & Monroe, K. B. (1989). The effect of price, brand name, and store name on buyers' perceptions of product quality: An integrative review. *Journal of Marketing Research, 26,* 351–357.

15. Ries, A., & Trout, J. (2001). *Positioning: The battle for your mind* (Twentieth anniversary ed.). New York, NY: McGraw-Hill.

16. McCarville, R. E., & Garrow, G. (1993). Name selection and response to a hypothetical recreation program. *Journal of Park and Recreation Administration, 11*(3), 15–27.

17. Bynum, M. (2004, July). Price pointers. *Athletic Business, 2004,* p. 40.

18. Meltsner, A. J. (1971). *The politics of city revenue.* Los Angeles: University of California Press.

19. McCarville, R. E., & Crompton, J. L. (1987). An empirical investigation of the influence of information on reference prices for public swimming pools. *Journal of Leisure Research, 19,* 223–235.

20. Economic Research Associates. (1976). *Evaluation of public willingness to pay user charges for use of outdoor recreation areas and facilities.* Washington, DC: Heritage Conservation and Recreation Service.

21. Reiling, S. D., Criner, G. K., & Oltmann, S. E. (1988). The influence of information on users' attitudes towards campground user fees. *Journal of Leisure Research, 20,* 208–217.

22. McCarville, R. E. (1991). An empirical investigation of the influence of cost information on willingness to pay for public aerobics classes. *Leisure Sciences, 13,* 85–96.

23. McCarville, R. E., Crompton, J. L., & Sell, J. A. (1993). The influence of outcome messages on reference prices. *Leisure Sciences, 15,* 115–130.

24. Kyle, G. T., Kerstetter, D. L., & Guadagnolo, F. B. (1999). The influence of outcome messages and involvement on participant reference price. *Journal of Park and Recreation Administration, 17*(3), 53–75.

25. Coalter, F. (2004). Reference pricing: Changing perceptions of entrance charges for sport and recreation. *Managing Leisure, 9*(2), 73–78.

26. Suarez, S. (1991). *Results of the Lake Farm Park visitors survey.* Lake Metroparks, OH.

27. Crompton, J. L., & Kim, S. (2001). Reactions to a large increase in admission price to state parks. *Journal of Park and Recreation Administration, 19*(4), 42–59.

28. Lemelin, R. H., McCarville, R., & Smale, B. (2006). The effects of context on reports of fair price for wildlife viewing opportunities. *Journal of Park and Recreation Administration, 24*(3), 50–71.

29. Folkes, V. S. (1988). Recent attribution research in consumer behavior: A review and new directions. *Journal of Consumer Research, 14,* 548–565.

30. Weiner, B. (1985, January). "Spontaneous" causal thinking. *Psychological Bulletin, 97*(1), 74–84.

31. Kelly, H. H. (1973). The process of causal attribution. *American Psychologist, 28*(2), 107–128.

32. Kelly, H. H., & Michela, J. L. (1980). Attribution theory and research. *Annual Review of Psychology, 31,* 457–501.

33. Bies, R. J. (1986). Identifying principles of interactional justice: The case of corporate recruiting. In R. J. Bies (Chair), *Moving beyond equity theory: New directions in organizational justice.* Symposium presented at the meeting of the Academy of Management, Chicago, IL.

34. Bies, B. J. (1987). The predicament of injustice: The management of moral outrage. In L. L. Cummings & B. M. Staw (Eds.), *Research in organizational behavior: Vol. 9* (pp. 289–319). Greenwich, CT: JAI Press.

35. Bies, R. J., & Shapiro, D. L. (1987). International fairness judgments: The influence of causal accounts. *Social Justice Research, 1,* 199–218.

36. Brockner, J., & Greenberg, J. (1989). The impact of layoffs on survivors: An organizational justice perspective. In J. Carroll (Ed.), *Advances in applied social psychology: Business settings* (pp. 45–75). Hillsdale, NJ: Lawrence Erlbaum Associates.

37. Fincham, F. D., & Jaspers, J. M. (1980). Attribution of responsibility: From man the scientist to man as lawyer. *Advances in Experimental Social Psychology, 13,* 81–138.

38. Urbany, J. E., Thomas, S., Madden, T. J., & Dickson, P. R. (1989). All's not fair in pricing: An initial look at the dual entitlement principle. *Marketing Letters, 1*(1), 17–25.

39. Xia, L., Monroe, K. B., & Cox, J. L. (2004). The price is unfair: A conceptual framework of price fairness perceptions. *Journal of Marketing, 68*(4), 1–15.

40. McCarville, R. E., Reiling, S. D., & White, C. M. (1996). The role of fairness in users' assessments of first-time fees for a public recreation service. *Leisure Sciences, 18,* 61–76.

41. Kahneman, D., Knetsch, J. L., & Thaler, R. H. (1986). Fairness as a constraint on profit seeking: Entitlements in the market. *American Economic Review, 76,* 728–741.

42. Bolton, L. E., & Alba, J. W. (2006). Price fairness: Good and service differences and the role of vendor costs. *Journal of Consumer Research, 33,* 258–265.

43. Maxwell, S. (2008). *The price is wrong: Understanding what makes a price seem fair and the true cost of unfair pricing.* Hoboken, NJ: John Wiley.

44. Vaidyanathan, P. A., & Aggarwal, P. (2003). Who is the fairest of them all? An attributional approach to price fairness perceptions. *Journal of Business Research, 56,* 453–463.

45. Petty, R. E., McMichaels, S., & Brannon, L. (1992). *The elaboration likelihood model of persuasion: Applications in recreation and tourism.* In M. J. Manfredo (Ed.), *Influencing human behavior* (pp. 77–102). Champaign, IL: Sagamore.

46. Petty, R. E., & Cacioppo, J. T. (1981). *Attitudes and persuasion: Classic and contemporary approaches.* Dubuque, IA: Wm. C. Brown.

47. Kahneman, D. (2011). *Thinking fast and slow.* London, England: Penguin.

48. Sherif, M., & Sherif, C. W. (1968). Attitude as the individuals' own categories: The social judgment-involvement approach to attitude change. In M. Sherif & C. W. Sherif (Eds.), *Attitude, ego-involvement, and change* (pp. 105–139). New York, NY: John Wiley.

49. Asch, S. E. (1940). Studies in the principles of judgments and attitudes: II. Determination of judgments by group and by ego standards. *Journal of Social Psychology, 12,* 433–465.

50. Spence, A. M. (1974). *Marketing signaling: Informational transfer in hiring and related screening processes.* Cambridge, MA: Harvard University Press.

Chapter 12

Strategies Informed by Prospect Theory to Reconcile Inconsistencies with Reference Price

- Enterprise fund effect
- Semantic framing of discounts and premiums
- Promotional price
- Bundling and unbundling multiple component services
- Hyperbolic discounting
- The endowment effect
- Sunk cost effect
- Odd number pricing
- Summary

Prospect theory was first articulated in 1979.[1] Its influence was profound and extensive. Indeed, this article was the second most cited paper in the field of economics during the period 1975 to 2000.[2] It has proved to be a conceptual foundation that informs explanations for multiple pricing heuristics. The theory was modeled on classical utility theory, but departs from it in fundamental ways. One of its founders stated: "Its goal was to document and explain systematic violations of the axioms of rationality in choices" (p. 271).[3] The theory has three central tenets.

First, price is *reference dependent*. Like adaptation-level and assimilation-contrast theories, prospect theory recognizes perceptions and judgments are relative, evaluations of the acceptability of a new price are made by comparing it to a reference price, and changes from the reference price rather than the actual price *per se* are what matter. However, it extends these theories by recognizing prices lower than the latitude of acceptance are perceived to be gains, while those higher than this reference range are perceived to be losses.

A consequence of this tenet is that the way an issue is framed will influence how it is perceived. Framing effects occur when "decision-makers respond differently to different but objectively equivalent descriptions of the same problem" (p. 150).[4] For example, the descriptions of a glass as "half full" or "half empty" are logically equivalent, but their different framing means they do not convey the same information. The former phrase implies the glass was originally empty so half full is a perceived gain, whereas the latter implies it was originally full and that reference point leads to it being perceived as a loss.[5]

When one group of participants was asked to judge (on a 10-point scale) "how large is the number 9," while another was asked "how large is the number 221," the averages of the two groups were 5.13 and 3.10, respectively. Why was 9 judged to be larger? The author suggested that subjects' reference point for 9 was one-digit numbers (i.e., 0 to 0), while for 221 it was three digits (i.e., 0 to 999). The judgment was strongly influenced by the implied reference point.[6]

The following scenario illustrates how different reference prices lead to different perceptions of a price:

- Bill and Jill have equal family incomes, and both recently moved into the community. They each purchase an annual family membership costing $500 at the community recreation center. At similar facilities in his previous community, Bill paid $800 for a membership, while in her town, Jill paid $200. Orthodox utility theory suggests they should be equally happy with the purchase because they received equal benefits from their $500 investment. However, in reality, their reactions are likely to be different because their evaluations are based on a different reference price. It is likely that Bill will be happy, whereas Jill will be unhappy.

Users will judge a service to be less expensive if they have previously encountered it in the context of higher priced services than if they have experienced it in the context of lower priced services.

A second tenet of prospect theory is a *diminishing sensitivity* to changes in price, so the value function is concave for gains and convex for losses. This has two relevant dimensions for leisure managers. First, each additional increment of gain or loss has a smaller impact than the equal amount preceding it. Consequently, gaining $100 is not 10 times as pleasurable as gaining $10, and losing $100 is not 10 times as painful as losing $10. This is illustrated by the following analogy:

If you add one pound to an empty backpack, it feels like a substantial increase in weight. But adding a pound to a backpack that's already laden with a laptop and some books does not feel like a big difference. This diminishing sensitivity to the pain of paying means that the first dollar we pay will cause us the highest pain, the second dollar will cause us less, and so on, until we feel just a tiny twinge for, say, the forty-seventh dollar. (p. 249)[7]

The second dimension of diminishing sensitivity is that it is proportionality rather than absolute value that is key to the acceptance of new prices. That is, the difference between a price increase from $70 to $78 is perceived to be much smaller than an increase from $10 to $18. It was recognized almost 300 years ago that "the psychological response to a change in wealth is inversely proportional to the initial amount of wealth" (p. 273).[3] However, on its own, this insight was incomplete because it ignored the influences of a reference point and of gains and losses, both of which are integrated into prospect theory.

The third tenet of prospect theory is that people are strongly influenced by *loss aversion,* so the degree of pain associated with losing money through a price increase is much greater than the joy obtained from gaining the same amount of money from a price decrease. There is asymmetry between the power of negative and positive expectations. Thus, an increase in the price of entry to a swimming pool from $5 to $8 is likely to meet substantial user resistance, while a decrease from $5 to $2 would probably create a much weaker sense of gain. Traditional economic theory states that people evaluate prospective purchases on the basis of utility or value (i.e., by comparing a service's benefits with the price being charged) and that losses and gains of equal size are valued the same. In contrast, prospect theory recognizes that people make their evaluations on the basis of gains and losses relative to a reference point, and they are valued differently with loss aversion being a more powerful influence than benefit gain. The comparison is not with actual value, but with anticipated changes in well-being.[8]

In this regard, the authors of prospect theory concluded from their experiments:

A salient characteristic of attitudes to changes in welfare is that losses loom larger than gains. The aggravation that one experiences in losing a sum of money appears to be greater than the pleasure associated with gaining the same amount. (p. 279)[3]

Research during the 35 years since prospect theory was first published has consistently reaffirmed the asymmetric effects of gains and losses and the robustness of loss aversion. Indeed, it has been claimed: "The concept of loss aversion is certainly the most significant contribution of psychology to behavioral economics" (p. 300).[3]

Prospect theory is graphically illustrated in Figure 12-1.[1] The horizontal axis represents the dollar gain or loss incurred in a given price change, while the vertical axis represents the perceived value of that gain or loss to an individual. The utility function plots the way losses and gains are perceived. The $10 loss or gain is of equal magnitude on the horizontal axis. However, in terms of perceived value on the vertical axis, Point A is closer to the origin than Point B. Thus, the utility function shows that a gain of equal magnitude to a loss has a smaller weight in decision making. The graph's salient feature is its S-shape, which indicates diminishing sensitivity as gains and losses mount, but the two curves of the S are not symmetrical. The psychological response to losses is stronger than the response to corresponding gains, reflecting the greater power of loss aversion compared to benefit gains.

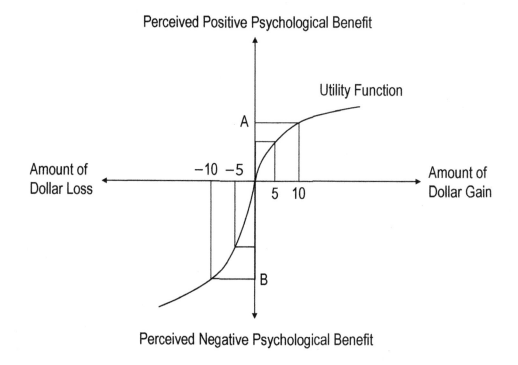

Figure 12-1. The Principles of Prospect Theory

Prospect theory explains why the latitude of acceptance shown in Figures 9-2 and 10-1 is asymmetrical with a smaller zone of acceptance for price increases than for price decreases. A review of numerous empirical studies led to the following conclusion: "The effect of a price increase (losses relative to the reference price) is about twice as large as the effect of a gain" (p. 290).[3]

Eight heuristics informed by prospect theory that can have a positive influence on participants' perceptions of price increases are described in this chapter: enterprise fund effect, semantic framing of discounts and premiums, promotional price, bundling and unbundling multiple component services, hyperbolic discounting, the endowment effect, sunk cost effect and odd number pricing.

ENTERPRISE FUND EFFECT

It was pointed out in Chapter 4 that an enterprise fund provides a "closed-loop" mechanism whereby those paying for a service can see the direct benefits that arise from their payments. This is consistent with prospect theory in that users are likely to perceive fees that are directed to a jurisdiction's general fund as a total loss because there is no direct nexus between their payments and provision of the service. In contrast, if their resources are directed to an enterprise-type fund, users are likely to perceive a direct gain from their payments.

It has been consistently demonstrated that "consumers are more likely to support user fees when such fees are used to maintain and improve the resource at which they are collected" (p. 288).[9] For example, a sample of 188 hikers was asked: "Assuming you were asked to pay a daily hiking fee, how much would you be willing to pay if the money was credited to: (a) the federal government's general treasury; (b) the federal agency that collected the fee; and (c) the local park or forest unit where the fee was collected?" The authors reported that the average amount these hikers were willing to pay was 4 times greater when this revenue was reinvested in improving the facility where fees were collected than when it went to the general treasury.[10]

Similarly, when 300 users of two backcountry wilderness areas were asked if they were prepared to pay fees to use the trails, 65 percent and 32 percent responded affirmatively. However, when they were later asked to assume "the quality of wilderness areas is likely to deteriorate unless user fees are charged," their numbers increased to 87 percent and 80 percent, respectively. The authors concluded: "This implies overwhelming support among users if fees are used to maintain deteriorating wilderness areas" (p. 107).[11]

Data were collected from 1,405 visitors to U.S. Army Corps of Engineers day use recreation areas, who were asked: "If fees were charged at day-use areas, the money collected should be . . ." A variety of allocation options were provided. The authors reported that 62 percent preferred the funds be returned to the site at which they were collected, 13 percent to any Corps day-use area, 11 percent to any Corps recreational area (scenic overlooks, campgrounds, etc.), 2 percent to non-recreational Corps initiatives and 1 percent favored such funds being returned to the U.S. Treasury. Respondents also had the opportunity to offer open-ended responses: "Consistent with the more quantitative responses, many stated explicitly that they would be willing to pay higher fees if such a payment resulted in site improvements" (p. 72).[12] The authors concluded:

> The results of this and previous fee studies clearly indicated that the disposition of the fee revenue is an important factor in people's acceptance of fees. Users of facilities prefer that fee revenue be used to maintain and improve the area where the fee was collected. If fees are allocated to other areas or projects that are not used by the people paying the fee, it is much more difficult to justify fees to users. Therefore, projects should exercise as much control over the allocation of fees as is allowed by the legislation authorizing the collection of fees. (p. 40)[13]

Parents of youth sport participants were asked: "What is the maximum amount of money you would pay for a season of soccer, basketball, or softball/tee ball if the additional monies collected could be retained by the Parks and Recreation Department and used for the development of athletic fields?" They reported they would be prepared to pay increases over the current prices of 73 percent, 72 percent and 65 percent, respectively.[14]

Preferences, rather than willingness to pay values, were sought from a phone sample of 3,515 U.S. residents, who were asked their opinions about how the National Park Service (NPS) should manage entrance fees. Three possible approaches were offered: (i) all entrance fee money could stay within the unit where it was collected, (ii) all entrance fee money could be sent to the NPS headquarters with a percentage going back to the unit where it was collected and the remainder distributed to other units or (iii) all entrance fee money could be sent to the U.S. Treasury with a relatively small percentage sent back to the NPS to cover costs of collecting the money. Respondents' preferences for the three options were 45, 47 and 6 percent, respectively.[15] In a related study, it was reported that a key element in securing user support for pricing on federal lands was "whether or not people believed the majority of funds would be returned to the local areas where they were collected, and used in a way they deemed important" (p. 223).[16]

The following anecdotes illustrate the forthcoming support for large price increases when they were perceived to be an investment that would yield direct benefits to users by facilitating improved resources:

- Existing prices were $109 for the slow pitch fields and $229 for the Little League fields. The city announced increases to $2,178 and $2,853, respectively. The leader of the slow pitch association said: "I have no problem paying the extra money, as long as it goes into servicing those diamonds . . . I don't mind paying top price as long as we get the service for it." The leagues had complained that the city had poor field maintenance compared with other municipalities in the area, and the city's parks and recreation director admitted they were not maintained as frequently as those in other municipalities.[17]

- After it lost general fund support for lifeguards and maintenance of its beaches, a city metered car parking in the area, which previously had been free. They publicized extensively that all the revenue from this source would be used to staff and maintain the beach. No one opposed the new fees. In this case, the enterprise fund effect was probably reinforced by the Principle of Dual Entitlement, which was discussed in Chapter 11.

Implications for Leisure Managers

The enterprise fund approach provides an economic incentive for those staffing a facility or program to be diligent about collecting fees. If those revenues go into a general fund or elsewhere, field staff at a park, for example, may elect not to man entrance stations to collect the fees. This would be a logical decision from their myopic perspective because while the staffing cost would be funded from the park's general fund, the park would not receive any of the revenue. Consider the following case:

- Many of the federal national wildlife refuges had established special recreation fee accounts that enabled them to retain revenues collected from activities such as wildlife tours conducted by staff, hunting blind rentals, camps along trails and primitive cabins. When Congress ruled those fees could no longer stay in the refuges and had to be conveyed to the Land and Water Conservation Fund for support of all activities authorized by that fund, two changes occurred. First, in the first year the change was implemented, one third of those refuges quit collecting fees because they lacked the economic incentive to do so. Second, many of the services were contracted out to local non-profit "friends of refuge" groups, who were able to retain the funds and reinvest them in the refuges.[18]

Financing "small-scale" facility renovations is a challenge for many leisure agencies. In the case of athletic fields, for example, this may include lighting, irrigation, shade structures, backstops, bleachers, windscreens, goals, bases and drinking fountains. The effective life span of such items is likely to be much shorter than 20 or 25 years, so it is inappropriate to fund them with long-term bonds because future taxpayers would be paying for assets that no longer exist. At the same time, their cumulative cost is likely to be too great for them to be consistently financed out of regular operational budgets. This has led some agencies to impose a surcharge on all teams using athletic fields to pay for the replacement of items that have deteriorated as a result of their use and for improvements in the existing standard of facilities the participants would like to have.

To establish the appropriate fee, agencies typically prepare a 10-year schedule that projects the annual renovations and improvements required at each athletic field complex. The costs of implementing the 10-year program are calculated, with allowances made for likely future cost increases, and divided into equal annual amounts. This rolling schedule is updated annually. The surcharge is fixed at a level sufficient to pay user groups' prorated share of the fields' annual renovations and improvements. The revenues are retained in a separate fund for each athletic field complex and are used exclusively for renovating or improving that complex.

Representatives from the athletic groups should be involved in setting the fee and in authorizing disbursements from the fund. If the fee is set too low and there are insufficient funds to pay for the renovations, the athletic groups have to accept responsibility for the deteriorated facilities because they failed to make adequate provision to retain the desired standard.

- A city council levied a 10 percent surcharge fee for golf on all annual passes and daily green fee charges. This revenue was conveyed to the Golf Surcharge Reserve Fund. The primary use of those surcharge funds was for course renovation and equipment replacement. Similarly, the city's 36 tennis courts needed resurfacing every 5 years at approximately $5,000 per court, giving a total cost of $180,000. This was done on a rotation basis, so $36,000 per year was needed to renovate the courts. A renovation surcharge was specified in the published tennis pricing schedules, and each year the courts benefiting from this designated fund were widely publicized so players were aware that the surcharge money was being spent as promised.

Frequently, agencies report that users are prepared to pay such surcharges when they are assured those funds are exclusively directed to upgrading or maintaining the facility they use.

One city's 10-year rolling projection of small item replacement costs for the 9 softball and 10 soccer fields at its main athletic park is illustrated in Table 12-1. It shows that during the next 10 years, the softball field renovations are projected to cost almost $245,000, while those for soccer are estimated at almost $187,000. Based on projections of the number of teams per year using the fields and the number of players per team, it was estimated that these costs could be met by a surcharge of $5 per player on every team. There was widespread acceptance and no resistance to this surcharge.

Table 12-1

Illustration of 10-Year Rolling Cost Estimates for Renovations in an Athletic Field Enterprise Fund

Athletic Field	Last Installed	Current Estimated Costs	Replacement Year											10-Year Total
			Year 1	Year 2	Year 3	Year 4	Year 5	Year 6	Year 7	Year 8	Year 9	Year 10	Year 11	
SOFTBALL FIELDS														
Turf/Infield (15 yrs)	Year 0	$12,000.00								$17,730.00				
Shade Structures (12 yrs)	Year 0	$160,000.00					$204,205.00							
Bleachers	Annually	$1,000.00	$1,050.00	$1,100.00	$1,150.00	$1,200.00	$1,260.00	$1,325.00	$1,390.00	$1,460.00	$1,535.00	$1,610.00	$1,690.00	
Bases	Annually	$420.00	$440.00	$460.00	$485.00	$510.00	$535.00	$560.00	$590.00	$620.00	$650.00	$685.00	$720.00	
Windscreens	Annually	$135.00	$140.00	$145.00	$150.00	$160.00	$170.00	$180.00	$190.00	$200.00	$210.00	$220.00	$230.00	
TOTAL	Annually		$1,630.00	$1,705.00	$1,785.00	$1,870.00	$206,170.00	$2,065.00	$2,170.00	$20,010.00	$2,395.00	$2,515.00	$2,640.00	$244,955.00
SOCCER FIELDS														
Turf/Infield (15 yrs)	Year 0	$31,500.00								$46,540.00				
Goals (15 yrs)	Year 0	$2,000.00								$2,955.00				
Drink Fountains (10 yrs)	Year 0	$5,000.00			$5,790.00									
Bleachers	Annually	$1,000.00	$1,050.00	$1,100.00	$1,150.00	$1,200.00	$1,260.00	$1,325.00	$1,390.00	$1,460.00	$1,535.00	$1,610.00	$1,690.00	
Irrigation	Annually	$1,000.00	$1,050.00	$1,100.00	$1,150.00	$1,200.00	$1,260.00	$1,325.00	$1,390.00	$1,460.00	$1,535.00	$1,610.00	$1,690.00	
Nets	1/2 Annually	$850.00	$895.00	$940.00	$985.00	$1,035.00	$1,085.00	$1,140.00	$1,200.00	$1,260.00	$1,325.00	$1,390.00	$1,460.00	
Lights	1/3 Annually	$5,985.00	$6,285.00	$6,600.00	$6,930.00	$7,275.00	$7,640.00	$8,020.00	$8,420.00	$8,840.00	$9,280.00	$9,745.00	$10,230.00	
TOTAL	Annually		$9,280.00	$9,740.00	$16,005.00	$10,710.00	$11,245.00	$11,810.00	$12,400.00	$62,515.00	$13,675.00	$14,355.00	$15,070.00	$186,805.00

SEMANTIC FRAMING OF DISCOUNTS AND PREMIUMS

People's reactions to information are strongly influenced by how it is framed and presented to them. Consider the following examples that were cited in Chapter 9:

- The short-term outcome of a surgery may be framed as:
  - The 1-month survival rate is 90 percent.
  - There is a 10 percent mortality in the first month.
- Similarly, cold cuts may be described as:
  - 90 percent fat free.
  - 10 percent fat.

In both examples, the outcome is logically the same.[3] However, in both cases, the second frame is much more effective than the first format. The negative connotations of mortality and fat evoke much stronger feelings than do the positive connotations of survival rate and fat free. This general principle has been termed "the reflection effect"[2] and recognizes that preferences tend to reverse when the sign or direction of the outcomes is reversed.

This role of semantic framing is important when differential prices are charged. Situations in which premiums could be charged so agencies could capture more of the consumers' surplus were discussed in Chapter 8. This terminology is conceptually correct because the word "premium" distinguishes its Benefit Principle pedigree from the term "discount," which stems from the Ability to Pay Principle. However, its connotations of "surcharge" and "paying more than others" are likely to be perceived as punitive and thus create controversy.

Implications for Leisure Managers

Consider the following situations:

- A state park agency charges residents $12 and non-residents $15 a night for camping.
- A city charges its residents $20 to play golf and non-residents $25.
- A golf course charges $40 a round on Saturdays, but $50 for rounds started before 10 a.m.
- Registration is $30, but if you register late, the fee goes up to $40.

In all of these cases, the regular price is established and then a surcharge is added for those who pay the premium price. Prospect theory suggests resentment to this is likely because paying the premium represents a loss to those users. If the premium price is framed as the regular price so it serves as the point of reference, this resentment is likely to be removed as no additional losses are incurred. Discounting from it becomes a gain to others. Thus, in the aforementioned examples, the price information should be presented differently:

- The state park agency price for camping is $15. Residents receive a $3 discount to $12.

- It is $25 to play golf. Residents receive a $5 discount to $20.
- The Saturday price for golf is $50. A $10 discount is given to those who start after 10 a.m.
- Registration is $40. A $10 discount is given to those who register early.

The asymmetry between a loss frame and a gain frame means discounts and surcharges "may be economically equivalent, but they are not emotionally equivalent" (p. 364).[3] Surcharges make people mad; discounts make them happy! This was verified when the framing effects were empirically analyzed in the context of golf. Golfers were presented with differential prices in the forms of a discount and a premium and rated these on a 5-point scale. The authors reported: "When the price was presented as a discount, customers viewed it as significantly more acceptable (mean = 2.96) than when it was presented as a premium (mean = 3.92)" (p. 340).[19]

PROMOTIONAL PRICE

Prospect theory provides the primary explanation for the effectiveness of promotional prices. Reductions in the price are invariably viewed as a gain to users when compared to a regular price because benefits remain the same, while the cost of purchase is lowered. Indeed, benefits may even increase because the discount may be perceived as a benefit, as brain recordings indicate that buying at low prices is a pleasurable event per se.[2]

A decision to participate in a program is usually the culmination of a process that may have started long before participation occurs. Users pass through a series of stages from first becoming aware of a service to finally using it on a regular basis. These stages are widely known as the purchase decision process.[20] The five stages shown in Figure 12-2 are *awareness,* in which a person becomes aware a given service exists; *interest,* which is characterized by effort to find out more detailed information about it; *evaluation/trial,* in which the individual mentally evaluates it or samples it; the *decision* is a commitment to use the service regularly; and *confirmation* is reassurance that regular use is a wise investment.

Typically, a promotional price is offered for only a short time because it is intended to incentivize those who are interested to take imminent action and try it. If an agency is willing to price a service at 30 percent less during a limited time that ends on (say) Sunday, why wouldn't they sell it at 30 percent off on Monday? The answer is loss aversion. If people are on the fence about trying the service, they are most likely to purchase it while it is on sale. Once Monday comes, they have lost the opportunity. If the agency does not stop the sale on Monday, people don't have the extra incentive to buy on Sunday. Loss aversion drives the success of promotion prices.

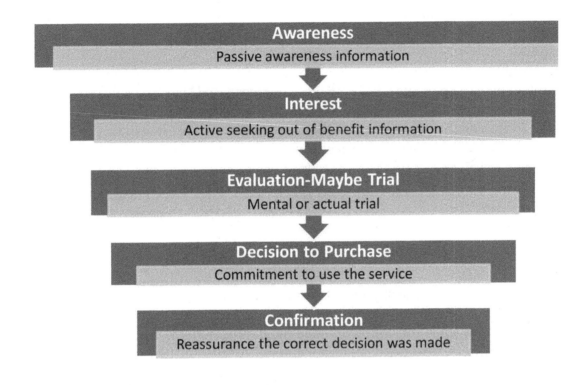

Awareness
Passive awareness information

Interest
Active seeking out of benefit information

Evaluation-Maybe Trial
Mental or actual trial

Decision to Purchase
Commitment to use the service

Confirmation
Reassurance the correct decision was made

Figure 12-2. The Purchase Decision Process

Further, it was noted in Chapter 9 that the current price users expect to pay is most strongly informed by the last price to which they were exposed. Hence, the danger is that a promotional price could become the reference price if it is offered for a long duration or if it is offered frequently. Price promotions are effective when they are considered exceptional opportunities. If they are short, temporary and infrequent, they are more likely to stay in short-term memory and not influence reference price rather than to be stored in long-term memory. The perception of them as rare, one-off opportunities can be enhanced by linking them with a special event, for example, a major sporting occasion or festival in the city, a national day/week of celebration or a city's founders day.

In some contexts, a zero price promotion may be appropriate and effective. This will guard against a discount lowering the reference price. Some potential users may be unsure of the benefits offered by a service, but after two or three trials, they may be convinced of them. Their reluctance to pay (say) $80 for a month's membership may disappear after they have experienced the service or facility. A zero price promotion has a distinctive emotional dimension because receiving something for free invariably feels good:

> Zero is a source of irrational excitement. Would you buy something if it were discounted from 50 cents to 20 cents? Maybe. Would you buy it if it were discounted from 50 cents to two cents? Maybe. Would you grab it if it were discounted from 50 cents to zero? You bet! (p. 49) . . . The difference between two cents and one cent is small. But the difference between one cent and zero is huge! (p. 62)[7]

For potential users, monetary loss is not possible, so ostensibly there appears no reason not to try the service, even if they are skeptical of its potential for delivering the benefits they seek.

An additional element likely to impact the effectiveness of a promotional price is the way it is physically presented. For example, "congruent" and "incongruent" versions of a sale price for a fictitious brand of in-line skates were developed and presented to respondents. In the congruent condition, the higher regular price appeared in larger font than the lower sale price; in the incongruent condition, the higher regular price appeared in smaller font than the lower sale price. They were reproduced as follows:

	Regular Price:	Sale Price:
Congruent:	$239.99	$199.99
Incongruent:	Regular Price:	Sale Price:
	$239.99	$199.99

As anticipated, the congruent protocol, for which the lower sale price was presented in a relatively small font, was more effective than the incongruent version. It was suggested this was because when consumers encoded the information, the difference in font size between regular and sale price reinforced and accentuated the perceived magnitude of the discount. In the incongruent version, the larger physical size of the sale price made it more difficult for people to encode and process the magnitude of the sale price.[21]

An alternative approach to a price promotion that further protects the regular reference price is to embrace the principle of customary pricing described in Chapter 10. Instead of a reduction in the regular price, this approach offers enhanced value and gain to potential users by adding benefits. Examples include a celebrity instructor for a class, a free sample session to try out a program before signing up or a fifth additional concert to first-time buyers of a four-concert package for the symphony orchestra.

Some leisure experiences require the presence of a threshold number of other participants to create the ambiance needed for a satisfying experience. For example, a symphony or pop concert, dance, athletic contest or special event is likely to be more enjoyable if the facility is full rather than half empty. The full facility creates a stimulating atmosphere for the performers, which is likely to inspire them to perform at a higher level. At the same time, the enthusiasm of a large crowd is contagious and enhances the experience for all present. In these situations, if audience numbers are increased by giving away heavily discounted or free tickets to build the crowd, it may result in a threshold number being reached that encourages more full-price customers to engage.

In these situations, the challenge is how to implement the promotional price to some, without alienating others who pay full price and lowering the reference price in people's minds. The solution is to use a "third party" for distributing the heavily discounted tickets with the understanding that those receiving the tickets will be unaware they are discounted. For example, an agency might give them to a major company in the community whose managers announce the tickets have been acquired and distributed by the company in appreciation of their employees' efforts. Thus, employees remain unaware they were discounted.

Implications for Leisure Managers

An especially challenging task for leisure managers is to move prospective users from the interest to the evaluation/trial stage of the purchase decision process. Many prospective participants are likely to be aware of and interested in an activity, but may have never taken the next step and tried it. Alternatively, they may have formerly participated in an activity, but discarded it when other priorities on their time arose, and may be receptive to re-engaging in it. The intent of a promotional price discount is to move people from the interest to the trial stage by offering a reduced price for a short time. A promotional price has to be restricted to new users, or those who have not participated in the program for (say) 2 years. If this is not done, many regular participants may take advantage of it, resulting in an overall reduction in revenue.

In this case, the regular price is positioned as the reference price criterion against which the magnitude of a discount is measured. For the discount to be effective in inducing trial behavior, the discount must be perceived as being sufficiently deep that it will generate awareness and stimulate action among people who might not otherwise have considered participating. Research in the marketing field suggests that to be perceived as offering a meaningful gain, most promotional discounts should be in the 30–50 percent range.[22, 23]

The effectiveness of a promotional price is influenced by how it is semantically framed as well as by the amount of the discount. Consider the following alternatives for presenting the same promotional price:

- Regularly $20; for 1 week $15.
- 25 percent off for 1 week.
- Save $5 this week.
- Special: $15 for 1 week.

All four formats have discount information and limited-time availability information.[24] However, all else equal, the first is likely to be most effective because it highlights the regular price and uses it as the external reference point.[25] This anchor resolves users' uncertainty about the depth of the discount and cues them to the magnitude of savings they will accrue. When this reference point is not provided, the regular price may be seriously underestimated so users conclude the posted discount is smaller than it actually is. In adaptation level terms, if objective points of reference are not provided, individuals compare sale prices to internal reference prices, and under those circumstances, they may seriously underestimate the size of the available discount.[25]

This was illustrated by respondents at a swimming pool who offered estimates of prices they last paid. Only 19 percent reported that they were reasonably certain the price they cited was accurate. The author suggested this meant many "may be unsure of the value being enjoyed as a result of any discount program. Consequently, discount programs should make 'regular' price levels clear" (p. 62).[26] This level of uncertainty about actual price was noted in Chapter 9 and has consistently been confirmed in the marketing literature. (It should be noted that it is illegal in the U.S. to inflate a "regular" price artificially to magnify the size of a discount. The external reference price must not be fictitious or misleading, and it has to have been in effect for a reasonable time.)

Dollar-off and percent-off framing affect users' perceptions differently. Both discount formulas involve arithmetic calculations to determine the final service price, but most users adopt simplifying heuristics to form an overall judgment.[27] In the discussion of the Weber–Fechner law in Chapter 10, it was pointed out that a price discount for higher priced services is most effective when it is presented in dollar, rather than percentage, terms, while the effect is reversed for lower priced services.[28, 29] A $2 swimming pool discount moving the price from $4 to $2 is small, but it is a 50 percent discount. The 50 percent figure is likely to attract more attention than is a $2 savings, so in this case, the proportionality discount should be promoted. A class discounted from $30 to $15 represents a relatively large monetary amount, so the $15 monetary savings rather than the proportionality should be stressed.

People are more likely to respond to discounts for higher priced services because the amount of money saved, and hence their gain, is relatively high. However, perceptions of "higher priced" will vary across target markets. A discounted swim admission from $4 to $2 may be of no interest to higher income groups because of their perception that a $2 savings is insignificant. In contrast, it may have a galvanizing effect on low income groups because they recognize that a family group of four people can save $8 on the admission price.

BUNDLING AND UNBUNDLING MULTIPLE COMPONENT SERVICES

Services that have multiple components can be bundled or aggregated and offered at a single price, or they can be unbundled or segregated so individual components are priced separately. Prospect theory's tenet of diminishing effect as gains and losses grow larger has implications for bundling and unbundling services and prices. Four potential pricing strategies emanate from this principle: (i) unbundle (segregate) gains, (ii) bundle (integrate) losses, (iii) bundle (integrate) smaller losses with larger gains and (iv) unbundle (segregate) smaller gains from larger losses.[30]

Unbundling gains into multiple smaller gains occurs when a discount of (say) 25 percent ($40 ➤ $30) is offered as a promotional price for admission to an ice rink and a skating class, but it is presented as two 25 percent reductions for the entrance fee ($10 ➤ $7.50) and the class fee ($30 ➤ $22.50) rather than as a single larger amount. The aggregate amount of the discount is the same. However, when it is disaggregated into multiple parts, the discount is likely to be perceived as superior because the principle of diminishing sensitivity to larger gains suggests that the two smaller gains will be perceived as being greater in aggregate than the single large gain.

In contrast, the concavity of the loss function in Figure 12-1 suggests that users perceive they are less negatively affected if *multiple losses are bundled together* because of the diminishing sensitivity associated with greater losses. A $5 price for a cup of coffee at an airport is salient when paid for in cash, but it does not appear significant when paid for as a part of a much larger monthly credit card bill.[31] Thus, if a facility is rented to a private group for $800, it is easier to induce the group to purchase additional complementary services for $100 each (e.g., party coordinator, disc jockey, post-event cleanup) at the time of the rental than it is to make the same sale separately. The psychological difference between $900 and $800 is not great. However, should a $100 item be purchased at a later date, the reference point is $0 and the jump to $100 seems much more daunting.

Concession operations frequently combine two or more items into a "value package" with a single price:

- Ski areas may package lift tickets with rental of boots and skis.
- Golf courses may bundle green fees and cart rentals.
- Food concessions offer value meals (e.g., hamburger, fries and soda) at a lower bundled price than if they were purchased separately.

As the bundled price increases, there is a diminishing sensitivity to the larger loss. This effect is complemented and reinforced by the anchoring influence of the individual prices against which the bundled package is compared. That is, in each case, the price of the added elements is small relative to the price of the main element being purchased and the aggregated price of purchasing them à la carte.

Some agencies organize vacation trips for their senior groups. If a fixed price for a package deal is adopted that includes meals, lodging and recreation, the extra costs of including the meals and recreation look relatively small when compared to the core transportation and accommodation costs. If the unbundled alternative is adopted, each small expenditure looks large by itself and is likely to be resented. Further, the piece-rate approach means the group's members will be constantly conscious of paying for items throughout the trip, "watching the meter running."[32]

Integrating smaller losses with larger gains recognizes that those who perceive a cost as simply reducing a large gain that has already been subject to diminishing returns find it less painful than seeing the cost as a loss that stands alone. Substantial efficiency improvements and cost savings in irrigation and ball-field lighting systems are often possible with investments in technology. Frequently, the challenge for managers in public agencies is to persuade elected officials to invest in the up-front cost for the technology. An alternative approach is to contract with equipment suppliers who will estimate the likely cost savings over (say) 5 years and charge a percentage of these savings spread over the time to pay for the equipment. Paying for the equipment by reducing a large gain is invariably more palatable than incurring the up-front cost, which represents an initial large loss.

Unbundling smaller gains from large losses is illustrated by the role of awards, trophies and other tangible recognitions. The cost of a youth sport program, for example, could be reduced (say) from $120 to $110, if the cost of providing these recognition elements were removed. However, when a substantial price is being spent, a small reduction will not have a large psychological impact. Recognitions are a meaningful gain for most participants, and the $10 investment in them will have a much greater impact. The awards are not an intrinsically necessary ingredient of participation in an activity. They remain part of the large loss, but they are presented as a separate unbundled small gain. Participants derive more pleasure from receiving this small gain as a distinctive element than from feeling the sense of reduced loss from a concomitant reduction in the program's cost. This pricing strategy is sometimes called the silver lining principle.[30] Because separate gains are valued more highly than reduced losses, the gains become a silver lining that reduces the pain associated with a larger expenditure.

HYPERBOLIC DISCOUNTING

Standard practice among economists, bankers and financiers is to discount future benefits and costs by some constant interest or discount rate. They assume there is timing consistency, meaning that if it is beneficial or painful to purchase a service now, it will be equally beneficial or painful to purchase it in the future. For example, if a discount rate of 6 percent is used, $100 today is worth $106 in a year and $112.36 in 2 years.

This means if they were offered $100 today or $150 in 1 year's time, people should invariably select the $150. Surprisingly, substantial evidence suggests that most people do not do this, but rather they select the $100. However, if the $100 and $150 were offered in 5 and 6 years' time, respectively, so there was also a 1-year time interval, most people, it has been found, would select the $150 option. There may be a rational explanation for these apparently contradictory decisions. The now, rather than in 1 year, decision may reflect the following:

- A distrust concern: Are you going to be here next year?
- A hassle concern: Will it be more difficult for me to get the money next year? Do I have to use extra resources to get it?
- A pocket-change perspective: The amounts are too small to be worth bothering about. I will take the $100 now and be done with it.
- Immediate need: The money may be needed now for rent or food.[33]

The reversal of their preference decision when the time is extended to 5 and 6 years may also be explained: The distrust and hassle concerns apparent in the short term are not differentiable in the longer term decision, the insignificance of the amount and longer time make the larger amount the logical decision, and the money is no longer relevant for addressing immediate needs.

However, many who do not have any of the rational concerns listed make these time inconsistent decisions. It has been widely documented: "There is substantial evidence that both people and lower animals spontaneously value future events in inverse proportion to their expected delays" (p. 47).[34] The way time is perceived is not rational. As points in time are pushed into the future, they are simply viewed as faraway points on a fuzzy horizon. The most important feature of hyperbolic discounting is that it causes individuals to rank near-term and long-term events differently. Hence, the further into the future that a price payment is deferred, the lower weighting it is given in a purchase decision. In prospect theory terms, delays in benefits are viewed as losses, while delays in costs are viewed as gains.

The hyperbolic discounting phenomenon is illustrated in Figure 12-3. At the time a leisure service is purchased, the perceived benefit (or cost) is high. The traditional exponential curve shows the rate of decay over 12 months is constant. In contrast, the hyperbolic curve shows the perceived benefit (or cost) decays substantially in the first three months and remains more or less constant after that period.

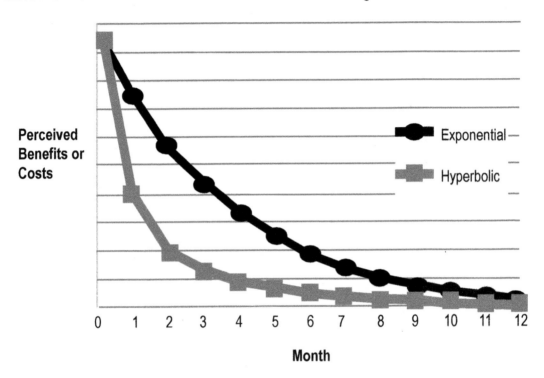

Figure 12-3. Comparison of Exponential and Hyperbolic Discount Decay Curves

When people pursue a long-term goal, similar hyperbolic discounting occurs. Assume in Figure 12-4 that this goal is a desired state of physical fitness. The exponential line shows a consistent rate of progress to accomplish it. The hyperbolic discount curve represents the natural tendency to give less weight to future actions or consequences. This means the focus on the long-term goal is not strong at the outset. Only as the goal becomes imminent does the curve accelerate sharply upwards, reflecting a substantial increase in perceived value and motivational impact.

Figure 12-5 shows how individuals typically respond when exposed to interim temptations before the long-term goal is reached. Intended regular visits to the gym are skipped in favor of watching television, a night of partying, napping or whatever. This results in a short-term hyperbolic detour, reflecting a willingness to enjoy the immediate benefit and to discount the larger long-term benefit.

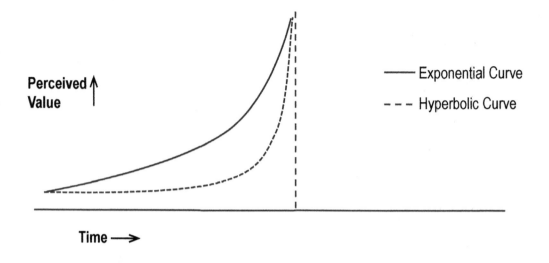

Figure 12-4. Comparison of Exponential and Hyperbolic Discount Curves

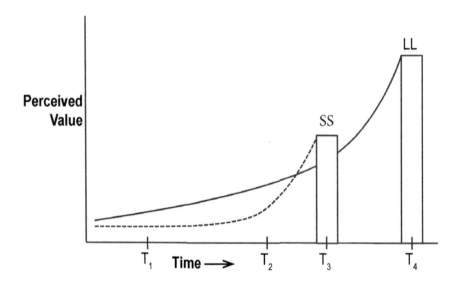

Imagine there is a smaller–sooner reward from an attraction at time T_3, and a larger–later benefit from a long-term goal at a time T_4. At a very distant, early time T_1, the solid line is preferred (the larger–later reward) because they are both far enough away that the time delay seems insignificant.

But as the time gets closer (T_2), the choice flips and the smaller reward (T_3) is more attractive.

Figure 12-5. The Influence of Temporary Short-Term Attractions on Long-Term Goals

Explanations for Hyperbolic Discounting

The timing inconsistency of hyperbolic discounting is explained by three phenomena: immediate gratification, procrastination and delusional optimism.

Long ago, the Scottish economist John Rae observed:

> Such pleasures as may now be enjoyed generally awaken a passion strongly prompting to the partaking of them. The actual presence of the immediate object of desire in the mind by exciting the attention, seems to rouse all the faculties, as it were to fix their view on it, and leads them to a very lively conception of the enjoyments which it offers to their instant possession. (p. 120)[35]

The tendency for individuals to attach too much weight to salient or vivid events and too little to non-salient events has been termed "a central principle of modern cognitive psychology"(p. 2).[36] It recognizes that people have an inherent immediacy bias manifested by them wanting the *gratification of benefits now* and willingly deferring and discounting costs associated with these benefits to a future time.

Evidence suggests that immediate gratification prevails because only the benefits associated with that action "excite the attention" (Rae above). If the costs or consequences are also explicitly presented, the frame is changed and enthusiasm for the short-term action is tempered. For example, when people were asked to choose between "$5 right now or $6.20 in 20 days," preference was overwhelmingly for the immediate reward. When the frame was changed to "$5 right now and $0 in 20 days, or $0 now and $6.20 in 20 days," the number selecting the immediate reward dropped substantially.[37]

Procrastination is the complement of immediate gratification. For the latter, people choose immediate short-term benefits over a long-term goal, whereas procrastination occurs when present costs are unduly salient in relation to future costs so there is a gap between intention and action. People know what they ought to do, but they are unable to bring themselves to do it. Thus, an unpleasant task, such as paying a large price, is deferred, even though the delay results in a greater long-term cost being incurred.

It has been observed:

> One of the most robust findings in the psychology of prediction is that people's predictions tend to be optimistically biased. By a number of metrics and across a variety of domains, people have been found to assign higher probabilities to their attainment of desirable outcomes than either objective criteria or logical analysis warrants. (p. 334)[38]

This phenomenon is termed *"delusional optimism."* It is the systematic tendency to make decisions based on over-confidence or a virtuous conscience rather than on a rational weighting of gains, losses and probabilities. It is accentuated when verification of the outcome will not be revealed until some distant future time. It has been observed that most people view "the goals we adopt as more achievable than they are likely to be" (p. 255).[3]

For example, at the beginning of each year, many people vow to exercise more. With laudable intention, they invest in a fitness club membership or program. However, after a few weeks, they skip workouts, rationalizing they are too tired or the workouts are preempted by more appealing uses of their time. The time, physical effort and opportunity costs of exercise are immediate and vivid in the mind, while the benefits are distant, vague and abstract. Thus, enthusiasm and commitment wane, and no progress is made. Once the money is spent, it becomes a sunk cost for the individual, and missing sessions becomes easier as the time increases from when the payment was made. (These implications of sunk cost are discussed later in this chapter.)

This scenario explains the general systematic tendency, illustrated in Figure 12-5, for people to switch from "virtues" that are seen as valuable in the long term toward pleasurable "vices" in the short term. Delusional optimism explains why some people persist in investing in virtues when they have a clear track record of selecting vices. The psychology underlying this can be explained by thinking about individuals as containing two semi-autonomous selves who coexist within them, which may be termed a *want* self and a *should* self.[39] They are susceptible to conflicting preferences. The *want* self is driven by the desires people affectively feel in the moment when a decision will take effect, whereas the *should* self is guided by more deliberative feelings about what ought to be done to accomplish long-term goals. Some have conceptualized these two selves as a farsighted "planner" and a myopic "doer":

> The individual can be modeled as an organization with a *planner* and a series of *doers,* one for every time period. Conflict arises because the current doer's preferences are always myopic relative to the planner's . . . Since the planner's preferences are consistent over time, it makes sense for him to adopt rules to govern the doer's behavior. (p. 396)[40]

Implications for Leisure Managers

The act of parting with money is painful and aversive.[41] Handing over cash and receiving change make a user aware of the price.[42] In contrast, a credit or debit card payment involves a quick signature or tap of a PIN. Changing the context by using such cards has been shown to alleviate the pain of parting with money[43] and facilitating spending.[44, 45] Transactions with a card are not as "real" or as immediately painful as those made with cash. As technology is being developed for increasingly convenient methods of making electronic payments, the loosening of the coupling between benefits and costs becomes more pronounced, and the payments are perceptually increasingly distant from a cash transaction.[46] This phenomenon has been explained in the following terms:

> In paying by cash, the payment is very salient in both physical form (i.e. it is easy to see the money is being spent) and in amount (i.e. since cash has to be counted and given, the amount is relatively memorable). In moving from cash to check payments, the salience of the physical form weakens somewhat, but the amount is reinforced (since it has to be written in words and numerals). With credit/debit cards, the salience of both the physical form and the amount is weaker (i.e. cards don't have the physical properties of cash, and the opportunities to reinforce the price are low). And with electronic and mobile payments, the salience is even lower. (p. 76)[47]

Thus, whenever leisure agencies facilitate the use of credit or debit cards, electronic payment mechanisms or automatic monthly payments with a bank draft, price resistance is likely to be reduced. The perceived loss is reduced by perceptually distancing and decoupling costs from benefits and by moving costs into the future and thus discounting them, while a service's benefits can be enjoyed immediately. Thus, the innate human preference for rapid reward and immediate gratification is reinforced.

Hyperbolic discounting explains the popularity of pledging in capital campaigns. If donations are needed to build a new facility, it is much easier for people to commit to contributing at some future date than to pay for it now. The satisfaction and perhaps recognition associated with altruism is enjoyed immediately, while the loss incurred by paying the donation is spread over a future time.

All three explanations of hyperbolic discounting (immediate gratification, procrastination and delusional optimism) reflect a failure of self-regulation. The internal conflict within individuals between the planner self, concerned with long-term benefit, and the want self, who is selfishly interested in the present, is a test of will—will being defined as "the faculty by which we impose some over-riding value of ours on the array of pressures and temptations that seem extrinsic" (p. 3).[34] Given the fallibility of will, without a mechanism that serves as an "external voice" to regulate and exercise authority over the want self, the desired planning outcome cannot be attained.[40] Thus, it is rational for people to impose adaptive controls to regulate their behavior. Recognition of this problem has led to the creation of two mechanisms, based on the prospect theory tenet of loss aversion, that are designed to sustain commitment to a long-term goal and counter the failures of self-regulation.

First, penalty payments may be imposed and be perceived as motivational fees because of the loss aversion phenomenon. As described in Figure 12-6, an app called GymPact was launched to counter this decay in sustaining commitment to a fitness regime.[48, 49]

After taking a class in behavioral economics and grasping the power of loss aversion, two students co-founded a new app for iPhones. GymPact rewards people for going to the gym, but penalizes them if they do not go. Users of the app decide how many days they want to go to the gym, along with the penalty they will pay if they fail in that commitment. The minimum commitment is 1 day a week for at least 30 minutes, and users can set the penalty at between $5 and $50 for each missed visit, with $5 being the minimum and default position.

GymPact has more than 40,000 gyms in its database, and users can easily add others. Every time users arrive at a gym, they hit the check-in button on the app and it confirms the location. At the end of each week, the credit card the company keeps on file is charged $5 for every missed visit (or more, if users raised the stakes above the minimum). For example, if someone committed to 4 days a week, but only went twice, $10 would be charged to the credit card. One experienced user of the app stated: "Set a fine that will hurt. While $5 is the suggested fine, pick a price that will motivate you to attain your goal."

If the commitment is fulfilled, users are rewarded with cash, which is drawn from the penalty payments of those who did not meet their commitments. The money is funneled into a PayPal account and winnings can be withdrawn once they reach $10. Each week the company calculates how much it collected from members who did not meet their pacts. The amount each user collects is based on how many days they committed to go, so if they signed up for 3 days, they are allotted "three portions" of the winnings. Typically, a portion amounts to approximately 50 cents, so someone who committed to 3 days would collect $1.50 a week or $6 a month. One user reported: "After using GymPact for two years and 390 workouts later, I've earned $147.27 and I highly recommend it to anybody who is serious about getting in shape."

The GymPact model expanded to embrace other forms of commitment and changed its name to Pact to reflect this:

A committer's goal might be to lose weight, eat vegetables for a certain number of days, quit smoking, exercise more frequently, improve grades, or the like. There is even a creative section for people with idiosyncratic goals: climb Mount Kilimanjaro while there is still ice at the summit (verification by photograph), travel to Mongolia (verification by passport stamp), learn to juggle seven oranges and watermelon (verification by video), run a marathon, save more money (less creative, to be sure), use less gas and electricity (not so creative but admirable) or whatever self-improvement people can conjure up and post on the website. (p. 231)[49]

Figure 12-6. Using Loss Avoidance to Motivate Sustained Commitment to a Fitness Regime[48]

An alternative approach recognizes that individuals have a strong tendency to procrastinate and remain at the *status quo* (which is a variant of the endowment effect discussed in the next section). There appear to be three reasons for this preference: aversion to loss, as preferring an existing option is less risky than switching to an alternative service whose benefits are unknown; the hassle costs involved in transitioning to another option make it more bother than it is worth; and the original choice presumably was based on good reasons, so there is no merit in re-examining it (even though those reasons may no longer be recalled).

This *status quo* effect can be used to the advantage of clients and agencies if leisure managers structure enrollment in their programs to be governed by an opt-out rather than an opt-in default position. When an opt-out system is used, if people take no affirmative action, they remain in the program. This meets their needs if it reflects the option that would lead to what they consider to be their best long-term outcome. Opt-out default rules work not only because of procrastination, but also because they create a different reference point as the anchor for making judgments. The judgment now is whether to opt out of seeking long-term benefits, which would represent a loss. The loss may loom large. In contrast, an opt-in default requires people to seek a benefit, which is a much less powerful motivator.[50]

Leisure agencies frequently offer classes every quarter. After the class ends, if people want to participate in the following quarter, they have to re-register; this is a lost opportunity. Instead of requiring users to re-register, the agency should set the default position to opt-out so they are enrolled automatically for the next quarter unless they act to the contrary. The combination of delusional optimism, loss aversion, procrastination and *status quo* bias indicates this default designation is likely to result in increased participation.

The data reported earlier in Figure 7-7 empirically confirms the common anecdotal reports of people paying more for fitness club programs than is warranted by their level of use.[43] This may be explained by delusional optimism in that when thinking about the future, people naïvely over-predict how frequently they will go to the gym. Alternatively, they could be using the contracts as commitment devices. That is, they signed unlimited gym use contracts to increase the likelihood their future selves would go to the gym regularly.

Whatever the rationale, from a revenue maximizing perspective, these actions confirm the default position should be to require people to be proactive in canceling their ongoing participation. It may only take a phone call, e-mail or letter, but given the human tendency to procrastinate and the strength of the planner or should self, reluctance to opt out is likely. This may take the form of repeatedly putting off such a defeatist act with its connotations of failure until some indeterminate future time.[51] This has been called the "yeah, whatever" heuristic.[49] When people have to make a phone call to cancel their membership, the likelihood of renewal is much higher than if they do not have to take action to cancel. This probably contributed to the findings described in Figure 7-7[52] and reinforces the case for using opt-out as the default position if the goal is to maximize participation and revenue.

THE ENDOWMENT EFFECT

Supreme Court Justice Oliver Wendel Holmes over a century ago observed:

A thing which you enjoyed and used as your own for a long time, whether property or opinion, takes root in your being and cannot be torn away without your resenting the act and trying to defend yourself. (p. 473)[53]

The endowment effect describes the tendency for people to demand much more to give up a service or product than they are willing to pay to acquire it. They ascribe more value to it merely because they own it (i.e., they have paid for it). Prospect theory suggests owners of a good or service regard its potential loss as more significant than non-owners regard its potential acquisition. Thus, for example, the price for which an individual would be prepared to sell a ticket to a popular sport event or a permit for a hunting opportunity is generally much higher than the price he or she would be willing to pay for it:

- Fans who had won the right to buy a pair of tickets for $325 or $400 each in a Super Bowl lottery were asked if they would have been willing to pay $3,000 a ticket if they had lost in the lottery and if they would have sold their tickets if someone had offered them $3,000 apiece. Ninety-four percent said they would not have bought for $3,000, and 92 percent said they would not have sold at that price. The author concluded: "Rationality was in short supply at the Super Bowl" (p. 29).[54]

In an early experiment demonstrating the endowment effect, respondents were presented with the following scenario:

Two avid sports fans plan to travel 40 miles to see a basketball game. One of them paid for his ticket; the other was on his way to purchase a ticket when he got one free from a friend. A blizzard is announced for the night of the game. Which of the two ticket holders is more likely to brave the blizzard to see the game?[55]

The overwhelming answer was the fan who paid for his ticket. His loss was greater and his sense of ownership was stronger because he bought a ticket and thus was now out of pocket as well as deprived of the game.

- The state of Wisconsin allocated early season, day goose hunting permits by drawing names at random from the pool of applicants. Nearly 14,000 such permits were issued, and each entitled a hunter to take at most one goose. In an experiment, when the state mailed permits to 237 of those whose names were drawn, the researchers enclosed a check for $1 to $200. The person was asked to return either the permit or the check. The average break-off point was $63. Those who received over $63 tended to keep the check, while those who received less tended to keep the permit.

  The researchers then approached a different group of 353 people who had received permits and made offers to buy back those permits. The average price for purchasing those permits was $101.

  Finally, 300 applicants who did not receive permits were asked how much they would pay to buy a permit. The average price offer was $21.[56]

These results illustrate the power of the endowment effect. While those who possessed the permit on average would sell it for $101, those who did not "own" a permit would pay only $21 to acquire one. The $67 cutoff among those who were given possession of the check and the permit was approximately midway between the other two values.

Similar results have been consistently reported. In a review of 59 studies, the authors concluded that selling prices typically were approximately 3 times higher than buying prices.[57] Among those studies, waterfowl hunters were willing to spend only $247 to continue hunting, but required $1,044 to sell their hunting rights.[58] Among elk hunters, the respective values were $15 and $69;[59] for deer hunting permits, they were $31 and $153;[60] and for bison hunting permits, they were $215 and $12,333.[61]

Implications for Leisure Managers

Ownership creates inertia and the endowment effect recognizes the reluctance of people to give up assets that have become part of their "endowment." This provides a rationale for the common marketing practice of many health clubs, fitness centers and weight loss clinics offering an initial trial membership either for free or at a nominal rate. People not familiar with or confident of a program's benefits might be tempted to try it because if it isn't worth the purchase price, they have lost nothing. At the end of the trial period, the hope is that trialists integrate the new service and benefits into their lifestyle routine so it becomes part of their endowment. This means its value to them will increase, making it difficult to reject appeals to continue with the program at regular rates.[8]

The endowment effect also explains why service users are more likely to show up and be more aggressive in protesting price increases or proposals to reduce or terminate a service. Non-users would likely gain because such actions would reduce a service's tax subsidy. However, prospect theory suggests that those who feel a sense of ownership and stand to lose will fight harder than those who stand to gain.

SUNK COST EFFECT

"Sunk cost" is the term used to describe irrecoverable costs. These are expenditures that cannot be reclaimed once they have been incurred. Traditionally, economists have argued that it is not rational to allow historical costs to influence future decisions. Individuals may regret an investment, but that money is gone. They should get over it and move forward rather than allow attempts to justify it to influence future decisions. A rational decision maker is only interested in the future consequences of current investments.

The tenet of loss aversion, however, induces sunk cost pressure and renders the traditional economic perspective incomplete. People often feel obligated to use a service despite not wanting to do so, because they have misgivings about "wasting" their investment. There is an "irrational perseverance" whereby people "give up rationality rather than give up the enterprise" (p. 267).[3] Consider the following scenario:

> A man pays a $500 yearly membership fee to join a tennis club. After one week of playing he develops tennis elbow. He continues to play (in pain) saying, "I don't want to waste the $500." (p. 47)[55]

He wants to feel he is getting "value for money." A sunk cost investment creates a level of emotional commitment to a course of action beyond that of others who have less "skin in the game." People are reluctant to walk away from an investment and accept it was unwise because doing so would mean admitting failure. Sunk cost pressure is defined as a "greater tendency to continue an endeavor once an investment in money, time or effort has been made" (p. 125).[62] Hence, while orthodox economic theory directs that use will decline when prices are increased, the sunk cost effect suggests that if the expenditure is large enough, it could result in sustained participation.[63]

The sunk cost influence may extend to ancillary or complementary expenditures. Someone who has invested heavily in, for example, ski or golf equipment may not be as sensitive to changes in prices for lift tickets or green fees because of these associated capital expenditures.

The emotional influence exerted by sunk cost pressure is likely to depreciate over time. When payment is made at the time of use, this pressure is high and people feel compelled to use a service to avoid feeling they have wasted their money. In contrast, if an annual pass is purchased, a decline in sunk cost pressure to use the service as the year progresses is likely.

As the pain of paying fades from memory, the decay effect is reinforced by adaptation, as the cost no longer forms part of an individual's financial *status quo*. The new *status quo* becomes the reference standard against which the decision to use a service is made. This has been termed "payment depreciation."[64] There is a gradual discounting of the initial price over time until ultimately the service takes on the characteristics of a free good. At that point, the reference standard is not the original monetary price paid. Rather, an individual evaluates only if the benefits accruing from the service outweigh the costs of immediate constraints associated with the activity, such as time availability, travel costs, amount of effort and adverse weather. The discounting or discarding of the initial monetary price increases the probability the service will not be used. If people cease to use a service over time, they are likely to balk when requested to renew their payment in the future.

Implications for Leisure Managers

This phenomenon was illustrated in a study of payment plans at a health club.[42, 64] The results are shown in Figure 12-7. All members paid the same annualized membership fee, but they could select from four payment plans: (a) pay the whole fee once a year, (b) pay half the fee every 6 months, (c) pay a quarter of the fee every 3 months or (d) pay one twelfth of the fee every month. The usage rate of the club's facilities among those selecting option (d) was approximately constant every month. These users felt sunk cost pressure to work out regularly each month to justify their investment. Those selecting the other three options felt this pressure immediately after their payment, but their drive dissipated as the pain of the cost faded into the past:

> Members who made a single annual payment used the club most frequently in the months immediately following payment, reflecting a strong nexus between service use and time of payment. But as time passed, the effect dissipated. By the final months, individuals seemed to be treating their memberships as if they were free and worked out at a rate that was only a quarter of what it had been in the first few months. The same pattern held for members who had paid on a semiannual or quarterly basis: Attendance was highest immediately following payment, only to decline steadily until the next payment. This resulted in a saw-tooth pattern of usage, spiking in the first and seventh months for semiannual payment members and every three months for quarterly members. (p. 94)[42]

Similar findings emerged in the study reported in an earlier chapter in Figure 7-7 in which those who chose a monthly contract at their health club were 17 percent more likely to stay enrolled beyond 1 year than were users choosing the annual contract.[52]

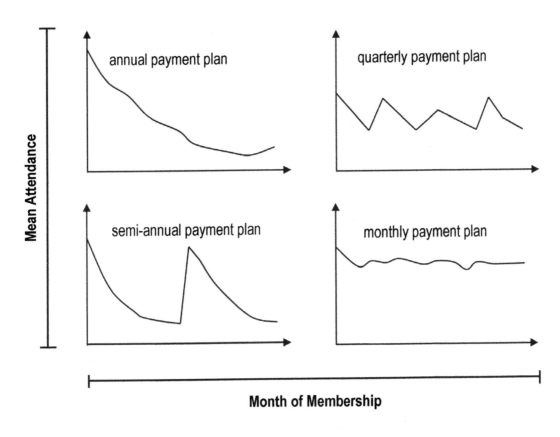

Figure 12-7. Patterns of Usage at a Health Club Linked to the Timing of Payments

The sunk cost pressure may have been reinforced by the endowment effect. That is, the monthly payers who participated regularly would have to give up an element of their lifestyle that had become part of their endowment, so it became difficult for them to terminate participating in the program. The obvious implication of these findings for leisure managers is to encourage monthly payments rather than an annual payment.

When services are bundled, the emotional attachment to sunk costs is typically weaker. There is a decoupling of transaction costs and benefits associated with each event, resulting in a much weaker sunk cost effect. It is a common strategy in sport and art events to bundle individual performances and sell them as packages. An analysis of ticket purchase and attendance data at a Shakespearean summer festival comprising four plays revealed the decreased attention to sunk costs brought about by price bundling:

> Some ticket holders had purchased tickets to a single play, some to two or three of the plays, and others to all four plays. What we found was that the no-show rate for people who had bought tickets to a single play was 0.7%, indicating that almost all ticket holders showed up. But the no-show rate for those purchasing tickets to two plays was 3.6%; for three plays, 13.2%; and for four plays, 21.5%. As the bundling of tickets increased from one to four plays, the likelihood of a person not showing up for one of the plays rose 35-fold. (p. 94)[42]

From an economist's perspective, the format of the payment should not matter because all who purchased tickets are assumed to consider the sunk cost of their investment equally when making an attendance decision. However, the bundling creates an ambiguity in determining which costs are paying for what benefits. In this case, those who purchased single tickets explicitly recognized that the performance cost them (say) $40, and their decision to attend would be influenced by sunk cost pressure not to lose that amount. In contrast, for some who purchased the four-play bundle option, the sunk cost effect had depreciated over time. They would ask themselves if they had derived enough benefit from the first three plays to offset this cost. If yes, they would be more willing to forgo the fourth play.

In a Colorado experiment, half of the subjects were told they had pre-purchased a single 4-day ski lift pass for $160, while the other half were told they had pre-purchased four 1-day ski tickets. They were shown the physical pass and 1-day tickets, respectively, to emphasize the format. They were then informed:

> It is now the morning of the last day of your vacation. You have had three excellent days of skiing with perfect conditions. Unfortunately, last night a warm rain hit the area. While skiing is still permitted, it may not be much fun. As an alternative, a friend suggests taking it easy, having a nice lunch, and leaving early to beat the traffic. You look at your [ski pass/remaining ski ticket] and are not sure if you want to go skiing or leave early. (p. 33)[46]

Those given the single pass format were significantly less likely to ski on the final day.

These findings indicate the "no-show" effect induced by bundling can be reduced by the physical form in which individual performance or day admission is facilitated. Season tickets or ski passes in the form of a booklet with individual tickets for each performance suggest a single transaction nexus between cost and that specific event and hence induce sunk cost pressure to attend. If admission is gained by showing a single card, it removes the coupling between costs and benefits and reduces the likelihood of attendance.

ODD NUMBER PRICING

In the commercial marketplace, prices of products and services ending with 9 are omnipresent. They are used in real estate, for which common strategies are to price homes at $599,000 instead of $600,000 or alternatively to price them at $601,000 knowing there will be subsequent negotiations, and a reduction to $599,000 will sound like a substantial concession to the buyer. In retail stores, inexpensive items are widely priced at 99 cents rather than $1. Odd-ending prices have been consistently demonstrated to be an effective strategy for increasing demand.[65-74] For example, it was reported in surveys that between 30 and 65 percent of all retail prices ended in the digit 9,[66] and in a series of eight studies published over 17 years, it was reported that prices ending in 9 increased sales by an average of 24 percent.[66]

Retailers initiated this practice in the early 1900s to reduce dishonesty among store assistants.[66] If a customer handed a clerk a $1 bill, the clerk could neglect to record the sale, slip the bill in his or her pocket and leave no one the wiser. The 9 digit ending re-quired employees to punch in a price to open the change drawer, as most people paid in even-dollar amounts. The cash register kept a record of the amount entered, and it was relatively simple to check the record against the cash, so it reduced opportunities to pocket the payment.

Nowadays, this practice has continued because it is believed it creates an illusion of substantially lower prices, and hence, consistent with prospect theory, it offers a mean-ingful gain. Several explanations have been offered to explain this phenomenon, but the most convincing is termed "truncation."[71] Truncation involves people cutting off reading a price's digits before all of them have been recognized and encoded. This derives from research demonstrating that despite years of school training to process numbers from right to left while adding and subtracting, people process prices from left to right. To il-lustrate, in the following examples, which program's price increase appears to be highest: A: $79 ➔ $93 or B: $75 ➔ $89? And which discount is perceived to be largest: A: $6.00 ➔ $4.95 or B: $6.05 ➔ $5.00? In both cases, most people are likely to select option A. It is suggested this occurs because of a tendency to reach a decision by comparing only the left-side digits, so the differences between 7 and 9, and 6 and 4 are perceived to be greater than those between 7 and 8, and 6 and 5, respectively.[71]

The magnitude of the numbers is encoded rapidly, and a conclusion is reached before all the digits are read. Thus, the price perception is anchored by the left-most digit(s). Because the left-most digits are the most important and people have a limited capacity to absorb information, this is a heuristic that enables them to simplify the complexity ema-nating from the bombardment of information to which they are subjected. Prospective purchasers are said to be "cognitive misers," so they ignore the right-hand digits because they are "trading off the low likelihood of making a mistake against the cost of mentally processing the digit" (p. 65).[71]

Odd-ending pricing has the most impact on price perceptions when the difference in the left-most digit alters the right-most digit. That is, $19.99 (vs. $20) is more effec-tive than $17.99 (vs. $18) because the left-most digit changes from 2 to 1.[72] Further, it is likely to be more effective at higher price levels because the perceived dollar gain is much greater. Thus, the gain from a $39.99 price if only the first digit is processed would be $10, compared to a $1 gain for a $3.99 price.

While truncation offers a strong and valuable explanation for why use of 9 is so ef-fective, it is not complete. Studies have shown, for example, that when a service is offered at $34, $39 and $44 not only are sales disproportionately larger at $39 compared to $44 price, but they are also higher at $39 than at $34. Truncation and mental rounding can-not explain such results. If only the first digits were considered, sales at both price points should be the same rather than being greater at the substantially higher $39 price.[71]

To accommodate this anomaly, it has been proposed that the truncation effect may be complemented by a more holistic response that is instinctive and associative rather than deliberative. It draws from associative knowledge structures in long-term memory and recognizes that sometimes a number spontaneously "pops up" first in a customer's mind, so it serves as an unintended heuristic in judgments. It may be the result of instinctive cognitive arithmetic that mentally completes rounded number comparisons quicker than it does non-rounded number comparisons. Alternatively, the associative structures may recognize that prices including a 9 tend to imply a discounted price, so it is the notion of a discount rather than the reduced amount that pops up unintentionally without users being aware of what is occurring. Thus, users infer meaning from the right-hand digits of price, and odd-ending prices are heuristics for low price.[72, 73] These processes rely on an instinctive representativeness heuristic rather than on rule-based reasoning, such as truncation.[72] Both are likely to contribute to the explanation for the effectiveness of odd number pricing.

A conceptual illustration of the influence of odd pricing on demand is shown in Figure 12-8. Consistent with classic economic theory, the figure shows that as price decreases from $45 to $18, the number of individuals enrolled in the program is expected to increase. However, at the prices of $39, $29 and $19, with the 9 digit, disproportionately more people enroll than at the rounded prices immediately above them. Thus, 10 people enroll at $40, but this increases to 15 at $39. Similarly, Figure 12-8 shows enrollment of 20 people at $30, but this number increases to 26 when the odd price of $29 is used.

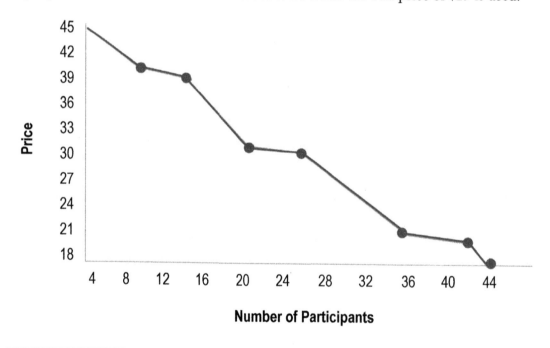

Figure 12-8. The Influence of Odd Pricing on Demand

Implications for Leisure Managers

If a price of $29.99 is rounded down to $29.00 assuming the last two digits are omitted or to $20.00 if only the first digit is processed, there would appear to be obvious advantages for leisure managers to adopt odd pricing. If this strategy is used for pricing recreation classes, for example, the agency could lower a user's perceived price by almost either $1 or $10 for the cost of one penny. By the same token, offering a discount of $10 will be more effective than a discount of $9.99 as it is likely to be perceived as being a much larger number.

Nevertheless, despite the widespread adoption of odd number pricing in the private sector, few public leisure agencies price their recreation classes at $29, $39 or $49; their swim pool admission at $5.99; or their annual passes at $199. Two reasons may explain this lack of adoption. First, there may be a lack of awareness of the strategy's framing potential for reducing perceptions of the magnitude of a price. Second, the absence of a tradition of odd number pricing in the field may cause managers to be reluctant to implement it because of a concern it will be controversial. Because the underlying intent of odd number pricing is to create an illusion, its adoption may be viewed as manipulative, deceitful, slick and exploitive; inconsistent with the criterion of fairness and the ethical standards expected of public agencies; and incongruent with a community's social norms and value system.

There is empirical support for this perspective, as it has been reported that the perceived quality and classiness of restaurants[75] and of retailers[76] are enhanced by the use of prices that end in 0 rather than 9. The implication is that prices ending in a 9 signify to users that they should buy because it is a good price, while those ending in 0 suggest they should purchase for quality reasons. This suggests that services aimed at users who are price sensitive may incorporate the 9, while those directed at higher end users should use round numbers.

Managers who have these reservations may argue against using this strategy when first pricing a recreational opportunity. However, they may consider odd number pricing to be appropriate in some price revision decisions.

- Consider a recreation class for which costs increase by $3 each year. Last year, this meant the price went from $24 to $27. It should be raised to $30 this year. To reduce price resistance and potential decreases in enrollment, there may be merit in raising it only to $29. Next year, the lost revenue could be recovered by setting a price of $33, as odd pricing suggests there will be no more resistance to $33 than there would be to $32 or $30. If more revenue needs to be generated in 2 years' time, the usual $3 increase could be raised to (say) $5 to move the price from $33 to $38. Given the first digit remains the same, there likely would be relatively little user resistance.

SUMMARY

The three core tenets of prospect theory are (i) evaluations are reference dependent, so change from a reference point rather than the actual price is the evaluative criterion and, importantly, prices lower than the latitude of acceptance are perceived to be gains, while those higher than this reference range are viewed as losses; (ii) there is diminishing sensitivity to changes in price, so each additional increment of gain or loss has a smaller impact than the amount preceding it, and proportionality rather than absolute values is evaluated; and (iii) people are more strongly influenced by loss aversion than by benefit gains.

The *enterprise fund effect* suggests that users are more likely to be supportive of price increases if their revenues are invested to maintain and improve the resource at which they are collected. This is consistent with prospect theory in that if these revenues disappear into a general fund, users are likely to perceive them as a loss, but if they are directed into an enterprise-type fund in which there is a direct nexus between their payment and quality of the service, they are likely to perceive a direct gain accrues to them.

Semantic framing of discounts and premiums recognizes that while use of the word "premium" is conceptually correct in some contexts, it is sometimes interpreted as a punitive surcharge, which leads to resentment among those expected to pay it. This alienation is likely to be removed if a premium price is presented as the regular price so it serves as the primary point of reference, and the former regular price becomes a discount. This approach adheres to the adage: Surcharges make people mad, while discounts make them happy.

Prospect theory informs the effectiveness of *promotional prices* in that users invariably view reductions in price not accompanied by loss of benefits as gains when compared to a regular price. The primary goal of a promotional price is to move people from the interest to the trial stage of the purchase process. To be effective, the promotional price should be between 20 and 50 percent and should be offered only for a short time so it incites action and does not reduce the existing reference price. A zero promotional price has a distinctive emotional appeal that makes it especially effective.

The effectiveness of a promotional price is influenced by how it is semantically framed. Three semantic guidelines are suggested. First, the promotional price should be related to the regular price so magnitude of the discount is clear to potential users. Second, a price discount is more effective when it is presented in dollar, rather than percentage, terms for higher priced services, while the effect is reversed for lower priced services. Third, comparisons of promotional prices to regular prices are likely to be most effective if font size of the two prices is congruent rather than incongruent.

The prospect theory principle of diminishing effect as gains and losses grow larger has implications for the *bundling and unbundling of multiple component services* and pricing component elements in ways that enhance users' perceptions. Four pricing strategies emanate from this principle: segment gains, integrate losses, bundle smaller losses with larger gains and segregate smaller gains from larger losses.

Hyperbolic discounting recognizes that the further into the future payment of a price is deferred, the lower weighting it is given in a purchase decision. Delays in benefits are viewed as losses, while delays in payments are viewed as gains. Hyperbolic discounting is explained by three phenomena: immediate gratification, which reflects people's desires to enjoy benefits now and their willingness to defer associated costs to a later time; procrastination, which defers unpleasant choices, such as paying a large price, to a future date; and delusional optimism, which is the systematic tendency to make decisions based on over-confidence or a virtuous conscience rather than on a rational weighting of gains, losses and probabilities. Delusional optimism recognizes that individuals have two semi-autonomous selves, a short-term want self and a long-term should self, which are often in conflict with each other.

Four implications for leisure managers emanate from hyperbolic discounting. First, credit card payments will reduce price resistance because using them is less painful than parting with cash. Further, the costs are moved into the future, so they are discounted. Second, seeking pledges rather than immediate cash makes it easier for people to commit to a capital project. Third, users may value external motivation to sustain momentum to a long-term goal that involves them in voluntarily paying a penalty if they veer from it. Fourth, opt-out default mechanisms are preferred to opt-in actions to keep users on track toward their long-term goals.

The *endowment effect* recognizes that people perceive a service to be more valuable when they "own" it (i.e., they have paid for it). Thus, the price for which an individual would be prepared to sell a ticket to a popular event or a permit for a hunting opportunity is invariably much higher than the price he or she would be willing to pay for it.

Sunk costs are expenses that cannot be reclaimed once they have been incurred. While an investment may be regretted, it cannot be recovered. Thus, rational decision makers should not allow sunk costs to influence future investment decisions. However, the emotional commitment to such investments often reflects people's aversion to accepting losses and admitting failure, and this pressure continues to influence future behavior. This sunk cost pressure depreciates over time.

Odd number pricing refers to pricing services so the price ends with the number 9. It has been consistently demonstrated that this creates an illusion of substantially lower prices, and hence, consistent with prospect theory, it offers a meaningful gain. Its effectiveness is primarily explained by truncation, which suggests a tendency to encode and compare only the left-side digits of numbers and ignore the right-side digits.

REFERENCES

1. Kahneman, D., & Tversky, A. (1979). Prospect theory: An analysis of decision under risk. *Econometrica, 47,* 263–291.
2. Wu, G., Zhang, J., & Gonzales, R. (2014). Decision under risk. In D. J. Koehler & N. Harvey (Eds.), *Blackwell handbook of judgment and decision making* (pp. 399–423). Malden, MA: Blackwell Publishing.
3. Kahneman, D. (2011). *Thinking fast and slow.* London, England: Penguin.
4. Levin, I. F., Schneider, S. I., & Gaeth, C. J. (1998). All frames are not created equal: A typology and critical analysis of framing effects. *Organizational Behavior and Human Decision Processes, 76,* 149–158.
5. Keren, G. (2011). On the definition and possible underpinnings of framing effects: A brief review and a critical evaluation. In G. Keren (Ed.), *Perspectives on framing* (pp. 3–34). New York, NY: Psychology Press.
6. Birnbaum, M. (1999). How to show that 9 > 221: Collect judgments in a between subjects design. *Psychological Methods, 1,* 241–249.
7. Ariely, D. (2009). *Predictably irrational.* New York, NY: HarperCollins.

8. Monroe, K. B. (2003). *Pricing: Making profitable decisions.* New York, NY: McGraw-Hill.

9. McCarville, R. E., & Crompton, J. L. (1987). Propositions addressing perceptions of reference price for public recreation services. *Leisure Sciences, 9,* 281–292.

10. Fedler, A. J., & Miles, A. F. (1988). Paying for backcountry recreation: Understanding the acceptability of user fees. *Journal of Park and Recreation Administration, 7*(2), 35–46.

11. Leuschner, W. A., Cook, P. S., Roggenbuck, J. W., & Oderwald, R. G. (1987). A comparative analysis for wilderness user fee policy. *Journal of Leisure Research, 19,* 101–114.

12. McCarville, R. E., Reiling, S. D. B., & White, C. M. (1996). The role of fairness in users' assessments of first time fees for a public recreation service. *Leisure Sciences, 18,* 61–76.

13. Reiling, S. D. B., McCarville, R. E., & White, C. M. (1998). *Demand and marketing study at Army Corps of Engineers day-use areas* (Miscellaneous Paper R-94-1). Washington, DC: U.S. Army Corps of Engineers.

14. Steele, C. (1984). *Participants' willingness to pay higher fees for parks and recreation services* (Unpublished master's thesis). Virginia Commonwealth University, Richmond, VA.

15. Ostergren, D., Solop, F. I., & Hagen, K. K. (2005). National Park Service fees: Value for the money or a barrier to visitation. *Journal of Park and Recreation Administration, 23*(1), 18–36.

16. Winter, P. L., Palucki, L. J., & Burkhart, R. L. (1999). Anticipated responses to a fee program: The key is trust. *Journal of Leisure Research, 31,* 207–226.

17. Sports clubs hit with higher user fees [Editorial]. (1993, July 6). *Kitchener-Waterloo Record,* p. B3.

18. Baldacchino, N. P. (1984). Recreation fees on national wildlife refuges. *Trends, 21*(4), 39–40.

19. Kimes, S. E., & Wirtz, J. (2003). Perceived fairness of revenue management in the U.S. golf industry. *Journal of Revenue and Pricing Management, 1,* 332–344.

20. Rogers, E. (1962). *Diffusion of innovation.* New York, NY: Glencoe.

21. Coulter, K. S., & Coulter, R. A. (2005). Size does matter: The effects of magnitude representation congruency on price perceptions and purchase likelihood. *Journal of Consumer Psychology, 15*(1), 64–76.

22. Kalyanaram, G., & Little, J. D. C. (1994). An empirical analysis of latitude of price acceptance in consumer package goods. *Journal of Consumer Research, 21,* 408–418.

23. Cram, T. (2006). *Smarter pricing: How to capture more value in your market.* New York, NY: Prentice Hall.

24. Howard, D. J., & Kerin, R. A. (2006). Broadening the scope of reference price advertising research: A field study of consumer shopping involvement. *Journal of Marketing, 70,* 185–204.

25. Mayhew, G. E., & Winer, R. S. (1992). An empirical analysis of internal and external reference prices using scanner data. *Journal of Consumer Research, 19,* 62–70.

26. McCarville, R. E. (1996). The importance of price last paid in developing price expectations for a public leisure service. *Journal of Park and Recreation Administration, 14*(4), 52–64.

27. Weisstein, F. L., Monroe, K. B., & Kukar-Kinney, M. (2013). Effects of price framing on consumers' perceptions of online dynamic pricing practices. *Journal of the Academy of Marketing Science, 41*, 501–514.

28. Gendall, P., Hoek, J., Pope, T., & Young, K. (2006). Message framing effects on price discounting. *Journal of Product and Brand Management, 15*, 458–465.

29. Krishna, A., Briesch, R., Lehmann, D. R., & Hong, Y. (2002). A meta-analysis of the impact of price presentation on perceived savings. *Journal of Retailing, 78*, 101–118.

30. Thaler, R. H. (1985). Mental accounting and consumer choice. *Marketing Science, 4*, 199–214.

31. Thaler, R. H. (1999). Mental accounting matters. *Journal of Behavioral Decision Making, 12*, 183–206.

32. Liu, M. W., & Soman, D. (2008). Behavioral pricing. In C. P. Haugtvedt, M. Herr, & F. R. Kardes (Eds.), *Handbook of consumer psychology* (pp. 659–681). New York, NY: Psychology Press.

33. R. Dudensing, personal communication, 2015.

34. Ainslie, G. (2001). *Breakdown of will.* New York, NY: Cambridge University Press.

35. Rae, J. (1834). *The sociological theory of capital* (Reprint 1834 ed.). London, England: MacMillan.

36. Akerlof, G. A. (1991). Procrastination and obedience. *The American Economic Review, 81*(2), 1–19.

37. Magen, E., Dweck, C., & Gross, J. J. (2008). The hidden zero effect. *Psychological Sciences, 19*, 648–649.

38. Armor, D. A., & Taylor, S. E. (2002). When predictions fail: The dilemma of unrealistic optimism. In T. Gilovich, D. Griffin, & D. Kahnemanz (Eds.), *Heuristics and biases: The psychology of intuitive judgment* (pp. 334–347). New York, NY: Cambridge University Press.

39. Bazerman, M. H., Tenbrunsel, A. E., & Wade-Benzoni, K. (1998). Negotiating with yourself and losing: Making decisions with competing internal preferences. *Academy of Management Review, 23*, 225–241.

40. Thaler, R. H. (1981). An economic theory of self-control. *Journal of Political Economy, 89*, 392–406.

41. Prelec, D., & Lowenstein, G. (1998). The red and black: Mental accounting of savings and debt. *Marketing Science, 17*, 4–28.

42. Gourville, J. T., & Soman, D. (2002, September). Pricing and the psychology of consumption. *Harvard Business Review, 80*, 90–96.

43. Prelec, D., & Simester, D. (2001). Always leave home without it: A further investigation of the credit card effect on willingness to pay. *Marketing Letters, 1*(12), 5–12.

44. Feinberg, R. A. (1986). Credit cards as spending facilitating stimuli: A conditioning interpretation. *Journal of Consumer Research, 13*, 348–356.

45. Monger, J. E., & Feinberg, R. A. (1997). Mode of payment and formation of reference prices. *Pricing Strategy and Practice, 5*, 142–147.

46. Soman, D., & Gourville, J. (2001). Transaction decoupling: How price bundling affects the decision to consume. *Journal of Marketing Research, 38*, 30–44.

47. Soman, D., & Ahn, H. K. (2011). Mental accounting and individual welfare. In G. Keren (Ed.), *Perspectives on framing* (pp. 65–92). New York, NY: Psychology Press.

48. Bernard, T. S. (2012, January 2). Gym-Pact fines you for not exercising. *New York Times*. Retrieved from http://bucks.blogs.nytimes.com/2012/01/02/gym-pact-fines-you-for-not-exercising/?_r=0

49. Thaler, R. H., & Sunstein, C. R. (2008). *Nudge: Improving decisions about health, wealth, and happiness.* New Haven, CT: Yale University Press.

50. Sunstein, C. R. (2013). *Simpler: The future of government.* New York, NY: Simon & Schuster.

51. Milkman, K. L., Rogers, T., & Bazerman, M. H. (2008). Harnessing our inner angels and demons. *Perspectives on Psychological Science, 3*, 324–338.

52. Della Vigna, S., & Malmendier, U. (2006). Paying not to go to the gym. *American Economic Review, 90*, 694–719.

53. Holmes, O. W. (1897). The path of the law. *Harvard Law Review, 10*, 457–478.

54. Krueger, A. B. (2001). Supply and demand: An economist goes to the Super Bowl. *Milken Institute Review: A Journal of Economic Policy, 3*, 22–29.

55. Thaler, R. H. (1980). Towards a positive theory of consumer choice. *Journal of Economic Behavior and Organization, 1*, 39–60.

56. Bishop, R. C., & Heberlein, T. A. (1979). Measuring values of extra market goods: Are indirect measures biased? *American Journal of Agricultural Economics, 61*, 926–930.

57. Horowitz, J. K., & McConnell, K. E. (2002). A review of WTA/WTP studies. *Journal of Environmental Economics and Management, 44*, 426–447.

58. Hammack, J., & Brown, G. H. (1974). *Waterfowl and wetlands: Toward bioeconomic analyses.* Baltimore, MD: Johns Hopkins Press.

59. Brookshire, D. S., Randall, A., & Stoll, J. R. (1980). Valuing increments and decrements in natural resource service flows. *American Journal of Agricultural Economics, 62*, 478–488.

60. Bishop, R. C., Heberlein, T. A., McCollum, D. W., & Welsh, M. P. (1988). *A validation experiment for valuation techniques.* Madison: Electric Power Institute, School of Natural Resources, University of Wisconsin.

61. Boyce, J. R., & McCollum, D. W. (1993). A market test of the contingent valuation method: The case of bison hunting permits in Alaska. In J. C. Bergstrom (Compiler), *Western Regional Research Project W-133, Sixth interim report. Benefits and costs transfer in natural resource planning* (pp. 1–26). Athens: Department of Agricultural and Applied Economics, University of Georgia.

62. Arkes, H. R., & Blumer, C. C. (1985). The psychology of sunk cost. *Organizational Behavior and Human Decision Processes, 35*, 124–140.

63. Thaler, R. H. (1991). *Quasi rational economics*. New York, NY: Russell Sage Foundation.

64. Gourville, J. T., & Soman, D. (1998). Payment depreciation: The behavioral effects of temporally separating payments from consumption. *Journal of Consumer Research, 25*, 160–175.

65. Soman, D. (2004). Framing, loss aversion and mental accounting. In D. J. Koehler & N. Harvey (Eds.), *Blackwell handbook of judgment and decision making* (pp. 379–398). Malden, MA: Blackwell Publishing.

66. Schindler, R. M., & Kirby, P. N. (1997). Patterns of rightmost digits used in advertised prices: Implication for nine-ending effects. *Journal of Consumer Research, 24*, 192–201.

67. Holdershaw, J., Gendall, P., & Garland, R. (1997). The widespread use of odd pricing in the retail sector. *Marketing Bulletin, 8*, 53–58.

68. Kalyanam, K., & Shively, T. S. (1998). Estimating irregular pricing effects: A stochastic spline regression approach. *Journal of Marketing Research, 35*(1), 16–29.

69. Manning, K. C., & Sprott, D. E. (2009). Price ending, left-digit effects and choice. *Journal of Consumer Research, 36*, 328–335.

70. Schindler, R. M., & Kibarian, T. M. (1996). Increased consumer sales response through use of 99-ending prices. *Journal of Retailing, 72*, 187–199.

71. Stiving, M., & Winer, R. S. (1997). An empirical analysis of price ending with scanner data. *Journal of Consumer Research, 24*, 57–67.

72. Thomas, M., & Morwitz, V. (2009). Heuristics in numerical cognition: Implications for pricing. In V. R. Rao (Ed.), *Handbook of pricing research in marketing* (pp. 132–149). Northampton, MA: Edward Elgar.

73. Quigley, C. J., Jr., & Notarantonio, E. M. (1992). An exploratory investigation of perceptions of odd and even pricing. *Developments in Marketing Science, 15*, 306–309.

74. Thomas, M., & Morwitz, V. (2005). Penny wise and pound foolish: The left-digit effect in price cognition. *Journal of Consumer Research, 32*, 54–64.

75. Naipaul, S., & Parsa, H. G. (2001). Menu price endings that communicate value and quality. *Cornell Hotel and Restaurant Administration Quarterly, 42*, 26–37.

76. Schindler, R. M., & Kibarian, T. M. (2001). Image communicated by the use of 99 endings in advertised prices. *Journal of Advertising, 30*, 95–99.

Index

SAGAMORE
P U B L I S H I N G

RELATED BOOKS

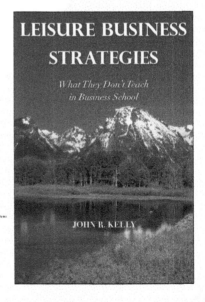